ECDL
Syllabus 5.0 Using Office 2003

Jenny Phillips
Peter MacBride
David Longworth
Rosemary Richards

Heinemann
Part of Pearson

Heinemann is an imprint of Pearson Education Limited, a company incorporated in England and Wales, having its registered office at Edinburgh Gate, Harlow, Essex, CM20 2JE. Registered company number: 872828

http://www.heinemann.co.uk/

Text © David Longworth, Peter MacBride, Jenny Phillips and Rosemary Wyatt 2008

First published 2009

12 11 10 09
10 9 8 7 6 5 4 3 2

British Library Cataloguing in Publication Data
A catalogue record for this book is available from the British Library

ISBN 978 0 435578 45 9

Edited by Alex Sharpe: additional text in Module 2 and Module 8 © Alex Sharpe 2009
Typeset by Standard Eight Limited www.std8.com
Original illustrations © Pearson Education Limited 2008
Cover design by Pearson Education Limited
Picture research by Helen Reilly/Arnos Design Ltd
Cover photo/illustration © iStockphoto/faberfoto_it
Printed in Great Britain by Scotprint

ECDL Foundation Disclaimer Text
European Computer Driving Licence, ECDL, International Computer Driving Licence, ICDL, e-Citizen and related logos are all registered Trade Marks of the European Computer Driving Licence Foundation Limited ("ECDL Foundation").

PEARSON EDUCATION LIMITED is an entity independent of ECDL Foundation and is not associated with ECDL Foundation in any manner. This courseware may be used to assist candidates to prepare for the ECDL Foundation Certification Programme as titled on the courseware. Neither ECDL Foundation nor PEARSON EDUCATION LIMITED warrants that the use of this courseware publication will ensure passing of the tests for that ECDL Foundation Certification Programme. This courseware publication has been independently reviewed and approved by ECDL Foundation as covering the learning objectives for the ECDL Foundation Certification Programme.

Confirmation of this approval can be obtained by reviewing the Partners Page in the About Us Section of the website www.ecdl.org

The material contained in this courseware publication has not been reviewed for technical accuracy and does not guarantee that candidates will pass the test for the ECDL Foundation Certification Programme. Any and all assessment items and/or performance-based exercises contained in this courseware relate solely to this publication and do not constitute or imply certification by ECDL Foundation in respect to the ECDL Foundation Certification Programme or any other ECDL Foundation test. Irrespective of how the material contained in this courseware is deployed, for example in a learning management system (LMS) or a customised interface, nothing should suggest to the candidate that this material constitutes certification or can lead to certification through any other process than official ECDL Foundation certification testing.

For details on sitting a test for an ECDL Foundation certification programme, please contact your country's designated National Licensee or visit the ECDL Foundation's website at www.ecdl.org.

Candidates using this courseware must be registered with the National Operator before undertaking a test for an ECDL Foundation Certification Programme. Without a valid registration, the test(s) cannot be undertaken and no certificate, nor any other form of recognition, can be given to a candidate. Registration should be undertaken with your country's National Licensee at an Approved Test Centre.

Photo acknowledgements

The author and publisher would like to thank the following individuals and organisations for permission to reproduce photographs:

Module 1 Pg 2 with kind permission from Hewlard Packard; pg 3 © iStockphoto/amaludin Abu Seman; pg 3 Dell; pg 5 © iStockphoto/Alex Slobodkin and © iStockphoto/Greg Nicholas; pg 7 © COLIN CUTHBERT/ SCIENCE PHOTO LIBRARY; pg 8 © iStockphoto/Viktor Gmyria; pg 9 Fotolia/Lance Bellers; pg 9 © iStockphoto/ Gustaf Brundin; pg 9 Fotolia/Pedro Nogueira; pg 10 Fotolia/luchschen; pg 10 dreamstime/Instamatic; pg 10 ©Nikon; pg 11 Dell; pg 12 © iStockphoto/Emrah Turudu; pg 12 © iStockphoto/Emrah Turudu; pg 13 with kind permission from Hewlard Packard; pg 13 Fotolia/motionero; pg 14 Pearson Education Ltd/GarethBoden; pg 14 © iStockphoto/En Tien Ou; pg 15 Fotolia/Marek Kosmal; pg 15 Fotolia/Marc Dietrich; pg 15 Fotolia/Vincent Duprez; pg 26 © iStockphoto/Ales Veluscek; Module 2 Pg 51 © iStockphoto/James Phelps; Module 3 Pg 119 Punchstock/stockbyte.

Screenshot acknowledgements

The authors and publisher would like to thank the following individuals and organisations for permission to reproduce material used in this book:

Microsoft screenshots throughout the publication: Microsoft product screenshot(s) reprinted with permission from Microsoft Corporation.

Module 1
Pg 22 iTunes player © Apple Inc. iTunes is a trademark of Apple Inc., registered in the U.S. and other countries. Disclaimer: Learn to Pass ECDL 5.0 Using Office 2003 is an independent publication and has not been authorised, sponsored, or otherwise approved by Apple Inc.
Pg 28 The [un]Happy Planet Index – http://www.happyplanetindex.org/
Pg 29 Amazon – http://www.amazon.co.uk/ECDL-Connect-Student-Book-Rom/dp/043549788/ref=sr_1_1?ie=UT F8&s=books&qid=1225878108&sr=8-1 © 2008 Amazon.com Inc. and its affiliates. All rights reserved.
Pg 33 Direct Gov – http://www.direct.gov.uk/en/Environmentandgreenliving/index.htm © Crown copyright
Pg 35 Sky – http://messageboards.sky.com/ThreadView.aspx?ThreadId=9929
Pg 44 ICO – http://www.ico.gov.uk/Home/what_we_cover/data_protection.aspx

Module 2
Pg 87 and pg 88 CA – CA product screenshot reprinted with permission form CA, Inc.

Module 7
Pg 375 Pearson Education Ltd – http://www.heinemann.co.uk/Series/Secondary/LearningToPassECDL/ LearningToPass ECDL.aspx
Pg 381 Pearson Education Ltd – http://www.heinemann.co.uk/FEAndVocational/ITAndOfficeTechnology/ ITAndOfficeTechnology.aspx
Pg 388 and pg 390 Wikipedia 'Arthur Wellesley, 1st Duke of Wellington', and pg 409 'Moore's Law' Copyright © 2008 Pearson Education Ltd. Permission is granted to copy, distribute and/or modify this document under the terms of the GNU Free Documentation License, Version 1.2 or any later version published by the Free Software Foundation; with no Invariant Sections, no Front-Cover Texts, and no Back-Cover Texts. A copy of the license can be found at the following website page entitled "GNU Free Documentation License": http:// en.wikipedia.org/wiki/Wikipedia:Text_of_the_GNU_Free_Documentation_License
Pg 403 Sky News home page – http://news.sky.com/skynews
Pg 407 Google Search page – http://www.google.co.uk/
Pg 408 Google Advanced Search page – http://www/google.co.uk/advanced_search?q=allintext:
Pg 411 Tucows – http://www.tucows.com/ (3 screenshots from the website)
Pg 412 NHS Direct Body Mass Index (BMI) calculator © Crown copyright

Every effort has been made to contact copyright holders of material reproduced in this book. Any omissions will be rectified in subsequent printings if notice is given to the publishers.

table of contents

Introduction

The European Computer Driving Licence is the world's leading computer user certification. More than 7 million candidates have completed the qualification worldwide, and it is one of the most recognised standards of computer literacy for employers.

Learning to Pass ECDL Syllabus 5.0 provides simple step-by-step instructions for developing the skills needed for the qualification. Each module is carefully signposted to match ECDL Syllabus 5.0 and includes learning objectives for easy reference and customisable learning. Clearly illustrated and packed full of practical tips, quick questions to test your understanding and practice exercises to help you apply your skills, this book will help you prepare for the ECDL exam.

If you're new to Microsoft Windows XP and Office 2003, then you can build your skills gradually by working through each module from the start. If, however, you are more experienced, you may want to use the test your understanding tests and practice exercises to assess where you need to build your knowledge and understanding.

The BCS Module I revised syllabus on IT Security for Users is covered in Module 8 on pages 450–462 of this book. BCS Module 2 Revised IT User Fundamentals syllabus inclusions are covered in Modules I and 2 of this book. A table has been produced on page 463 to show where BCS does not map directly to ECDL syallabus 5.0.

Good luck with your studies!

In this module you'll learn about what a computer is and about some of the thousands of ways in which computers are used today.

Amazingly, the history of commercial computing goes back only to around 1960, when the first computers were used by a very few large organisations to perform repetitive tasks such as processing the company payroll. These computers were massive, occupying whole floors in office blocks, and yet had only a fraction of the computing power of a modern pocket calculator. The computer that controlled the first manned spaceship to the moon in 1969 had less calculating capability than a modern mobile phone!

MODULE 1.
concepts of ICT

Computer hardware

Note

ICT (I.4.I.I)

The term Information and Communication Technology (ICT) refers to the use of computers, and devices like fax machines and telephones which contain tiny computers, to process and transfer information. Computers are commonly used to communicate information, as well as performing tasks like word processing or calculations. You may hear the term IT or Information Technology used instead of ICT.

Learning objectives

By working through this lesson you will learn:
- ⊙ about hardware and software
- ⊙ about types of computers
- ⊙ about the components of a computer
- ⊙ about what affects a computer's performance
- ⊙ about input and output devices
- ⊙ about data storage.

Hardware (I.I.I.I)

In order to work, a computer needs two things: hardware and software.

Hardware is the physical part of a computer – the bits you can see and touch. The casings for computers and their associated pieces of hardware, such as monitors and printers, are usually made of tough plastic. The hardware inside the casings is made up of electronic switches and integrated circuits (known as 'chips') mounted on **printed circuit boards** (PCBs), along with disk drives, transformers, fans and other components.

Figure I.I Inside a PC case

Types of computers (I.I.I.2–3)

Different types of computers are used for different applications.

Mainframe computers

These machines are large, fast and expensive. They are used by very big organisations such as electricity companies, banks and multinational companies. Hundreds or thousands of users may be connected to and using a mainframe at the same time.

Each user has a **computer terminal** that is connected to the mainframe. Some types of terminal cannot be used for anything unless they are connected to the mainframe – these are known as **dumb terminals**. All the computer's calculations take place in the mainframe. Alternatively, an ordinary PC may be connected to a mainframe and this can do useful work even when it is not connected. A PC used in this way is sometimes known as an **intelligent terminal**.

The terminals connected to a mainframe computer may be in different parts of the country or even overseas.

Personal computers

A **personal computer** or PC has become an almost indispensable piece of equipment for office workers, from the managing director down to the humblest clerical worker.

The most popular type of PC is the **desktop** model. The main system unit is designed to sit on top of the user's desk. **Tower** models are also popular as the system unit can be sited on the floor, so taking up less desk space.

If the computer is only ever going to be used in the same place, a desktop model is the best choice. You get more memory, a faster processor, a larger hard disk and wider screen on a desktop PC than on a laptop for the same price – and desktop PC keyboards are much more comfortable to type on.

Tip!

Hardware devices such as the screen, keyboard, mouse etc. connected to the main system unit are all types of **peripherals**.

Portable computers

These were introduced so that users could easily transport their PC to different locations and even do some work en route, perhaps on a train journey. There are two main types: laptops and tablet PCs.

Laptop computers (sometimes called notebook computers) are portable computers that have an integral keyboard and monitor and a rechargeable battery.

A **tablet PC** is a slate-shaped mobile computer with a touch-sensitive screen. It is operated using a stylus or digital pen, and does not normally have either a keyboard or mouse, though these can be attached to some versions. The pen can be used for selecting items on screen, and data can be entered either through an on-screen keyboard display or by handwriting recognition.

Figure 1.2 A laptop

Hand-held devices

Personal Digital Assistants (PDAs, sometimes referred to as palmtops) are hand-held computers small enough to hold in your hand or fit into your pocket. They were originally developed as electronic personal organisers, after the success of the paper-based Filofax™ in the mid-1980s. The first models had only diary, address book and notepad functions, but over time more features have been added as the devices have become more powerful. Recent models include spellcheckers, small games and

Figure 1.3 A PDA

notepad functions, and some models with larger screens now have handwriting-recognition software. PDAs tend to fall into two categories: keyboard- and pen-based devices. Both types normally have cut-down versions of PC applications and can be easily connected to a PC to transfer data.

Smartphones combine PDAs and mobile phones. They can be used not only to make and receive normal phone calls, but also to access the Web, for email and text messaging, and many have a built-in camera and/or video camera, MP3 and video player. The most popular ones currently are the Blackberry, which has very good email facilities, and the iPhone, based on the iPod® audio and video player.

The iPod® and other **multimedia players** have a lot of computing power built into them, but here the power is devoted to playing and organising the music and video collections.

Type	Capacity	Speed	Cost	Typical users
Mainframe	Very large disk storage. Very large main memory.	Very fast in order to process vast amounts of data.	Extremely expensive.	Large companies (often multinational), Health Authorities etc.
PC	Probably smaller disk storage and RAM capacity than a server (especially if networked).	Fast – measured in GHz.	Becoming cheaper all the time.	Employees in all sizes of organisation, home users etc.
Laptop	Similar to a PC.	Similar to a PC.	Often more expensive than comparable PC due to miniaturisation.	Mostly business users, commuters etc.
PDA	Much smaller disk storage capacity and main memory than PC.	Slower than a PC.	Relatively expensive compared to a PC.	Mostly business users, commuters etc.
Smartphone	As PDA.	As PDA.	Relatively expensive.	Business and home users.

PC components (I.I.I.4)

Figure I.4 on page 5 shows the main parts of a desktop PC.
- ◉ Screen: displays information from the computer.
- ◉ System unit: contains the CPU (Central Processing Unit), memory, hard disk drive, removable disk drives and power supply.
- ◉ Mouse: lets you control the computer without typing.
- ◉ Keyboard: press the keys to give commands or enter data into the computer.
- ◉ Printer: to print out your work onto paper.

more slowly because instructions and data are being copied from disk to memory as needed. Thus, the **number of applications** running at any one time also affects the performance of a computer.

Processing power and memory are also required to run the computer's screen display. With simpler applications, the screen can be managed using just the graphics chip on the motherboard and a section of the main memory, but for more demanding jobs such as editing photos or videos, and computer games, especially 3-D action games, more is needed. A separate **graphics card**, with a dedicated processor and set of memory chips, will provide faster, smoother displays.

Input devices (1.1.4.1)

All the data that is fed into a computer is called **input**. The items of hardware used to input data are called **input devices**. Some of the most common input devices are described below.

Keyboard

The most common way to enter data into a PC is by keyboard. Computer keyboards have their keys arranged in a similar way to those on a typewriter. This arrangement is called QWERTY because of the order in which the keys appear in the first row of letters. Extra keys carry out specific jobs depending on the software being used.

Some keyboards, especially on laptop computers, incorporate a tracker ball or touch pad that performs the function of a mouse.

Figure 1.6 A QWERTY keyboard

RAM has these two major characteristics.

- Each location in RAM has its own unique address. It can be randomly accessed – that is, the computer can be instructed to fetch the data it needs from any given address in memory.
- RAM is **volatile**. Its contents are lost when the power is switched off.

A PC will also only have a very small amount of ROM. Unlike RAM, its contents can never be changed, and all the instructions held in ROM have to be 'burned' into the memory chip before it leaves the factory. The contents of ROM are not lost when the computer is switched off. A tiny program held in ROM starts running as soon as you switch on the computer. This program tells the computer to start loading the operating system (e.g. Windows) from disk.

ROM has these two major characteristics.

- ROM cannot be written to or used to hold ordinary user application programs such as word-processing software.
- ROM is **non-volatile**. Its contents are NOT lost when the power is switched off.

Tip!

Many household machines contain ROM chips – for example a washing machine, dishwasher or video recorder. You can, for example, select which washing program to use, but you cannot change how many minutes the cycle takes or use the washing machine to cook your dinner instead!

Computer performance (1.1.2.1–2)

Two main factors impact on a computer's performance: **processor speed** and the **amount of RAM**.

Processor speed is measured in hertz (cycles per second). One kilohertz (kHz) is 1,000 cycles per second, 1 megahertz (MHz) is 1,000 kHz and 1 gigahertz (GHz) is 1,000 MHz.

Each year, as technology advances, processor speed increases. Twenty years ago a computer with a processor speed of a few hundred kilohertz would have been considered very powerful. Now a processor speed of 3.6 GHz is not unusual – that is about 12,000 times faster!

The other factor in determining the performance of a computer is the amount of memory (or RAM) it has. Modern software takes up a huge amount of memory.

When you open Word to write a letter, for example, the software program (Word) has to be copied into RAM (which may have a capacity of, say, 512 MB) before the computer can execute the program instructions which enable you to type your letter. If a computer does not have enough memory to hold all of Word in RAM at once, it will swap bits of the program in and out of memory from disk as they are required. This takes time.

The same happens when you have several programs running at once. They all take up memory space, and a computer may run

Figure 1.5 RAM chips on a PCB

Memory (I.I.3.I–2)

A computer has a 'memory' which stores data. There are two kinds of memory: **Random Access Memory** (RAM) and **Read-Only Memory** (ROM).

RAM (sometimes known as **immediate access memory**) is divided into millions of addressable storage units called **bytes**.

Each byte consists of 8 bits or binary digits. A bit can be set either ON or OFF, depending on whether an electric current is switched on or off, representing a 0 or a I. All numbers, text, sounds, graphics etc. are held as different patterns of 0s and Is in the computer.

One byte can hold one character, or it can be used to hold a code representing, for example, a tiny part of a picture, a sound or part of a computer program instruction. The total number of bytes in main memory is referred to as the computer's memory size.

Measurement	Power of 2	Size (bytes)	Symbol
I kilobyte	2^{10}	1,024 (just over I thousand)	KB
I megabyte	2^{20}	1,048,576 (just over I million)	MB
I gigabyte	2^{30}	1,073,741,824 (just over I billion)	GB
I terabyte	2^{40}	1,099,511,627,776 (just over I trillion)	TB

For example, this paragraph contains approximately 180 characters or bytes. The text in this module is stored as a **file** which contains approximately 60,000 characters (approximately 59 KB). Files are organised into **directories** or **folders**. Files and folders are given names so that they can easily be found on the computer.

The amount of memory that comes with a standard PC has increased exponentially over the past 25 years. In about 1980, BBC microcomputers with 32 KB of memory were bought in their thousands for home and school use. In 1981, Bill Gates of Microsoft made his famous remark '640 KB ought to be enough for anybody'. By 2007, a PC with 512 MB or I GB of memory was standard, costing less than £500 including bundled software. Instructions and data being processed are held in RAM. For example, if you are writing a letter using Microsoft Word, both Word and your letter will be held in RAM while you are working on it. If you accidentally switch off the machine, or there is a power cut while you are working, you will lose the letter if you have not saved it and, when you restart the computer, you will have to load Word again (i.e. the Word software will be copied from your hard disk into RAM). When you finish your letter, save it and close Word so RAM is freed up for the next task.

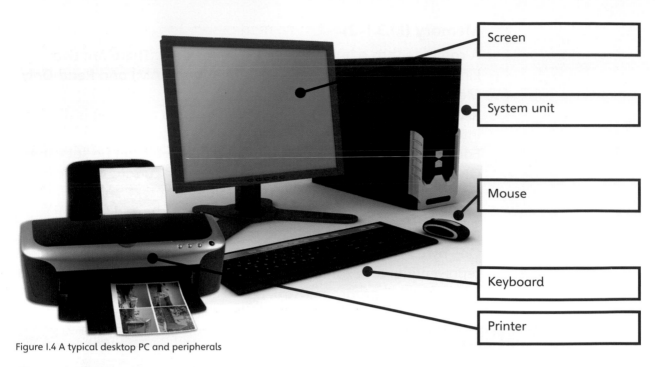

Screen

System unit

Mouse

Keyboard

Printer

Figure 1.4 A typical desktop PC and peripherals

◉ Speakers: allow you to listen to music and other sounds from your computer.

Central Processing Unit

The main brain of the computer, the **Central Processing Unit** (CPU), is within the system unit. The CPU is where all processing and calculations take place. It consists of two different parts:

◉ the processor
◉ memory.

The processor

The processor consists of two main components: the **control unit** and the **arithmetic/logic unit** (ALU). The control unit fetches instructions from the computer's memory, decodes them and synchronises all the computer's operations.

The arithmetic/logic unit (ALU) is where all of the work is carried out. The ALU can perform two sorts of operations on data. **Arithmetic** operations include addition, subtraction, multiplication and division. **Logical** operations consist of comparing one data item with another to determine whether the first data item is smaller than, equal to or greater than the second data item. Physically the processor is a small silicon **chip**, which consists of complex electronic circuits. This chip, together with other chips that do different jobs, are mounted on printed circuit boards (PCBs).

Mouse

A **mouse** is a small hand-held input device which has a ball fitted underneath. When the mouse is moved, the signal created by the movement of the ball is transmitted to the computer. This controls a pointer on the screen which moves in a direction corresponding to the direction of the mouse movement. Once the user has pointed the arrow on their screen at something it can be selected by clicking a button on top of the mouse. There are usually two or three buttons on a mouse. The left-hand button is normally used to make selections.

Figure I.7 A cordless mouse

A **tracker ball** is also a type of pointing device. It is often used instead of a mouse on portable computers. The user rotates a ball to move the cursor over the screen.

Touch pads can also replace the mouse. They are also often found on the keyboards of portable computers. The user moves their finger over the surface of the pad to move the cursor.

Graphics tablet

A graphics tablet consists of a flat surface upon which the user may 'draw' with a stylus (see below) to create an image on the computer screen. A tablet is far more accurate than a mouse for creating and editing graphics.

Microphone

If your computer has a sound card it will have the ability to receive sound input from a microphone through the sound card microphone port. This may be useful for recording voice or sounds on your computer.

Figure I.8 A microphone and headset

Light pen

A light pen is a small pen-shaped wand which contains light sensors. The light pen is used to choose objects or commands on the screen either by pressing it against the screen or by pressing a small switch on its side. This sends a signal to the computer, which then works out the exact location of the light pen on the screen. They have largely been replaced by styluses.

Stylus

A stylus is a pencil-shaped pointer, typically made of plastic, used to interact with the touch-sensitive screens of PDAs, graphics tablets and tablet PCs. It is used instead of a finger, partly because the fine tip allows more accurate work, but mainly to avoid getting the natural oil from one's hands onto the screen.

Figure I.9 Using a stylus

Scanner

Scanners are used to input text, diagrams and pictures to the computer. They can be hand-held but usually they are 'flat-bed' devices which sit on the desk. Printed text can be scanned using OCR (Optical Character Recognition) software so that it can be word-processed. Images can be

Figure 1.10 A flat-bed scanner

scanned and loaded into graphics software where they can be altered or enhanced.

Joystick

Figure 1.11 A joystick

A joystick is often used to play games on a PC. It controls the way things move on the screen and can control movement from side-to-side, up and down and diagonally. A joystick normally has at least one button that can be used in a game, for example to make a character jump or fire a missile.

Digital camera

A major benefit of using a digital camera is that you can transfer photos directly to your PC without sending off a film to be developed. A cable supplied with the camera can connect it to a port on the PC.

Using a digital camera is very similar to using a traditional camera. They both use the same basic components such as a lens, flash, shutter and viewfinder. Most digital models now incorporate an LCD screen so that you can get a good view of your subject as you take the photo, and you can then review the picture afterwards. The quality and number of digital pictures that can be taken will depend on

Figure 1.12 Digital cameras

the amount of memory in the camera. The on-board memory is usually very small, but can be increased greatly by the use of small memory cards. Some modern PCs have memory card reader slots which offer a simple way to transfer data from a camera to a computer. When the card is plugged into the reader, it can be read and its files handled in much the same way as a disk drive.

Webcam

This is a small, low-resolution video camera that feeds its images directly into the computer where they can be broadcast through a web page. Webcams have two main uses: people can use them on a one-to-one basis to see each other while they talk; they can also be set up to monitor a location, for example for tourist viewing or traffic management.

Output devices (I.I.4.2–3)

The information that a computer produces is called output. The items of hardware that receive this output are called **output devices**. The most common output devices are described below.

Screen

A screen or monitor displays the output information from a computer. The size of a monitor is measured in inches diagonally across the screen; 15, 17, 19 and 21 inch monitors are the most common sizes. The picture on a monitor is made up of thousands of tiny coloured dots called pixels. The quality and detail of the picture on a monitor depends on the resolution, which is measured in pixels going across and down the screen. The more pixels the screen has, the higher the resolution and the better the picture. Resolutions typically range from 800 × 600 to 1,600 × 1,200. Another factor which affects the quality of the

Figure I.I3 An LCD screen

image is its refresh rate. This is measured in hertz (Hz) and indicates how many times per second the image on the screen is updated. To avoid flickering images, which can lead to eyestrain and headaches, the refresh rate of a monitor should be at least 72 Hz.

Older monitors work in the same way as televisions where electrical signals are converted into an image on the screen by a Cathode Ray Tube (CRT). New flat-screen monitors take up much less desk space than CRTs. These Liquid Crystal Display (LCD) screens are similar to those provided on portable computers.

Printer

A good printer can help you produce professional-looking printed output from your PC. There are three main categories of printer, each of them suitable for different types of job.

Many PCs are supplied with an inkjet printer. These print pictures or characters by forcing small dots of ink through tiny holes. The ink is stored in replaceable cartridges, normally separate for colour and black ink. Inkjet printers can print on envelopes, labels, acetates and other specialist paper.

Figure 1.14 An inkjet printer

Laser printers produce very high quality printed output very quickly. They are suitable for large volume printouts. Colour laser printers are relatively expensive (but getting cheaper). Black and white laser printers can cost less than £100 and are common in many large and small businesses. The main running expense is the cost of replacement toner (powdered ink) cartridges every few thousand pages.

Dot matrix printers have steel pins which strike an inked ribbon to create a pattern of tiny dots which form a character. How good the print is depends on how many pins the machine has; 24 pins will produce better quality print than 9 pins.

Figure 1.15 A laser printer

This type of printer is not normally supplied with a PC for home use, as the quality is not as good as an inkjet or laser printer. As they work by striking the paper, they are called impact printers and are often used by businesses to print on multi-part stationery for producing documents such as invoices. A top copy goes to the customer, a second 'carbon copy' may be used as a delivery note and a third copy may be kept in the office. Laser printers and inkjet printers cannot print two or more copies of a document simultaneously in this way.

Plotter

A plotter is another device for producing hard-copy from a computer. It uses several coloured pens to draw the computer output on paper. Plotters can produce very accurate drawings and are often used in Computer-Aided Design (CAD) applications to produce engineering or architectural drawings.

Figure 1.16 A typical plotter

Speakers and headphones

External speakers are supplied with multimedia PCs, usually with a sound card and CD-ROM drive. The system can then combine text, sound and graphics to run programs such as games. The quality and volume of the sound can be adjusted either from within the software or on the speakers themselves.

Computers with speech synthesiser software can output the electrical signals to speakers that convert them into sound waves sounding like a voice. Telephone enquiry systems or similar services sometimes replicate human speech this way – the electrical signals are sent directly down phone lines for conversion to sound by speakers in the telephone handset. Sound software can be used to mix musical sounds and create new sounds.

Headphones are an alternative to speakers. They might be used so the audio output does not bother, or cannot be overhead by, other people. The sound quality can be as good as that from speakers.

Figure 1.17 A pair of speakers

Tip!

(I.I.4.3) Some devices can be classed as **input or output devices**.

A **touchscreen** allows the user to touch an area of the screen rather than having to type the data on a keyboard. They are widely used in tourist centres, where tourists can look up various local facilities and entertainments, in fast-food stores for entering customer orders, in manufacturing and many other environments.

A **headset** combines headphones and a microphone. It is useful for Internet telephony (see page 37).

Connections (I.I.I.5)

Computers can be connected to a variety of devices, and the connections are made through a number of standard ports located on the front and back of a PC, and either at the back or sides of a laptop.

- **Parallel** ports – mainly intended for printers, but also used for connecting Zip drives. This port is often no longer used.
- **Serial** ports – mainly used to connect a modem, but the mouse, keyboard and printer can also be connected via serial ports.
- **Universal Serial Bus** (USB) ports – a faster alternative to the serial port. This has become the standard way of connecting any peripheral to a computer. Modern PCs typically have four USB ports at the back and another two at the front.
- **Firewire** ports – a high-speed serial port, mainly used for connecting multimedia devices, for example camcorders.
- **Network** ports – for connecting the PC to a local area network. These are normally rectangular sockets (RJ-45 connectors) suitable for Ethernet networks. USB ports can also be used for networking.

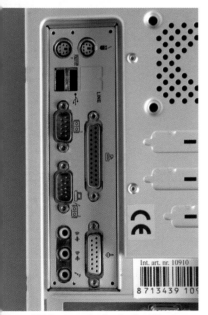

Figure I.18 Ports on the back of a PC case

Figure I.19 Ports on the side of a laptop

Storage devices (1.1.3.3)

Disk storage

Before you turn off a computer you need to save your work onto a disk or other storage medium. There are four main types of disk: floppy disk, hard disk, CD-ROM and DVD.

A **floppy disk** is not floppy at all (although the actual disk is made of flexible plastic). It has a hard protective casing and a storage capacity of 1.44 MB. Floppy disks can be used for backup storage of small quantities of data or for moving files between machines, but they are steadily falling out of use. CD-ROMs and DVDs (see below) offer much more storage capacity at less cost.

Figure 1.20 A floppy disk

Most computers have a **hard disk** permanently housed inside them. Hard disks have a much larger storage capacity than a floppy disk, and transfer data to and from the computer memory much more quickly.

The capacity of hard disks is measured in megabytes (MB) or gigabytes (GB). Most modern PCs have a hard disk with a capacity of at least 40 GB.

PCs are often fitted with a DVD/CD drive. This can be used to play standard music CDs and video DVDs, but also to read and write data. A CD-ROM (Compact Disc Read-Only Memory) can hold up to 650 MB of programs or data. DVD-ROMs can hold up to 4.7 GB of data. Software is normally supplied

Figure 1.21 A hard disk

on CD-ROM or DVD, but these are read-only disks which means that you cannot save any data on them, only read what is already there.

Almost all PCs since 2000 have been able to write to CDs; most

Figure 1.22 A compact disc

modern ones can also write data onto DVDs. There are two ways to do this. With a **CD-R** (CD-Recordable) or **DVD-R**, you can write once to the disk, whether the data fills it or not. With a **CD-RW** (Re-Writable) or **DVD-RW** you can write data in several sessions and erase data already written.

Removable storage

- **External hard disks** offer a fast and efficient form of removable storage, with capacity of anything up to 500 GB. These will normally plug into a USB port and are automatically recognised by a PC. They can then be used just like an internal hard drive, but with the advantage that they are portable and can be plugged into another computer elsewhere.

- **Zip drives** read and write on removable Zip disks. These are a little larger and thicker than floppy disks and can hold up to 750 MB of data. A Zip drive is sometimes fitted as an option on a PC, but one can be added as an external drive. They are faster than floppy disks, but they are still much slower than hard disks.

- **Rev drives** are the big brother of Zip drives. They use similar technology but the disks have a larger capacity of up to 120 GB.

- **USB flash drives** have memory chips that can store data even when the power is off. They plug into a USB port and have uses similar to portable disks. They are tiny, offer very fast data transfer rates and are highly portable. In 2008, the largest could hold 32 GB, but their capacities are increasing all the time.

- **Memory cards** have the same kind of memory chips as flash drives, but embedded in a small card. They are used in digital cameras, mobile phones, hand-held computers and similar devices where space is at a premium. Modern computers often have special ports into which memory cards can be plugged for data transfer.

- **Magnetic tape** or **DAT** (Digital Audio Tape) is used almost exclusively for backups and for archiving old data that needs to be kept but which will probably never be used. Large amounts of data can be stored very cheaply and compactly using this medium. The tape is housed in a cartridge. Tapes are much slower to access than a floppy disk, Zip/Jaz disk or CD-ROM.

The table on the next page gives a comparison between the different types of removable PC storage.

> ### Note
>
> Flash drives are sometimes referred to as memory sticks or pen drives.

Device	Capacity	Approximate price of drive	Approximate price of media
Floppy disk	1.44 MB	£25	£0.50
Zip	750 MB	£60	£10.00
Rev	120 GB	£400	£30.00
Flash drive	32 GB	£20	–
CD	650 MB	£25	£0.50
DVD	4.7 GB	£25	£1.20
DAT	60 GB	£250	£100
External hard drive	750 GB	£60	–

These prices are changing all the time, so only use this table for the sake of comparison.

Online file storage

Files can be stored online using specialist web-based storage firms. Selected files or folders can be uploaded as required, or the store can be set up for automatic backup, so that new or changed data is uploaded regularly. Some sites offer small amounts of storage for free, but there is normally a fee of £5 to £10 per gigabyte per year.

Test your understanding

1. A friend tells you that his new PC has 100 GB of RAM. Is this likely? Look up some advertisements for PCs to find typical figures for RAM and hard disk capacity.

2. Describe **two** differences between RAM and ROM; give a typical use for each.

3. a) Describe briefly a typical user of:
      i) a personal computer
      ii) a laptop
      iii) a palmtop.
   b) What unit is the speed of a CPU measured in?
   c) Name the **two** main parts of the CPU and describe the function of each.

4. Explain the terms **Information Technology, hardware** and **software**.

⑤ Describe the functions of each of the following devices and state whether they are input or output devices.
a) Touchpad
b) Plotter
c) Joystick
d) Scanner

⑥ Suppose you have typed a page of text that contains about 2,000 characters including spaces. Approximately how much RAM will this text occupy?

⑦ What type of printer would you recommend for each of the following users? Justify your answers.
a) An author working at home on her latest novel.
b) A small garage printing purchase orders for spare parts. Three copies of each purchase order are required.
c) A student who needs to print out his geography project in colour at home.

⑧ A graphic artist needs to send artwork that he has created on his computer to his client. The graphics files are 50 MB. Name and justify a suitable medium for storing and posting the files.

⑨ Describe **two** typical uses of each of the following devices attached to a PC.
a) Touchscreen
b) Speakers
c) DVD drive

You can find the answers to the questions on the CD-ROM saved as **Answers to TYU questions I.I**. How did you do? Go back over anything that you are unsure of.

Software

Software is the list of instructions that are coded in a special way so the computer can understand them. These are computer **programs** and they tell the computer exactly what to do. There are two main types of program in a computer system.

- **Operating system software**, such as Microsoft Windows, which manages the hardware and forms a base on which applications software can run.
- **Applications software** such as a word processor or an email package.

All software is continually being updated to provide more flexibility and features for the user. It is usually possible to upgrade from one version to the next. Updates to improve the reliability and security of software are often supplied free of charge by the manufacturer. For example, Windows Service Pack updates and Office Service Pack (or Release) updates can be downloaded from the Microsoft website (www.microsoft.com) to keep a PC up to date with the latest versions.

You need to know which software you are working with, since, for example, you may not be able to open a document created in Word 2003 on a PC with Word 97.

Operating system software (1.2.1.2/4)

An operating system is a series of programs that organise and control a computer. The computer will not work without it. Most PCs use an operating system called Microsoft Windows. There have been several versions of Windows and there are bound to be more versions in the future. The main functions of an operating system are:

- to provide a user interface so that the user can communicate with the computer
- to communicate with all the peripheral devices such as keyboard, screen and printer – for example when a user gives an instruction to print, the operating system checks that the printer is switched on and ready
- to organise the storage and retrieval of data from disk – the operating system has to keep track of where every file is stored on disk so that it can be retrieved quickly

Learning objectives

By working through this lesson you will learn:

- about operating systems
- about different types of systems and applications
- about how some software can make computers more accessible.

Note

Many common household devices, such as washing machines, microwave ovens, video recorders and digital alarm clocks contain computer hardware and specialised software to make them perform the tasks they are designed to do.

◉ to manage the smooth running of all the programs currently in RAM – the operating system will allocate processing time to each program in turn, for example while you are thinking what to type into Word, the computer may be busy receiving an email message or saving a spreadsheet you have just been working on.

Other operating systems

Examples of other operating systems include MS-DOS, UNIX and Linux. MS-DOS (Microsoft Disk Operating System) was developed for the first IBM PCs. It is a text-based system, and users type commands to manage files and to run programs. UNIX, and Linux, which grew out of UNIX, were also text-based though they now have GUI interfaces for easier handling. Linux is open source, meaning that its source code can be read and adapted freely.

Figure I.23 Microsoft Windows XP default desktop screen

Applications software (I.2.I.3–4)

Application packages are available for specific tasks. The most commonly used applications on a PC are word processing, spreadsheets, databases and Internet/email software.

◉ **Word-processing** software deals mainly with words. You can type all kinds of documents such as letters, CVs, reports etc. When you have finished a document you can save it on a disk and print it. One of the most popular word-processing packages is Microsoft Word.

- **Spreadsheet** software deals mainly with numbers. It is very useful for calculations involving money. One of the most popular spreadsheet packages is Microsoft Excel. Most spreadsheet packages are fairly similar in use.
- **Database** software is used to store data about people or items. It allows you to sort the data and find a particular record very quickly. Microsoft Access is one of the most popular database packages.
- **Internet browser** software, such as Internet Explorer and Netscape Navigator, allows you to surf the World Wide Web. Internet Explorer is supplied as part of Windows and is therefore one of the most popular web browsers.
- **Email** software allows you to send messages to other people who have a mailbox, for example colleagues, family and friends. Many people use this to keep in touch with family who live abroad. Outlook Express is supplied as part of Windows, and you will probably find it installed on your PC. There are alternatives such as Eudora and Netscape Messenger.
- **Presentation** software helps the user to create visual slide show presentations on a personal computer. These can display text, graphics, limited sound and some animation. The slides can also be printed onto acetates for use in an OHP presentation. Microsoft PowerPoint is often used to produce this type of presentation.
- **Desktop publishing** software, such as Microsoft Publisher, is used to produce many different types of documents from simple party invitations to more complex applications such as professional-looking newspapers and magazines. Professional users in the publishing industry often use more powerful packages such as QuarkXPress or Adobe® InDesign.
- **Accounting** software helps businesses take control of bookkeeping and accounting tasks, such as calculating VAT returns, producing invoices, tracking cash flow and managing payment and receipts. Sage software is one of the most widely used accounting packages.
- **Media players** can play digital music or videos. Some, such as Windows Media Player and Apple's iTunes (see Figure 1.24 on page 22), can also be used to organise your media collections, copy music and videos from CDs/DVDs onto your hard drive, and download media files from the Web.
- **Photo-editing** software allows you to resize, crop, retouch, adjust the colours and manipulate picture files in many ways – think of it as the darkroom for digital photography.

- **Video-editing** software can turn your PC into a cutting room. With it, a digital video can be separated into short clips, or individual frames, which can be cut, moved, repeated or reorganised as required, then titles, voice-overs and music can be added.
- **Games** software covers a huge range of different types of entertainment, from Windows' own Solitaire and Minesweeper through to 3-D shoot-'em-ups and flight simulators; from single player games or those for a few friends grouped around a PC to games involving, perhaps, hundreds of people linked through the Internet.

Figure I.24 Apple iTunes

Accessibility software (I.2.I.5)

There are programs that are designed to make the computer more accessible to people with disabilities. Some of these are included in the Windows package, others are separate programs. Some examples of accessibility software are:

- a **screen magnifier**, which uses a strip across the top of the screen to display a bigger view of whatever is beneath the cursor in the main screen area
- **high contrast** and **large type display** options to make the screen more readable for people with visual disabilities

- an **on-screen keyboard** that can be 'typed' on using the cursor, for people who cannot manage the physical keyboard. The letters here can be selected by mouse, joystick or any other pointing device
- **cursor control through the key pads**, for people who cannot use the mouse
- **voice recognition software**, as an alternative to typing. Once you have 'trained' the software, by reading set phrases, it can convert your spoken words into text
- a **screen reader**, which reads aloud the text beneath the cursor and any descriptions that are attached to images.

Test your understanding

1. a) Name the **two** main types of software found on a PC.
   b) Why are there often several different versions of software packages, each with their own version number? Name an example of some software that has at least two versions.
   c) Give **two** reasons why a user may decide to upgrade software to the latest version.

2. a) Explain what is meant by a Graphical User Interface (GUI).
   b) Give **two** reasons why a computer user may find a GUI interface easier to use than an alternative where commands have to be typed in.

3. Describe briefly the main functions of the operating system.

4. Think of **four** types of disability that may make it difficult to use a computer. In each case, what ways are there by which software can make the computer more accessible?

You can find the answers to the questions on the CD-ROM saved as **Answers to TYU questions 1.2**. How did you do? Go back over anything that you are unsure of.

Information networks

Local area networks (1.3.1.1–2)

Although a PC will function perfectly well as a 'stand-alone' machine, there are many advantages to an organisation of connecting all the computers together into a network.

A **local area network** (LAN) links together computers on the same site, for example within one building. This enables the users connected to the network to share information and to share resources such as printers that are connected to the network. If you are studying at a college, your computer will probably be connected to a LAN.

In a **client–server** network, a powerful computer called a **server** controls the network and stores data which can be used by other computers on the network. The other computers are referred to as the **clients**.

Storing data centrally, on a single computer, is essential where users are working on the same files. Where each user has their own separate files, central storage makes backing-up simpler. If the server is a mainframe computer, rather than a high-specification PC, the clients will send data to it for processing, and not just for storage.

The Internet also works on the client–server model. Here client programs, such as web browsers, access information on server computers elsewhere on the Web.

In most networks, the computers are connected by cables, either linked one to the next in a continuous chain, or with each client cabled directly to the server in a star pattern.

Today wireless links sometimes replace cables. A **wireless local area network** (WLAN) is easier to set up, to extend or to adjust as it does not need cables to be run through a building. Data can be transferred just as quickly as through cables, but there is some concern about the security of data in the wireless transmissions.

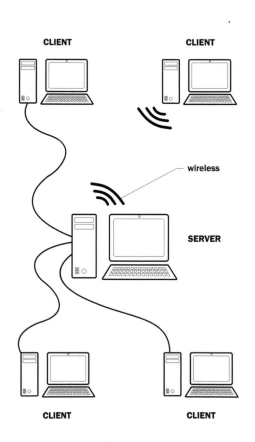

Figure I.25 A typical client–server network

Advantages of networks

- Workstations can share devices like printers. This is cheaper than buying a printer for every workstation.
- Users can save their work centrally on the network server. They can then retrieve their work from any workstation on the network.
- Users can communicate with each other and transfer data between workstations very easily.
- One copy of each application program can be loaded onto the file server and shared by all users. When a new version comes out it only has to be loaded onto the server instead of onto every workstation.

Disadvantages of networks

- Special security measures are needed to stop users from using programs and data that they should not have access to.
- Networks are complicated to set up and must be maintained by skilled ICT technicians.
- If the file server develops a serious fault all the users are affected.
- If a virus enters the network all the users may be affected.

Wide area networks (1.3.1.1)

A **wide area network** (WAN) connects computers in different geographical locations all over the world. They are connected by cable and wireless links through the telephone system. Large multinational companies depend on this type of network to communicate between different parts of their organisations within a country or in different countries.
The **Internet** is an example of a WAN. It is a worldwide computer network made up of smaller networks.

Telephone connections (1.3.2.1–5)

There are three main types of telephone lines which can be used for network connections. The type of line determines the speed at which data is transmitted (the **transfer rate**). This is measured in bits per second (bps), kilobits per second (kbps) or even megabits per second (Mbps).

Figure I.26 A modem

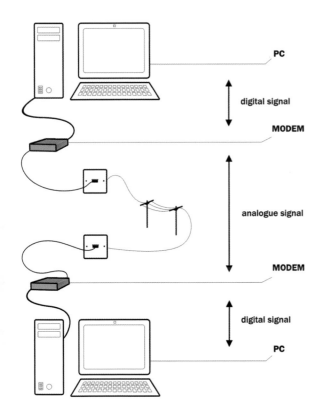

Figure I.27 Using a modem

PSTN

Short for **Public Switched Telephone Network**, this is the international telephone system that we are all familiar with for regular telephone calls. It is also referred to as POTS (the Post Office Telephone Service or the Plain Old Telephone Service as it later became known). Data can be transferred through the PSTN at up to 56 kbps. At this rate it takes a little over two minutes to transfer I MB of data.

A '**dial-up**' connection to the Internet is one made through the PSTN. It is called that because you dial the Internet Service Provider phone number to get online.

A modem is required for communication between computers over telephone lines. This device converts digital data from the computer into a varying electrical (analogue) signal that the telephone system can handle, and converts incoming analogue signals into a digital data stream for the computer to use.

ISDN

The amount of data that can be sent over a line depends partly on the bandwidth, which is the range of frequencies that the line can carry. The greater the bandwidth, the greater the rate at which data can be sent. This also means that several messages can be transmitted simultaneously. A network that is capable of sending voice, video and computer data requires a high bandwidth and is called an **Integrated Services Digital Network** (ISDN). ISDN can transfer data twice as fast as a PSTN line.

ADSL

Asymmetric Digital Subscriber Line (ADSL), commonly known as **broadband**, is a newer technology which enables existing copper wire telephone lines to be used to transmit computer data at extremely fast rates. The subscriber needs an ADSL router (equivalent to a modem) and a 'splitter' or filter, which separates the telephony signal from the ADSL signal. This means that telephone calls can be made at the same time that data is being sent or received (i.e. a customer can use the Internet to surf the Web or send/receive emails, and still make telephone calls). Broadband transfer rates are far higher than either PSTN or ISDN, typically reaching 8 Mbps. In theory, at this speed, 1MB of data can be transferred every second. In practice it tends to be a little lower, as bottlenecks at various parts of the network slow things down.

ADSL is 'asymmetric' in that data travels faster in one direction (from the Internet) than the other (from the user's computer). This works well for most Internet use. When accessing a web page, for example, the user sends the web page address (a few bytes) and the web server sends back the text and images that make up the page (possibly many kilobytes).

As the connection is always open, there is an increased danger of intruder attack – of people gaining access to the computer, through the Internet. To prevent this, the computer should have a firewall installed and active. The firewall limits how far external programs can access a computer.

With a broadband connection you normally pay a flat fee for the line, no matter how much you actually use it (some providers set a limit to the amount of data that can be downloaded, but none set a limit to the length of time). Many users stay online all the time that their computer is running because the phone can be used while the Internet connection is active. This is why broadband connections are sometimes referred to as 'always on'.

Wireless connections

Twenty years ago almost all telephone connections were made through cables and wires. Today a large part are wireless.

- The major links across the oceans are through satellites.
- Most of our one-to-one conversations are through mobile phones. These connect into the network through a grid of transmitting/receiving stations on towers and buildings.
- Wireless networks are now found in many homes, offices, schools and colleges. At the centre of each network is a router which handles the external connection to the Internet through a telephone land-line, and communicates with the internal computers through short-range radio signals. Wireless networking is based on Wi-Fi technology. Wi-Fi capability can be built into laptops, game consoles, mobile phones and other devices. Wi-Fi hotspots are places with open access wireless links to the Internet, that anyone can use.

Warning!

In a Wi-Fi broadband setup, any Wi-Fi-enabled computer within range of the router may be able to access the Internet – even without the router owner being aware of it. Going online through someone else's Internet connection without their permission is known as 'piggy-backing'. It is easily stopped, as access to a router can be controlled by setting up a network name and password. On a home network, this should be done. It doesn't just stop piggy-backing, it will also prevent outsiders gaining access to your computers and their files.

The Internet (I.3.I.3)

The **Internet** is a huge number of computers – including yours – connected together all over the world. Using the Internet you can look up information on the World Wide Web on any subject you can imagine, send and receive messages using email, download music and videos, interact with other people in real-time, communicate by text or maybe video, or play online games.

Figure I.28 A typical web page

To connect to the Internet you will need a PC with at least a 486 processor and Windows 95. You will also need a modem or broadband router installed and connected to a phone socket. You will then need to choose an **Internet Service Provider** (ISP) to connect you to the Internet. Most ISPs offer unlimited broadband or dial-up access for a flat monthly fee; some offer dial-up access for occasional users, with no fee but a slight charge on the phone bill. Their software does all the installation for you. There are free trial CDs for dial-up services on offer in high street shops and magazines.

The World Wide Web

The most active area of the Internet is the **World Wide Web** (often referred to simply as the Web). This is made up of many millions of websites. Every website consists of one or more documents called pages. A home page is the first page of a website and serves as an introduction to the whole site. Every page on the Web has its own address, or **Uniform Resource Locator** (URL).

The growth of the Internet over the past 15 years has been phenomenal. In 1989, Tim Berners-Lee introduced the World Wide Web to his colleagues at CERN (the European particle physics research organisation). In 1993, there were 130 servers on the Web. A year later there were 500. By the middle of 2007, there were over 500 million. Virtually every organisation now has their own website, finding it as indispensable as the telephone.

E-commerce (electronic commerce) has become an important Web activity. Many companies now do a significant part (or all) of their business through websites, both with other companies and with customers.

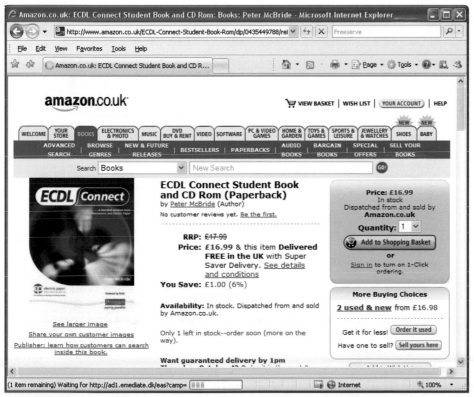

Figure 1.29 A typical e-commerce web page

The Web is now huge. There are literally billions of pages on it, and there is no central index to tell you where anything is. However, **search engines**, such as Google, offer simple ways to search for and find information on any topic (see page 405).

Email (I.4.2.I)

Email (electronic mail) is another major use of the Internet. It has become one of the most popular forms of communication.
Here are some of its advantages over regular mail.

- An email message arrives almost instantaneously anywhere in the world.
- It is very quick and easy to reply to an email.
- The same message can be sent to several people at once.
- Long documents or photographs can be sent as attachments.
- A message can easily be forwarded to another person.

To send and receive emails you need software such as Outlook, part of the Microsoft Office suite, or Outlook Express, which is supplied with Windows.

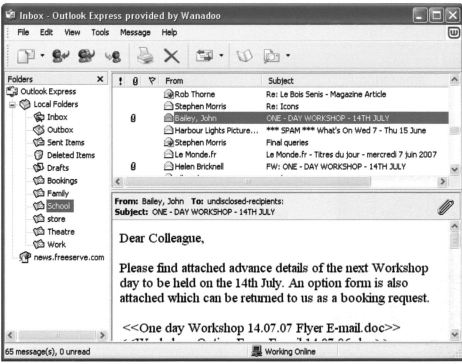

Figure I.30 Microsoft Outlook Express

Instant messaging (I.4.2.2)

Instant messaging services such as Skype and Windows Messenger allow people to exchange text messages, images and files interactively. If the users at both ends have fast broadband connections, the exchanges are almost instant – hence the name.

Intranets and extranets (1.3.1.4)

An **intranet** is similar to the Internet but is internal to an organisation. It is owned and used only by people in the organisation. It allows employees to share information, fix up appointments with each other, circulate important documents internally and co-operate in many other ways. Remember that in a large organisation not everybody will be working on the same site or even at the same time.

Whereas an intranet is accessible only to people who are members of the same company or organisation, an **extranet** provides various levels of access to users outside of the local network. A business might allow its clients access to parts of the network so that they can follow the progress of their jobs, place orders or check their accounts. A college might use an extranet to open its resources to its students.

You must have a valid username and password to access an extranet and your identity determines which parts of the extranet you can view.

Test your understanding

1. Explain what is meant by a client–server network.
2. a) Distinguish between a wide area network (WAN) and a local area network (LAN).
   b) Describe briefly three advantages of connecting PCs into a network rather than using stand-alone computers.
3. What hardware is needed to connect to the Internet?
4. Name **two** advantages of ADSL over PSTN for connecting to the Internet.
5. What is the function of a modem?
6. Explain the terms **intranet** and **extranet**. Why might an organisation choose to have an intranet?
7. Describe four functions provided by an email package such as Outlook Express.
8. Describe **four** advantages of email over ordinary mail.

You can find the answers to the questions on the CD-ROM saved as **Answers to TYU questions 1.3**. How did you do? Go back over anything that you are unsure of.

ICT in everyday life

Learning objectives

By working through this lesson you will learn:
- about how the Internet can be used by governments, commerce and education to provide information, goods and services to people
- about publishing on the Web through websites, blogs, podcasts and other media
- about some health issues relating to computer use
- about how computer users can minimise their impact on the environment.

E-commerce (electronic commerce) (1.4.1.2)

Everything from travel tickets to office supplies can be purchased on the Web, often more cheaply than from a high street store. Some online stores, such as Amazon (www.amazon.co.uk), operate only through the Internet; others, such as W H Smith (www.whsmith.co.uk), have grown out of high street stores. Most stores deal in physical goods (e.g. books, CDs, groceries) which are then sent by post or by the company's delivery vans to the customer. Some sell data, in the form of software, images, music, videos, fonts, e-books and information of all types, and this can be 'delivered' by downloading.

E-banking (1.4.1.2)

Banking, insurance and other financial services are much cheaper to run through websites than high street offices. The advantages of online banking to the customer include access to their account details at any time without the need to travel to a high street branch. Many people are still concerned about the level of security of these systems and the lack of personal contact if problems arise. The main advantage to the banks is a reduction in the cost of running and staffing branches. Fewer high street premises can lead to job losses.

A high proportion of bookings for plane, train and coach tickets, car hire, hotel rooms and theatre tickets is now through websites. Interactivity (the ability to choose from the available seats, rooms or vehicles, and to reserve it immediately) is one of the key attractions of online bookings.

E-government (1.4.1.2)

National and local governments, and other services, are increasingly accessible online. They also appreciate the advantages of the Internet. Using the Web, you can now:
- pay your income tax and VAT
- apply for a driving licence, book a test and pay your vehicle tax

- find out about local schools and childcare facilities
- do your tax returns online, claim benefits and check your premium bonds
- apply for energy grants, order a compost bin etc.
- watch MPs at work in Parliament and in committees
- contact the police
- find a job and find out your rights as an employee
- find a doctor or a dentist
- and much more.

Figure I.3I E-government

E-learning (I.4.I.3)

ICT is spreading rapidly in education, from primary schools through to universities and adult learning. With ICT firmly on the National Curriculum, students now gain invaluable experience of ICT in the classroom before they embark on a career.

Spending on ICT facilities in educational establishments has increased dramatically over the last decade, and the majority of schools and colleges have dedicated ICT staff and management. Most schools and colleges operate their computers on a network basis so that students can access their files and materials from any terminal in their institution. Some can gain access remotely, for example from home, which is especially useful to those who cannot attend school for whatever reason.

Publishers and organisers of distance learning material routinely provide some or all of their learning material on the Web. The material may be simple read-only text, but is often multimedia, combining text, images, sounds and videos, and interactive simulations. Testing during the course can be used to direct students to suitable material, and the final assessment can also be done online.

E-learning can be highly flexible, allowing users to choose when and where to do their studying. It can also be more cost-effective than classroom-based teaching, especially where only small numbers of students can be brought together at any one time.

Teleworking (1.4.1.4)

This term means replacing the journey to work that many people make each day with the use of telecommunications and computers. When teleworking first became acceptable business practice, it was often programmers who had no daily face-to-face contact with other people who became teleworkers. Now, more and more organisations, particularly large ones, are allowing employees to spend time out of the office working from home, for some or all of their weekly hours. The number of teleworkers in Europe has grown from under 10 million in 2000 to nearly 25 million by 2008, with further steady growth expected.

The benefits to employees of teleworking include:

- reduced cost of travelling
- long commuting journeys are avoided
- the opportunity to work in the comfort of their own home environment
- greater ability to focus on one task
- flexible schedules (with the knock-on effect of easier childcare arrangements).

The drawbacks include:

- a lack of personal contact with fellow workers
- a lack of teamwork and participation with shared projects
- home distractions may interfere with work
- home workers may not be given the same benefits as in-office employees, for example medical plans, pensions and bonuses.

For the company, the main benefits are:

◉ reduced space requirements
◉ a happier workforce, which may lead to increased productivity.

Virtual communities (1.4.3.1)

People get together online to form virtual communities. 'Virtual' because community members never, or rarely, meet face to face. These communities can be found in the following.

◉ Chat rooms, where groups of people meet and 'chat' by typing text messages into a shared area.

◉ Online games, which range from computer versions of card or board games, through to multi-player graphic adventure games. In these, players take on a game character and enter into a virtual world where they can co-operate or compete with other players.

◉ Social networking sites, which people use to find new partners, friends or business contacts. Users post details about themselves, their interests and the sort of people they want to meet. Contact is typically by messages through the site, though some also have chat rooms where groups can meet.

◉ Forums, or message boards, are sites where people can post messages to discuss things or to answer each others' questions. A forum will normally be dedicated to a specific topic. Computing, technology and games are popular forum topics, as are politics, fashion and celebrity culture – but there is a forum for almost every interest.

Warning!

(1.4.3.3) For some people, one of the advantages of virtual communities is that you can hide your real name, age, sex, height, weight etc. so that other people can relate to the person inside – the 'real you' – rather than to your appearance. The other side of this is that you cannot be sure what sort of person you are talking to. It is dangerous to give out personal data to those that you do not know. Keep your profile private, and be careful about the information you share, so that strangers cannot locate you in the real world. If you upload photos or videos to networking or video-sharing sites, remember that if you post them in a public area, anybody can see them.

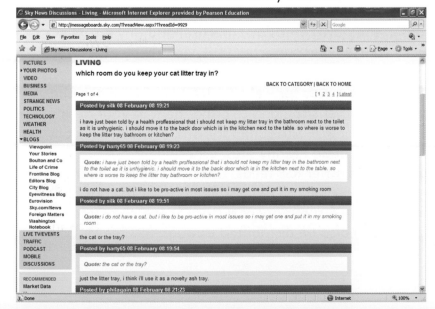

Figure 1.32 Example of a virtual forum web page

Publishing on the Web (I.4.2.4–6/I.4.3.2)

When the Web first started, if people wanted to publish their ideas, or images, or products on the Web, they did this on web pages. This is still one of the best ways to tell people about your company, organisation or society, but there are now many other ways to distribute your material.

- A **blog** (web log) is a form of interactive diary/notice board. Someone running a blog can add new material at any point, and can allow others to post their own comments. Bloggers (people who run blogs) often link to each other's blogs, to share ideas and reach a wider public.

- **Podcasts** are audio recordings downloaded from the Internet, and are designed to be listened to on an iPod or on a PC. Anyone can create a podcast – it is only a matter of having a microphone and suitable recording software on your PC, and having something to say (or sing or play). Some podcasts are one-offs; others are offered as a continuous service that you can subscribe to. To download, manage and listen to podcasts you need special software. There are several alternatives, all of them free, including iTunes, My Yahoo! and Google Reader.

- People can share their videos on sites like **YouTube** (www.youtube.com). Some of these are commercial promotional videos for bands or movies, but many are home movies and 'candid camera' shorts.

- **Wiki** sites are where people collaborate to create material. The first of these was Wikipedia, a form of encyclopedia. Anyone who registers with the site can write entries or edit existing ones. Generally speaking, people only write about things in their own areas of expertise, and any errors are usually spotted and corrected fairly quickly by other users. The entries are then available for anyone to access.

- **RSS** feeds are a way for websites to share headlines and stories with other sites, and to bring them to your desktop. (RSS stands for RDF Site Summary, and casually as Really Simple Syndication.) Many sites, especially those of news organisations, offer RSS feeds. Once you have subscribed to an RSS site, you will get regular 'feeds' sent to your browser. A feed may be a summary of a story or the complete story. Podcasts can also be distributed through RSS feeds.

Web phones (1.4.2.3)

VoIP (Voice over Internet Protocol) allows people to talk to each other through the Internet, in almost the same way with almost the same quality as through the normal telephone system. All that's needed is a headset or speakers, a microphone and an account with an Internet phone service, such as Skype. Calls to other users' computers are free. Calls can also be made from a computer to a landline or mobile phone. These are charged at the local rates in the other person's country (plus a small surcharge), rather than at international rates.

Ergonomics (1.4.4.1/3–4)

As people spend more and more time using computers it is essential to create an **ergonomic** working environment. Ergonomics refers to how design and functionality affect the ability of a person to do their work. It encompasses a range of factors.

- **Lighting**. The room should be well lit. Computers should neither face windows nor back onto a window so that the users have to sit with the sun in their eyes. Adjustable blinds should be provided.
- **Ventilation**. The room should have opening windows to allow free circulation of air and to prevent overheating.
- **Furniture**. Chairs should be of adjustable height and set so that a user's feet are flat on the floor with their knees level with their hips. It should give support to the lower back, and should swivel on a stable five-point base. The relative heights of the desk and chair should mean that the forearm is roughly horizontal when typing on the keyboard.
- **Accessories**. Document holders, mouse mats, paper trays, foot rests etc. should be provided where appropriate.
- **Hardware**. The screen should tilt and swivel and be flicker-free. Ideally it should be positioned so that it avoids reflecting light. A removable monitor filter can be useful to prevent glare. The keyboard should be separately attached so that it can be positioned to suit the user.

All computer users should be encouraged to take frequent breaks away from the computer. Short, frequent breaks (e.g. a 5–10 minute break after working 50–60 minutes) are best, but if the job means spending long periods at a screen, then longer breaks should be taken between sessions. Ideally the break should involve some exercises to stretch muscles, and to relax the eyes.

Health and safety issues (1.4.4.2–4)

A computerised office can be hazardous.

- All cables should be safely secured. If they have to cross a floor where people walk, they should be protected by a sturdy cover.
- Power points should not be overloaded. Use a surge protector to prevent power spikes from damaging the equipment. If a sudden shut-down could cause expensive loss of data, install an uninterruptible power supply (UPS – a battery-backed system that gives you time to shut down safely).
- Working surfaces should be clean and tidy.

Computers can be held responsible for many health problems, from eye strain to wrist injuries and back problems.

- **Repetitive Strain Injury** (RSI). This is the collective name for a variety of disorders affecting the neck, shoulders and upper limbs. It can result in numbness or tingling in the arms and hands, aching and stiffness in the arms, neck and shoulders, and an inability to lift or grip objects. The Health and Safety Executive says that more than 100,000 UK workers suffer from RSI.
- **Eye strain**. Computer users are prone to eye strain from spending long hours in front of a screen. Many computer users prefer a dim light to achieve better screen contrast, but this makes it difficult to read documents on the desk. A small spotlight focused on the desktop can be helpful. There is no evidence that computer use causes permanent damage to the eyes but glare, improper lighting, improperly corrected vision (through not wearing the correct prescription glasses), poor work practices and poorly designed workstations all contribute to temporary eye strain.
- **Back problems**. Poor seating and bad posture while sitting at a computer screen can cause back problems.

Simple techniques can reduce these problems.

- Take a 1–2 minute stretch break every 20 minutes, and take a 5–10 minute break or do something away from the computer every hour.
- Relax your eyes while you take your breaks. Rest them by covering them with your palms for 10–15 seconds, or refocus them by looking out of the window or elsewhere in the distance.
- Sit up properly when working.

Note

The UK Health and Safety at Work Act (1974) legislates on health and safety in the workplace. It is supported by numerous regulations, such as:

- the Control of Substances Hazardous to Health (COSHH) Regulations (2002)
- Manual Handling Operations Regulations (1992)
- Workplace (Health, Safety and Welfare) Regulations (1992)
- Health and Safety (Display Screen Equipment) Regulations (1992)

The environment (1.4.5.1–2)

There are a number of measures that computer users can take to help the environment.

- Ensure that the computer's energy-saving routines are turned on, so that it powers down when left unattended. (See Power options on page 90.)
- Recycle printer toner and inkjet cartridges.
- Ensure that used paper goes to recycling, not the bin, and buy recycled paper for printing.
- Do not print out if you can read something on a screen.
- CD-ROM materials, electronic documents and on-screen help all reduce the need for printed materials.
- Old CDs, that have been used for file transfer or backups and are no longer wanted, can be recycled. CD recycling is a specialised business but you should be able to find a local collection point through the Internet or your local recycling centre.
- Dispose of old equipment, especially laptop batteries, carefully. Old computers in working order, or repairable, can be sent to charities for reuse by other people in this country or overseas.

Note

Businesses need to comply with the Waste Electrical and Electronic Equipment (WEEE) Directive when recycling and disposing of IT equipment.

Note

Power options (1.4.5.2)

There are four levels of power saving:

- Turn off the monitor.
- Turn off the hard drives.
- Standby – turns off the monitor and hard drives.
- Hibernate – saves open documents and desktop configuration, then shuts down completely. On restarting, the desktop and documents are restored to where they were.

The more you turn off, the more power you save, but the longer it takes to restart.

Test your understanding

1. Give **three** advantages and **three** disadvantages of shopping over the Internet compared with shopping in a high street store.
2. a) What type of software do you need to surf the World Wide Web?
   b) Describe briefly **three** advantages to a company of having its own website.
3. Give **three** advantages and **three** disadvantages of computer-based training in a school or company.
4. Describe briefly **three** health hazards associated with working long hours at a computer. In each case, describe one method of minimising the hazard.
5. a) Describe briefly **three** ways in which users can minimise the detrimental effects of computers on the environment.
   b) Describe **three** ways in which computers could be said to be contributing positively towards preserving the environment.

You can find the answers to the questions on the CD-ROM saved as **Answers to TYU questions 1.4**. How did you do? Go back over anything that you are unsure of.

Legal issues and security

Learning objectives

By working through this lesson you will learn:

- about how to keep data safe by controlling access, making backups and protecting your devices
- about computer viruses and how to avoid them
- about copyright and software licences
- about the Data Protection Act and the protection of data.

Access controls (1.5.1.1–2)

Most networks require a user to log on with a **user ID** and **password** before they can gain access to the computer system. The user ID is normally assigned to you, and is open to view. The password is secret and does not appear on the screen when you type it in – the letters may be replaced by asterisks as you type. You can change your password whenever you like.

If you are authorised to access particularly sensitive data which only certain people are allowed to view, you may need to enter a second password. For example, on a company database the accounts clerks may be able to view customer records but they may not be allowed access to personal data about colleagues. These **access rights** are used to protect the privacy of individuals and the security of confidential data.

There are some basic rules you should follow when using a password.

- Never write the password down. Commit it to memory.
- Never tell your password to another person.
- Do not use an obvious word or name as a password. A combination of at least six letters and numbers is best.
- Change your password regularly.

Backup procedures (1.5.2.1)

Computer data can be very valuable and can be all too easily lost. Backups ensure that you have a recent copy of your data in case disaster strikes. For home users it may be enough to make a backup once a week, or after any significant work has been done or new files loaded. In businesses, backups are typically made on a daily basis, or more frequently, depending on the nature and importance of the data.

Backing up data involves copying it to a removable storage device such as magnetic tape, CD-ROM, Zip drive, flash memory etc. The backup media must be clearly labelled and should be stored in a fireproof safe, or better still on a different site, so that should a disaster or emergency occur, the backup media will be safe.

Theft (1.5.2.3)

The theft of a desktop or laptop computer, PDA or mobile phone can have disastrous consequences for the owner if they have not backed up their data. Confidential files, lists of phone numbers which could be misused, contact details or months of work can be lost if they are not properly protected and backed up. Also, data can be stolen without actually removing the computer. This can be even more damaging as the owner will not know the data has been stolen until someone starts to misuse it.

Steps should also be taken to prevent the theft of computers, and computer data, from within the premises.

- Visible security marks make hardware less attractive to steal.
- Security cables make it harder to remove devices.
- Backup disks must be kept under lock and key. In transit, they must be protected and monitored at all times.
- Password-protected access to disk drives, folders and files all help to keep data safe.

Computer viruses (1.5.3.1–3)

Viruses are programs designed to cause damage to computer files or, at the very least, cause inconvenience and annoyance to computer users. They are disguised as innocent files, hidden in other programs or documents, but become active once the program is run or the document opened. (A document cannot itself do anything, but it may contain macros – mini programs – which can contain viruses.) A key feature of viruses, and why they are called 'viruses', is that they create copies of themselves and attempt to infect other files and computers.

These are other types of **malware** (malicious software).

- **Trojan horses** – programs hidden within other programs and designed to become active under certain conditions, for example a set date or when a specific operation is run.
- **Spyware** – sends information about the websites you visit and other aspects of your computer use to their hosts. This may just be measuring the effectiveness of web advertising, but they can be more intrusive.
- **Worm** – a program that copies itself and tries to spread over a computer network. Unlike a virus, this is not hidden in another program and they are not usually meant to do any damage to files. They do damage to networks simply because they can take up so much processing power as they copy and spread.

Note

If a virus infects your computer, it can corrupt files and spread to other computers on your network or belonging to your email contacts. You must take steps to prevent viruses getting into you computer, removing any that do make it through the defences.

The best protection is good anti-virus software, which must be updated regularly so that it is able to recognise new viruses as they are developed.

There is more on viruses and anti-virus software in Module 2, see Virus protection on page 86.

Firewalls (I.5.2.2)

A firewall is a hardware or software device that controls the flow of data over a network. When a computer is connected to the Internet, it is possible for other people elsewhere on the Internet to gain access to the computer, to read its files or store other files there. A firewall prevents this. It allows you to specify which sites, if any, can have access to your machine, and to set the level of access, if any.

Copyright (I.6.I.I–4)

Figure I.33 About Internet Explorer

Computer software is **copyright** material. This means it is protected in the UK by the Copyright, Designs and Patents Act (1988). Software is owned by the software producer and it is illegal to make unauthorised copies. When you buy software it is often supplied in a sealed package on which the terms and conditions of use are printed. This is called the **software licence** and when the user opens the package they are agreeing to abide by the licence terms (often referred to as the End User Licence Agreement). The CD or package will have a unique Product ID number which you may need to type in when installing the software. Once installed, you can see the Product ID number by clicking the Help menu and selecting an option such as, for example, About Internet Explorer.

Software licences usually permit the user to use one copy on any single computer. It is considered to be in use if it is loaded into either the computer's temporary memory (RAM) or onto the hard disk drive. With network licences the software is often loaded onto the file server and the licence specifies how many users on the network can access it at any one time.

It is illegal to make copies of the software, except for backup purposes, so you are breaking the law if you copy some software from a friend onto removable media such as floppy disk, CD or memory stick to use on your own computer.

Some software is classed as **shareware**. This can be downloaded from the Internet for evaluation. If you like the program you pay a fee and register with the manufacturer. Most programs of this type allow you to use them a limited number of times and then they cease to run correctly when the evaluation period expires. **Freeware** programs can be downloaded from the Internet and used at no cost.

Some software is **open source**. This means that the source code – the lines of programming instructions from which the software is produced – is available for anyone to download and change or reuse freely. The Linux operating system and applications are all open source, and have been developed by co-operation between individual programmers, working for the fun of it.

Files downloaded from the Internet containing text, graphics, audio or video clips may also be copyright. It is illegal to use such material in your own publications without the consent of the author or creator.

Personal privacy (1.6.2.1)

The **right to privacy** is a fundamental human right and one that we take for granted. Most of us, for instance, would not want our medical records freely circulated, and many people are sensitive about revealing their age, religious beliefs, family circumstances or academic qualifications. In the UK even the use of name and address files for mail shots is often felt to be an invasion of privacy.

With the advent of large computerised databases it became quite feasible for sensitive personal information to be stored without the individual's knowledge and accessed by, say, a prospective employer, credit card company or insurance company to assess somebody's suitability for employment, credit or insurance, respectively.

The Data Protection Act (1998) (1.6.2.2–3)

The **Data Protection Act (1998)** came into force on 1 March 2000. It sets rules for processing data about people and applies to paper records as well as those held on computers. It is intended to protect the privacy of individuals.

Case Study

James Wiggins – A true story

In the USA, James Russell Wiggins applied for and got a $70,000 post with a company in Washington. A routine pre-employment background check, however, revealed that he had been convicted of possessing cocaine, and he was fired the next day, not only because he had a criminal record but because he had concealed this fact when applying for the job. Wiggins was shocked. He had never had a criminal record, and it turned out that the credit bureau hired to make the investigation had retrieved the record for a James Ray Wiggins by mistake, even though they had different birthdates, addresses, middle names and social security numbers. Even after this was discovered, however, Wiggins didn't get his job back.

If the pre-employment check had been made before Wiggins was offered the job, he would not have been offered it and no reason would have been given. The information would have remained on his file, virtually ensuring that he would never get a decent job – without ever knowing the reason why.

The data protection principles

Anyone holding personal data must comply with the eight enforceable principles of good practice. They say that data must be:

- fairly and lawfully processed
- obtained only for specific purposes
- adequate, relevant and not excessive
- accurate and up to date
- not kept longer than necessary
- processed in accordance with the data subject's rights
- not transferred to other countries without adequate protection
- secure from others who do not have rights to it, for example other employees and hackers.

Any organisation holding personal data about people (e.g. employees or customers) must register with the Data Protection Registrar. They have to state what data is being held, the sources and purposes of the data and the types of organisations to whom the data may be disclosed.

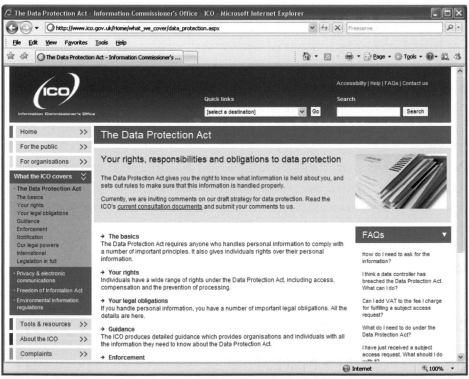

Figure I.34 The Information Commissioner's Office (ICO) website

- As an individual you are entitled, on making a written request to a data user, to be supplied with a copy of any personal data held about yourself. The data user may charge a fee of up to £10 for each register entry for supplying this information but in some cases it is supplied free.
- Usually the request must be responded to within 40 days. If not, you are entitled to complain to the Data Protection Registrar or to apply to the courts for correction or deletion of the data.
- With some exceptions, data cannot be held about you without your consent.

For more information on data protection visit the Information Commissioner's website at www.ico.gov.uk (Figure 1.34).

Data security

One of the legal requirements of the Data Protection Act is that data about individuals must be kept secure. This means that it must be properly protected from unauthorised view or loss. Moreover, the data held on a computer system can be one of the most valuable assets of a company. Security controls must be put in place to protect it from damage and unauthorised access.

To deal with security risks, most organisations have an information security policy. A typical security policy will cover:

- administrative controls such as careful screening of prospective employees and disciplinary procedures in the event of security breaches
- backup procedures
- control of access to data by means of smartcards, ID badges, sign-in/sign-out registers
- protection against fire and flood
- access controls to computer systems and data by means of user IDs, passwords and access rights
- procedures for reporting security incidents
- training to make staff members aware of their responsibilities.

Staying safe and good practice

When using ICT-based communications, bear in mind the following principles:

- Protect personal information to minimise the risk of identity theft or fraud.

- Avoid the misuse of images which will offend others or break the law.
- Use language appropriate to the topic and recipient of any messages, and do not offend others. Check all recipients on a copy list should receive a particular message before you send it.
- Respect confidentiality.

See Module 7, page 397, for more on staying safe.

Test your understanding

1. List **three** ways in which you can help to keep your password secure.
2. Why is it important to backup data? How can you best keep your backups safe?
3. a) What is a computer virus?
   b) Name **three** measures you can take to minimise the possibility of your computer being infected with a virus.
4. Before using a photograph that you have downloaded from the Internet in a publication of your own, what should you do?
5. What is meant by the terms shareware and freeware? Explain whether or not you can use such software on your computer without paying.
6. a) What is the name of the Act that protects the privacy of personal data held on a computer?
   b) List **four** provisions of this Act.
7. What rights do you have as an individual regarding the holding of personal data about yourself on a computer?

You can find the answers to the questions on the CD-ROM saved as **Answers to TYU questions I.5**. How did you do? Go back over anything that you are unsure of.

In this module you will learn to become competent in using a personal computer and its operating system. You will learn how to use the Desktop and work with Desktop icons and windows, manage files and folders, use simple editing tools and Windows' print management facilities.

MODULE 2.
using the computer and managing files

Windows basics

Learning objectives

By working through this lesson you will learn:

◉ how to start your PC

◉ about the parts of the Desktop and what you might find on it

◉ about the mouse and the effects of clicking its buttons

◉ about the structure of windows and how to open, close, move and resize them

◉ how to end a session safely

◉ how to deal with a program crash.

First steps

This module shows you how to use your computer's **operating system – Microsoft Windows**. The version used here is Windows XP, but you will find that other versions of Windows work in much the same way. The things you will learn in this module will help you to organise the work that you do and the documents that you create using applications such as word-processing software. It will also help you to 'troubleshoot' and know what to do when something unexpected happens.

Switching on (2.1.1.1)

❶ If there is a floppy disk drive on your computer, check that there is not a disk in it.

❷ Press the power switch on the front of the system unit. Switch on the screen and the printer.

❸ If the computer has been set up for multiple users, you will probably be asked to enter a **user ID** and **password**. Do that now. For security reasons, the password will not be displayed on the screen.

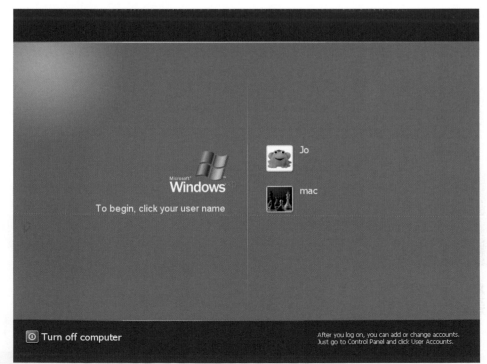

Figure 2.1 Microsoft Windows XP log on screen

④ Wait for the screen to stop changing. It should end up showing some small symbols (called icons) on a coloured or picture background. This is called the **Desktop**.

Figure 2.2 Microsoft Windows XP Desktop

Depending on how your computer has been set up you may see a different background and a different set of icons. Later in this module you will learn how to select a different background for your Desktop. Let's look more closely at the Desktop.

Icons (2.1.3.1)

Desktop icons come in a variety of forms. Here are some of the common ones.

● A **folder** (sometimes called a **directory**). You can double-click a folder icon to open the folder. Then you can select a file from the folder. (We will be looking at files and folders in the next section, and mouse clicks later in this section.)

● A **file**. Double-click a file icon to open the file in the appropriate application – in this case Microsoft Word.

● An **application**. You can double-click an application icon to open the application.

● The **Recycle Bin** (a 'wastebasket'). When you delete a file from your hard drive, it goes into the Recycle Bin. You can retrieve it from there if you change your mind about deleting it, so long as you haven't emptied the bin!

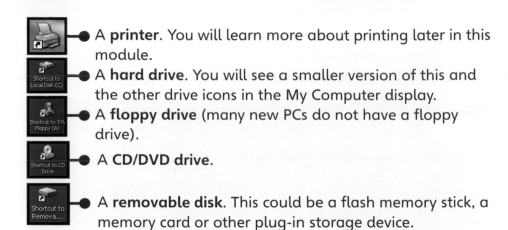

A **printer**. You will learn more about printing later in this module.

A **hard drive**. You will see a smaller version of this and the other drive icons in the My Computer display.

A **floppy drive** (many new PCs do not have a floppy drive).

A **CD/DVD drive**.

A **removable disk**. This could be a flash memory stick, a memory card or other plug-in storage device.

Taskbar

The **Taskbar** at the bottom of the screen shows application programs that are currently open. Hover the mouse pointer (i.e. do not click a mouse button) over any icon on the Taskbar. A screen tip appears telling you its function.

On the left-hand side, next to the **Start** button is the **Quick Launch** toolbar. Its icons give you a quick way to start some key applications – and notice **Show Desktop**. This hides all the open applications and shows a clear Desktop. On the far right is the clock, which shows the current time.

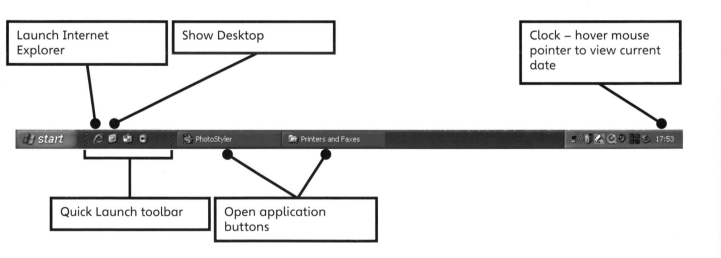

Launch Internet Explorer

Show Desktop

Clock – hover mouse pointer to view current date

Quick Launch toolbar

Open application buttons

Figure 2.3 Microsoft Windows XP Taskbar

Using the mouse

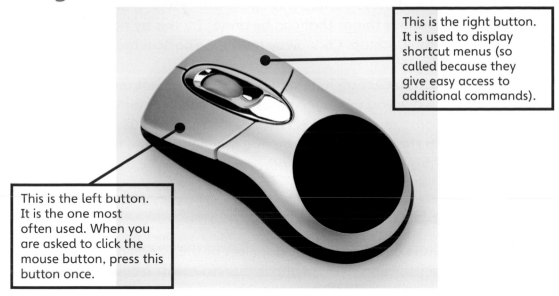

This is the right button. It is used to display shortcut menus (so called because they give easy access to additional commands).

This is the left button. It is the one most often used. When you are asked to click the mouse button, press this button once.

Figure 2.4 Using the mouse buttons

Depending on where the mouse pointer is on the screen, or on what the computer is doing, a different icon appears. Here are some examples.

- This is the general pointer and means the computer is ready for you to do something.
- The hourglass shows the computer is busy, maybe loading a program, and you should wait until the normal pointer appears before you do anything.
- When the pointer changes to a two-headed arrow you can resize a window.

Mouse clicks (2.1.3.2)

There are basically three different ways of clicking a mouse button. You will also need to drag to select or move text or objects.

- ◉ Single-click. When you are told to 'click', this means click the left button once. Clicking once selects an item. Try clicking on one of the Desktop icons. It changes colour but nothing else happens.
- ◉ Double-click. Generally speaking, clicking selects an item, and double-clicking activates it, but there are plenty of exceptions to this rule. Try double-clicking the **My Computer** icon, for example, to open the **My Computer** window. You can leave this window open on the Desktop for now.

Tip!

If the icon won't move, right-click the Desktop and select **Arrange Icons By** from the menu. Make sure **Auto Arrange** is not selected.

Figure 2.5 Auto Arrange option

◉ Right-click. When you are told to right-click, click the right-hand button once. This opens a shortcut menu showing various things that can be done. Try this by right-clicking on the Desktop. Click away from the shortcut menu to close it again.

◉ Drag. Click an item and hold down the left mouse button while you move the mouse. The selected item will be dragged in the direction you move the mouse in. Try moving a Desktop icon by dragging it. Releasing the mouse button drops the icon in the new position.

The Start menu

The **Start** button at the bottom left of the screen opens a menu where you can select an application to run or a task that you want to do – including shutting down your computer!
We'll open a games application now.

❶ Click the **Start** button.
❷ On the menu that appears, click **All Programs**.
❸ On the submenu, click **Games**.
❹ On the next menu, click **Solitaire**.

Tip!

There are two different styles for the **Start** menu. We are using the default XP style. In the 'Classic' style, the menu looks as it did in earlier versions of Windows. To switch between the two, right-click the Start button and click **Properties**. Go to the **Start Menu** tab, where you can select a Start menu option. Try both styles, and see which you prefer.

Figure 2.6 Starting Solitaire

❺ The Solitaire window opens.

If you can tear yourself away from the game, or cannot figure out how to play, we'll look now at the parts of a window.

The parts of a window (2.1.4.1)

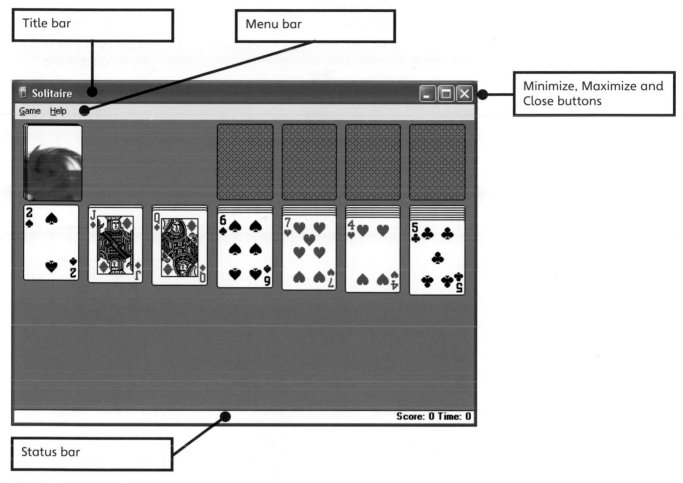

Title bar

Menu bar

Minimize, Maximize and Close buttons

Status bar

Figure 2.7 Parts of a window

You should have two windows open on the Desktop – the **My Computer** window and the **Solitaire** window. You'll notice that each of them has the following parts in common.

- A **Title bar** showing the name of the program. Click in the **Title bar** of each window in turn to bring it to the foreground.
- A **Menu bar** that has labels that when clicked produce drop-down menus with options to choose from.
- A **Status bar** which provides information about the current state of what you are viewing in the window.

- A **Minimize** button. ▬ Click this button once in the Solitaire window. The window disappears to the Taskbar, but the application is still open. Look in the Taskbar and you will see a button named Solitaire.

  [🃏 Solitaire]

  Click it to restore the window to the Desktop.
- A **Maximize** button. ▢ Click this once on the Solitaire window. The window now occupies the full screen. Notice that the Maximize button has now changed to a **Restore Down** button. ▣ Click this once now to restore the window to its original size.
- A **Close** button. ✕ You would click this once to close the window. Don't do this now. If you do close one of the two open windows, open it up again!
- Horizontal and vertical scroll bars that can be moved to allow you to see all parts of the window.

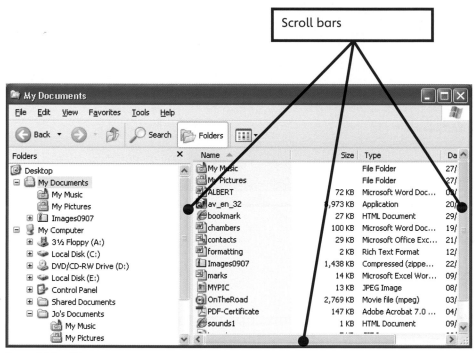

Figure 2.8 Scroll bars

Moving and resizing a window (2.1.4.2–3)

- To switch between open windows, either click the buttons on the Taskbar or click any visible part of the window that you want to bring to the front.
- To move a window around on the screen, drag its Title bar.

- ◉ To change the size of a window, move the cursor over one of its borders so that the pointer changes to a double-headed arrow. Drag the border out or in to make the window bigger or smaller.
- ❶ Try making the **My Computer** window smaller so that scroll bars appear. You can drag a scroll bar to see parts of the window that are hidden from view. Notice that this window also has a toolbar with buttons which you can click.
- ❷ Try arranging the windows on the Desktop so that they don't overlap. A quick way to do this is to right-click in the Taskbar and from the shortcut menu, select **Tile Windows Horizontally** or **Tile Windows Vertically**.

Figure 2.9 Tiling windows

Do it!

Close both the open windows when you have finished practising. Click the **Close** button.

Creating and removing a Desktop icon (2.1.3.3–4)

You can create a shortcut on the Desktop for any program so that you can open it quickly, instead of using the Start menu.

- ❶ Click **All Programs** on the **Start** menu and find the **Solitaire** program as you did earlier.
- ❷ This time right-click the word **Solitaire** and move the mouse pointer over **Send to**.
- ❸ Click **Desktop (create shortcut)** on the menu. A shortcut icon will appear on the Desktop.

- ❹ Drag and drop the icon in the position you want.
- ❺ Try opening the **Solitaire** program using your new shortcut icon.
- ❻ To remove a shortcut, right-click it and select **Delete**. This only removes the icon, not the program.

How about...?

You can also create a shortcut icon by pointing to the filename, holding down the right mouse button and dragging onto the Desktop.

The Windows Help and Support Center (2.1.1.5)

If you have problems with any of the tasks we have covered so far you can visit the **Windows Help and Support Center**.

① Click **Help and Support** on the **Start** menu.

② You can either click a Help topic or type a keyword into the **Search** box.

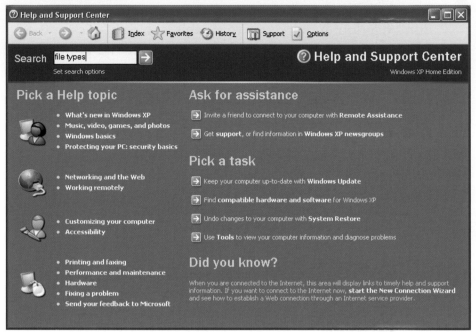

Figure 2.10 The Windows Help and Support Center search screen

Each individual application that you run on your computer (e.g. a game, word processor, spreadsheet etc.) has its own Help system too.

Ending a session (2.1.1.4)

Before you switch off your computer you should close any open programs. If you don't do this and just switch off, you may lose data from the files that you have been working on, and it will certainly take your computer longer to start up next time, as it will run through a series of checks.

When you have closed all your programs you should see only the Desktop on the screen.

① Click the **Start** button.

◉ If you are on a network and want to leave the PC running for another user.

② Click **Log Off**.

③ In the box that appears click **Log Off**.

Figure 2.11 Logging off from Microsoft Windows

- ◉ If you are on a stand-alone PC, or want to shut down a networked PC.
- ② Click **Turn off** Computer.
- ③ In the box that appears, click **Turn Off**.
- ④ Wait for the screen to go black, or for a message to say that it is safe to turn off your computer and then switch off the computer.

Figure 2.12 Turning off Microsoft Windows

Tip!

With Windows 2000 or later versions, the PC switches itself off.

Restarting your computer (2.1.1.2)

Instead of closing down your computer you can choose to restart it. You may want to do this if you have loaded some new software and its installation guide tells you to restart Windows.

- ◉ When you reach the **Turn off** computer box, click the **Restart** option.

Shutting down a non-responding application (2.1.1.3)

From time to time, just when you think things are going really well and that you are getting to grips with using a PC, everything suddenly grinds to a halt and it refuses to respond. An application has 'crashed'!

If the application locks up so that you cannot use the keyboard or mouse, you can try to find out which program is causing the problem.

1 Press the Ctrl, Alt and Del keys on the keyboard (all at the same time – this is usually written as **Ctrl+Alt+Del**). This opens the **Windows Task Manager** window.

Figure 2.13 The Task Manager

On the **Applications tab**, you will see a list of the programs currently running on your computer. One of them will probably show a status of **Not Responding**. This will be the offending program.

2 Click the program name and click **End Task** to shut it down.

This should close down the faulty program and allow you to carry on working. If it doesn't, follow the shut down procedure above to safely close down your PC.

Unfortunately, either way you will lose anything you have been working on in the application, for example all the changes to a document since you last saved it. The only lesson to be learned is to save your work every few minutes. Everything that you have saved to a floppy disk or hard disk is safe.

Tip!

A quick way to save a document you are working on is to press **Ctrl+S** (Ctrl and S together) on the keyboard, or click the Save icon.

Test your understanding

1. Switch on your computer and look at the Windows Desktop. Write down the answers to the following questions.
   a) Do you have to enter a Windows username and password?
   b) What are icons?
   c) Write down the names of all the icons you can see.
   d) What is the Recycle Bin icon used for?
   e) Where would you find the current date and time on your Windows Desktop?
   f) What does it mean when you see an hourglass on the screen?
   g) Describe how you would open the Solitaire game.
2. Open the My Computer window and the Solitaire game and answer the following questions.
   a) Describe the purpose of the window Minimize and Maximize buttons.
   b) Describe how you would resize a window.
   c) Draw a rough sketch of a screen with two windows tiled vertically.
3. Why shouldn't you just switch off your computer without closing down correctly?
4. How would you restart your computer?
5. Give **one** example of when you might need to restart your computer.

You can find the answers to the questions on the CD-ROM saved as **Answers to TYU questions 2.1**. How did you do? Go back over anything that you are unsure of.

Files and folders

Learning objectives

By working through this lesson you will learn:

- ◉ about the drives on your computer
- ◉ how files are stored in folders
- ◉ how to explore the files and folders in your computer
- ◉ about file types and file extensions
- ◉ how to use a text-editing application
- ◉ how to create simple documents in Word
- ◉ how to print a file
- ◉ how to change a file's name or its status
- ◉ how to sort files in the display
- ◉ how to select files, and to copy and move them
- ◉ about the drag-and-drop copying/moving technique.

Tip!

If the **My Computer** window has a blue pane on the left, click the Folders button to display the **Folders** list. This makes working with files and folders easier.

Disk drives on your computer (2.2.1.1–2/2.2.2.1)

As you learned in Module I, data can be stored on a number of different types of devices. Your computer will have at least one hard drive and probably a CD/DVD drive. There may also be a floppy drive and a flash memory stick or other removable drive. If it is attached to a network, there may also be storage space on one of the network's servers.

Windows assigns a letter to each drive on the computer. The floppy drive is usually **A:**, the hard drive **C:**, the CD/DVD drive **E:** and so on. On a network the hard drive is usually divided or 'partitioned' into several 'logical drives' called, for example, F:, G:, H: etc.

You can see what drives your computer has and how much free space there is on each disk.

❶   Go to the Desktop. To do this, click the Desktop icon on the left of the Taskbar, next to the **Start** button, or right-click the Taskbar and select **Show the Desktop**.

❷   Double-click the **My Computer** icon. You should see a window similar to the one below.

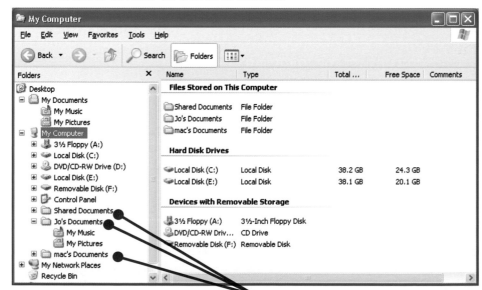

Two people share this computer. They each have their own folder for storing files, and there is a shared one which they can both use. Each user's folder has two subfolders: one for music and one for pictures. More folders can be set up as needed so files can be stored in an organised way.

Figure 2.14 My Computer showing users' folders

Figure 2.14 shows two hard disk drives, C: and E:, plus a DVD/CD-RW drive (D:) and a removable disk (F:). What drives do you have on your computer?

Your screen may still look different. You can change the appearance of the window by clicking the **Views** button, and selecting one of the other options.

Views of files

Figure 2.15 **Views** options

- ⦿ **Thumbnails** give little previews of the files (if possible).
- ⦿ **Tiles** shows the name and key details of each file, along with a large icon to identify its file type.
- ⦿ **Icons** shows the filename and a file type icon for each file.
- ⦿ **List** shows the filename and a small icon, packing more into a window.
- ⦿ **Details** lists the files, with their key details.

Windows Explorer (2.2.2.2)

Another way of looking at and manipulating your files and folders is by using **Windows Explorer**.

- ⦿ Right-click the **Start** button and select **Explore**.

You will see a screen similar to the one you opened from **My Computer**.

Folders (2.2.1.1/2.2.2.1/2.2.3.5)

All the documents you create on your PC are referred to as **files**. These files have to be given names (you can use up to 255 characters) and it is a good idea to use meaningful filenames so that you can easily find a particular file later on.

As you use your computer more and more you will store many files on your hard drive (**C:**). You will need to keep your work organised so that you can quickly go to the files you want.

Files are organised by saving them into named folders (sometimes called directories). Folders can contain subfolders. One very important folder that Windows has set up for you is My Documents. This is where Windows expects you to create your own folders to store your work. When you set up a folder, you need to give it a name. As with a filename, this should identify it clearly.

Figure 2.16 (overleaf) is an example of a folder structure within **My Documents**.

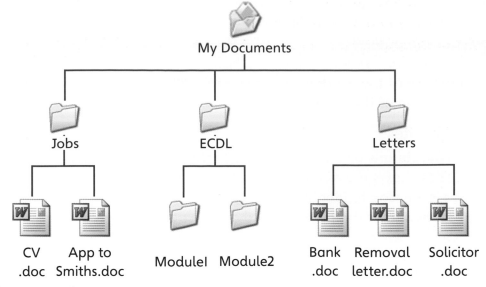

Figure 2.16 Example tree structure

The location of files is specified by their pathname. For example, in the diagram above, the pathname to the word-processed file Removal letter.doc is as follows:

C:\My Documents\Letters\Removal letter.doc

❶ In **My Computer**, double-click the **C: drive** icon.

You will now see a window displaying the folders on the C: drive. (Your window will have different folders.)

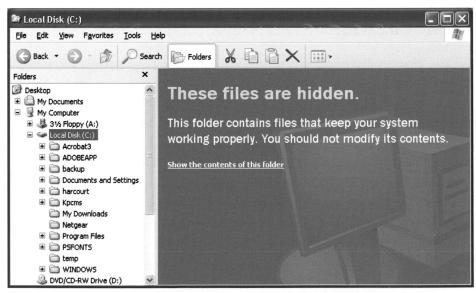

Figure 2.17 Notification of hidden files

By default, Windows hides files on the C: drive to protect them from accidental deletion or change – there are some essential ones here! If you see a blue **These files are hidden** panel, click **Show the contents of this folder**.

② Click the Folders button if it is not already selected. This shows you a more detailed view.

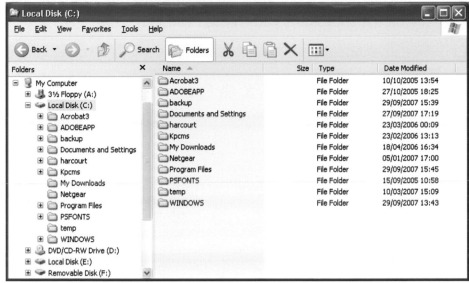

Figure 2.18 Detailed view of folders

Tip!

The view shown in Figure 2.18 is the **Details** view. Use the **Views** button to change to this if your screen looks different.

Creating a new folder (2.2.2.4)

We will set up the folders and subfolders shown in the example.

① Double-click **My Documents**. The **My Documents** folder opens.

② Click **New** on the **File** menu, then **Folder**.

③ Replace the default name **New Folder** by typing the name **Jobs** in its place.

④ Click the **Back** button to go back to the **My Documents** folder.

Do it!

Create the other two folders, **ECDL** and **Letters**, in the same way. Then select the **ECDL** folder and create two subfolders **Module1** and **Module2** inside it (see Figure 2.19).

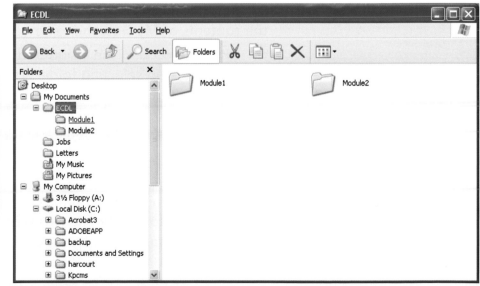

Figure 2.19 The created subfolders **Module1** and **Module2**

Navigating to a file or folder (2.2.2.2–3)

◉ In the left-hand pane, click **My Documents**. Now you should see all the subfolders you created within it.

Tip!

If you right-click a folder and select **Properties**, you can see the total size of the folder and the number of subfolders and files it contains.

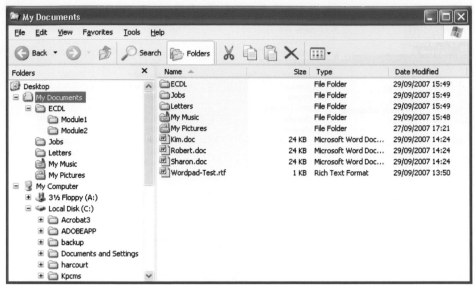

Figure 2.20 My Documents with newly created folders

Notice that you can now see the hierarchy of folders and files. When you clicked **My Documents**, the little + sign beside it in the left-hand window changed to a – sign. The + sign indicates that there are subfolders within this folder, which can be viewed by clicking to expand the structure.

This needs practice. For example, if you click the + sign beside the **ECDL** folder, you will see it expanded in the left-hand window, but it is not the selected folder so the right-hand pane will still show the contents of **My Documents**, the selected folder.

◉ Practise clicking the + sign and the – sign beside various folders, and selecting folders and subfolders, until you are clear about how the system works. Leave your screen looking like the one shown in Figure 2.20 for the next task.

File types (2.2.3.1)

Tip!

Later you will learn how to rename a file. However, you have to be careful not to change the extension because the software will not recognise the file type and will not know how to handle your file.

Windows recognises many different file types. The type depends on which application the file was created in. Here are some examples of common file types, each identified by the three-character extension which forms part of the filename.

File extension	File type
.avi, .mpeg, .mov	Different types of video file
.bmp	A bitmapped graphic created in a graphics package
.doc	A word-processed file produced in Microsoft Word
.exe	An executable file, that is a program
.htm	A web page file
.jpg, .gif, .tif	Different types of graphics file
.mdb	A database file created in Microsoft Access
.mp3, .mid, .wav	Different types of audio file
.pdf	A Portable Document Format (PDF) file which can be opened in Abobe® Reader
.ppt	A presentation file created in Microsoft PowerPoint
.rtf	A Rich Text Format file which can be opened in most word processors
.tmp	A temporary file
.txt	A plain text file
.xls	A spreadsheet produced in Microsoft Excel
.zip	A compressed file

Tip!

The three-letter file type extensions can be hidden. If you cannot see them after the filenames, open the Tools menu and select **Folder Options....** Switch to the View tab on the **Folder Options** window, and under **Advanced settings:,** click **Hide extensions for known file types** to clear its tick box.

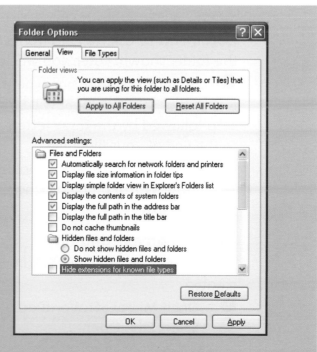

Figure 2.21 Folder options

Using a text-editing application (2.2.3.2)

First we will create a short document and save it.

① From the **Start** menu, select **All Programs**, **Accessories**, **WordPad**.

WordPad is a simple word processor that is supplied free with Windows. It has all the features that you may need for writing letters, essays, reports and other documents that use formatted text, perhaps with inserted images.

② Type this short sentence – you can be more imaginative if you like!

This is a test document created in WordPad.

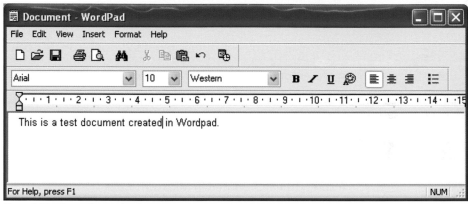

Figure 2.22 Microsoft WordPad

③ Click **Save** on the **File** menu.

The **Save As** dialogue box (Figure 2.23 on page 67) will open, probably showing the default **My Documents** folder in the **Save in:** box. If it shows something different, you can navigate to **My Documents** or ask for help from your tutor. Alternatively, save it in the folder shown. Later, you will learn how to move it.

④ In the **File name:** box type the name **Wordpad-Test**.

Notice that the document will be saved in **Rich Text Format**. A full stop followed by the three letters **rtf** (the extension) will be added to the end of your filename.

⑤ Click **Save** to close the dialogue box.

⑥ Close **WordPad** by clicking the **Close** icon ☒ or by selecting **File**, **Exit**.

Opening an existing file

Now practise re-opening WordPad and opening the new file you created.

① Open **Microsoft WordPad**.

② Select **File**, **Open...**

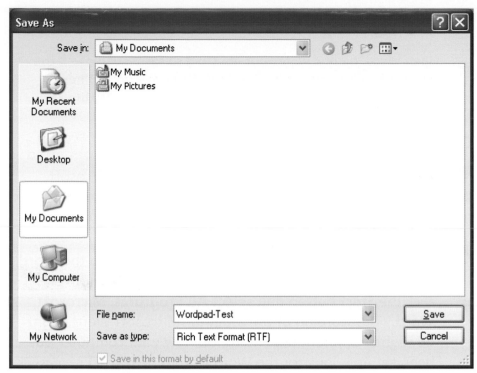

Figure 2.23 The **Save As** dialogue box

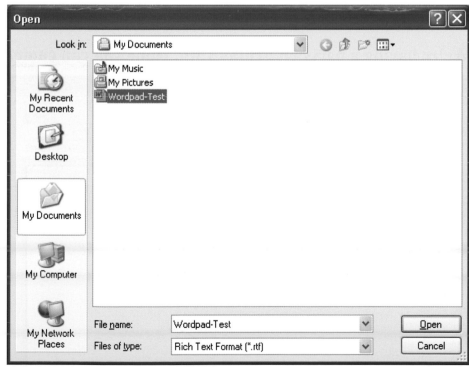

Figure 2.24 Opening a file in Microsoft WordPad

The **Open** dialogue box will be displayed (Figure 2.24).

❸ Navigate to the correct file and select it.

❹ Click **Open**.

How about...?

You can open a file by double-clicking it in the **Open** dialogue box.

Creating a Word document

Next we'll create three very short documents using Microsoft Word – a more advanced word processor than WordPad. We need some files so that we can practise moving them, copying them, renaming them and so on.

1. Open **Microsoft Word**. You can do this by clicking the **Word** shortcut icon on the **Desktop** (if it is there). Alternatively, click the **Start** button and select **All Programs**, **Microsoft Word**. (The wording of the label for Microsoft Word might be slightly different depending on how your computer has been set up – look for the Word icon to help you.)

2. Type a short invitation to your friend Kim as follows:

Dear Kim

We're having a party on Friday 13th. Hope you can come!

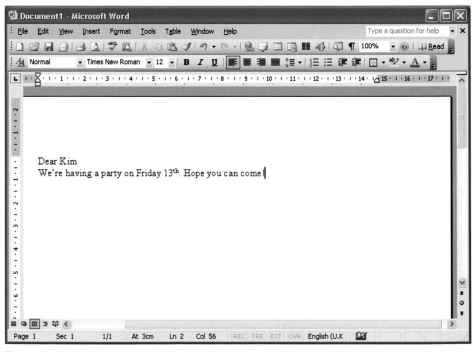

Figure 2.25 Example Word document

3. Click **Save** on the **File** menu. Save the document in the same folder as before, with the name **Kim**.

④ Now edit the letter by changing the name **Kim** to **Robert**.

⑤ This time, you don't want to click **Save** on the **File** menu because that would simply overwrite the contents of the original file, leaving you with a letter to Robert with the filename Kim. Instead, select **Save As...**

⑥ Type a new filename **Robert**.

⑦ Edit the letter once more, to send an invitation to Sharon.

⑧ Save this file as **Sharon**.

Warning!

If you do not have a printer installed on your computer, go to page 97 before you do anything else. You need to be able to print!

Printing a file (2.4.2.I)

① Click **Print...** on the **File** menu.

The Print dialogue box allows you to choose many options including which printer you want to use, which pages to print (for longer documents) and the number of copies.

② Check that there is paper in the printer.

③ Make sure that only one copy is selected and click **OK**.

Your letter will print.

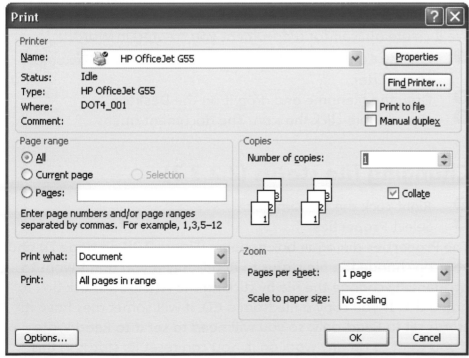

Figure 2.26 The Print dialogue box

Renaming a file (2.2.3.6)

You can rename any file or folder.

| Open |
| Edit |
| New |
| Print |
| CA Anti-Virus |
| Open With ▶ |
| Send To ▶ |
| Cut |
| Copy |
| Create Shortcut |
| Delete |
| Rename |
| Properties |

Figure 2.27 Renaming a file

❶ Run **My Computer** and navigate to **My Documents**.
❷ Right-click the file **Sharon.doc**. Then select **Rename**.
❸ Change the filename to **Tom.doc** by typing the new name over the old one and pressing Enter. If you do not enter the file extension **.doc** correctly, you will be warned that changing the extension may make the file unusable. Be sure to get it right!

Creating and using a file icon (2.1.3.4)

If you are in the middle of writing a book, a long report or any other project which is likely to take a few weeks, it is useful to have the file icon on the Desktop. You can then open the document in the correct software (e.g. Word or Excel) simply by clicking the icon.

We'll create an icon for a document you created in Word.

❶ Use **My Computer** to navigate to a document, for example **Sharon.doc**.
❷ Drag the filename and drop it on the **Desktop**.
❸ Now double-click the icon. The document opens.

Changing file status (2.2.3.3)

❶ Right-click the file **Kim.doc**.
❷ Select **Properties**.

The **Properties** dialogue box appears (Figure 2.28 on page 71) and you can change the file status to **Read-only** if you don't want to accidentally change the file by clicking the **Attributes:** tick box to add a tick. If you copy a file from a CD, it will sometimes have its status set to Read-only, so you will need to set it to Read/Write if you want to do any work on it. You can reset its status in this dialogue box by clicking the tick box to remove the tick.

Tip!

When a file is set to Read-only, you won't be able to save any changes you make to it without giving it a new name first. This means the original remains unaltered.

Figure 2.28 The **Properties** dialogue box

Do it!

Change the name of **Robert.doc** to **Bill.doc**, and set it to **Read-only**.

Actually, that was a mistake. Change the name back to **Robert.doc**, after all the invitation is to him.

Sorting files (2.2.3.4)

If you display files in **Details** view, you can change the order in which they appear by clicking the header bar on **Name**, **Size**, **Type** or **Date Modified** to sort the files and folders.

◉ Click **Name** once. The files will be sorted in alphabetical order of name, from A–Z.

◉ Click **Name** again. The files will be sorted in sequence from Z–A.

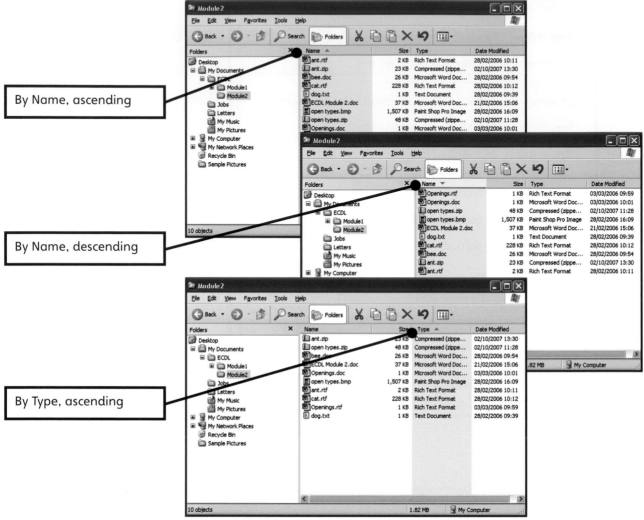

By Name, ascending

By Name, descending

By Type, ascending

Figure 2.29 Sorting files

Selecting files and folders (2.2.4.1)

Sometimes you need to reorganise your files, perhaps moving them into different folders. Other times you may want to copy one or more files into a different folder or onto a removable disk as a backup.

You can move, copy and delete files and folders individually, but alternatively you can select all the files you want to manipulate and then work with them in one operation.

⊙ To select several adjacent files or folders, click the first filename, then hold down the **Shift** key while you click the last filename you want to select.

- To select non-adjacent files, hold down the **Ctrl** key while you select each one.

If you decide you do not want the files you have selected, click the highlighted background to deselect them.

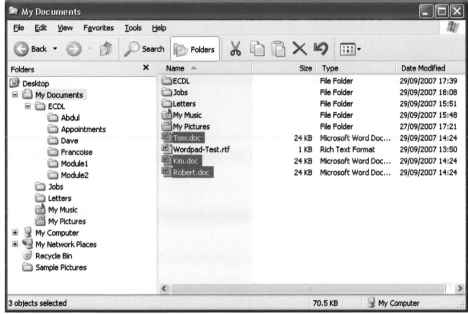

Figure 2.30 Selecting more than one file

Do it!

Navigate to a folder that contains several different file types. Sort the files into **Name** order and select all the .doc files. Deselect them. Now sort the files into **Type** order and select the .doc files again. Which was easier?

Copying and moving files and folders (2.2.4.2–3)

You can copy a file to another folder or disk drive by first copying it to the **Clipboard**, and then pasting it to the desired location. We will copy all the Word documents to the **Letters** folder.

1. Select the .doc letter files you created and click **Edit**, **Copy**. This copies all the files to the **Clipboard**.
2. In the left-hand window, click the **Letters** folder.
3. Select **Edit**, **Paste**. The files will be copied to the **Letters** folder.

There are now two copies of each of these files: one in **My Documents** and another in **Letters**.

Note that folders can be copied in the same way. When you copy a folder, all its contents are copied too. You can copy to another drive, such as the A: drive, in exactly the same way.

Tip!

The **Clipboard** is a temporary storage area that holds files or folders that you cut or copy. By default, the next time you cut or copy something, the previous contents will be overwritten, although you can set the **Clipboard** to display several previous cut or copied items.

Making backup copies (2.2.1.4–5)

Copying files for backup purposes is an essential skill for everyone using a computer! Sooner or later some disaster will occur such as your hard disk crashing, your laptop being stolen or your file being infected with a virus. That's when you will be glad you have a recent copy of your work on a memory stick in your pocket or in an online file store (see pages 40 and 85 for more on backups).

Drag and drop

Another way of copying or moving files is to select them and then drag and drop them to the new location.
Be aware of the following.

◉ Dragging and dropping a file or folder to a new location on the same drive moves the file or folder.

◉ Dragging and dropping a file or folder to a different drive copies the folder.

If you want to drag and drop a copy of a file to a new location on the same drive, hold down the **Ctrl** key while you drag.

We'll use the drag and drop technique to move the .doc files you created to the folder **Module2**, which is a subfolder of **ECDL**.

❶ Restore the C: window to the **Desktop**. It may be minimised in the **Taskbar**.

❷ Click the + sign next to the **ECDL** folder name so that its two subfolders are visible.

❸ Click **Tom.doc**, then hold down **Ctrl** and click **Robert.doc** (Figure 2.3I).

❹ Hold down the left mouse button while you drag the files and drop them into **Module2**.

Figure 2.3I Two selected files

Test your understanding

In this exercise you are asked to create a folder structure which will help organise the computerised files of a double-glazing sales office.

1. Create a folder named **Sales** on your disk. Create **two** subfolders within the **Sales** folder. Name these folders **Quotes** and **Appointments**.

2. Create **two** simple word-processed files and save them in the **Sales** folder. Name these files **Windows.doc** and **Conservatories.doc**.

3. Create the following subfolder structure within the **Appointments** subfolder as represented by the diagram below.

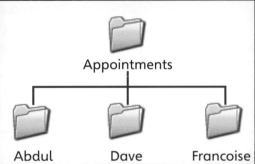

4. Copy the files **Windows.doc** and **Conservatories.doc** to the **Quotes** folder.

5. Rename the folder **Francoise** to **Francis**.

Learning objectives

By working through this lesson you will learn:
- about deleting files, and restoring files deleted by mistake
- how to navigate through folders when looking for files in an application
- about the Print Manager.

Tip!

You use **Edit, Cut** instead of **Edit, Copy** to move files. This means the file(s) is deleted from its original location instead of leaving it. You may find it's safer to copy them first and then delete the ones you don't want!

Tip!

If you realise a mistake immediately, the easiest way to get your files back is to click the **Undo** button.

Deleting files and folders (2.2.5.I)

You can delete the documents from their original location.

1. Click **My Documents**.
2. Select the **.doc** files again.
3. Press the **Delete** key on the keyboard. Alternatively, you can click the **Delete** button on the toolbar.

You will see a message (Figure 2.32).

Figure 2.32 Confirming a file deletion

4. If you are sure you have selected the correct items, click **Yes**.

The Recycle Bin (2.2.5.I–3)

When you delete a file or folder from a hard drive, it is not completely deleted. It is moved to a storage area called the **Recycle Bin**. This is very useful because it means that if you deleted the wrong file by mistake, you can retrieve it from the bin, as long as you haven't emptied the contents of the bin!

Suppose you have deleted **Tom.doc** by accident and you want to restore it.

1. Go to the **Desktop**.
2. Double-click the **Recycle Bin**.

A window opens (Figure 2.33) showing the contents of the **Recycle Bin**.

3. Right-click **Tom.doc** and select **Restore** from the shortcut menu.

Your file will be restored to where it originally came from, in this case the **My Documents** folder.

You can restore deleted folders, complete with their contents, in exactly the same way.

Sharon.doc	C:\Documents and
Robert.doc	C:\Documents and
Tom.doc	C:\Documents and

Figure 2.33 Files in the Recycle Bin

Do it!

Restore **Robert.doc** – we will need it again!

Emptying the Recycle Bin

The contents of the **Recycle Bin** take up space on your hard disk and it is a good idea to empty it now and then.

❶ On the **Desktop**, right-click the **Recycle Bin** and select **Empty Recycle Bin**. You will be asked to confirm your request, because once the bin is emptied the contents are really gone!

Figure 2.34 Emptying the Recycle Bin

Warning!

The Recycle Bin only works with the files and folders on your hard drive. Files deleted from a floppy drive or CD are deleted immediately. Data deleted from a network drive won't go into the bin either, but networks normally have their own recovery methods for files deleted in error.

Navigating within an application

Very often you need to find a file, save a file in a particular folder, create a new folder or delete a file from within an application such as Word.

For example, suppose you want to open the file **Kim.doc** in Word.

❶ Open **Word**.

❷ Click **Open…** on the **File** menu.

The following screen appears.

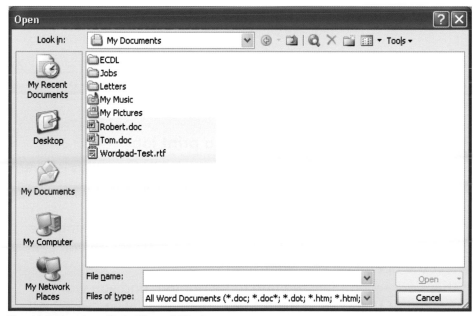

Figure 2.35 Opening a file in Microsoft Word

Now suppose you can't remember where the file is saved and you decide to look in Module2. You double-click ECDL to display its subfolders. Then double-click Module2 – no, it's not there!

You need to navigate back through the folder structure and across to Letters. There should be a copy of Kim.doc in there. You can do this either by clicking the down-arrow on the right of the **Look in:** box and navigating through the folder structure, or by clicking the **Up One Level** button until you are back at **My Documents** and then opening folders until you reach the one you are looking for.

Note that you can create a new folder in this window by clicking the **Create New Folder** button. You can also delete a selected file using either the **Delete** key on the keyboard or the **Delete** button in this window.

Controlling the printer (2.4.2.2–3)

Figure 2.36 The System Tray

When you send a document to a printer to be printed, a printer icon appears in the **System Tray** at the right-hand side of the **Taskbar**.

Right-click this and select the name of the printer to open its **Print Manager** dialogue box. You can see what the printer is doing, and sometimes sort out problems from here.

Figure 2.37 A file in a print queue

Pausing, restarting or cancelling a print job

Figure 2.38 Cancelling a print job

In the screenshot for the print job (Figure 2.37), the status is given as **Error**. (In this case it was because the printer was not switched on.)

You can pause, restart or cancel a print job by right-clicking the document name. A shortcut menu appears from which you can select the operation you want.

If there are several files waiting to be printed, and you want to cancel all of them, open the **Printer** menu and select **Cancel All Documents**.

Creating a printer icon

You can also add a printer icon to your Desktop so that you can open its dialogue box from there – the Taskbar icons are very tiny!

❶ From the Start menu, select **Control Panel, Printers and Other Hardware, Printers and Faxes.**

❷ Drag and drop the default printer icon (the one with the tick mark against its name) onto the Desktop.

Test your understanding

1. Run WordPad and start a new document.
2. Enter the following text:

Different file types include the following:

3. Move to a blank line by pressing Enter and type in the names of as many common file types as possible. Leave a couple of spaces between each one.
4. Save this document as **File types.rtf** in your My Documents folder. Leave WordPad running.
5. Run Microsoft Word and start a new document. Describe how you would access the Desktop Print Manager and explain what it does.
6. Save this document as **Print Manager.doc** in your My Documents folder.
7. Click your document, **File types.rtf**, on the Taskbar and print it.
8. Return to **Print Manager.doc** and print that too.
9. Add some more text to the document **Print Manager. doc** to explain how to close a non-responding application.
10. Save the document with the name **Useful tips.doc** and print a copy.
11. Close the file **File types.rtf** and close WordPad.
12. Close **Print Manager.doc** and **Useful tips.doc** and close Word.

Better file management

Learning objectives

By working through this lesson you will learn:

- ⦿ about compressing files, and extracting files from compressed folders
- ⦿ how to search for files
- ⦿ about the recently used files list
- ⦿ about viruses and anti-virus software.

Tip!

Go to Module I page 6 to remind yourself about how file size is measured.

Compressing files (2.2.1.3/2.3.1.1–2)

If you want to send a large file as an attachment to an email, zipping or compressing the file will normally reduce its size making it faster to send and receive. Some ISPs, and the email services of some organisations, will not accept large files. As a general rule if the size of the file you are sending is more than half a megabyte (500 KB) then you should compress it. Compression software uses complex mathematical techniques to reduce the size of files. Versions of Windows from XP onwards have compression software built in.

❶ In **My Computer**, go to your **ECDL/Module2** folder and locate **opentypes.bmp**. This is a large bitmap file, and the bitmap format is very wasteful of storage space.

❷ Right-click the file and choose **Send to**, then select **Compressed (zipped) Folder**.

Figure 2.39 Compressing a file

A copy of the file will be compressed and stored in the new folder. This will have the same name as the file. You can compress several files at a time, packing them into one folder. It will take the name of the first file in the set.

In the next screenshot (Figure 2.40) you can see the original **open types.bmp** file, and the new compressed folder **open types. zip**. Notice the difference in size – from 1.5 MB down to 48 KB.

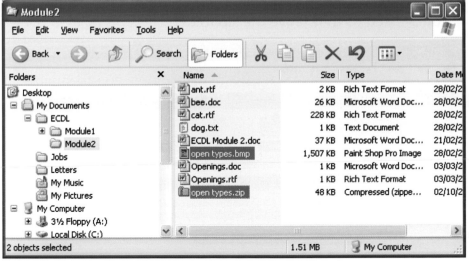

Figure 2.40 Comparing file sizes – compressed and normal

Extracting a compressed file (2.3.1.3)

To unzip the file, right-click it and select **Extract All...**. The **Extraction Wizard** will appear. Follow the steps to extract the file.

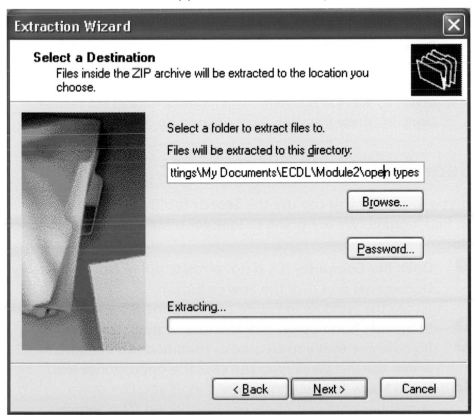

Figure 2.41 The Extraction Wizard

If the compressed folder contains several files and you only want to extract some of them, double-click it, and it will open like any other folder. If you want to work on the files, it's best to copy or move them into a normal folder – they are automatically uncompressed as they leave the zip folder.

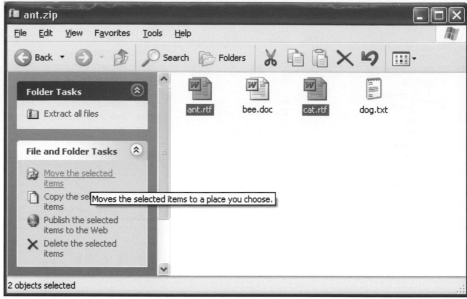

Figure 2.42 Files in a zip folder

Do it!

Go to the **ECDL/Module2** folder. Select all the files, then look at the **Status bar**. On the right it will show the total size of the selected files. (If the Status bar is not visible, turn it on by ticking its name in the View menu.) Make a note of the number. Compress those files. How big is the new zip file?

Searching for files (2.2.6.1–4)

If you lose a file you can use the **Search** facility in **My Computer** to find it again. We are going to look for a file called **openings. doc**.

❶ Open **My Computer** if it is not already open. Navigate to **My Documents** and click the **Search** button.

You will see the window in Figure 2.43 on page 83.

❷ In the left-hand pane, click the second item, **Documents**.

❸ If you know that you created or modified the document within the last week, you can click the appropriate box.

❹ If you know the filename, type it in. If you can only remember part of it, that may be enough. The Search routine will list all the files with matching names, and you may be able to pick it out from there.

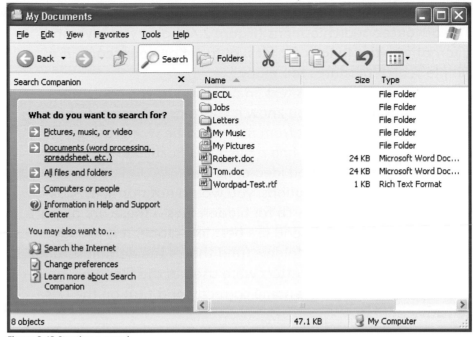

Figure 2.43 Starting a search

5 Ignore **Use advanced search options** at this stage and click **Search**.

The computer will find the file you are looking for.

You can open the file in Word simply by double-clicking it.

Figure 2.44 Search criteria

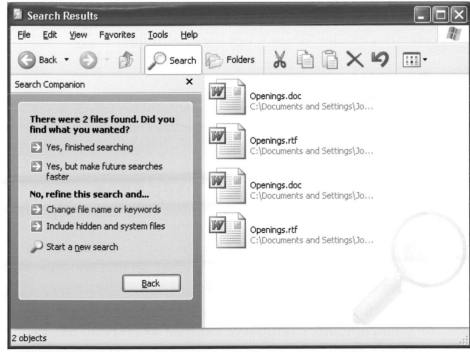

Figure 2.45 Search results

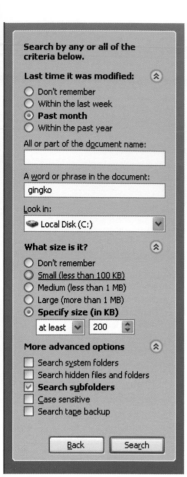

Figure 2.46 Advanced search options

Advanced search options

The advanced search options (Figure 2.46) give you several alternative ways to look for files, or to refine your search if a simple search produces too many.

If the document contains text, in any format, you can enter a word or phrase that you know it contains – it needs to be something a bit different from normal to be worth using. Setting the size can help find a file if it is particularly large or small, or you have a good idea of its size.

In the more advanced options, you would not normally look in the system folders or search for hidden files – these are all part of the operating system and are best left alone. It is usually worth searching the subfolders (and that is the default setting). If capitals and lower case letters were used in the filename, and you know how, then type the name correctly and turn on the **Case sensitive** option.

Wildcards

If you can only remember very little of a filename, you can use the wildcards in place of characters. The wildcard **?** represents a single character, and ***** represents any number of characters. So, for example, instead of the filename you could enter ***.doc** to find all files with a **.doc** extension, or **mu*.doc** to find all Word documents starting with the letters **mu**. If the Status bar is present, it will show a count of the number of files found. (***.*** will, of course, find all files, which is not very helpful!)

Do it!

In My Computer, go to your My Documents folder. Search to see what rtf files there are on your PC within My Documents or its subfolders.

Viewing a list of recently used files (2.2.6.5)

You might want to open or search for a recently used file. Rather than search for it as described in the previous section you can select it from a list of recently used files.

◉   Click **My Recent Documents** or just **Documents**, depending on your computer's setup (see Figure 2.47 on page 85), on the **Start** menu. A list of recent documents will be displayed and you can open any of them by clicking on the filename.
Hover the mouse pointer over a filename to show its location.

Figure 2.47 Opening recent documents

Backups

A backup is a copy of a file, kept on a different disk or other removable media, and preferably stored in a different place, so that if the original file or its computer becomes damaged or lost, the data can be replaced from the backup copy.

Businesses, schools and other larger organisations will usually have special software and hardware to manage the backups, to ensure that copies are made regularly. In a small firm or at home, backups can be made on CDs, DVDs or flash drives.

The **Search** facility can be used to identify those files that are new or have been changed since the last backup. These can then be copied onto the storage media. If a backup has not been done for some time, several disks or flash drives may be needed to hold the files.

Backups should be labelled, dated and stored safely, away from the PC.

Online file stores

There are now websites that offer online storage facilities, at low cost or free (for small storage amounts). These can be used for backing up, but have other uses.

- Files in the stores can be accessed from any computer, anywhere in the world that is linked to the Internet.
- You can share your files with others, anywhere in the world, by giving them the access details.

Virus protection (2.3.2.I–3)

Viruses can be spread in programs downloaded from the Internet, or passed between computers on disks or flash drives, but are most commonly spread through emails. If an incoming email is allowed to infect a computer, it will normally try to send copies of itself to the people whose email addresses are stored on the computer.

Precautions to avoid your PC being infected with a virus include the following.

- You should not share or lend floppy disks or flash drives that could introduce viruses into your system without first checking them for viruses.
- Care should be taken when downloading files from the Internet. The proliferation of viruses over recent years is partly due to email communication. Never open an email message or an email attachment from someone that you don't recognise – it could well introduce a virus to your system. You will generally see a message like the one shown in Figure 2.48 when you attempt to open an email attachment.

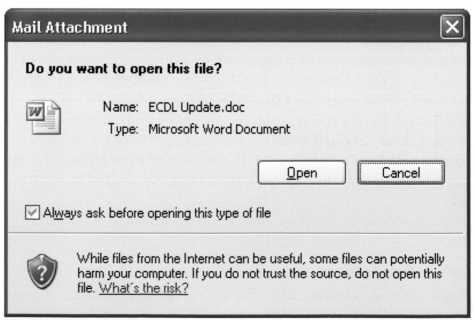

Figure 2.48 Open confirmation query

⊙ **Anti-virus software** should be installed on all computer systems. This automatically checks for any infected data when the computer is started up, and scans any new files as they are introduced into the computer. Checks can also be run manually on floppy disks, CDs and flash drives before their files are accessed. As approximately 300 new viruses are unleashed each month it is a good idea to install a virus checker that provides an automatic or manual online update service. With the latter, you will automatically receive a message to update. The virus checker software should be capable of not only detecting the virus, but also of removing it from the infected file. This is called disinfecting the file.

Using anti-virus software

Typical anti-virus software enables you to specify which drives, folders or files you wish to scan and disinfects the file (i.e. removes the virus) if a virus is found. In this example drive F: (the memory stick) is being scanned.

❶ Click the anti-virus software you have installed from the program list on the **Start** menu.

❷ Browse through your files and folders and select which drive, folder or file you wish to scan.

❸ Start the anti-virus scanner (Figure 2.49).

The software will check all the files on drive F: and report any problems (Figure 2.50 on page 88).

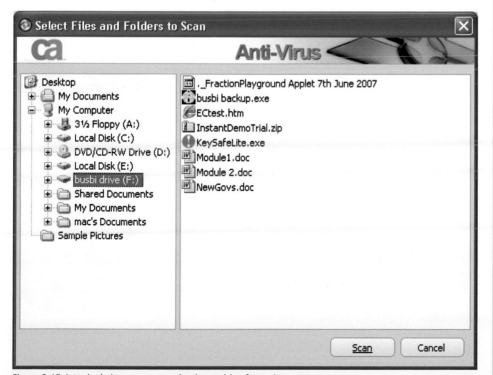

Figure 2.49 A typical virus scanner: selecting a drive for a virus scan

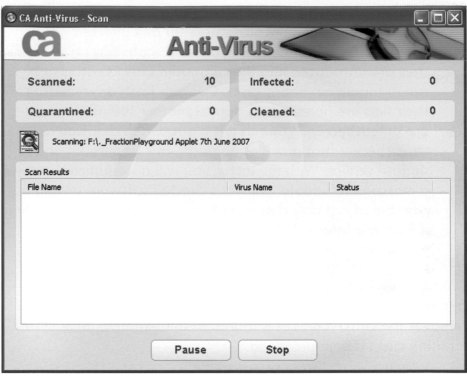

Figure 2.50 A typical virus scanner: results of a scan

Test your understanding

1. Use My Computer to search for a large file on your disk drive.
2. Send this to a compressed folder and see how much smaller it becomes.
3. Use the Search facility within My Computer to find the file **Useful tips.doc** you created in an earlier exercise.
4. Make a note of how large this file is.
5. Enter some text giving three tips to help prevent your computer being infected by a virus.
6. Next enter some text explaining how you can view recently used files.
7. Edit the document so that each section of text has an appropriate heading.
8. Save and print this file.
9. Use My Computer to check the size of this file after the extra text was added.

Customising your computer

Learning objectives

By working through this lesson you will learn:
- ◉ about creating desktop icons
- ◉ how to view system information about your computer
- ◉ how to customise the appearance of your desktop
- ◉ how to set up a screen saver
- ◉ how to change the date and time
- ◉ how to add another keyboard language
- ◉ how to format a floppy disk
- ◉ about installing software
- ◉ how to use the Help and Support Center
- ◉ how to install a printer.

Basic system information (2.I.2.I)

It is useful to be able to view basic information about the computer system you are using.

❶ Click **Control Panel** on the **Start** menu.

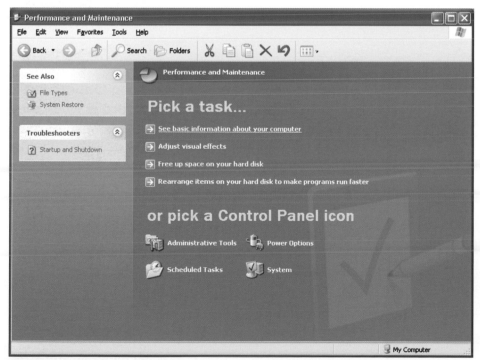

Figure 2.5I The Windows Control Panel

Tip!

If your **Control Panel** shows a set of icons, instead of the tasks on a blue background, you are in **Classic** view. Click the link in the left-hand pane to switch to **Category** view. It's the one we will be using.

❷ Click **Performance and Maintenance** in the category list, then click **System**.

❸ Click the **General** tab on the **System Properties** window (see Figure 2.52).

Figure 2.52 The System Properties window

This tells you which operating system and version number you are using (e.g. Microsoft Windows XP Professional Version 2002, Service Pack 2). It also tells you which processor type is installed and its speed (e.g. Intel Pentium III 930 MHz). Finally it tells you how much RAM is installed in the system (e.g. 256 MB).

This kind of information can be useful if you are reporting a fault on your computer or want to check whether your computer has the recommended minimum amount of RAM to run a new software package.

Do it!

Find out about the PC that you are using. Which version of Windows is installed? How much RAM does it have? What speed is its processor?

Figure 2.53 Selecting a power scheme

Power options

All modern PCs have energy-saving routines that can turn off components automatically when they are not in use. You can control these through the **Power Options Properties** window.

❶ Click **Control Panel** on the **Start** menu.

❷ Click **Performance and Maintenance**, then double-click **Power Options**.

❸ Select an option that matches your computer from the **Power schemes** drop-down list.

❹ If necessary, adjust the turn-off times for the monitor and hard disks.

❺ When you have finished, click **OK**.

Changing the Background (2.1.2.2)

If you don't like the **Desktop Background** you can easily change it.

❶ Right-click the mouse anywhere on the **Desktop Background** to see a shortcut menu.

❷ Click the **Properties** option to open the **Display Properties** window.

❸ Click the **Desktop** tab.

Figure 2.54 Display Properties – Desktop

❹ Scroll down the list and click a background. You will see a preview of what it looks like.

❺ When you find one you like, click **OK**.

Setting up a screen saver (2.1.2.2)

A screen saver is a moving picture or pattern that appears on your screen when you have not used the mouse or keyboard for a specified period of time. As well as being interesting and entertaining these can help protect the screen from burn-out in particular spots.

❶ Open the **Display Properties** window, as you did to change the Background.

❷ Click the **Screen Saver** tab.

> ## Tip!
>
> To scroll up and down a list of items click one of the arrows on the scroll bar.

Figure 2.55 Display Properties – Screen Saver

❸ Click the down arrow to view a list of screen savers. Click the **Preview** button to see what the option you choose will look like.

❹ Set the time before the screen saver activates.

❺ When you have finished, click **Apply** or **OK**.

Changing the screen resolution (2.1.2.2)

Screen resolution is the setting that determines the amount of information that appears on your screen, measured in pixels. Low resolution, such as 800 × 600, makes items on the screen appear large and 'blocky' and you have relatively small windows. High resolution, such as 1,600 × 1,200, makes individual items such as text and graphics appear small but clearly defined, and you can have larger windows, or view more windows at once.

❶ Open the **Display Properties** window at the **Settings** tab.

❷ Drag the slider to change the resolution. Start with the highest possible setting, then come back and adjust to a lower one if text is too small for your comfort.

❸ Click the **Apply** button. The screen will momentarily go black and then the **Display Properties** window will be redisplayed.

❹ If you like the look of the screen, click **OK**, otherwise go back and try a different setting.

Figure 2.56 Display Properties – Settings

Do it!

Change the background of your Desktop. Try a patterned background. Do you like it? How about a picture? Set up a screen saver – try one where you can customise the settings.

Other display settings (2.1.2.2)

Using the Display Properties **Themes** tab, you can set up themes which comprise a background plus a set of sounds, icons and other elements to help you personalise your computer. If you click the **Appearance** tab you can change the appearance of fonts, windows and dialogue boxes.

Changing the date and time (2.1.2.2)

You shouldn't need to change the date and time as it should have been set up correctly for the correct time zone by the manufacturer. However, if you do need to it's quite straightforward.

1. Click **Control Panel** on the **Start** menu, then **Date, Time, Language and Regional Options**.
2. Click **Change the date and time**.
3. Make any changes in this dialogue box and click **OK**.

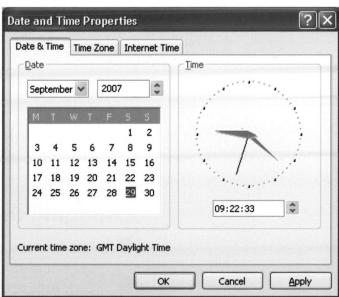

Figure 2.57 Setting the date and time

Changing keyboard language (2.1.2.3)

Your computer will have a language set as default, probably English (United Kingdom).

If you need to enter text in a different language you can add different keyboard layouts.

Text Services and Input Languages

Settings | Advanced

Default input language
Select one of the installed input languages to use when you start your computer.

English (United Kingdom) - United Kingdom

Installed services
Select the services that you want for each input language shown in the list. Use the Add and Remove buttons to modify this list.

EN **English (United Kingdom)**
   Keyboard
      • **United Kingdom**
FR French (France)
   Keyboard
      • French

Add...
Remove
Properties...

Preferences

Language Bar... | Key Settings...

OK | Cancel | Apply

Figure 2.58 Setting the language

❶ In the **Control Panel**, select **Date, Time, Language and Regional Options**.

❷ Click **Add other languages**. A dialogue box will open with the **Languages** tab displayed.

❸ Click the **Details...** button.

❹ Click the **Add...** button and select the language to add and click **OK**.

❺ Back at the **Languages** tab, click **Apply**.

❻ Switch to the **Regional Options** tab.

Regional and Language Options

Regional Options | Languages | Advanced

Standards and formats
This option affects how some programs format numbers, currencies, dates, and time.

Select an item to match its preferences, or click Customize to choose your own formats:

English (United Kingdom) | Customize...

Samples

Number: 123,456,789.00

Currency: £123,456,789.00

Time: 21:32:59

Short date: 29/09/2007

Long date: 29 September 2007

Location
To help services provide you with local information, such as news and weather, select your present location:

United Kingdom

OK | Cancel | Apply

Figure 2.59 Setting regional options

❼ Check that the right region is selected, and change it if necessary, using the drop-down list.

❽ Click **OK**.

Changing the volume settings (2.1.2.2)

❶ Click **Control Panel** on the **Start** menu, and then **Sounds, Speech and Audio Devices**.

❷ Click **Adjust the system volume** to display the **Volume properties** window.

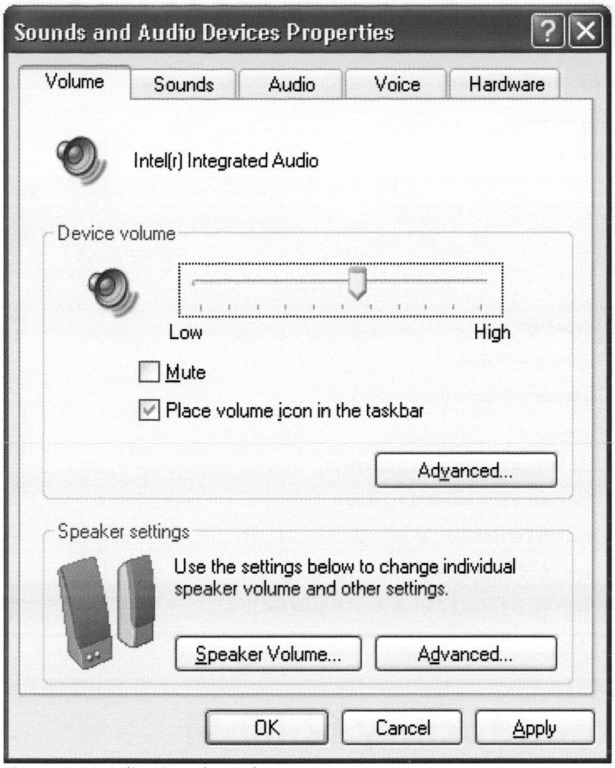

Figure 2.60 Adjusting the volume

❸ Drag the bar to adjust the sound level.
❹ Turn on the option **Place volume icon in the taskbar**. This gives you a simpler way to adjust the volume.
❺ Click **OK**.

Installing/uninstalling a software application (2.1.2.4)

Most application programs today are supplied on DVD or CD-ROM. The disk will automatically run when it is inserted into the drive and on-screen instructions will explain how to proceed. If you no longer need an application, it should be removed properly to ensure that all its files are deleted. This also removes its Start menu entries and clears its details from the Windows system. Some applications place an Uninstall routine in the Start menu. Otherwise you should use **Add or Remove Programs** in the Control Panel.

❶ From the Start menu, select **Control Panel**, **Add or Remove Programs**.
❷ Click **Change or Remove Programs** to uninstall an application.
❸ Click **Add New Programs** to install a new application.

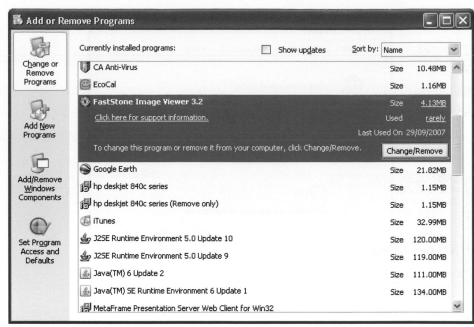

Figure 2.6I Adding or removing programs

Tip!

You can see what has been copied to the **Clipboard** by selecting **Edit**, **Office Clipboard...** in any Microsoft Office application. This opens the Clipboard on the right-hand side of the screen. Click any item to paste.

Print screen facility (2.1.2.5)

Sometimes it is useful to be able to take a screenshot of what is on your screen and paste it into a document. You can either capture the whole screen or just the current window.

◉ Press the key labelled **Prt Scr** (or Print Screen) on the keyboard.

This copies a picture of the whole screen to the **Clipboard**. If you now open a new or existing Word document, you can paste it in by selecting **Paste** from the **Edit** menu.

To capture just the current window, press the **Alt** key (to the left of the Space bar) at the same time as **Prt Scr**.

Do it!

Run Word. If its window fills the screen, switch to Restore mode and adjust the size so it's half the width and height of the screen. Take a screenshot of the Word window. Click in Word, and use Edit, Paste to copy the image of the Word window into the Word document. Add some text to describe what you have done. Save it as PrintScreen.doc and print one copy.

Changing the default printer (2.4.1.1)

The default printer is used when you click the **Print** button.
To change the default printer

① Click **Printers and Faxes** on the **Start** menu.

② Right-click the printer to use as the default, then click **Set as Default Printer**.

The tick indicates the default printer.

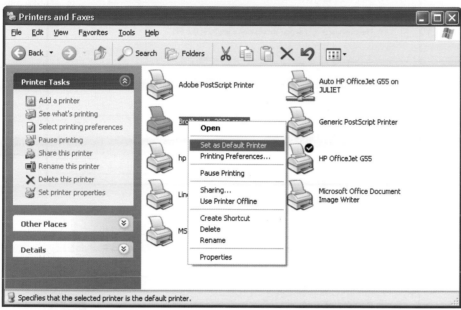

Figure 2.62 The printer list

Installing a new printer (2.4.1.2)

Most printers are now termed 'Plug and Play' devices. This means that you can attach a device to your PC and begin using it right away, without having to configure it or install software. An older printer may not be 'Plug and Play'. In this case you should use the **Add Printer wizard** to install it.

① Open the **Control Panel** and select **Printers and Other Hardware**.

② Select **Add a printer**.

③ When the wizard starts, click the **Next** button.

④ On the following screen select whether you are installing a network printer or a local printer (i.e. directly connected to your PC).

⑤ Click **Next**.

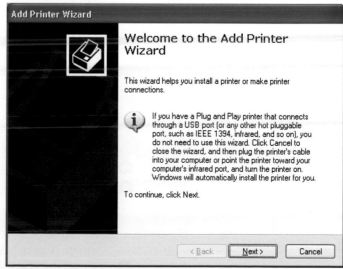

Figure 2.63 The **Add Printer** wizard – step I

6 Follow through the remaining stages of the wizard: you will be asked which printer port you want to use (Figure 2.64).

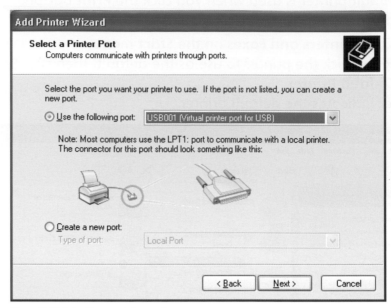

Figure 2.64 Selecting a printer port

7 Select a port and click **Next**.You will then be asked for manufacturer and model of the printer (Figure 2.65).

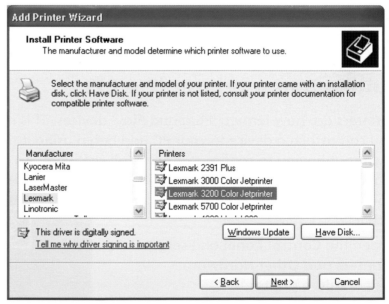

Figure 2.65 Selecting your printer

8 Make your selection and click **Next**.
9 On the next two screens assign a name to the printer and select whether or not you want to share the printer with other network users. You will also be given the option to print a test page.
10 Click **Finish** on the final screen to complete the installation.

Test your understanding

1. Open **My Computer** and navigate to the file **Useful tips. doc**.
2. Create a shortcut to this document on the Desktop.
3. Open the document using the shortcut icon.
4. Use **My Computer** to view the basic system information about your computer.
5. In the **Useful tips.doc** document make a note of the type of processor and amount of RAM your computer has.
6. Now enter some text to describe how you would change the Desktop Background.
7. Open the **Printer and Faxes** dialogue box from the **Start** menu to view the printers that your computer has access to.
8. Take a screenshot of this and paste it into the **Useful tips.doc** document together with some notes on how to change the default printer.
9. Save and print the word-processed document.
10. Close the file and close Word.

Maintenance

As with anything, things can go wrong with your computer system when you use it: the hardware can break and software might cease to function as expected. The probability of some of these things happening can be lessened by carrying out preventative maintenance to keep your system in good order, but inevitably moving parts (such as fan motors) or parts that are subject to repeated handling will need to be replaced when they break or wear out.

Hardware

Modern computer hardware is extremely reliable so long as it is used as the manufacturer intended. Quality control techniques have increased hardware life to the point where it rarely fails before the technology becomes obsolete. However, failures can still occur, sometimes bringing disastrous consequences (such as data loss or even fire) to individuals or companies.

Some examples of hardware that can fail are:
- bearings in disk drives
- motors in fans and disk drives
- backup batteries
- fuses and power supply components (e.g. capacitors)
- electronic components (including PCBs, keyboard switches, LED indicators, infrared transceivers etc.)
- displays (especially VDU tubes)
- laptop screen hinges and cables
- CD-ROM tray mechanisms
- power cables, and other cables and connectors
- moving parts in printers and scanners

Many of these examples are not easy to repair without the correct tools and specialist technical knowledge, so in some cases replacing the part is the best option.

Most hardware comes with an owner's manual or disk that details the component parts of the equipment, with part numbers, maintenance instructions, and support contacts (such as telephone numbers and websites). The manufacturer's guidelines on what can be repaired or replaced and how the maintenance should be carried out must always be followed to ensure that the work is performed correctly and safely.

Repairs and replacements such as described above are non-routine maintenance tasks because they are needed infrequently and at irregular intervals (if at all). However, routine maintenance can be easily and safely performed to ensure the hardware continues to work correctly and so the user can use it efficiently. Some examples of routine maintenance of any ICT hardware are:

- Clean all ventilation grilles. Excessive build-up of dust will prevent air flow through the equipment casing. This will cause electronic components to overheat and eventually fail. Also clean or replace air filters if this can be done safely.
- Clean keyboards. Dust and dirt falling between the keys will eventually jam the key switches making the keyboard unreliable.
- Clean screens and plates. Grease (from fingers) and dust will build up on the glass of LCD and CRT screens making them difficult to use. Unless the glass plates of flat-bed scanners are kept clean, the marks will also be scanned and appear on the reproduced image.
- Clean cases. Regular cleaning, if only dusting, of exposed surfaces keeps the equipment looking new and protects your investment. Infrared signals between hardware devices might be degraded by dirt on transmitters and receivers, so it is important to keep these clean.
- Check connectors and cables. Most connectors have integral clips or screws to hold them in place. However, because another user of the equipment might have been less than diligent, it is good practice to routinely check that connectors are correctly and firmly seated. Cables should be routinely tidied, making sure that cable runs (both in desks and floors etc.) are used if available. This will ensure that the workspace is less hazardous and that the equipment is more reliable and more efficient to use.
- Clean the ball and rollers on corded mice.

Warning!

Cleaning materials such as solvents can be dangerous. They are often toxic and flammable. Protect yourself and the environment by always following the cleaning product's instructions on safe use and disposal.

Warning!

Soap and cleaners containing alcohol will damage the anti-glare and anti-static coating on screens.

Tip!

Always read the manufacturer's guidelines on what can and should be routinely maintained, and how often.

Cleaning can usually be done using a soft damp cloth or brush. Marks on screens and cases should be removed using a suitable solvent spray or impregnated wipe. Always follow the hardware manufacturer's guidelines about what solvents can be used.

Printers

Printers are hardware and are subject to similar routine and non-routine maintenance requirements as described above. However, because they use up materials (consumables) in the printing process, such as ink and paper, routine maintenance also includes the replacement of the materials.

The methods of replacing consumables depend on the type of printer (e.g. impact, inkjet, laser), the printer model and the manufacturer. Therefore it necessary to read the manufacturer's guidelines to ensure that the correct procedure is followed and the correct replacement parts are installed.

Routine maintenance on printers includes:

Replenishing the print medium

Refill the paper tray or feed hopper with the recommended paper (i.e. correct weight and finish) or transparency film for the type and model of printer. Some printers will only take one size of paper, but if different sizes can be used, then make sure that the feed guides are correctly positioned so the paper enters the printer without misalignment.

Impact printers often use continuous feed (fan-fold) paper with holes in tear-off strips down the side edges. This type of paper needs to be fed into the printer so the holes are aligned with the sprockets that pull the paper through the printer.

Replacing ink

Laser printers: Toner is contained in a cartridge that can be easily replaced when empty. The user guide for the printer will give the part number of the recommended replacement cartridge and installation instructions. Often cheaper alternatives are available, or toner cartridge refills are offered, but unless the source is highly recommended there is a risk of printer damage and sub-standard printing (e.g. poor colour reproduction). Using the incorrect parts and ink is likely to invalidate the manufacturer's warranty.

New toner cartridges are carefully packaged to prevent toner leakage while in store or transit. It will be necessary to follow the instructions that come with the cartridge to prepare it before putting it in the printer. This usually involves removing plastic protection strips, and shaking it to evenly spread out toner that has settled while in store.

Empty toner cartridges should be sent back to the manufacturer for refilling and resale. Most manufacturers provide this as a pre-paid service to encourage recycling.

Inkjet printers: Depending on the make and model of the printer, inkjet cartridges are single colour or multi-colour. The cartridges are usually held in a cradle that moves at right angles to the direction of paper feed through the printer. When not being used, the cradle is 'docked' to one side of the printer and can often be unreachable. For this reason, the cradle needs to be moved into an accessible place before the cartridge can be changed. The printer's user guide will describe how to move the cradle, remove the empty cartridge and replace it.

The ink cartridge is simply a container for the ink which is fed to the print head on the cradle. Some new cartridges have a seal to prevent ink leaks. The seal is broken when the cartridge is installed in the printer. The delicate electronics on some makes of cartridge are protected by a plastic strip that has to be removed before the cartridge is installed.

Like toner cartridges, only approved cartridges and ink should be used. Most makes of inkjet cartridge can be recycled.

Impact printers: The ink in the ribbon that is struck by the character keys will eventually run out or the ribbon fabric itself will wear too thin causing the printed characters to appear faded. The ink-soaked ribbon is usually contained in a plastic cassette for easy replacement in a printer.

Plotters: A plotter's coloured pens will need replacing according to the manufacturer's guidelines.

Improving print quality

Running out of ink will obviously degrade the print quality: the printed characters will first appear faded and then disappear altogether. However, with toner, this can happen unevenly across the width of a page.

Poor (uneven) print quality from inkjet printers usually means that the print heads need cleaning. This can happen if the printer is unused for long periods. Read the user guide to find out how to clean the heads for a particular printer.

After a new ink cartridge has been installed, the printer automatically aligns the print heads to ensure the best quality print out. However, the heads might need realigning between cartridge changes: vertical lines become misaligned and

Tip!

The life of the toner cartridge can be extended by gently rocking it a few times to redistribute the toner more evenly along its length.

Warning!

Do not vigorously rock the toner cartridge because this might cause toner to leak out.

Tip!

Use the printer's test page facility to view the print quality to help you decide whether or not the print heads need cleaning or aligning.

horizontal banding appears. The printer's user guide will explain how to align print heads to improve the print quality.

Plotters that are used for highly accurate drawing usually need calibrating by a specialist.

Clearing paper jams

During the printing process, sheets of paper are fed through the printer by a series of rollers. The printing process in laser printers is more complicated than in inkjet printers, and so the sheets of paper are more likely to become jammed in the mechanism, especially if the incorrect quality paper is used or the inside of the printer has not been kept clean. It is therefore important to follow the manufacturer's guidelines regarding approved media, and to keep clean the accessible areas inside the printer.

Laser printers have panels that can be opened to view the location of the paper jam and to allow the jammed paper to be cleared. The component parts of some large laser printers can also be taken out to help clear the blockage.

The paper's route through most inkjet printers is more or less entirely visible, and the mechanism is simpler, making jams less likely, and easier to clear if they do occur.

Software

Software doesn't fail unless the program code becomes corrupted. However, over time, applications can show signs of slowing down when they access data or fetch new parts of their code from the hard disk.

Defragmenting a disk

Program and data files are rarely stored contiguously on the computer's hard disk. This means that the files are broken up and stored in different locations on the disk with the disk operating system managing where they are placed. This situation is made worse as files are deleted and the disk operating system stores parts of new files in the locations that become unused. This break-up of files causes the disk to become fragmented. The time to retrieve files from a severely fragmented disk slows down because the disk operating system needs to access many more storage locations.

Non-routine maintenance of software should include defragmenting the hard disk from time to time to ensure that the stored files are located more contiguously and unused locations are not scattered.

Warning!

Some jams in laser printers can occur before the fuser unit. This means that the toner will not have been fused to the paper and is easily transferred to whatever the paper comes into contact with: skin, clothing, desktops etc. Carefully dispose of the unwanted paper and use cold water if it is necessary to clean any toner smudges.

Tip!

Make sure that there are no programs (including the screen saver) running on the computer because any interruptions caused by these programs will slow down the defragmentation process.

❶ Click **All Programs** on the **Start** menu and select **Accessories, System Tools, Disk Defragmenter**.
❷ The **Disk Defragmenter** window is displayed (Figure 2.66). Select the disk you want to defragment.
❸ Click the **Defragment** button to start defragmenting the selected disk.

Maps of the estimated disk usage before and after defragmentation are displayed in the **Disk Defragmenter** window.

> **Tip!**
>
> Click the **Analyze** button to view whether or not the disk will benefit from being defragmented before starting the process.

❷ The selected disk

The free space on the disk

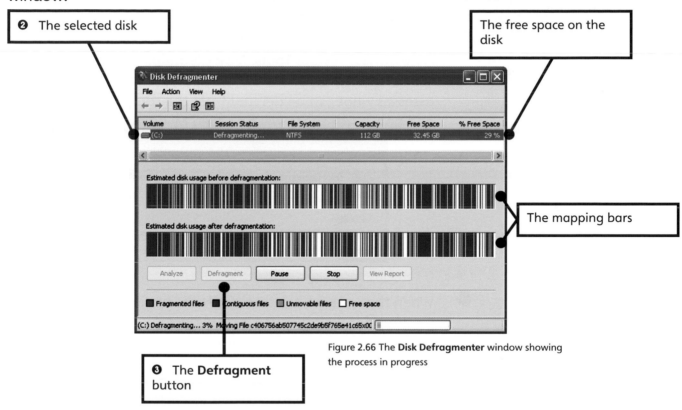

The mapping bars

❸ The **Defragment** button

Figure 2.66 The **Disk Defragmenter** window showing the process in progress

Deleting unwanted files

Over time, a computer's hard disk will become cluttered with unwanted files. These might be old program files, old data files or temporary files that have not been deleted automatically by the operating system. These all fill the hard disk and cause the system to run more slowly.

Uninstall unwanted programs using the method described in **Installing/uninstalling a software application** on page 95 of this module.

All data held on the computer's hard disk should be reviewed regularly to check its relevancy, and deleted if it is no longer required (see page 76 – **Deleting files and folders**). In any case, the Data Protection Act (see page 43) requires that personal data should be kept no longer than is necessary. Data that is required, but infrequently, should be backed-up to archive storage.

> **Tip!**
>
> Make sure you have the original source media for the application file before you uninstall the it from the hard disk. You can then reload the software at any time if you find that you need it again.

Tip!

You can find and delete temporary files by searching for files with a tmp extension on your hard disk. For example, type *.tmp in the search facility (see page 82) to find all the temporary files on the hard disk. Other temporary files have a tilde (~) symbol as the first character.

When an application is run, temporary files are created on the hard disk as part of the normal operation of the program. When the application is closed correctly, these files are automatically deleted from the hard disk. If, for any reason, an application or the computer crashes (i.e. an incorrect shut-down procedure happens), then the temporary files will remain on the hard disk, using valuable disk space that will eventually slow down the operation of the system.

Microsoft Windows also provides a clean-up utility to help you choose which files can safely be deleted.

❶ Click **All Programs** on the **Start** menu and select **Accessories**, **System Tools**, **Disk Cleanup**.

❷ A dialogue box (Figure 2.67) is displayed while the system assesses what can be deleted from the computer's hard disk and how much space will be saved by doing so.

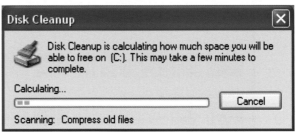

Figure 2.67 Assessing how much space could be freed on a hard disk

❸ When the system has assessed the hard disk, the **Disk Cleanup for** dialogue box is displayed (Figure 2.68). Click the **Disk Cleanup** tab if it is not already selected.

Tip!

A description of the different types of temporary files is displayed in the **Description** section of the **Disk Cleanup for** dialogue box when you click the file type in the **Files to delete:** section.

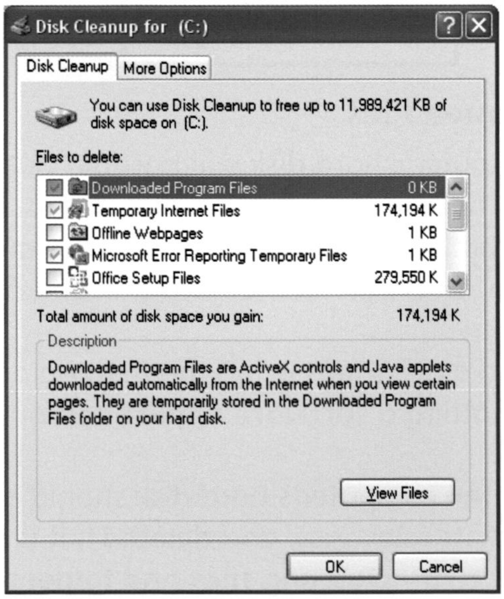

Figure 2.68 The **Disk Cleanup** tab on the **Disk Cleanup for** dialogue box

Tip!

Temporary Internet Files are discussed more fully in Module 7 on page 394.

④ Click the boxes to the left of the file types listed in the **Files to delete:** section of the dialogue box to select which files you want to delete.

⑤ Click **OK** to delete (or compress) the selected files.

The **More Options** tab (Figure 2.69) on the **Disk Cleanup for** dialogue box gives three further clean-up options. A brief description of the options is given in each section. Click the **Clean up...** button to select the option.

Figure 2.69 The **More Options** tab on the **Disk Cleanup for** dialogue box

Windows components – These are optional features of Windows that may have been included in the original installation of Windows and that you may never use.

Installed programs – This opens the **Add or Remove Programs** dialogue box that is explained on page 95.

System Restore – **System Restore** points are discussed below. Selecting this option deletes all but the most recent restore point, thereby freeing up disk space.

System restore

Microsoft Windows has a facility that allows you to return your system to a configuration that worked at an earlier point in time. This is useful if, for example, the system ceases to work correctly after you have installed new software.

① Click **Control Panel** on the **Start** menu and then select **Performance and Maintenance**.

② Click **System Restore** in the **See Also** panel in the left-hand panel of the **Performance and Maintenance** window (Figure 2.70 on page 108).

③ Click **Restore my system to an earlier time** on the **Welcome to System Restore** window and click the **Next** button.

Note

The **Files to delete:** section of the **Disk Cleanup for** dialogue box also allows you to compress files without deleting them. This will provide you with more usable hard disk space.

Tip!

Run the **Disk Defragmenter** after cleaning up the hard disk to optimise the use of disk space released by deleting files.

Tip!

You can set how much disk space is allocated to system restore files by clicking **Start**, **Control Panel**, **Performance and Maintenance**, **System**, and selecting the **System Restore** tab. Move the **Disk space usage** slider to change the disk space used, or click the **Turn off System Restore** box to turn off the facility.

Note

Windows automatically sets restore points but you can set your own restore point for the current configuration as well. Click **Create a restore point** to set your own restore point, then click the **Next** button. Type a descriptive name and click the **Create** button.

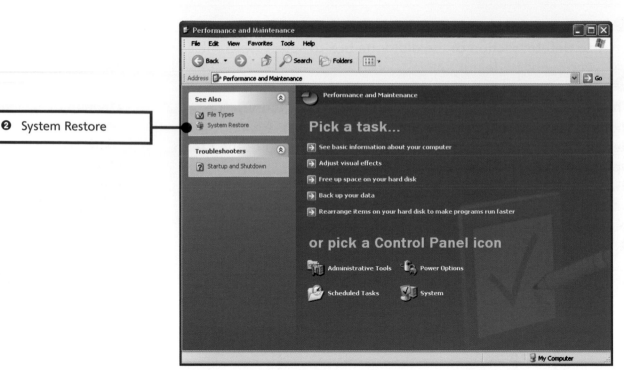

❷ System Restore

Figure 2.70 The **Performance and Maintenance** window

❹ Select a restore date and restore point using the calendar and descriptions shown on the **Select a Restore Point** window.

❺ Click the **Next** button and confirm that the restore point is the one you wish to use.

❻ Read the on-screen notes and then click the **Next** button to begin the restoration.

Memory resident programs

The number of programs resident in the computer's memory at any particular time will affect the performance of the computer. The more programs that are running, the less memory is available to an application you are using. Some memory resident programs are necessary to the well-being of your computer (e.g. anti-virus software) and should not be closed down. However, other utilities might have been loaded automatically when the system was booted up or you might have left open an application you used earlier for a specific purpose and forgot to close it after you had finished with it. You should close down any programs you are not using, especially if your computer has limited memory and/or you experience your applications slowing down.

Software updates

Most software goes through rigorous checks before being released for sale. The manufacturer will specify what the minimum system requirements are to guarantee that the product will work. However, it is impossible to test program code on every type of computer and with every type of program that it might be run alongside.

Sometimes a genuine 'bug' might be present and updates that patch the error will need to be installed. Many software providers provide free updates to registered users of the application. These updates are downloaded to the computer automatically or on demand. Sometimes the computer will need to be rebooted for the patch or update to take effect.

Microsoft regularly release updates that correct discovered flaws in the Windows operating system and in Internet Explorer that could affect the security of a system.

❶ Click **Control Panel** on the **Start** menu and select **Security Center**.

❷ Make sure that the **Automatic Updates** option is set to **On** in the **Security Center** (Figure 2.71).

Tip!

Use the **Help** feature in an application to find out about updates for that application.

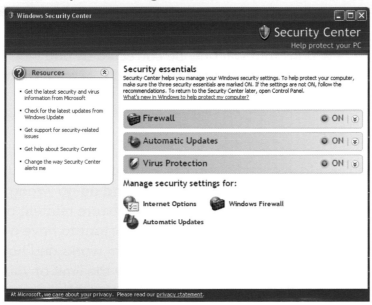

Figure 2.71 The **Security Center** window

Note

You might be asked to reboot the computer after an update before the update will take effect.

Drivers

Sometimes a piece of hardware (e.g. a printer) that worked on one system might not work on another. This might be because the driver for that hardware (i.e. the software that allows communication between the hardware and the computer) is out of date or incompatible. Drivers can be downloaded from the manufacturer's website.

Other reasons why an updated driver might be needed include:

◉ the original driver has been corrupted/deleted
◉ an updated driver might include new features not previously available.

Upgrading

At some time in the life of a piece of software, the manufacturer will decide to release a new version. There are several reasons for this, including:

- The number of patches released on the previous version now justify a new version of the software that incorporates them all.
- Technology has advanced and techniques have changed.
- The market demands new features.
- A new version keeps the manufacturer's name in the public's eye.

The advantages of upgrading include having the latest version of the software thereby ensuring that any previous problems have been eradicated. Compatibility with the latest hardware is ensured, meaning that you do not have to download drivers for any new hardware you might have.

However, the new features in the upgraded software might introduce new bugs that will only be corrected as and when the manufacturer finds out about them and a patch is made available.

Problems

In an ideal world every time you use your computer it should work perfectly. Unfortunately, things can and do go wrong. The types of problem might be hardware or software related, or a combination of the two, therefore it is important to have a good understanding of how your computer system works and how it is configured. It is also important to know the limit of your understanding and where to get help with a problem.

Typical hardware and software problems that might occur include:

- an inability to print
- lost Internet access
- program lock-up and not responding
- unable to save
- incorrect or unexpected operation caused by virus
- slow operation
- intermittent operation
- error messages.

The list cannot be exhaustive, and each problem might be caused by any number of reasons, both hardware and software related. As an example, if faced with an inability to print, you will need to investigate the following in no particular order:

- Is the printer turned on? Is it connected?
- How is the printer connected – standalone or network?
- If standalone, is the cable connected at the printer? Is it connected at the computer?
- If networked, is it a wireless or cable network?
- If cable networked, is the network cable connected at the printer? Is it connected to the router? Is the computer communicating with the network correctly? Has the computer lost other network connectivity? If so, has the network card failed?
- If wireless networked, has the signal path been blocked? Has the wireless router failed? Is your computer communicating with the network correctly?
- Is there paper in the printer? Is there a paper jam?
- Has the printer hardware failed?
- Is the printer driver corrupted?
- Is your print job stuck in a long print queue?
- Are you using the software correctly?
- Is the printer there? Has it been changed to a different model? (In a corporate environment, it has been known for a printer to be moved or changed without all the users being informed!)

These are only some of the reasons that a print problem might occur, but it shows the questions needed to resolve the issue and why an understanding of the system helps.

Most manufacturers provide help and support in the form of manuals and on-screen help pages on disk and/or web-based (for example, the **Help and Support Center** in Microsoft Windows – see page 56). Often the problem is identified by asking you to answer a series of 'troubleshooting' questions that eventually tell you how to correct the difficulty.

You might not be able to solve some of the problems you encounter. This might be because the problem is related to hardware that needs a technician to repair or replace it, or because it is related to software which you cannot change. In these cases, you will need expert help. Most manufacturers offer some type of support. This might be free, free for a limited period, or charged for. It might be necessary to pay to speak to an expert immediately, or, alternatively, free email support might be given by an expert providing you are prepared to wait until your query reaches the top of a queue.

In a corporate environment, the IT department will run a help desk that you can contact for on-site help. The technicians on the help desk will be experts in the systems used by the company.

When you report a fault, you are likely to be asked for specific details about the software and computer system you have. Make sure you take details of any error messages that appear and be prepared to give the exact details of what you were doing when the problem occurred.

This module shows you how
to word process from the
beginning up to intermediate
level. If you already have some
word-processing skills, you will
be able to use the instructions
and tasks to start later in the
chapter. You will learn how to
carry out everyday tasks such
as creating, saving, formatting
and printing small documents.

Each lesson begins with a quick
check of your knowledge and
understanding before you
begin so that you can start at
a point that suits you. At the
end of each lesson you can
quiz yourself to find out how
much you have learned. There
are pointers to help you revise
any parts you need to go over
again.

MODULE 3.
word processing

Using the application

Tip!

All actions using the mouse require only a single click on the left-hand mouse button, unless you are told differently.

Note

Giving the computer instructions using different methods

There are several different ways to give your computer the same instruction. Some of these are described in this module.

Try different ways so you can decide which way suits you best. You might prefer to use a number of different methods or you might favour one method in particular. For example, you might prefer to use the mouse for most actions or you might find the shortcut keys a quicker option. You will be given options throughout this module for using the keyboard shortcuts, toolbar buttons, menus and mouse shortcut menus.

It is also a good idea to use a range of methods which can help prevent Repetitive Strain Injury.

Working with documents

Word processing simply means working with words on a computer. It enables you to change the appearance of text after it has been typed at the keyboard or entered into the computer by another means.

Note

Microsoft Word can be opened by more than one method – as can any other Microsoft Office application.

Open and close Word, and Word documents (3.1.1.1)

1. Click the **Start** button on the Taskbar.
2. Click **All Programs**.
3. Click **Microsoft Office**.
4. Click **Microsoft Office Word 2003**.

As Word loads you will see an **hourglass** icon ⧗ to let you know that something is happening and you need to wait.
Word looks like this when it first opens.

The **Vertical** ruler

The **Horizontal** ruler

The **Standard** toolbar

The **Formatting** toolbar

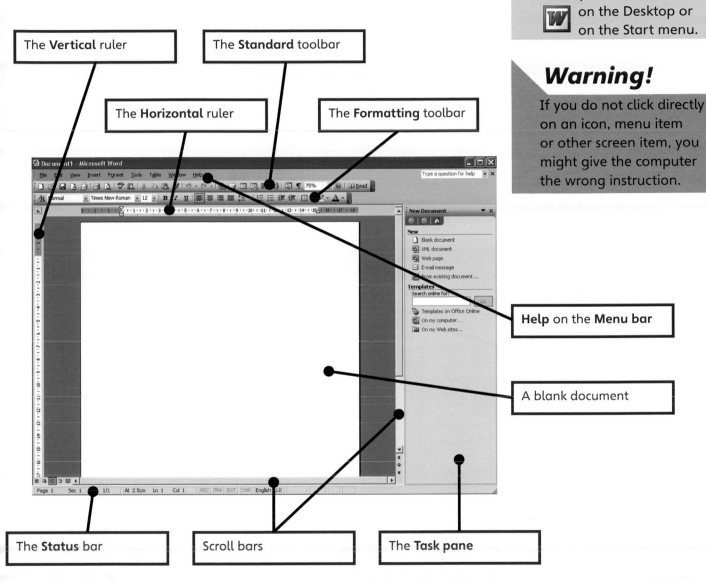

Help on the **Menu bar**

A blank document

The **Status** bar

Scroll bars

The **Task pane**

Figure 3.1 The Microsoft Word opening screen

You are going to open a document (a file) that is given to you on the CD-ROM. It has been produced in Word. The file is called **A day in the garden.doc**. Later you will need to save the file to your hard drive in your **My Documents** folder, but for now all you need to do is to open it.

How about...?

Alternatively, press **Ctrl+O** to open a new document.

❶ Put the CD-ROM in your computer's CD drive.

❷ Click the **Open** button 📂 on the **Standard** toolbar. This lets you open an **existing** document, not create a **new** one.

The **Open** dialogue box (Figure 3.3) appears.

Note

Toolbar buttons

A button (or icon) is an image or symbol which represents a program, a task or an option. They are used to represent instructions. Rest the mouse pointer over a button to see a screen tip that explains its function.

Figure 3.2 shows the Word **Standard** toolbar.

Figure 3.2 The Word **Standard** toolbar

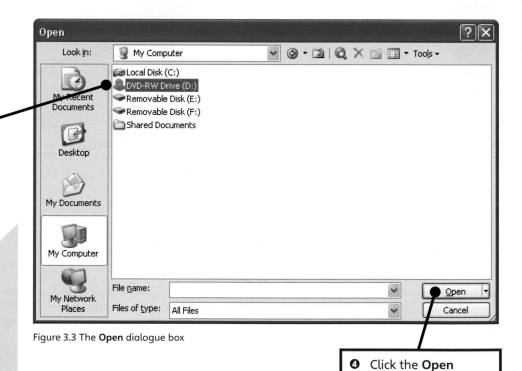

❸ Navigate to the CD-ROM drive and the file

Figure 3.3 The **Open** dialogue box

❹ Click the **Open** button

Note

Depending on your learning circumstances, you might find the file is located on a device other than the CD-ROM (e.g. on a network drive or on a USB storage device). You will need to find out where it has been saved and navigate to that location rather than on the CD-ROM. Navigating to open a file within an application is covered in Module 2 on page 77.

❸ Navigate to the file **A day in the garden.doc** on the CD-ROM.

❹ Select the file and click the **Open** button.

You will work more with this file later, but for the time being close the file and exit Word.

❺ Close the program without making any changes to the document by clicking **File**, **Exit**.

How about...?

Try exiting Word by clicking ☒ (top right) or ☒ (top left). These will close all the open documents and the application. Pressing **Alt+F4** will also do the same.

If you have carried out any activity at all, such as typing any text (even if you deleted the work leaving you with a blank document), Word will offer you the option to save the changes. In this case, click **No**.

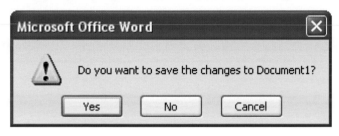

Figure 3.5 Exit prompt to save changes

All Microsoft Office applications have similar icons and dialogue boxes. If you have already opened any other Microsoft Office applications, you will notice how familiar the screen and instructions look.

Create a new document using the default template (3.1.1.2)

A **template** is a pattern or model that has been produced to help you. Even the blank document that opens when you first start Word is based on a default template (the Normal template). It contains formatting (i.e. the layout, fonts etc.) to help you save time. You can change the template formatting, but the changes only affect the document you save, not the template, which remains the same for future use. (You will learn how to change formatting in Formatting on page 139.)

❶ Click the **New** button ☐ on the **Standard** toolbar.

Note

Word, like other Microsoft Office applications, opens with a new (blank) document when you run it, so you do not need to open another. The default settings might be slightly different depending on how your computer has been set up. You will learn how to change these settings in **Options and preferences** (3.1.2.1) on page 127.

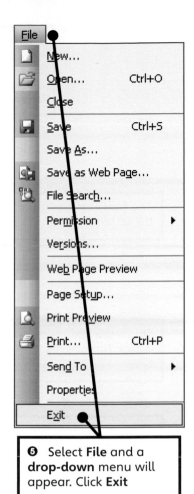

❺ Select **File** and a **drop-down** menu will appear. Click **Exit**

Figure 3.4 Exiting Word

Tip!

The underline means that if you press that letter on the keyboard the command will execute (type **Alt+letter** to open the drop-down list). It is a keyboard alternative to using the mouse. Dots at the end of a menu item tell you that there are more stages to follow (such as a dialogue box).

How about...?

Alternatively, press **Ctrl+N** to open a blank document.

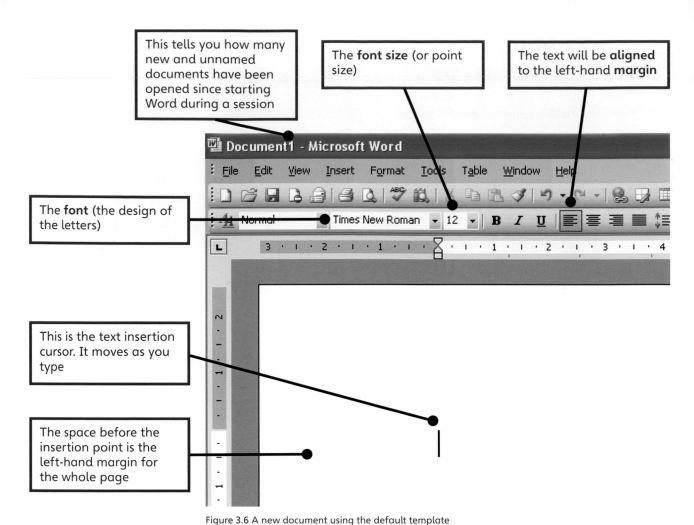

This tells you how many new and unnamed documents have been opened since starting Word during a session

The **font size** (or point size)

The text will be **aligned** to the left-hand **margin**

The **font** (the design of the letters)

This is the text insertion cursor. It moves as you type

The space before the insertion point is the left-hand margin for the whole page

Figure 3.6 A new document using the default template

When you type text on a keyboard into Word, you will find that the word processor does much of the hard work for you! For example, when you type lines of text, you do not need to press the Return key to move to the next line (unless you want to start a new paragraph).

The table below Figure 3.7 on page 119 tells you what the different keys are for.

2 Type the following text, inserting your name in place of <insert your name here>. Remember to press the spacebar once after each word and after a full stop.

My name is <insert your name here>. This is my first word-processed document. I opened Word and was immediately able to start typing. I did not need to think about how I wanted the text to be formatted. If I want to change how it looks, I will learn how to do this in a later lesson.

There is a file called **My first document.doc** on the CD-ROM. You can open it to see what your document should look like.

Note

What to do when you get to the edge of the page

If you want to leave a blank line between one piece of text and another, such as between paragraphs, then you need to press the Return key for each empty line you need (but see 3.3.2.7 on page 146). Do not press it at the end of every line or you will start a new paragraph each time and your text layout will look strange.

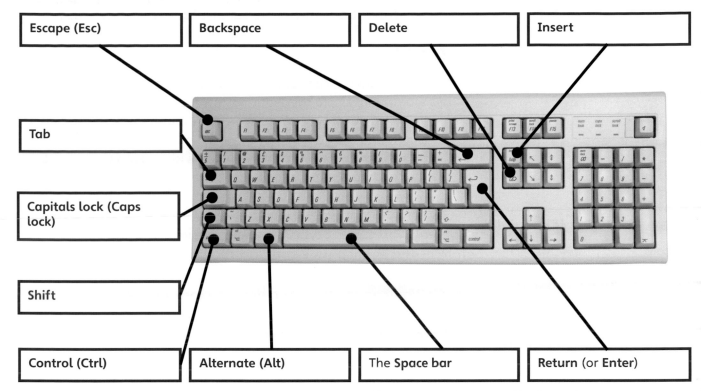

Escape (Esc)	Backspace	Delete	Insert
Tab			
Capitals lock (Caps lock)			
Shift			
Control (Ctrl)	Alternate (Alt)	The **Space bar**	**Return** (or **Enter**)

Figure 3.7 A typical keyboard (some key positions might be different, but their functions will be the same)

Key name	What it does
Escape (Esc)	Press to de-activate a menu option, to clear a dialogue box etc.
Tab	Each press will move the cursor from one tab position to another.
Capitals lock (Caps lock)	Press this to get all capital letters.
Shift	Press at the same time as pressing a letter to give a capital letter. Holding down this key will also give you the keyboard symbols (e.g. those above the number keys and punctuation keys like %, & and @ etc.).
Control (Ctrl)	Holding down this key will give you access to shortcut commands when pressing other keys at the same time.
Alternate (Alt)	Holding down this key when using other keys gives you extra functions.
Space bar	Press this bar to get a space.
Return (or Enter)	Press this to move the cursor to the next line.
Backspace	Press this to erase the character immediately to the left of the cursor.
Delete	Press this to erase the character immediately to the right of the cursor.
Insert	Press this once and you will overtype any characters that are in front of the cursor. Press it again and you will be able to insert characters.
Page up (PgUp) Page down (PgDn)	Press this to move the cursor up or down a screen page.
Arrows	These keys move the cursor forwards, backwards, up or down.

❸ Now read through the text to check for any errors. You will learn more about this in Prepare outputs on page 178.

Note

You should always carefully check every document you produce to make sure there are no mistakes. You should check for spellings, punctuation and layout. It helps to look at the document and ask yourself if you would be happy to receive it. Reading the document word for word will also help you to check the grammar and punctuation.

Look at where the insertion point (cursor) is on completing your document. You cannot type text after the insertion point, only before it. This is because Word doesn't 'know' the document exists after this point. In other words, the document grows as you create it. You can scroll up and down to look at the whole page (see Module 2, page 54). A new page will appear when you have typed enough text to fill the first page.

At this stage it is important to save your document. You could lose your work if you do not save it.

Save a document (3.1.1.3)

❶ Click the Save button 💾 on the **Standard** toolbar. The **Save As** dialogue box will appear.

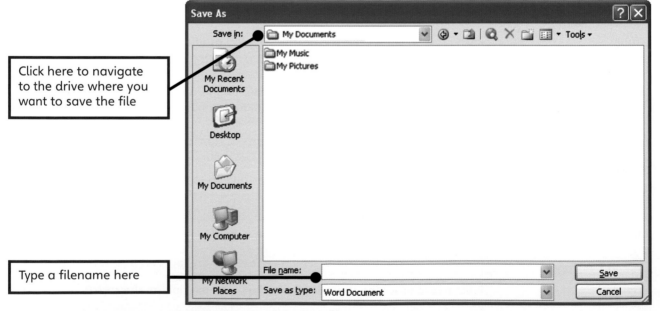

Figure 3.8 Naming and saving a file

Click here to navigate to the drive where you want to save the file

Type a filename here

Tip!

If you want to print your first document, click the Print button 🖨 on the **Standard** toolbar. Your document will print to the default printer for your computer.

Think carefully before printing to avoid wasting paper and increasing your carbon footprint!

❷ Type the filename **My first document**.

❸ Look at the name in the **Save in:** box. It should show **My Documents**. This is where your file will be stored.

❹ Click **Save**.

Saving your file does not close it. You can choose to close your file without saving, but Word will ask you if you're sure.

If your file already has a name, every time you click the **Save** button, Word will save any changes you have made since the last time the file was saved. This is called **overwriting** a file. The name of your file will not change unless you want to change it.

Do it!

Saving an existing file with a new name in a new location

You are going to create a copy of **My first document** with a new name in a new folder on your hard drive.

❶ Create a new folder called **How to** in your **My Documents** folder. If you need to, remind yourself how to create new folders in Module 2, page 63.

❷ Open **My first document.doc** (if it is not already open).

❸ Click **File, Save As…** to open the **Save As** dialogue box.

❹ Navigate to the **How to** folder you created in step I.

❺ Change the filename shown in the **File name:** text box to **How to save a file.doc** and make sure that the **Save as type:** box shows the **Word Document** format.

You can save documents in other formats. You will learn about these formats and how to save files in them in **Save a document as a different file type (3.1.1.4)** on page 124.

❻ Click the **Save** button.

You have now made an identical copy of your file by saving it with a new name in a new location on your hard drive.

❼ Delete the existing text and type some instructions telling somebody how to save the file.

❽ Save your instruction document.

Create a new document using other types of default templates (3.1.1.2)

Earlier you learned how to type text into a new document using the **Normal** template (page 117). Word also gives you a selection of other templates to use, for example for memos, faxes and agenda. This means you don't have to create the document from scratch each time which saves time and also means that each time you produce another memo or fax etc. it will look similar, making it look more professional.

When you first open Word the **Task pane** is displayed at the right-hand side of the Word screen, showing the **Getting Started** options.

Tip!

Always give your file a name that is meaningful – in other words, a name that describes the document. Although Word will offer you a suggested filename you will see that it takes the name from the first line of your document. This may not be the best name for your file because you might not be able to remember it if you want to find it again. It is best not to name your files with your name but give the file a name that makes sense.

Tip!

The **Getting Started** Task pane lists documents that you have recently worked on. Click a document in the list to open it.

How about...?

You can open the **New Document** Task pane by clicking **File** and then **New...** from the drop-down list.

① Click **Create a new document....**

The **Task pane** now provides you with options to start different types of blank document, including those based on templates other than the **Normal** template.

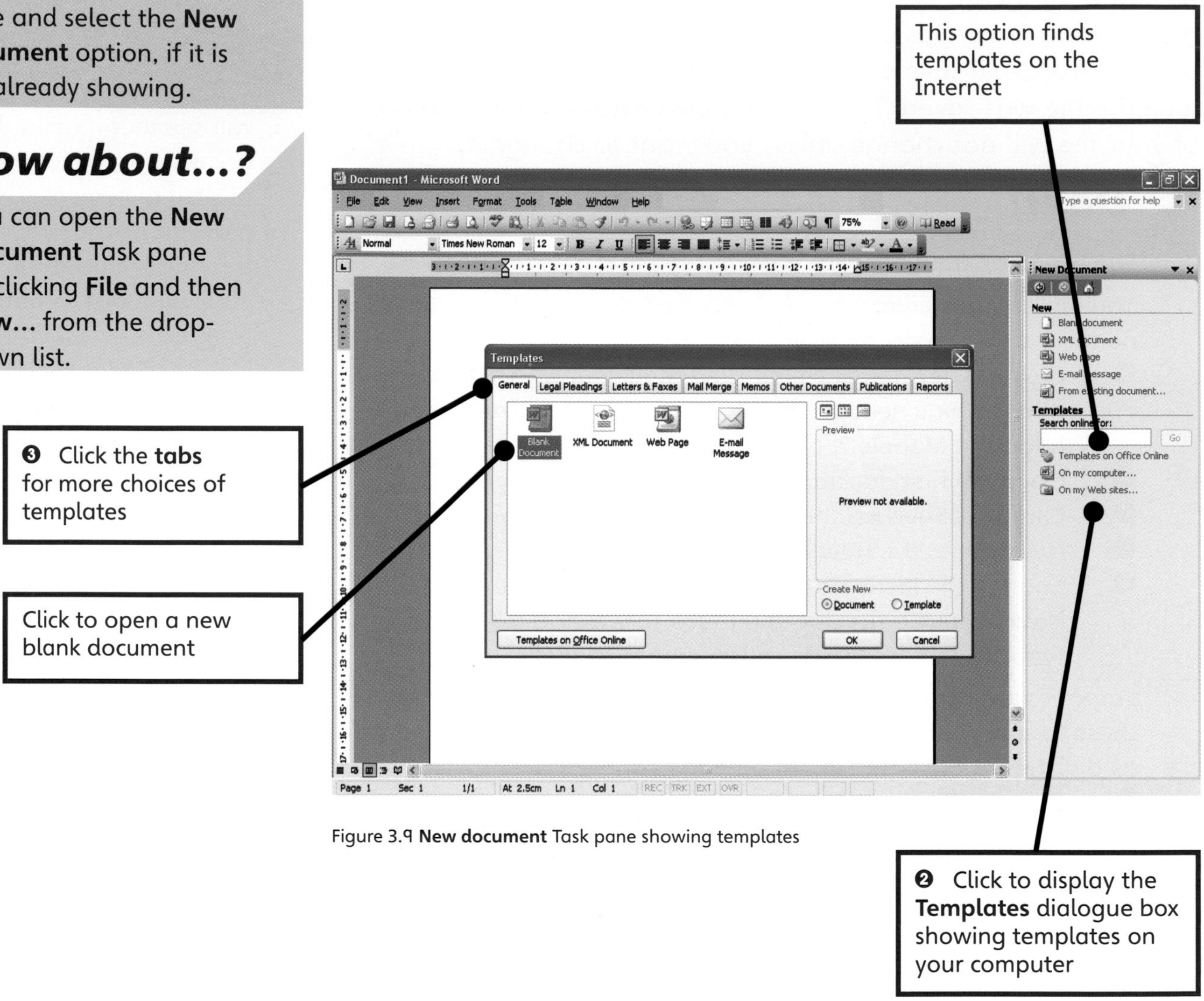

This option finds templates on the Internet

❸ Click the **tabs** for more choices of templates

Click to open a new blank document

Figure 3.9 **New document** Task pane showing templates

❷ Click to display the **Templates** dialogue box showing templates on your computer

❷ Click **On my computer...** under **Templates** on the Task pane.

❸ The **Templates** dialogue box will display.

❹ Select the **Memos** tab.

❺ Select **Contemporary Memo** and click the **OK** button. The document will open showing the layout of and instructions for using the memo template.

❻ Read the instructions on the template to familiarise yourself with using the template.

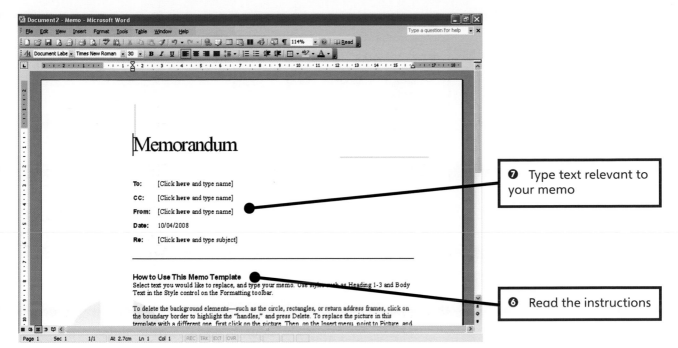

Figure 3.10 The Contemporary Memo template

❼ Type the following into the relevant template areas:

To: Jo Smith
CC: Ahmed Patel
From: your name
Date: today's date
Re: How to use a template

❽ In the body of the memo, type how you used this template as if you were giving instructions to a colleague or friend.

❾ Save your file by clicking on the **Save** icon or selecting **File, Save As…**. Name your file **How to use a memo template. doc**. Save your file in your **How to** folder.

Tip!

It is a good idea to save your document as soon as you begin, and save it again periodically as you work on it. By doing so you will always have a recent copy of your work should your computer crash or if there is a power failure as you work.

Do it!

See what other templates are available on your computer

❶ Open one of the fax templates and create a fax to a company's IT Support team letting them know that the toner needs to be replaced on one of the printers you use. Mark the fax as urgent and save it as **My first fax using the template.doc**.

❷ Close the document.

❸ Locate and open the **Agenda Wizard** template.

Continues…

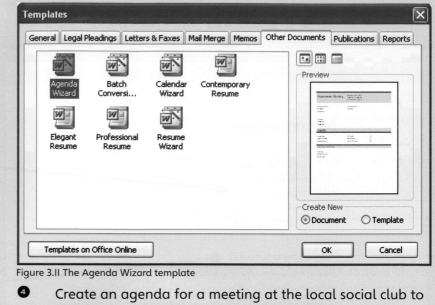

Figure 3.11 The Agenda Wizard template

4 Create an agenda for a meeting at the local social club to organise a party. The agenda items to be included are:

Welcome and apologies
Purpose of meeting
Dates for party
Entertainment
Any other business
Date of next meeting

5 Save your agenda as **My first agenda using the template. doc**.

6 Close the document.

Save a document as a different file type (3.1.1.4)

You can save a Word file as a different type of file. You might want to do this because you are giving the file to somebody who uses an earlier version of Word (one that does not support all the features of Word 2003), or to somebody who uses a different word-processing package. In the latter case, for example, Word files can be saved as WordPerfect files or as Rich Text Format (rtf) files which can be opened by most other word processors.

1 Open your file called **How to save a file.doc**.

2 Click **Save As...** on the **File** menu.

3 Click the down arrow to the right of the **Save as type:** box on the **Save As** dialogue box.

4 Select **Rich Text Format** from the list and save with the same filename.

5 Click the **Save** button.

Your document will be saved with the same filename as before but with a **.rtf** extension and format.

Another common file type you might come across is the text file (.txt). This type of file takes up less storage space on the computer because it doesn't include advanced formatting features.

Saving different versions of a file (3.1.1.4)

You can save different versions of a file. This is useful, for example, if you are working on long documents such as an assignment, or on a document that might differ slightly depending on how it is going to be used.

❶ Open your file **How to save a file.doc**.

❷ Click **Versions...** on the **File** menu.

The Versions dialogue box will display.

Tip!

You can use Windows Explorer (page 61) to navigate to the **How to** folder to check that the file has been created. You should see two files called **How to save a file**: one with a .doc extension and one with a .rtf extension.

Tip!

If you create a file that you want to use again and again (e.g. a letter that has your address and perhaps a logo), you can save that file as a template (.dot).

❸ Click **Save Now...**

Tick this box if you want to automatically save a version each time you close the file

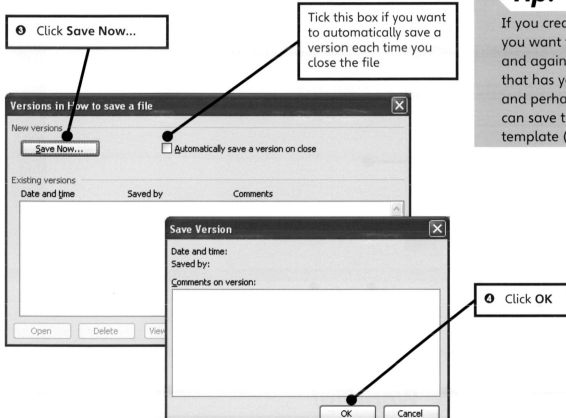

❹ Click **OK**

Figure 3.12 Saving versions

❸ Click the **Save Now...** button.

❹ Click **OK**.

Using this method saves space on your storage device because Word saves only the differences between versions, and does not save the complete file each time. You can open the files and check the changes between versions. You can also print, and delete earlier versions.

Switch between open documents (3.1.1.5)

You might often find that you have more than one document open at a time, so it's useful to know how to flick between them.

1. Open **How to save a file.doc**.
2. Open **My first document.doc**. **How to save a file.doc** will be hidden behind it.
3. Click the **Window** menu.
4. Select **How to save a file**.

> ❸ Click **Window** to show the files that are open

> ❹ Click **How to save a file**

> The Word screen with at least two documents open, one on top of the other

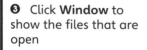

Figure 3.13 Switching between open documents

> Open files are shown on the Taskbar

How about...?

Here are some alternative ways of switching between open files.

- ◉ On the keyboard, press the number next to the file you want.
- ◉ Click the **Taskbar** button for the file you want to display.
- ◉ Use **Alt+Tab** to move through all the open files on your computer. Release the **Alt** key when you reach the file you want to display.

Warning!

The more files and applications there are running at any one time on a computer, the harder it has to work, potentially slowing it down.

Prove it!

Use Word to write a letter detailing your services as an administrator to a possible employer. Remember to include your address and the date, and explain briefly your recent experience and the skills you have to offer. Don't forget to mention you are studying for the ECDL award! Save it with the filename **Administrator.doc**.

Enhancing productivity

Options and preferences (3.1.2.1)

The default options in Word can be changed if you want to save all or most of your files in a different location. Module 2, Files and Folders, covers storing files in different locations (drives and folders). You can change the default location where Word stores files.

❶ Click **Options...** on the **Tools** menu to display the **Options** dialogue box.

❷ Select the **File Locations** tab.

❸ Select the **Document** file type and click the **Modify...** button.

❹ Navigate to a new location in the **Modify Location** dialogue box that is displayed.

❺ Click **OK**.

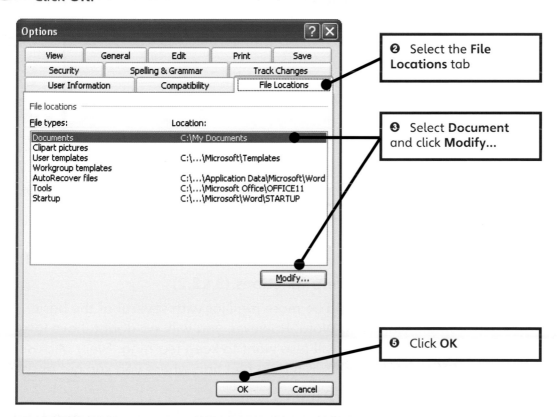

Figure 3.14 File locations options

Changing the default location for saving your files also means that Word will take you direct to the same location when you open a file.

You can set a username that is added to certain more advanced features of Word, such as **Properties**, **Comments** and **Reviewing**. The username allows you and others to see who wrote the document.

❶ Click **Options…** on the **Tools** menu to display the **Options** dialogue box.

❷ Select the **User Information** tab.

❸ Type in the name and initials by which you would like to identify yourself on your documents.

❹ Click **OK**.

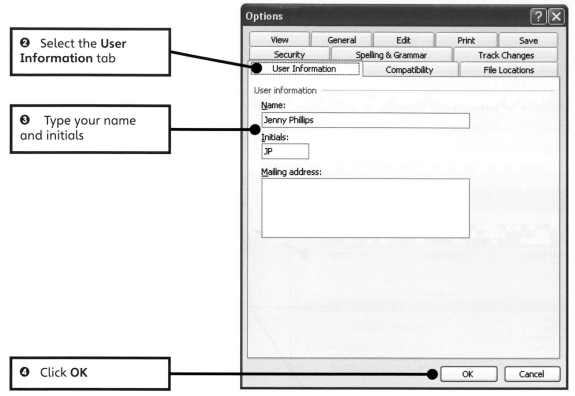

❷ Select the **User Information** tab

❸ Type your name and initials

❹ Click **OK**

Figure 3.15 User Information options

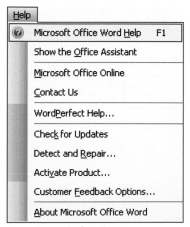

Figure 3.16 Help functions

Use available Help functions (3.1.2.2)

By now you should be more familiar with several of the basic options for using Word. However, you will, no doubt, have lots of questions and will also want to keep learning. Every Microsoft Office application has a Help function where you can get answers.

❶ Click the **Help** menu.

❷ Click **Microsoft Office Word Help** from the drop-down menu.

The Task pane will change to display the Word Help features.

❸ Type **how to use help** in the **Search for:** text box.

❹ Click the green arrow to begin searching.

❺ Word will display a list of topics relating to your search criteria. Click on any topic to display the help text available.

How about…?

You can also access Help by pressing **F1**.

❸ Type **how to use help**

❹ Click to begin a search

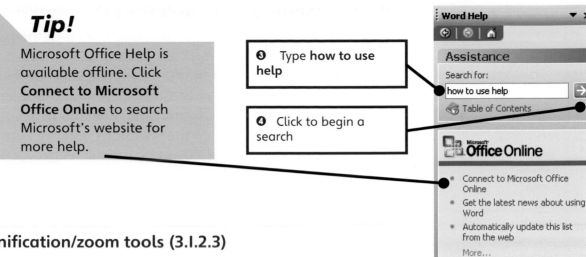

Figure 3.17 The **Help** Task pane

Use magnification/zoom tools (3.1.2.3)

It is likely that at some time you will want to magnify the displayed text. This means that it will appear larger on the screen, but doesn't change the font size of the characters themselves (i.e. they will print at the correct size). You can do this by zooming in (or out to make smaller) using the zoom option.

❶ Click **Zoom...** on the **View** menu to display the **Zoom** dialogue box.

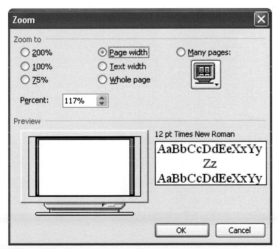

Figure 3.18 The **Zoom** dialogue box

❷ Select the option you require by clicking the relevant radio button, or select a percentage.

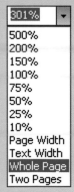

Figure 3.19 The Toolbar list

Display, hide built-in toolbars (3.1.2.4)

Word has many features, and obviously not all of them can be made accessible at the same time as they would clutter your computer screen. Some of the functions are very specialised, and so can be hidden until you need them. Windows toolbars group like features together (e.g. formatting, mail merge etc.). The most commonly used toolbars are the **Standard** and the **Formatting** toolbars, and these are displayed by default. However, they too can be hidden if you want to clear more space on your Word screen.

◉ To find toolbars, click **Toolbars** on the **View** menu. You can then select/deselect which toolbars are visible by clicking the toolbar name from the list.

Test your understanding

1. What is a word-processing application?
2. What is another name for a document?
3. a) What is a template?
   b) Name **five** different templates available in Word.
4. Describe the difference between **Save** and **Save As**.
5. What should you check just before saving a document?
6. Where are Word documents usually stored by default?
7. Describe **two** ways to create different versions of the same document.
8. Name some file formats in which you can store a Word document, explaining why you might want to do so.
9. Describe **two** ways to switch between open Word documents.
10. Does the **Zoom** tool make the characters larger on a printed document?
11. Describe how to change the default location for saving files.

You can find the answers to the questions on the CD-ROM saved as **Answers to TYU questions 3.1**. How did you do? Go back over anything that you are unsure about.

Document creation

Learning objectives

By working through this lesson you will learn:
- ◉ about page view modes
- ◉ how to enter text in a document
- ◉ how to insert special characters
- ◉ how to display and hide non-printing characters
- ◉ how to select characters, words, lines, sentences, paragraphs and entire text
- ◉ how to search for and replace text
- ◉ how to delete, copy and move text
- ◉ about the Undo and Redo commands.

Entering text

Page views (3.2.1.1)

You can change the appearance of the page on your Word screen. The default setting shows your page in **Print Layout**. This view shows the margins although you may not see all the page displayed in the space available. You might prefer to view your document in **Normal** view which shows the text extending fully across the Word screen.

In addition to these two views, you can view a document in **Web Layout** (to see how the document might appear if it was viewed as a website), **Reading Layout** (to view the document without toolbars and menus) and **Outline** (to show how the document is organised) views.

◉ Select the view from the **View** menu.

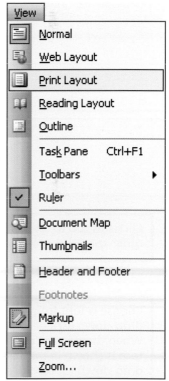

Figure 3.20 The **View** menu

Inserting text and punctuation (3.2.1.2)

❶ Open **A day in the garden.doc**.

❷ Click to position the text insertion cursor between **August** and **and** (immediately before the letter **a** in **and**).

❸ Type in **2008** and press the spacebar once after the **8**.

❹ Move the text insertion cursor to the end of the document and type the text **THE END** on a new line.

❺ Save your file as **A day in the garden with new text.doc** and close it.

❷ Click to place the insertion point between the words (note the position, leaving a space before the text to be inserted)

A day in the garden - Microsoft Word

File   Edit   View   Insert   Format   Tools   Table   Window   Help   Adobe PDF   Acrobat C

Normal   Times New Roman   12   **B** *I* <u>U</u>

It was a nice day in August [and I decided]
garden.

I opened the back door and went outside. '
blue. It was nice to see the sunshine as it h
flowers looked lovely around the edge of f
lawn was over hanging the flowerbeds a li
my lawn.

I needed something to sit on so I went bac
out of the kitchen or should I have a nice s
on a kitchen chair in case it got dirty. I car

What was I going to do? Should I sit and a
would read a book. I went back inside to a

Figure 3.2I Inserting characters

Inserting special characters and symbols (3.2.1.3)

Not all the symbols you might need when typing documents are immediately available on the keyboard, for example characters such as © (copyright), ® (registered), ™ (trademark) and other symbols such as ☺, ☹, ✓, ✗ and foreign language characters. You can access many special characters using Word (but the range will depend on which fonts are installed on your computer). Figure 3.22 shows the special characters available in the Wingdings font.

Click this tab to find other special characters

Choose a font from the drop-down list.
When the **normal text** font is shown in this drop-down list box, the characters will match the font style you are currently using

Scroll to see all the symbols

If you prefer to use the keyboard, make a note of the shortcut keys (if they are displayed)

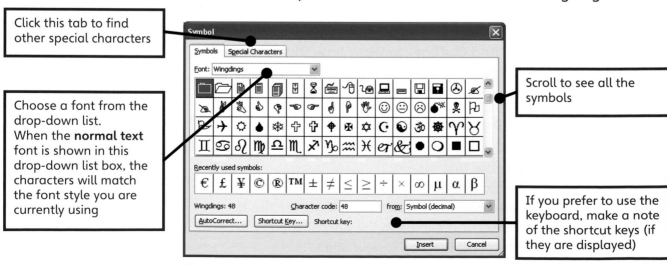

Figure 3.22 The Wingdings font characters

1. Open a new document and click the **Insert** menu.
2. Select **Symbol...** from the drop-down menu.
3. Choose a font by clicking from the **Font:** drop-down list.
4. Click the symbol you need from the displayed characters.
5. Click the **Insert** button and then close the **Symbol** dialogue box.

The symbol will be inserted in the document.

6. Close the file without saving it.

Select and edit text

Selecting text to edit (3.2.2.2)

Once you have typed text into a document, you will probably want to add and delete words, and perhaps move whole paragraphs so the text makes more sense. You need to be able to select (highlight) the text you are working with.

1. Place the insertion point at the start (or very end) of the text you want to highlight.
2. Hold down the left mouse button and drag the cursor over the text you want to select. The highlighted text will appear white on a black background.
3. Let go of the mouse button when you have highlighted all the text you want to work with.
4. To clear any highlighting after formatting, or if you change your mind:
- either click in an area which is not highlighted (but remember you might need to move the insertion point back to where it was if you want to try highlighting the same text again)
- or press one of the arrow keys.

Do it!

1. Open the file called **A day in the garden.doc**.
2. Highlight the first paragraph, then de-select the highlighting.
3. Highlight the third word in the first sentence, then de-select it.
4. Highlight one letter, then de-select it.
5. Highlight the whole document, then de-select it.
6. Close the document without saving any changes.

Tip!

There are shortcut keys for some characters. For example, typing **Alt+Ctrl+C** will give ©, **Alt+Ctrl+R** will give ® and **Alt+Ctrl+T** will give ™.

Warning!

If you let go of the mouse button before you have finished highlighting, or you click the mouse button again after highlighting but before giving Word an instruction, you will lose your highlighting and need to do it again.

How about...?

Alternatively, set the insertion point and press the shift key while you use the arrow keys. Practise using the different keys to see how they highlight the text in different directions.

Tip!

You might find that using the keyboard method gives you more control over the highlighting, particularly if you only need to highlight one letter.

Tip!

Press **Ctrl+A** to highlight the whole document.

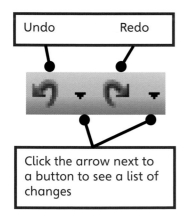

Click the arrow next to a button to see a list of changes

Figure 3.23 The **Undo** and **Redo** buttons

Edit (3.2.2.3) and delete text (3.2.2.7)

You will learn here how to use the **Insert**, **Delete** and **Backspace** keys to edit your document.

1. Open the file **A day in the garden with new text.doc**.
2. Save the file immediately with the new name **A day in the garden with edited text.doc**.
3. Highlight the sentence in the second paragraph **The birds were singing and the sky was blue**, making sure you highlight the final full stop and the space after it so that the space between the remaining sentences will not be too wide. (You will see that that the background becomes black and the text becomes white.) Press the **Delete** key.
4. Highlight **nice** in the next sentence and type **lovely**.
5. Highlight **lovely** in the next sentence and type **pretty**.
6. In the last sentence of that paragragh, place the insertion point immediately before the first **a**. Press the **Insert** key and type **quite a lot**.
7. Press the **Insert** key again, press the spacebar once and type **as**.
8. Place your insertion point after **thirsty** in the eleventh paragraph. Press the **Backspace** key to delete each letter.
9. Type the word **hard**, remembering to put in the space before or after the word if you have deleted it.
10. Save your document.

Use the Undo and Redo commands (3.2.2.8)

If you type in or delete some text and decide it was a mistake, you can undo the mistake straight away. You might even decide that now you have undone the mistake you want to redo the change. The **Undo** and **Redo** buttons are on the **Standard** toolbar.
You do not need to highlight first or move the cursor to where the change is to be made.

1. In **A day in the garden with edited text.doc**, delete the word **lot** and replace it with **little**.
2. This obviously does not make sense, so click on the **Undo** button to change it back again.
3. Practise undoing and redoing the change to get used to how these commands work, but leave the text as **lot** when you have finished. Save the file and close the document.

Use a simple search command (3.2.2.4)

Word can search for words and phrases in a document to save you time.

① Open **A day in the garden with edited text.doc**.

② Select the **Edit** menu.

③ Click **Find…** on the drop-down menu.

④ Type the word or phrase you want to find into the **Find what:** text box.

⑤ Click the **Find Next** button to find the first occurrence of the word or phrase in the open document.

⑥ Click **Find Next** again to move to the next occurrence.

⑦ Press **Escape** to close the **Find** dialogue box when you have found the word or phrase you want.

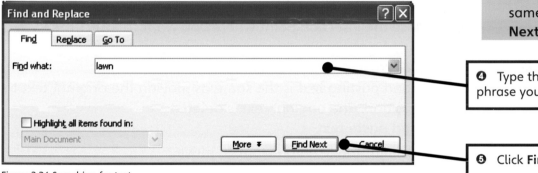

Figure 3.24 Searching for text

④ Type the word or phrase you want to find

⑤ Click **Find Next**

How about…?

Ctrl+F opens the **Find** dialogue box.

Tip!

Don't include any punctuation in the search criteria unless you want to limit your search.

How about…?

Pressing **Return** is the same as clicking the **Find Next** button.

Use a simple replace command (3.2.2.5)

① Click **Replace…** on the **Edit** menu to display the **Find and Replace** dialogue box.

② Type the word or phrase to be replaced in the **Find what:** text box.

③ Type the replacement word or phrase in the **Replace with:** box.

④ If you are sure that you want to replace every occurrence of the word or phrase, click the **Replace All** button. Otherwise, replace each occurrence individually by clicking the **Replace** button. The search will move on to the next occurrence after each replacement.

How about…?

Ctrl+H opens the **Find and Replace** dialogue box.

Do it!

Find and replace the first two occurrences of the word **secateurs** with the word **clippers**. Save and close the file.

Figure 3.25 Replacing text

② Type the word or phrase to be replaced

③ Type the replacement word or phrase

Copy, cut and paste (3.2.2.6)

A word processor lets you copy text (words, sentences, paragraphs and even whole documents) without you having to retype them. This can save you time and make your documents appear similar. You can copy text in the same document and between other open documents. Earlier you learned how to save a document with another name, therefore if you want to copy all the text from a document into another you might choose to open the file containing the text and then save it with another filename. Copying and pasting text means that the original text remains. Each time you paste you create a duplicate of the original.

To copy and paste text

1. Highlight the text you want to copy.
2. Click **Copy** on the **Edit** menu.
3. Place the insertion point where you want to insert the copied text.
4. Click **Paste** on the **Edit** menu.

Cutting and pasting text is the same as moving the original text to a new position. The original text is deleted.

To cut and paste text

1. Highlight the text you want to move.
2. Click **Cut** on the **Edit** menu.
3. Place the insertion point where you want to insert the cut text.
4. Click **Paste** on the **Edit** menu.

Display, hide non-printing characters (3.2.2.1)

Sometimes it is not clear why a document does not look as you intend, for example word spacing or line spacing might look odd. This is often caused by extra, invisible marks such as spaces, paragraph breaks and tabs.

◉ Click the **Show/Hide ¶** button **¶** on the **Standard** toolbar to view these marks. They can help you to find out what the problem is, so you can correct it.

Figure 3.26 on page 137 shows some of the hidden marks in the document.

Do it!

1. Open **A day in the garden with edited text.doc**.
2. Highlight the paragraph beginning **I decided I needed a hat.** and ending **... a really lovely, relaxing day.**
3. Move it to before the paragraph above that starts **I could do with a cushion...**
4. Delete any additional paragraph rows if they appear.
5. Save and close the document.

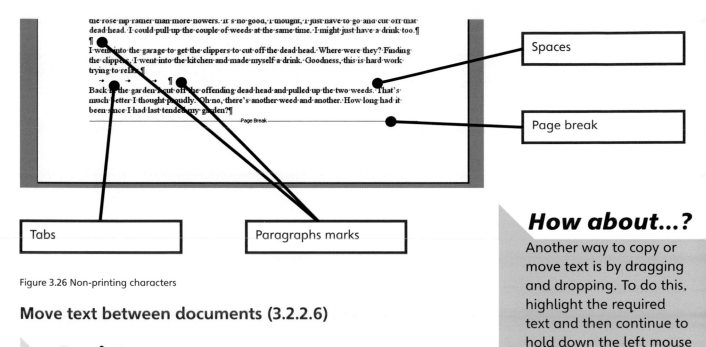

the rose hip rather than more flowers. 'It's no good,' I thought, 'I just have to go and cut off that dead head. I could pull up the couple of weeds at the same time. I might just have a drink too.¶

¶

I went into the garage to get the clippers to cut off the dead head. Where were they? Finding the clippers, I went into the kitchen and made myself a drink. Goodness, this is hard work trying to relax.¶

Back in the garden I cut off the offending dead head and pulled up the two weeds. That's much better I thought proudly. Oh no, there's another weed and another. How long had it been since I had last tended my garden?¶

————————————————————Page Break————————————————————

Spaces

Page break

Tabs

Paragraphs marks

Figure 3.26 Non-printing characters

Move text between documents (3.2.2.6)

Do it!

❶ Open **My first document.doc** and **A day in the garden with edited text.doc**.

❷ Highlight your name in **My first document**.

❸ Switch to **A day in the garden with edited text**.

❹ Put your insertion point at the end of the document, and press **Return** twice.

❺ Paste your name into this document, close and save changes.

❻ Close **My first document**.

How about...?

Another way to copy or move text is by dragging and dropping. To do this, highlight the required text and then continue to hold down the left mouse button. You will note that the cursor arrow shows a small box attached to it which means cut or move. To copy a piece of text you need to hold down the **Ctrl** key at the same time – a small + sign appears on the arrow.

Prove it!

Produce a business letter using the **Contemporary Letter** template. Open the letter you created earlier (**Administrator. doc**) introducing your services as an administrator. Make up a name for your own company. Copy and paste your address and the content (body) of the letter into the template. Save it as **Administrator letter.doc**.

1. What is **overtyping**?
2. What is the shortcut key combination for **Undo**?
3. How many times can you paste?
4. How can you delete a space?
5. What is the quickest way to find a word and replace it with another?
6. What is the difference between **copy and paste** and **cut and paste**?
7. Explain the difference between the different **Page Views** available in Word.
8. What are non-printing characters?

You can find the answers to the questions on the CD-ROM saved as **Answers to TYU questions 3.2**. How did you do? Go back over anything that you are unsure about.

Formatting

Formatting text

Once you have typed text into a document, you will probably want to format some or all of it to make it look more professional. For example, the formatting might include making a word (or character) appear italicised, or you might want to make a whole paragraph stand out from the others by making it appear as darker (bold) or coloured text.

It is good practice to apply formatting after you have typed in the text. To apply formatting, you need to select (highlight) the text or character that is to be affected.

Change text formatting: font sizes, font types (3.3.1.1)

There are two main types of fonts (or character design): **serif** and **sans serif**.

Serif fonts have 'tails' and probably the most commonly used is Times New Roman, which is the one being used in this sentence.

Sans serif means 'without tails'. This sentence is written in a commonly used sans serif font: Arial.

Your computer has a range of fonts and font sizes already installed, but it is possible to add many more.

The following demonstrates two ways of changing the font of selected text.

Method I: Using the Font dialogue box

❶ Open **My first document.doc**.

❷ Highlight **name** (the second word from the beginning).

❸ Click **Font...** on the **Format** menu.

❹ Change the font to **Comic Sans MS** and the size to **10**. Use the scroll bars to see fonts higher or lower on the list.

❺ Click **OK**.

❻ Save the document.

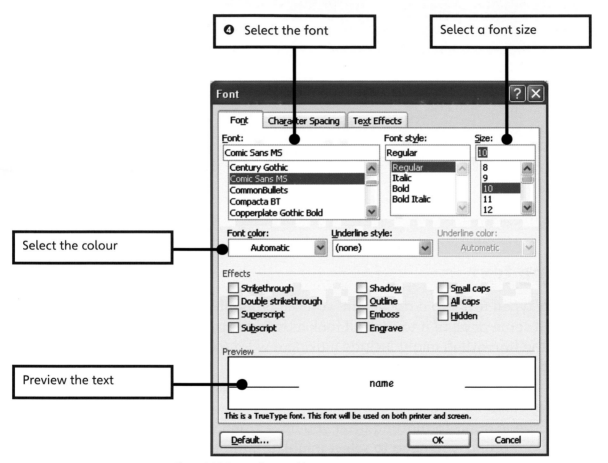

Figure 3.27 Formatting text (I)

Method 2: Using the Formatting toolbar

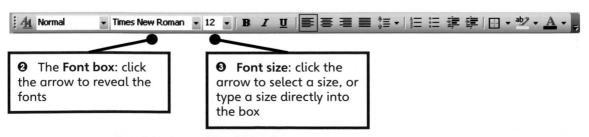

Figure 3.28 The Word **Standard** toolbar

1. Highlight the last sentence in your document.
2. Click the down arrow on the right-hand side of the **Font** box on the **Formatting** toolbar and change the font to **Courier New**. (You can choose another font if you like the look of a different one.)
3. Click the down arrow on the right-hand side of the **Font Size** box on the **Formatting** toolbar and change the size of the selected text to **11**.
4. Save the document as **My first document with new fonts. doc** and close it.

Apply text formatting: bold, italic, underline (3.3.1.2)

Once you have chosen a font and font size, you can change the appearance of the text, for example by making it appear bold, italic, underlined etc.

1. Highlight the text to which you want to apply the emphasis.
2. Click **Font...** on the **Format** menu to display the **Font** dialogue box.
3. Select a font style (e.g. **Bold**, **Italic** etc.) by clicking it in the **Font style:** box.
4. Underline text by clicking the arrow on the right-hand side of the **Underline style:** box and selecting the style you want.
5. Click **OK** to apply the formatting.

Tip!
You can select any of these options before inputting (typing) text. Try it!

Warning!
Do not use too much emphasis as it can make text difficult to read.

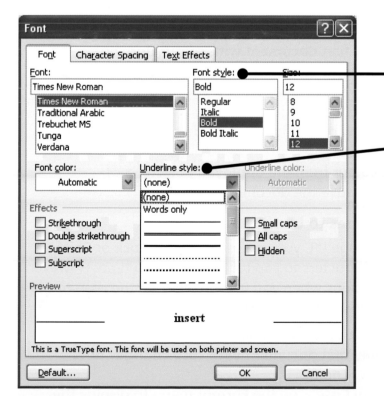

Figure 3.29 Formatting text (2)

How about...?
Alternatively, you can also apply bold, italic and underline formatting by clicking the Bold, Italic or Underline buttons on the **Formatting** toolbar.

B *I* **U**

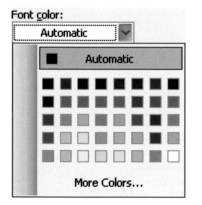

Figure 3.31 Selecting a colour

Do it!

❶ Open **My first document with new fonts.doc**.
❷ Use the **Find** function to locate the word **first**.
❸ Highlight **first** and embolden it (make bold).
❹ Find and underline the word **immediately**.
❺ Find and italicise the **If I want to**.
❻ Save the document as **My first document with emphasis. doc** and close it.

Apply superscript and subscript (3.3.1.3)

You might want to format characters in superscript or subscript style. They are widely used in measurements (e.g. an area in square metres is written as m^2) or in chemical symbols (e.g. the symbol for water is H_2O).

❶ Select the text you want to display in superscript or subscript.
❷ Click **Font...** on the **Format** menu to display the **Font** dialogue box.
❸ Click the tick box for **Superscript** or **Subscript** in the **Effects** section.

Apply different colours to text (3.3.1.4)

Another way to format text for emphasis is to change its colour. You might want to do this if you are producing a leaflet, notice or invitation.

❶ Open **My first document.doc**.
❷ Save it as **My first document with colour.doc**.
❸ Highlight your name.
❹ Click **Font...** on the **Format** menu to display the **Font** dialogue box.
❺ Click the arrow at the right-hand side of the **Font color:** drop-down list.
❻ Choose a colour from the displayed palette.
❼ Click **OK** and save the document.

Apply case changes to text (3.3.1.5)

As explained on page 119, you can use the **Caps Lock** or **Shift** keys to change characters to capital letters as you type. However, there will be occasions when you want to change the case of the characters after you have finished typing.

❶ Open **My first document.doc**.
❷ Save it as **My first document with case changes.doc**.
❸ Highlight your name.
❹ Click **Change Case...** on the **Format** menu to display the **Change Case** dialogue box.

5. Select **UPPERCASE** by clicking the radio button adjacent to the option.
6. Click **OK**. Your name will now appear in upper case characters.
7. Save and close the document.

Tip!

Holding down **Shift**, press **F3** to step through the case options.

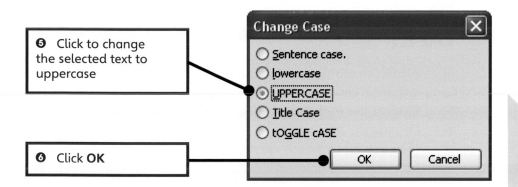

❺ Click to change the selected text to uppercase

❻ Click OK

Figure 3.32 Changing case

Note

If you want to change only one letter, say to a capital, then it is probably easier to simply delete the character and re-type it.

Apply automatic hyphenation (3.3.1.6)

Word automatically works out how to space text across consecutive lines. This is called **wrapping**. However, there will be occasions when you will want to control how words are split across lines. Some words can be split at the end of a line by using a **hyphen**. Word can do this automatically so you don't have to decide where a hyphen should be placed. This is particularly useful when **justifying** text, which you will learn about in Paragraphs on page 145 (see section 3.3.2.4).

1. Open **A day in the garden more pages.doc**.
2. Select the **Tools** menu.
3. Rest the mouse pointer over **Language** until the list expands.
4. Select **Hyphenation...** to display the **Hyphenation** dialogue box.

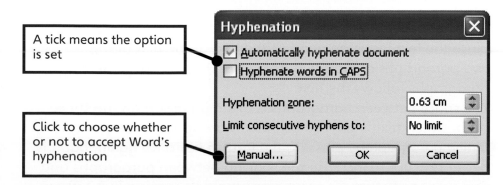

A tick means the option is set

Click to choose whether or not to accept Word's hyphenation

Figure 3.33 Setting hyphenation options

Tip!

You might prefer to use the **Manual...** option to avoid overuse of hyphens.

⑤ Click the tick box for **Automatically hyphenate document** so a tick is shown.

⑥ Click **OK**.

You will see some words at the end of lines are split with a hyphen.

⑦ Save the document as **A day in the garden with hyphens. doc**.

Do it!

Open **Administrator letter.doc** that introduces your services. Carry out these changes.

- ⦿ Change the font to a sans serif font of your choice.
- ⦿ Change the font size to 12.
- ⦿ Format your company name by changing the colour of the font and underlining it.
- ⦿ If you have left **Dear Sir or Madam** change **Sincerely** to **Yours faithfully**. If you have put the recipient's name (e.g. Dear Mr Smith), change **Sincerely** to **Yours sincerely**.
- ⦿ Remove all punctuation after the introduction and any that exists after Yours faithfully/sincerely, or in the address.
- ⦿ Highlight the automatic date and delete it. Replace it with today's date in the form 11th April 2008 (i.e. using superscript after the number).
- ⦿ Include a reference after the introduction and before the body of the letter (e.g. **RE: Administration services**) and embolden.
- ⦿ Save and close the document.

Paragraphs

Create and merge paragraphs (3.3.2.1)

Word automatically wraps text at the end of a line onto a new line, but to start a new paragraph you need to force the text insertion point onto a new line. To do this, simply press the **Return** key.

Tip!

Until you have had more practice, show the hidden characters when you merge paragraphs. ¶ This way you can see when you have deleted the paragraph symbol.

Conversely, if you want to merge two paragraphs, simply place the text insertion point at the end of the first of the two paragraphs and press **Delete** until the second of the two paragraphs follows the first.

The space between paragraphs is often greater than the space set between text lines. You can add more space when you create a new paragraph by pressing the **Return** key once again, but it is better practice to increase the spacing between paragraphs and use only one **Return** (see text on paragraph spacing (3.3.2.8) on page 148).

1. Open **A day in the garden with hyphens.doc**.
2. Find the first occurrence of a sentence beginning **I laid down on the lounger...**
3. Place your cursor at the beginning of the sentence.
4. Press **Enter** twice to make a new paragraph.
5. Save the document as **A day in the garden with new paras. doc**.
6. Show the non-printing characters.
7. Delete the paragraph marks between the first and second paragraph.
8. Check the space marks between the full stop and new sentence. Insert a new space if needed.
9. Save and close the document.

Line breaks (3.3.2.2)

A manual line break ends a line and forces the text which is in front of the cursor onto the next line in a similar way to when you create a new paragraph. However, instead of applying paragraph spacing (which might be greater than the line spacing), it keeps the line spacing that exists within the paragraph. A manual line break is often called a **soft return**, and it can be recognised on the page by its hidden character ↵ .

- Press **Shift+Enter** to insert a manual line break.
- To delete a manual line break, use the **Backspace** key if your cursor is positioned after the space or the **Delete** key if your cursor is before the space.

Align text left, centre, right, justified (3.3.2.4)

You can use Word's alignment options to easily line up lines of text in several different ways. Here are some examples of how text can be aligned in Word.

This paragraph is **aligned left**. All the left edges of the lines are lined up. The right edges appear ragged.

This paragraph is **justified**. This means that the all left edges of the lines are lined up and all the right edges are lined up. To do this, the spacing between words becomes unequal. This alignment is often used to make extracts or quotations stand out from the surrounding text.

These two paragraphs are **centred**. Both the left and right edges of the text appear ragged.
Text might be centred for an address at the top of a letter or for a heading. Centred text is also used to emphasise information, for example in a notice.

This paragraph is aligned right. All of the right edges of the lines are lined up. You might choose to right align text for a date in a letter, or to right align page numbers on the bottom of a page.

① Open **A day in the garden with new paras.doc**.
② Save it as **A day in the garden with title and date.doc**.
③ Place your insertion point in the first paragraph, which is currently left aligned.

Tip!

You do not need to highlight all the text in a paragraph to apply alignment formatting. Simply click in the paragraph and choose the alignment you want.

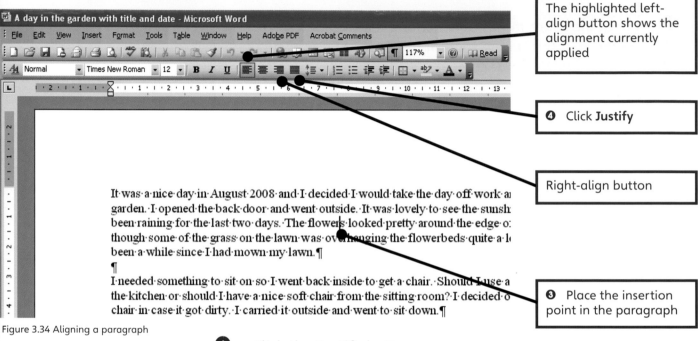

The highlighted left-align button shows the alignment currently applied

④ Click **Justify**

Right-align button

③ Place the insertion point in the paragraph

Figure 3.34 Aligning a paragraph

④ Click the **Justify** button.
⑤ Place the insertion point at the beginning of the document and insert the title **A DAY IN THE GARDEN** and format as bold.
⑥ Press **Return** twice to create a new paragraph between the heading and the first paragraph.
⑦ Move the insertion point to the title and **centre** the text.
⑧ Follow steps 6 and 7 again only this time insert the date, underlined not emboldened.
⑨ Save and close the document.

Tip!

A day in the garden with title and date.doc shows how your document should look after applying the paragraph alignment.

Good practice (3.3.2.3 and 3.3.2.7)

You will have already realised that there are more ways than one of doing things in Word. Some of the different ways are equivalent, but there are good reasons for doing others in a particular way. It is good practice to change your way of doing things to suit the situation.

When you align text, you might be tempted to make the gaps between word bigger by repeated use of the space bar. It will not result in neatly aligned words and columns, and so this is bad practice!

Warning!

If you have inserted too many spaces or line breaks, your text will not fully justify and will have gaps in it. You will need to delete the extra spaces first.

Remember to align text with:

- ◉ the left, center, right and justified buttons (see 3.3.2.4 on page 145)
- ◉ indents (see section 3.3.2.5 below)
- ◉ tabs (see section 3.3.2.6 on page 149).

Also, when you add space between paragraphs, do not be tempted to keep pressing the **Return** key. You should always apply good practice and adjust the space before and after the paragraph as explained in 3.3.2.8 on page 148.

Indent paragraphs (3.3.2.5)

Another way to format a paragraph is to indent the first line, or you can indent all of the left side, the right side or both sides.

> A short paragraph that requires emphasis can be indented at both edges like this. You might also find it helpful to adjust the line spacing within the paragraph (see Apply line spacing (3.3.2.8) on page 148). This paragraph is indented on both sides and the text is fully justified. You should fully justify the paragraph when indenting text from both margins.

1. Open **A day in the garden with title and date.doc**.
2. Save it as **A day in the garden with indents.doc**.
3. Place the insertion point into the first (justified) paragraph.
4. Click **Paragraph…** on the **Format** menu to display the **Paragraph** dialogue box.
5. Click the **Indents and Spacing** tab if it is not selected.

Tip!

Click the **Increase** and **Decrease Indent** buttons on the **Formatting** toolbar to change the left-hand indent.

⑥ Type or click the up/down arrows to adjust the indentation

Preview the text

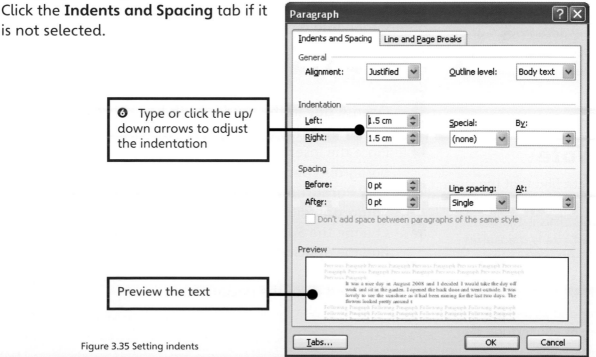

Figure 3.35 Setting indents

6. Set the left and right indentations to **1.5 cm**.
7. Click **OK**.
8. Save and close the document.

Apply line spacing within paragraphs (3.3.2.8)

In addition to emphasising text by colour, style, alignment etc., you can also adjust the space between each line of text. The default line setting is single. You can change the setting for a paragraph or whole document.

1. Open **A day in the garden with indents.doc**.
2. Save it as **A day in the garden with line space.doc**.
3. Click in the first paragraph.
4. Click **Paragraph…** on the **Format** menu to display the **Paragraph** dialogue box.
5. Click the arrow to the right of the **Line spacing:** drop-down list, and select **1.5 lines**.
6. Click **OK** to confirm the settings.
7. Save and close the document.

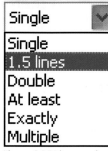

Figure 3.36 Line spacing

Apply spacing above, below paragraphs (3.3.2.8)

You might come across occasions when you don't want to change the line spacing within a paragraph, but do want to provide more space before and/or after a paragraph. For example, you might have been asked to leave a specific amount of space to insert a photograph into a document at a later date.

You might be tempted to just hit the return key a few times. However, this space is unlikely to be accurate and it is also easy to delete.

1. Open **A day in the garden with line space.doc**.
2. Save it as **A day in the garden with para space.doc**.
3. Place the insertion point in the blank line before the paragraph beginning **I decided upon a hat**.
4. Click **Paragraph…** on the **Format** menu to display the **Paragraph** dialogue box.
5. Change the **Spacing Before:** to **5 cm** and the **Spacing After:** to **3 cm**.
6. Click **OK**.
7. Save and close the document.

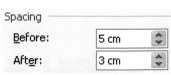

Figure 3.37 Spacing above and below paragraphs

Do it!

1. Open **My first document with case changes.doc**.
2. Save it as **My first document with space for ticket.doc**.
3. Add **5 cm** spacing after the paragraph.
4. Click **OK**.
5. Place the text insertion point at the end of the paragraph and press **Return** to move the text insertion point to the start of the new paragraph.
6. Type:

   However, I am now adding to this document as I want to include a fixed space where I could attach a used train ticket to give to someone else as proof of travel.
7. Change the text to a **sans serif** font in size **10**.
8. Change the text colour.
9. Save and close the document.

Set, remove and use tabs (3.3.2.6)

Tabs enable you to line up text without having to guess. For example, if you try to space out columns by using the spacebar, you will find that any characters included before the space will make it almost impossible to accurately line up the text. Also, if you fully justify text, the size of a space will vary from line to line! Tabs are accurate and are unaffected by changes to text either side of the alignment mark.

There are four types of tabs that you are likely to use: left, right, center and decimal. The most commonly used tab is the **left tab** where text will line up to what could be called a temporary margin. This is a stopping point which is used to line text equally. The **right tab** lines up text as if it was right justified and the **center tab** lines up text centrally around the tab stop. The tab stop is the point at which the tab is set on the ruler. The **decimal tab** is used to line up numbers which include a decimal point. Because most fonts use proportional spacing, the text and numbers take up different amounts of space depending on the size of the character or symbol. If you use the spacebar it will be guess work and text won't line up equally although it might look like it on the screen!

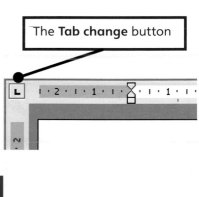

The **Tab change** button

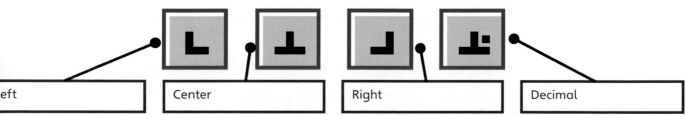

Left   Center   Right   Decimal

Figure 3.38 Tab buttons

Scenario:

You are going to produce a letter to a manufacturer of doll's house furniture. Your family are putting their money together to buy the furniture for your little sister's birthday, and you said you would write the letter as you want to practise your skills.

1. Create a new blank document.
2. Type the following letter, filling in the text between < > with your personal details. Use the tab key to space the columns in the table.

Centre your personal details

Press the tab key once between each 'column'. Default tabs are preset at regular intervals

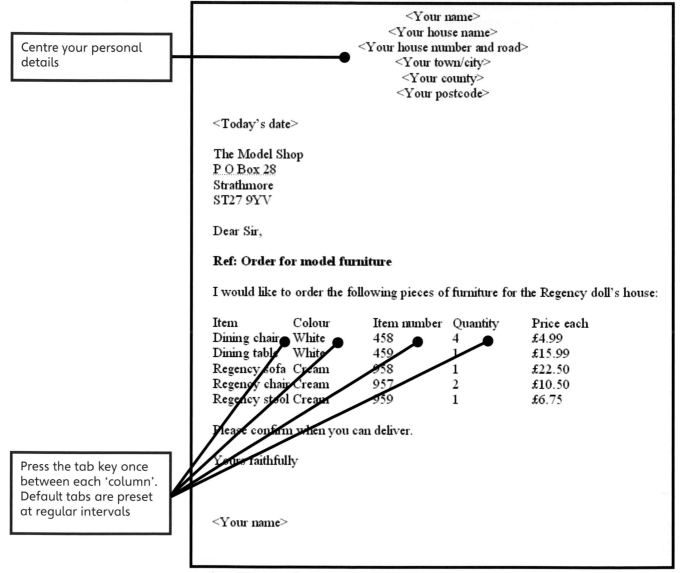

<Your name>
<Your house name>
<Your house number and road>
<Your town/city>
<Your county>
<Your postcode>

<Today's date>

The Model Shop
P O Box 28
Strathmore
ST27 9YV

Dear Sir,

Ref: Order for model furniture

I would like to order the following pieces of furniture for the Regency doll's house:

Item	Colour	Item number	Quantity	Price each
Dining chair	White	458	4	£4.99
Dining table	White	459	1	£15.99
Regency sofa	Cream	958	1	£22.50
Regency chair	Cream	957	2	£10.50
Regency stool	Cream	959	1	£6.75

Please confirm when you can deliver.

Yours faithfully

<Your name>

Figure 3.39 Using tabs

You will notice that the columns of text are not even and some are squashed. You can improve the column spacing by setting appropriate tabs at suitable spaces.

3. Highlight the text where you used the tab key.

Item	Colour	Item number	Quantity	Price each
Dining chair	White	458	4	£4.99
Dining table	White	459	1	£15.99
Regency sofa	Cream	958	1	£22.50
Regency chair	Cream	957	2	£10.50
Regency stool	Cream	959	1	£6.75

4   Click the ruler once at 3.5 cm to set the first tab, and at 6 cm, 9 cm and 12 cm to set subsequent tabs.

Don't panic! Your list might look incorrect at this stage. This is because in some places you have two tabs between columns, and now you have set up the spacing so there should be only one. You need to delete the extra tabs.

5   Click **Show/Hide ¶** to show the tab marks.

6   Place the text insertion point at the start of your table, and move through the list using the right arrow key, deleting tabs so there is only one between each column entry.

7   Save the document as **Letter to the model shop using tabs. doc**.

8   Close the document.

When you look at the letter you have produced you might consider ways in which it could be improved. For example, you might decide to make the headings of each column bold so they stand out. One way to make the letter look more professional is to set tabs that line up the columns according to the type of data in each one. For example, the item number might be better presented using a center tab while the price of each would be neater using the decimal tab. For the quantity, you will use a right tab. The colour will remain lined up using the left tab.

1   Open **Letter to the model shop using tabs.doc**.

2   Save it as **Letter to the model shop with tab types.doc**.

3   Highlight from **Dining chair** to **£6.75** (not the headings).

4   Click the **Tab change** button to change the type of tab to a center tab.

5   Place your cursor on the ruler and drag the left tab set at **6 cm** onto your document and 'throw it away'.

6   Click on the ruler at **7 cm** which will place a center tab.

7   Replace the existing left tab at 9 cm with a **right** tab at **10 cm**.

8   Replace the existing left tab at 12 cm with a **decimal** tab at **13 cm**.

9   Save and close the document.

Tip!

If you click in the wrong place or too many times and extra tabs appear, drag and drop them onto your page. This 'throws' them away and they will disappear.

Note

If the ruler is not displayed, click **Ruler** on the **View** menu.

Tip!

If you find it difficult to set a tab at an exact point on the ruler, hold down the **Alt** key at the same time as sliding the tabs along the ruler.

How about...?

You can view, set, clear and alter your tab settings by using the **Tabs** dialogue box. Click **Tabs...** on the **Format** menu.

Figure 3.40 The **Tabs** dialogue box

Bullet and number lists (3.3.2.9)

Bullet points are applied to lists of information or to small lines of information.

❶ Open **Letter to the model shop with tab types.doc**.

❷ Save it as **Letter to the model shop with extra items.doc**.

❸ Delete **Please confirm when you can deliver** and type the following:

> **When you confirm the delivery date, please could you also confirm the price of the following items and if you have them in stock:**
>
> **King size bed**
> **Single bed**
> **Dressing table and stool**
> **Wardrobe**

❹ Highlight from **King size bed** to **Wardrobe**.

❺ Click the **Bullets** button ⬚ on the **Formatting** toolbar to apply the default bullet style to the list.

❻ Click **Bullets and Numbering...** on the **Format** menu.

7 Click the **Bulleted** tab on the **Bullets and Numbering** dialogue box, and select an alternative style for the bullets.

8 Click **OK**.

9 Insert a new list item for a **Double bed** between **King size bed** and **Single bed** by placing cursor after **King size bed** and pressing **Return**, and then typing **Double bed**.

10 Save and close the document.

If the list is a sequential series of instructions, you should use a numbered list rather than a bulleted list.

◉ Click the **Numbering** button ≣ on the **Formatting** toolbar to apply the default number style to a list. You can change the style by selecting the **Numbered** tab on the **Bullets and Numbering** dialogue box.

1 Open **Garden Party without formatting.doc**.

2 Save it as **Garden Party with lists.doc**.

3 Format the lists of fun and games and things to bring, as bullet lists.

4 Change the bullets from dots to something suitable for a party invitation.

5 Format the directions as numbered lists.

6 Change the number style to a style without full stops after the numbers.

7 Save and close the document.

To delete a bulleted or numbered item from a list, place the insertion point at the beginning or end of the item and press **Delete** or **Backspace**, respectively.

Tip!

If you find an unwanted bullet appears when you next press **Return**, use the **Backspace** key to remove it.

Do it!

Open **Garden Party with lists.doc** and save it as **Garden Party with formatting.doc**. Carry out the following formatting tasks.

1 Format all text in a **sans serif** font. **Centre** the heading on the first line and change it to font size **18**, **blue**.

2 Format the remainder of the heading (down to **2 pm**) in font size **14**.

3 Centre the heading lines (down to **2 pm**).

4 Set all text to **1.5** line spacing.

5 Set all the remaining text in font size **12**.

6 Remove the existing numbering from the **Directions from the south** list.

7 Highlight the **Directions from the south** heading and list, and set a **left** tab at **8 cm**. Tab the heading and list to the new position.

8 Reapply the numbering to the list.

9 Underline 'fun' and 'games'.

10 Save and close the document.

Add a box border and shading to a paragraph (3.3.2.10)

Applying a border to an invitation or notice is likely to make it more attractive. You can apply a border to a whole page, part of a page or to a paragraph.

To identify the area where you require a border, highlight the text first. Although there is a toolbar button for applying borders ⊞ on the **Formatting** toolbar, you will find more choice by selecting **Borders and Shading...** from the **Format** menu.

① Open **Garden Party with formatting.doc**.

② Save it as **Garden Party with border.doc**.

③ Highlight the heading **Come to a Garden Party**.

④ Click **Borders and Shading...** on the **Format** menu to display the **Borders and Shading** dialogue box.

⑤ Click the **Borders** tab.

⑥ Select a line style

⑦ Select the borders to be affected

⑥ Select a colour from the list

⑥ Select a line width

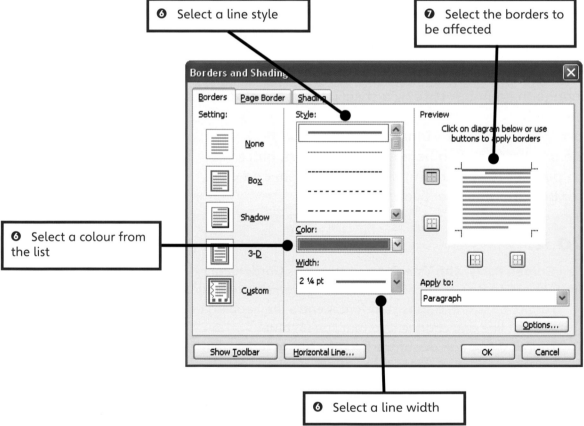

Figure 3.41 The **Borders and Shading** dialogue box (I)

⑥ Select the solid, **Green, 2 ¼ point** wide line for the border.

⑦ Select a top border only.

⑧ Click **OK**.

⑨ Carry out the same process to apply a border to the bottom of the page.

⑩ Save the document.

To format with a whole-page border

❶ Open **Garden Party with border.doc** if it is not already open.

❷ Highlight the whole document.

❸ Click **Borders and Shading...** on the **Format** menu to display the **Borders and Shading** dialogue box.

❹ Select the **Page Border** tab.

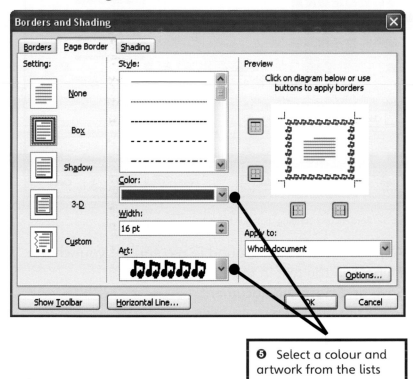

❺ Select a colour and artwork from the lists

Figure 3.42 The **Borders and Shading** dialogue box (2)

❺ Set a colour and artwork for the border, and click **OK**.

❻ Save the document.

To format selected text with a border

❶ Open **Garden Party with border.doc** if it is not already open.

❷ Highlight the heading from **On** to **2 pm**.

❸ Apply a **4 ½ point**, **red** border to the top and bottom of this portion of text only.

❹ Save the document.

To apply shading as background to text

❶ Open **Garden Party with border.doc** if it is not already open.

❷ Highlight the area from **On** to **2 pm** (i.e. between the red borders).

❸ Click **Borders and Shading...** on the **Format** menu to display the **Borders and Shading** dialogue box.

Note

You may need to install Word's optional border art component from CD if it is not already installed.

④ Select the **Shading** tab.

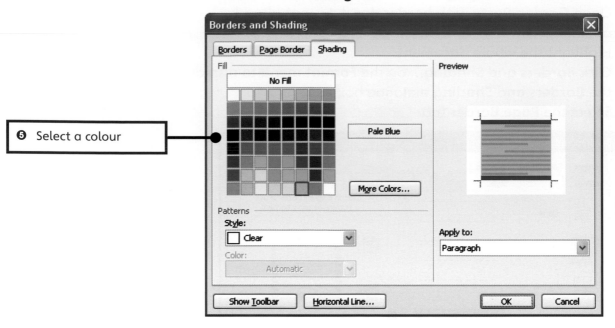

⑤ Select a colour

Figure 3.43 The **Borders and Shading** dialogue box (3)

⑤ Apply a shaded background in a colour of your choice.
⑥ Embolden the text in the shaded area.
⑦ Save and close the document.

Prove it!

Create a short newspaper article about water shortages with the heading H_2O. Apply a border and shading to the heading. Use a blue font every time **water** or **H_2O** appears in the text. Include a list of dates of water shortages and use bullets to emphasise the list.

Styles

Applying automatic styles (3.3.3.1 and 3.3.3.2)

You have already seen how to apply different fonts and sizes to characters and words by selecting them from the **Font** and **Font size** boxes on the **Formatting** toolbar (see Change text formatting: font sizes, font types (3.3.1.1) on page 139).

Word also allows you to define styles for paragraphs. This means that you can consistently apply complicated formatting to text in one click without having to select each element of the formatting. For example, you might be writing a book and you want each chapter title to be in Tahoma, bold, 30 pt, italic, right aligned, with a drop capital first letter, with a 2 cm space after it. You can define this as a style so that every time you write a chapter title, you simply click it and the text is formatted correctly.

Styles can be copied between documents, and between computers, so that consistency is ensured if, for instance, a series of documents, perhaps written by different authors, is being produced. Styles can be linked to automatic functions, for example they can be used to create indexes and contents lists. Defining your own styles is beyond the scope of this book, however Word comes with some preset styles which you can use.

❶ Highlight the text you want to format.

❷ Click the arrow on the right-hand side of the **Style** box to display a drop-down list of predefined styles.

❸ Click a style on the list to apply it to the selected text.

Do it!

❶ Open **A day in the garden with para space.doc**.

❷ Save it as **A day in the garden with style.doc**.

❸ Type the following:

The start of the day after the heading and date, and before first paragraph.

Making myself comfortable before the paragraph starting **I needed something to sit on...**

Getting bored before the paragraph starting **What was I going to do?**

Sun protection after the single sentence ending **... sit on my chair**.

Still not settled before the paagraph starting **I picked up the book but the sun was in my eyes**.

❹ Place the insertion point anywhere in the main title **A DAY IN THE GARDEN**.

❺ Select the **Heading I** style from the style list.

❻ Place the insertion point in the new text **The start of the day** and apply the **Heading 2** style.

❼ Apply the **Heading 2** style to all the other new headings you typed in step 3.

❽ Click in the first paragraph (starting **It was a nice day...**) and select the **Normal** style. This resets the paragraph style to the document default.

❾ Remove the spacing above and below the paragraph starting **I decided I needed a hat** by clicking the **Normal** style.

❿ Save and close the document.

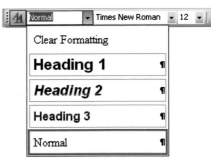

Figure 3.44 The **Styles** list

Copy a style (3.3.3.3)

A style can be copied. Instead of having to select the style from the style list each time, you can use the **Format Painter** 🖌 .

Do it!

❶ Open **A day in the garden with style.doc**.

❷ Save it as **A day in the garden with more style.doc**.

❸ Type the following:

Gardening before the paragraph starting **So I went into the garage...**

Time to relax before the paragraph starting **I went back to my lounger...**

The end of a perfect day! before paragraph starting **It can't be...**

❹ Click to place the insertion point in the heading **Still not settled**.

❺ Click the **Format Painter** button on the **Standard** toolbar.

❻ Click the new text **Gardening**. The **Heading 2** format is applied to the new text.

❼ Repeat steps 4–6 to apply the **Heading 2** style to the new text **Time to relax** and **The end of a perfect day!**

❽ Save and close the document.

Tip!

If you want to format only parts of a word or paragraph, highlight the area first.

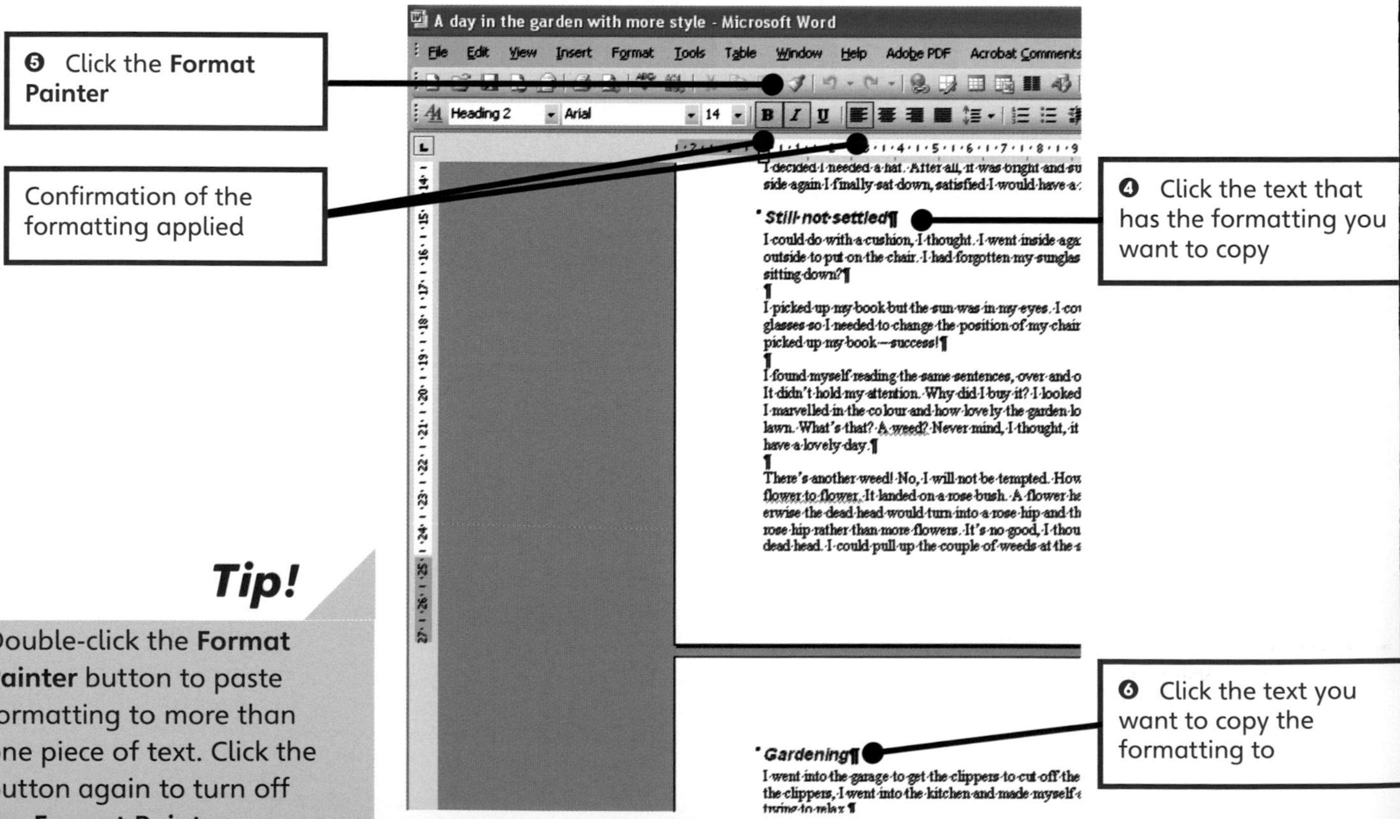

❺ Click the **Format Painter**

Confirmation of the formatting applied

❹ Click the text that has the formatting you want to copy

❻ Click the text you want to copy the formatting to

Tip!

Double-click the **Format Painter** button to paste formatting to more than one piece of text. Click the button again to turn off the **Format Painter**.

Figure 3.45 Using the **Format Painter**

Prove it!

Create a CV to accompany your application letter for the post of administrator that you created earlier. Use the formatting techniques you have learned so far to make the CV look professional, thereby increasing your chance of being selected for the post. Save the document as **My CV.doc**.

Test your understanding

1. What is the difference between a **serif** and **sans serif** font?
2. What type of font is **Comic Sans MS**?
3. What is the difference between **superscript** and **subscript**?
4. How do you underline text?
5. How can you delete a line break?
6. What does **justified** mean?
7. How do you ensure a paragraph is exactly **0.5 cm** away from a margin?
8. What are tabs used for?
9. What are bullets used for?
10. How do you apply an existing paragraph style to one or more paragraphs?
11. Name a quick way of copying formatting from one piece of text to another.

You can find the answers to the questions on the CD-ROM saved as **Answers to TYU questions 3.3**. How did you do? Go back over anything that you are unsure about.

Learning objectives

By working through this lesson you will learn:
- about tables and how to create and format them
- about graphical objects and how to manipulate them.

Creating tables

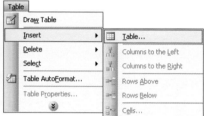

Figure 3.46 The Table menu

Create a table ready for data insertion (3.4.1.1)

Tables are not only quick to create but are, perhaps, an easier way to present information than using tabs or columns. Forms are often laid out using a table to define the columns and rows.

❶ To create a table, start a new document or place your cursor in the space where you want to insert it.

❷ Select **Insert** and then **Table** from the **Table** menu to display the **Insert Table** dialogue box.

❸ Select the number of rows and columns you want in your table.

❹ Click **OK** to insert the table into your document.

How about...?

Alternatively, you can use the **Insert Table** button on the **Standard** toolbar to insert a table.

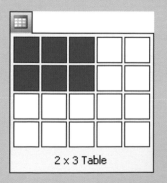

Slide mouse pointer over the number of columns and rows you want, then click to insert the table.

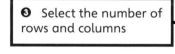

❸ Select the number of rows and columns

Figure 3.47 The **Insert Table** dialogue box

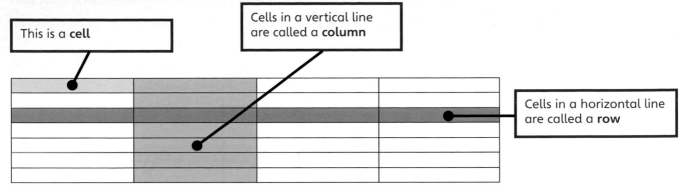

Figure 3.48 A typical Word table

When the table appears in your document it is already formatted with a border around the table and every cell in the table. You can move your cursor around in the table by using the mouse or the tab key. To move backwards from one cell to the previous cell on the same row, use **Shift+Tab**.

Insert and edit data in a table (3.4.1.2)

❶ Start a new document and save as **Shopping list.doc**.
❷ Insert a table with **4** columns and **10** rows.
❸ The text insertion point is in the top-left cell. Type the heading **Item**.
❹ Type the next three headings **Category**, **Type**, **Quantity**.
❺ Complete the table as shown in the figure.

Tip!

Use copy and paste to save typing words which are repeated.

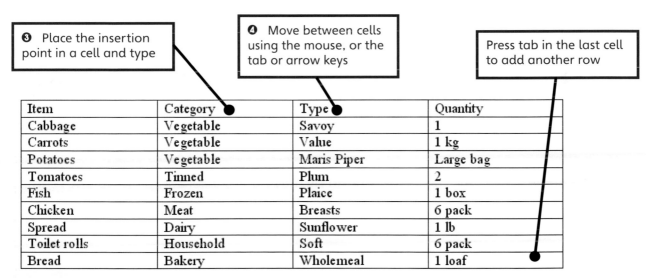

❸ Place the insertion point in a cell and type

❹ Move between cells using the mouse, or the tab or arrow keys

Press tab in the last cell to add another row

Item	Category	Type	Quantity
Cabbage	Vegetable	Savoy	1
Carrots	Vegetable	Value	1 kg
Potatoes	Vegetable	Maris Piper	Large bag
Tomatoes	Tinned	Plum	2
Fish	Frozen	Plaice	1 box
Chicken	Meat	Breasts	6 pack
Spread	Dairy	Sunflower	1 lb
Toilet rolls	Household	Soft	6 pack
Bread	Bakery	Wholemeal	1 loaf

Figure 3.49 Completed example table

❻ Change **Maris Piper** to **King Edward**.
❼ Change **Plum** to **Chopped**.
❽ Save and close the document.

Tip!

You could practise using **Find and Replace** to make these changes.

Select rows and columns, cells and the whole table (3.4.1.3)

To select parts of a table, perhaps to format a cell, row or column, you need to make sure the entire area is selected. For example, if you only select the text in a cell, it is only the text that will be formatted. You need to select the whole cell(s).

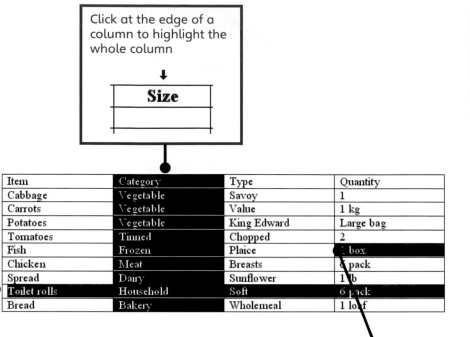

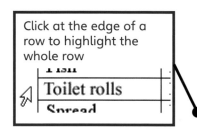

Figure 3.50 Selecting cells, rows and columns

- ◉ Select a cell by moving the mouse until the insertion point is over the left side of the cell. Click when it has turned into a black arrow.
- ◉ Select a row by moving the insertion point to the left of a row. Click when it has turned into a white arrow.
- ◉ Select a column by moving the insertion point to above the column. Click when it has turned into a black arrow.

Do it!

1. Open **Shopping list.doc**.
2. Save as **Shopping list with formatting.doc**.
3. Select the header row and apply bold formatting.
4. Select the **Quantity** column and align the text in it centrally.
5. Save and close the document.

Insert and delete rows and columns (3.4.1.4)

You might not always get your table correct first time, for example you might need to add another row or column in the middle of those already there.

❶ Place your insertion point in any cell in the row below or above where you want the new row to appear, or in any cell in the column to the left or right of where you want the new column to appear.

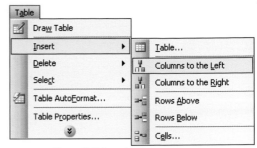
Figure 3.51 Insert columns

❷ Click **Insert** on the **Table** menu, and then click:
◉ **Rows Above** to insert rows above the current row
◉ **Rows Below** to insert rows below the current row
◉ **Columns to the Left** to insert columns to the left of the current column
◉ **Columns to the Right** to insert columns to the right of the current column.

For example, in **Shopping list with formatting.doc**, if you want to insert a new row between **Fish** and **Tomatoes** and the cursor is anywhere in the Tomatoes row, you need to insert a row below.

You can also delete rows and columns that you no longer require.

❶ Highlight the column(s) or row(s) to be deleted.
❷ Click **Delete** on the **Table** menu, and then click:
◉ **Rows** to delete the row(s)
◉ **Columns** to delete the column(s).

How about...?

Alternatively, you can use the buttons on the **Table and Borders** toolbar to insert/delete rows and columns. See page 130 to learn how to show toolbars.

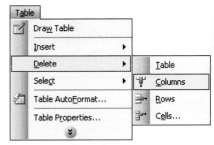
Figure 3.52 Delete columns

Do it!

❶ Open **Shopping list with formatting.doc** and save it as **Shopping list with new column.doc**.
❷ Insert a new column at the right-hand side of the table.
❸ Type the column heading **Weight**.
❹ Add **six** rows to the bottom of the table.
❺ Insert a column between **Type** and **Quantity**.
❻ Type the column heading **Size**.
❼ Enter the following data in the rows immediately after the last one already containing text.

T-shirt	Clothing	White cotton	Medium	2
Beef	Meat	Mince		I kg
Socks	Clothing	Black	9–11	3 pairs
Sweetcorn	Tinned	Value		2

❽ Change the heading **Quantity** to **Weight/Quantity** and delete the **Weight** column.
❾ Delete the last two (empty) rows.
❿ Save and close the document.

Warning!

If you press **Delete** on the keyboard rather than use the menu command, you will only delete the text in the cell.

Tip!

You don't have to highlight the whole row or column to delete it. As long as you place the text insertion point in a cell in the row/column you want to delete you can follow the steps again using the **Table** menu to delete.

Formatting tables

Modify column width, row height (3.4.2.I)

When checking the layout of data in a table, you might find that some columns are wider than they need be. Others might be too narrow. You can change the width of columns and the height of rows by using the mouse and sliding the border between them.

Place the mouse pointer directly on the border between cells, when the pointer becomes **+‖+** hold down the left mouse button and drag to the right or left to adjust the column width. When the pointer becomes **÷** drag up or down to adjust row height.

Item	Category	Type	Size	Weight/Quantity
Cabbage	Vegetable	Savoy		1
Carrots	Vegetable	Value		1 kg
Potatoes	Vegetable	King Edward		Large bag
Tomatoes	Tinned	Chopped		2
Fish	Frozen	Plaice		1 box
Chicken	Meat	Breasts		6 pack
Spread	Dairy	Sunflower		1 lb
Toilet rolls	Household	Soft		6 pack
Bread	Bakery	Wholemeal		1 loaf
T-shirt	Clothing	White cotton	Medium	2
Beef	Meat	Mince		1 lb
Socks	Clothing	Black	9–11	3 pairs
Sweetcorn	Tinned	Value		2

Figure 3.53 Adjusting column width and row height

If you need to be more precise, you can set the dimensions in the **Table Properties** dialogue box (Figure 3.54 on page I65).

Do it!

You are going to make the **Weight/Column** column slightly wider.

1. Open **Shopping list with new column.doc**.
2. Save it as **Shopping list with adjustments.doc**.
3. Place the insertion point anywhere in the **Weight/Quantity** column.
4. Click **Table Properties...** on the **Table** menu to display the **Table Properties** dialogue box.
5. Click the **Column** tab.
6. Change the **Preferred width** to **4 cm**.
7. Save and close the document.

Tip!

Change the heights of all the rows, or the widths of all the columns, by first selecting the entire table and then opening the **Table Properties** dialogue box.

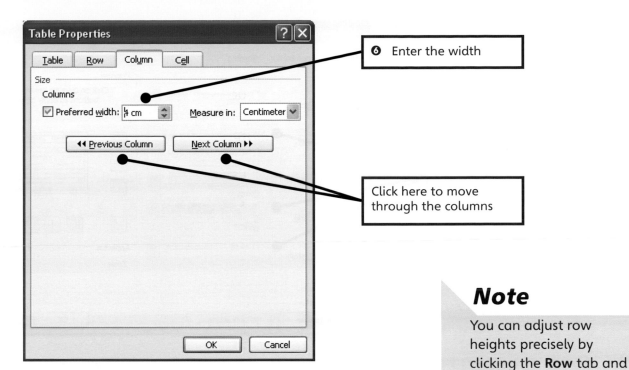

Figure 3.54 Table column properties

Note

You can adjust row heights precisely by clicking the **Row** tab and specifying the height.

Modify cell border line style, width, colour (3.4.2.2)

To modify the border around all or part of a table, you need to first select the area you want to affect. For example, if you want to change the border around the outside of a table you need to select the entire table first. If you want to change the line underneath the titles, simply highlight the row. However, if you want to change the border or part of the border of a single cell, you need to highlight the whole cell and not only the data within it.

How about...?

Alternatively, you can use the buttons on the **Table and Borders** toolbar to modify cell borders. See page 130 to learn how to show toolbars.

Do it!

1. Open **Shopping list with adjustments.doc** and save it as **Shopping list with borders.doc**.
2. Select the entire table.
3. Click **Borders and Shading...** on the **Format** menu to display the **Borders and Shading** dialogue box.
4. Select the **Borders** tab if it is not already selected.
5. Click **Box**.
6. Select the **double line** style, **pink** as the colour, and 1½pt as the width.
7. Click **OK**.
8. Save the document.
9. Add a similar border to that in step 6, around each of the header row cells.
10. Save the document.

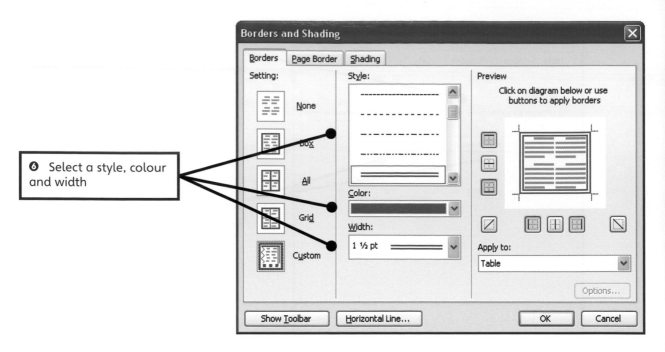

Figure 3.55 Applying a border

Warning!

Use colour for borders and shading sparingly as too much can have the opposite effect to what you want, and detract from the important data contained in the table.

How about...?

Alternatively, you can use the buttons on the **Table and Borders** toolbar to add shading to cells. See page 130 to learn how to show toolbars.

Add shading to cells (3.4.2.3)

Putting a border around cells and applying colour to them can make a table more professional by making it easier to use. Simple shading can also help by highlighting headings or other important cells.

Do it!

1. Open **Shopping list with borders.doc**.
2. Save it as **Shopping list with shading.doc**.
3. Highlight the entire heading row.
4. Click **Borders and Shading...** on the **Format** menu to display the **Borders and Shading** dialogue box.
5. Select the **Shading** tab if it is not already selected.
6. Select a colour for the fill.
7. Click **OK**.
8. Change the headings to upper case.
9. Save and close the document.

Prove it!

Create a table of your friends' and family names, addresses and birthdays. Save it as **Address book.doc**.

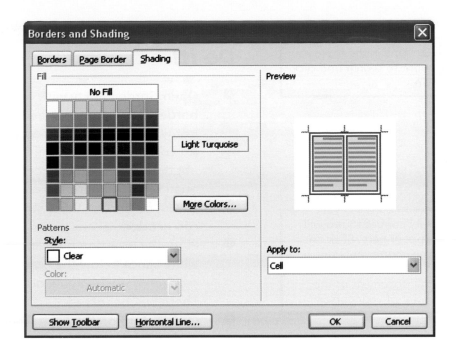

Figure 3.56 Applying shading to cells

Graphical objects

Although Word is not a drawing program, it is useful to have some drawing features and be able to insert images, pictures and drawings, and even charts or graphs. These are called **objects**. You might want to do this if you are producing a report and want to refer to a graph in order to explain its meaning. You might want to send a letter to a friend and include some digital images of your home or family with the text.

When you insert an object, you do not need to make room as Word will automatically make space. Simply place your insertion point where you want the object to be placed.

Insert a picture, image, chart or drawn object (3.4.3.l)

Word has a bank of images called **Clip Art**, which are mostly cartoon type images and can be searched by topic, for example 'school', 'fun', 'driving' etc.

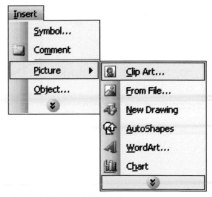

Figure 3.57 Insert Clip Art

❶ Click **Picture** on the **Insert** menu, and select **Clip Art...** to open the **Clip Art** Task pane Clip Art list.

❷ Type a topic in the **Search for:** box and click **Go**.

❸ The images matching your search criterion are displayed in the Task pane.

❹ Check that the insertion point is where you want the image to appear, and then click the image you would like to insert.

Warning!

The images found by Word differ between the precise versions of Word.

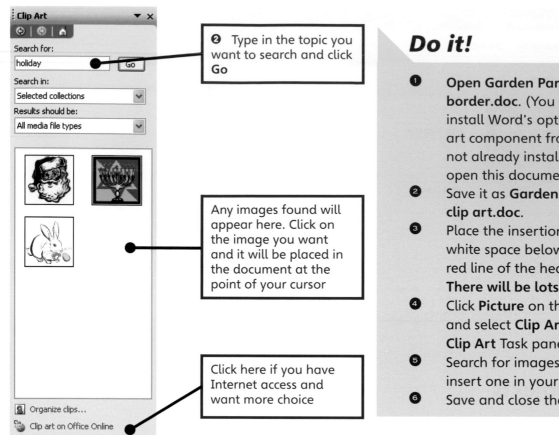

Figure 3.58 Searching for a Clip Art image

❷ Type in the topic you want to search and click Go

Any images found will appear here. Click on the image you want and it will be placed in the document at the point of your cursor

Click here if you have Internet access and want more choice

Do it!

❶ **Open Garden Party with border.doc.** (You may need to install Word's optional border art component from CD if it is not already installed, in order to open this document.)

❷ Save it as **Garden Party with clip art.doc**.

❸ Place the insertion point in the white space below the bottom red line of the heading, above **There will be lots of…**

❹ Click **Picture** on the **Insert** menu, and select **Clip Art…** to open the **Clip Art** Task pane Clip Art list.

❺ Search for images of **fun** and insert one in your document.

❻ Save and close the document.

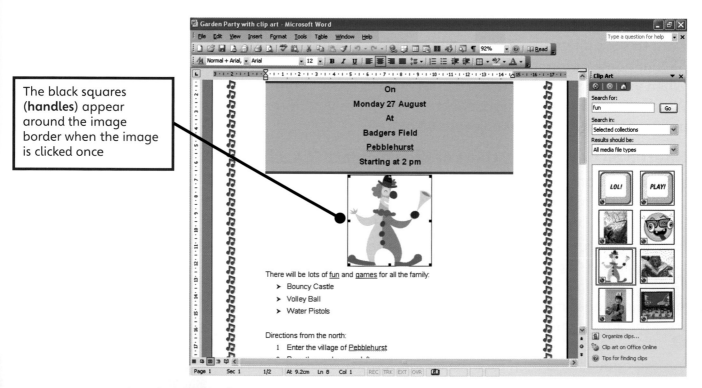

The black squares (**handles**) appear around the image border when the image is clicked once

Figure 3.59 An image inserted into a document

To insert an image from file (e.g. a photo, graph or a drawn object)

❶ Place the insertion point where you want the image to appear.

❷ Click **Picture** on the **Insert** menu, and select **From File...** to open the **Insert Picture** dialogue box. This will probably open at the **My Pictures** folder. If the image is located elsewhere, navigate to it in the usual Windows fashion (see Module 2, page 77).

❸ Select the image file and click the **Insert** button to insert the image at the insertion point.

Select an object (3.4.3.2)

To format an object, you first need to select it.

◉ Click the object to display a border with black squares (called handles) (Figure 3.59).

Copy, move an object within a document, between open documents (3.4.3.3)

You can copy or move any image within a document, between documents and even between applications.

To copy within a document

❶ Select the **object**.

❷ Click **Copy** on the **Edit** menu.

❸ Place the insertion point where you want the copy to be placed.

❹ Click **Paste** on the **Edit** menu.

To move an object within a document

❶ Select the **object**.

❷ Click **Cut** on the **Edit** menu.

❸ Place the insertion point where you want the object to be placed.

❹ Click **Paste** on the **Edit** menu.

To copy/move between documents

❶ Select the **object**.

❷ Click **Copy** (or **Move**) on the **Edit** menu.

❸ Open the destination document.

❹ Place the insertion point where you want the copy (or object) to be placed.

❺ Click **Paste** on the **Edit** menu.

How about...?

Alternatively, you can right-click a selected object and choose **Cut**, **Copy** or **Paste** from the shortcut menu that is displayed.

Do it!

1. Open **Garden Party with clip art.doc** and save it as **Garden Party with two images.doc**.
2. Click the clip art image to select it (i.e. display its handles).
3. Copy the object.
4. Place your cursor in the space between **Last house on the left** and **Please bring with you:**
5. Paste a copy of the image.
6. Centre align the image.
7. Re-select the first image and **Cut** it.
8. **Paste** the image between **Water Pistols** and **Directions...**
9. Centre align the image.
10. Save and close the document.

Do it!

Try copying the image from **Garden Party with two images.doc** to a new document. Close both files without saving when you have finished.

Resize and delete an object (3.4.3.4)

One type of routine formatting you will need to be able to do is to resize an object. When you insert an image it could appear far too large for your document. The images on the Garden Party invitation take up too much space, so you need to reduce their size.

When resizing an object, use the handles at any corner to resize the object in proportion, or the handles at the centre of the edges to reduce the height or width.

1. Select the object.
2. Place the mouse pointer over any corner handle until the pointer becomes a double-headed arrow ↗ .
3. Hold down the left mouse button and drag inwards to make smaller, outwards to enlarge.
4. Click away from the object when finished.

Note

To delete an object, select it, then press the **Delete** key.

Do it!

1. Open **Garden Party with two images.doc**.
2. Save it as **Garden Party with resized images.doc**.
3. Resize the images proportionally.
4. Reduce the font size of the text to make sure the invitation all fits onto one page.
5. Save and close the document.

Prove it!

Produce an invitation or a greetings card. Format it with borders and include some suitable clip art.

Test your understanding

1. What is a table?
2. How do you move around between the cells of a table?
3. What happens when you press the Enter key in a cell?
4. How do you remove the borders from a table?
5. How do you insert a row or column?
6. How do you modify the height of a row or width of a column?
7. How do you shade a column or row?
8. What is an object?
9. How do you resize an object?
10. How do ensure the object stays in proportion when it is resized?
11. How do you copy or move or delete an object?

You can find the answers to the questions on the CD-ROM saved as **Answers to TYU questions 3.4**. How did you do? Go back over anything that you are unsure about.

Learning objectives

By working through this lesson you will learn:
- about mail merge and how to prepare mail merged documents using a provided address list.

Preparation and output (3.5.1.1–3/3.5.2.1–2)

The Word mail merge feature helps you to save time when you want to send out several identical letters to different addresses. For example, you might be moving home and you need to inform utility companies, banks, friends etc.

In order to create mail merge documents, you need to either create a **List of addresses** containing the data to merge into a main document (e.g. a letter) or you can use the data in an existing list to merge with your letter. The list of addresses is effectively a database and is the data source.

Figure 3.60 Selecting **Mail Merge**

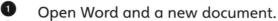

① Open Word and a new document.

② Type a brief note to say what your old and new addresses are.

③ Click **Letters and Mailings** on the **Tools** menu, and select **Mail Merge...** to display the **Mail Merge** Task pane.

④ Choose the type of document you are creating by clicking the radio button. (This is the document which will be the end product, for example a letter which will have a recipient's address at the top of each page.) Go to the next step.

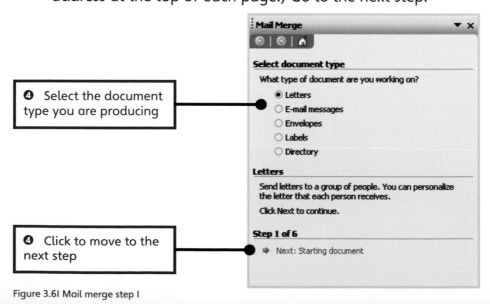

❹ Select the document type you are producing

❹ Click to move to the next step

Figure 3.61 Mail merge step 1

⑤ Select the starting document by clicking the relevant radio button. Go to the next step.

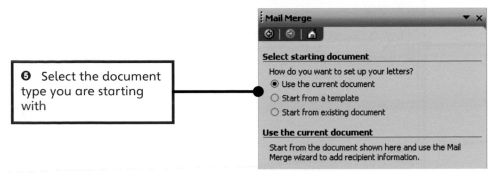

⑤ Select the document type you are starting with

Figure 3.62 Mail merge step 2

⑥ If you need to create a list of addresses, select **Type a new list**. If you already have a list, select **Use an existing list**. These instructions assume that you will use the mailing list supplied on the CD-ROM, so click **Use an existing list**.

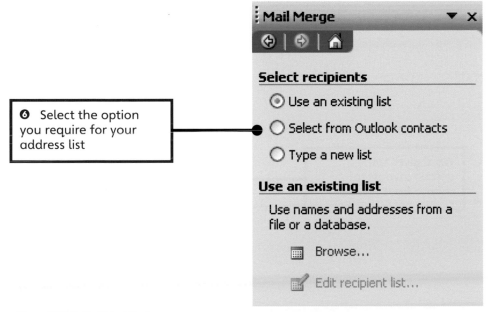

⑥ Select the option you require for your address list

Figure 3.63 Mail merge step 3

⑦ Click **Browse...** to navigate to where the address list is located.

The address list supplied on the CD-ROM is called **Friends Address List.mdb**. By default Word will look for this file in the **My Data Sources** folder on your computer. You might need to navigate to a different location if the address list is elsewhere.

⑧ Open the list, then click the **OK** button.

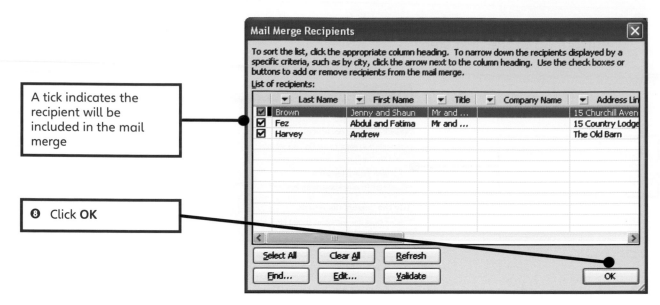

A tick indicates the recipient will be included in the mail merge

❽ Click **OK**

Figure 3.64 Mail merge recipients

❾ Click on the bottom of the Task pane to open the next step.

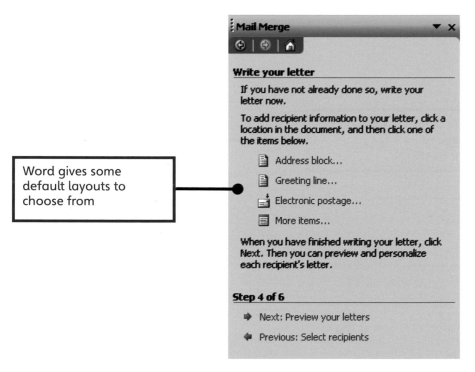

Word gives some default layouts to choose from

Figure 3.65 Mail merge step 4

Step 4 of the mail merge process prompts you to write your letter if you haven't already done so. Remember at the beginning of this section, you learned that you could use an existing document (e.g. letter) or create one from new. To help you do this, Word provides you with a number of choices.

❿ Click **Address Block...** to open the **Insert Address Block** dialogue box.

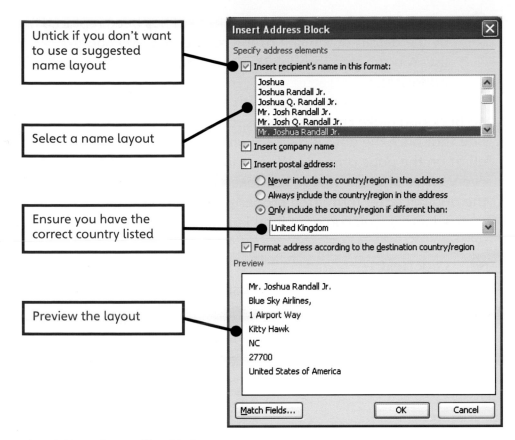

Untick if you don't want to use a suggested name layout

Select a name layout

Ensure you have the correct country listed

Preview the layout

Figure 3.66 Inserting an **Address Block**

⓫ Click **OK** to use the default settings. You will see the text **<<AddressBlock>>** has been inserted into your document.

⓬ Click **Next** to preview your letters.

Note

You can manually edit the mail merge document later if you find you do not want to use any of the default formats.

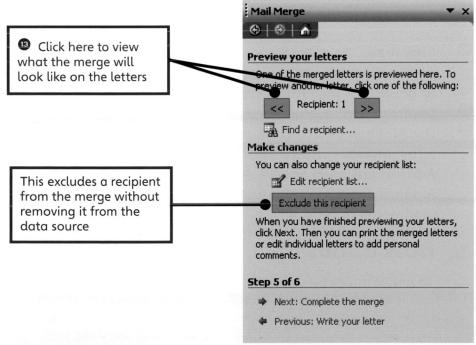

⓭ Click here to view what the merge will look like on the letters

This excludes a recipient from the merge without removing it from the data source

Figure 3.67 Mail merge step 5

(13) Notice that the <<AddressBlock>> field has been replaced by the details of the first of the recipients in the address list. You can step through the letters to see all of merged addresses.

Having checked your document with the merged data, you can go back and make changes. This is really important as you might find that once the data is merged with the letter that it doesn't all fit on the page properly. What you don't want to do is change every letter after the merge has taken place. You need to get the original letter formatted properly so that when the data is merged into it, you can print it all knowing you won't have any waste.

(14) Click **Next**.

Note

You can merge address list records with label and envelope documents by clicking the document type in step I of the Mail Merge wizard and following the step-by-step instructions.

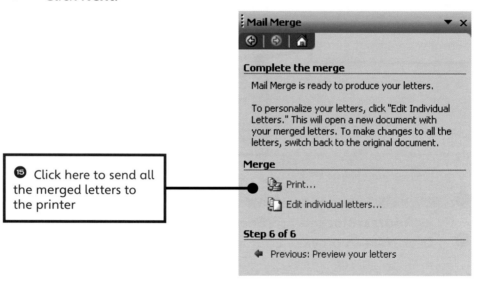

Figure 3.68 Mail merge step 6

The instruction to print will default to **All**.

(15) Click here to send all the merged letters to the printer

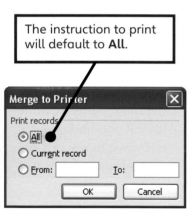

Figure 3.69 Mail merge print

(15) Click **Print...** to output the mail merged letters to the default printer connected to your computer. Notice you can choose to print all of the letters, the current one, or a range.

(16) Save your mail merge documents.

(17) Use **Mailmerge letter.doc** to see the completed mailmerge letter. **Mailmerge letter.doc** contains a fixed link to **Friends Address List.mdb**. Follow the instructions in the file **Mailmerge letter opening instructions.doc** in order to open **Mailmerge letter.doc**.

Note

Saving the mail-merged letters is not strictly necessary as you can easily generate the letters from scratch. The only files you need to keep are the address list and, perhaps, the original document that contains the merge fields (so you have a copy of the layout).

How about...?

Alternatively, you can select **Toolbars** from the **View** menu, then select **Mail Merge**. The toolbar button lets you set up mail merge documents in a similar way to the wizard. Rest the mouse cursor over a button to show a screen tip telling you what the button is for.

Test your understanding

1. What is mail merge used for?
2. Why should you check the merged document before printing?
3. What are mail merge fields?

You can find the answers to the questions on the CD-ROM saved as **Answers to TYU questions 3.5**. How did you do? Go back over anything that you are unsure about.

Setup

Figure 3.70 Page Setup

Change document orientation and paper size (3.6.1.1)

By default, Word prints documents in **Portrait** orientation (i.e. the height of the page is greater than its width – as you might find with a photo of a person). There are likely to be occasions when you want to display your work in **Landscape** orientation (where the width of the page is greater than the height – as you might find with a photo of a view). You can change the orientation of your document and the printer will automatically print on the paper in the layout you have selected.

❶ Click **Print Setup...** on the **File** menu to display the **Page Setup** dialogue box.

❷ Select the **Margins** tab if it isn't already selected.

❸ Click the orientation you want for your document.

You might be using a different size paper from the default size on your computer. In the UK and Europe, the most common size of paper used is **A4**. In the USA, the size most likely to be used might be **Letter**. When you change the paper size, your document will be automatically adjusted to the paper size without you having to do anything else.

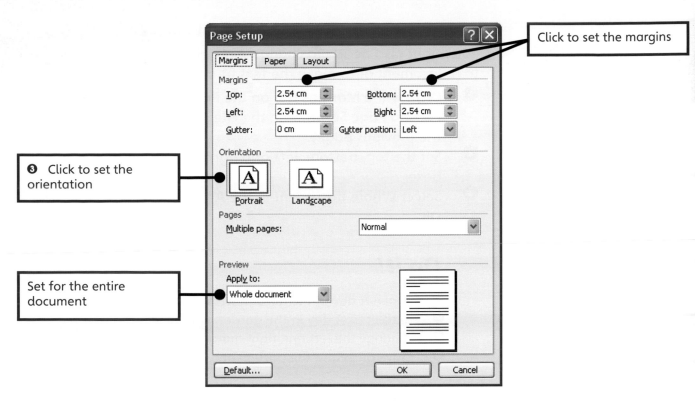

Figure 3.7I Changing page orientation and margins for the whole document

④ Select the **Paper** tab.

⑤ Click the arrow to the right of the **Paper size:** list box and select the size for your printer.

⑥ Click **OK**.

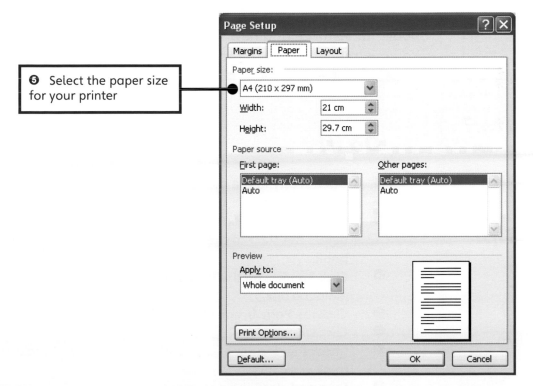

Figure 3.72 Changing paper size

Change margins of entire document (3.6.1.2)

You might also decide to change margins for a neater appearance to a document or to make the text fit on a single page.

① Display the **Margins** tab on the **Page Setup** dialogue box by clicking **Page Setup...** on the **File** menu (see Figure 3.71 on the previous page).

② Set the top, bottom, left and right margins in the **Margins** boxes.

③ Select **Whole document** in the **Apply to:** list box and click **OK**.

Do it!

① Open **A day in the garden with more style.doc**.
② Save it as **A day in the garden with new margins.doc**.
③ Change the left and right margins to **3 cm**.
④ Save and close the document.

Insert, delete a page break in a document (3.6.1.3–4)

When you changed the margins in the document **A day in the garden with new margins.doc** you will have seen how it changed the appearance of the document – some of the paragraphs might have been split across the page break. You can correct this by 'forcing' a new page to start where you want it to.

You might want to manually insert a page break to start a new page, for instance at a new section or chapter of a book.

You might be tempted to press the **Return** key until a new page appears, however good practice is to insert a page break.

Insert

| Break... |
| Page Numbers... |
| Date and Time... |
| AutoText ▶ |
| Field... |
| Symbol... |
| Comment |
| Reference ▶ |
| Web Component... |
| Picture ▶ |
| Diagram... |
| Text Box |
| File... |
| Object... |
| Bookmark... |
| Hyperlink... Ctrl+K |

Figure 3.73 Insert Break

How about...?

Alternatively, press **Ctrl+Enter** to insert a page break.

Tip!

Place the insertion point at the start of the paragraph otherwise if you place it in the blank space between paragraphs, you will get a blank line at the top of the next page.

Do it!

① Open **A day in the garden with new margins.doc**.
② Save it as **A day in the garden with page breaks.doc**.
③ Put the insertion point near the bottom of the first page before the start of the sentence beginning **Finding my book...**
④ Click **Break...** on the **Insert** menu to display the **Break** dialogue box.
⑤ Click the **Page break** radio button to select it.
⑥ Click **OK**.
⑦ Check the document and add any other page breaks you think necessary.
⑧ Save and close the document.

Figure 3.74 Setting a page break

Using headers and footers (3.6.1.5)

Headers and footers are areas at the top and bottom of a page that are repeated on all the pages in a document (unless you specify for them not to be shown).

❶ Open **A day in the garden with page breaks.doc**.

❷ Save it as **A day in the garden with headers footers.doc**.

❸ Click **Header and Footer** on the **View** menu to display the **Header and Footer** toolbar. Note also that the header area is displayed on the document. The footer is diplayed at the bottom of the page.

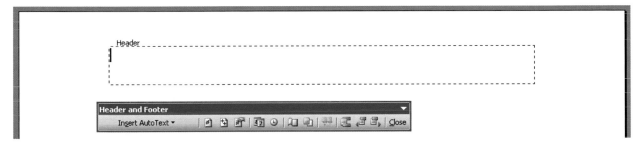

Figure 3.75 The Header and Footer toolbar and area on document

❹ For the moment you can ignore the toolbar except for the **Switch Between Header and Footer** button 🗐 . Click this now to show the **Footer** area.

❺ Type your name at the text insertion point in the footer.

❻ Click the **Close** button on the **Header and Footer** toolbar.

❼ Save the document.

❽ Scroll through the document to see your name at the bottom of each page.

Tip!

If you are working in **Normal View** you will not be able to see the header and footer. Select **Print Layout View** or **Print Preview** to see them.

Tip!

Click the **Format Page Number** button  on the **Header and Footer** toolbar to see the formatting options that you can apply to page numbers.

How about...?

Alternatively, you can insert page numbers without using the **Header and Footer** toolbar.

1. Click **Page Numbers...** on the **Insert** menu, to display the **Page Numbers** dialogue box.

2. Select the position and the alignment from the drop-down lists.

3. Click **OK**.

How about...?

Alternatively, press **F7** to open the spellchecker.

Add fields in headers and footers and page numbering (3.6.1.6–7)

Headers and footers are useful for putting in page numbers, dates, names, and filenames so they appear throughout the document. They are added to a document as fields which are automatically updated. This means you do not have to remember to alter them when you modify a file.

1. Open **A day in the garden with headers footers.doc**.
2. Save it as **A day in the garden with page numbers.doc**.
3. Click **Header and Footer** on the **View** menu to display the **Header and Footer** toolbar.
4. In the header, press the tab key twice, and click `Insert AutoText ▼` on the **Header and Footer** toolbar.
5. Click **Filename** on the drop-down list.
6. Click the **Switch Between Header and Footer** button and move the insertion point to after your name.
7. Press the tab key and type **Page** followed by a space.
8. Click the **Insert Page Number** button  on the **Header and Footer** toolbar.
9. Press the spacebar once and type **of** followed by another space.
10. Click the **Insert Number of Pages** button on the **Header and Footer** toolbar.
11. Save and close the document.

Check and print

Spellcheck a document and add words to the dictionary (3.6.2.1–2)

Word has a built-in spellchecker that lets you check a document for incorrectly spelt words and duplicated words.

1. Open **A day in the garden with mistakes.doc**.
2. Save it as **A day in the garden with corrected spelling.doc**.
3. Make sure that the insertion point is at the beginning of the document.
4. Click **Spelling and Grammar...** on the **Tools** menu, to display the spellchecker.

Figure 3.76 Spelling and Grammar

The checker immediately displays the first mistake it can find – in this case, a duplication of the word **the**.

5. Before correcting this, click the **Check grammar** tick box to remove the tick and turn off Word's grammar checker for the purposes of this example.

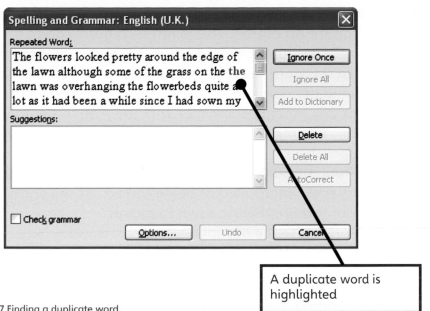

Figure 3.77 Finding a duplicate word

A duplicate word is highlighted

6 Click the **Delete** button to remove the duplicated word. The checker immediately moves to what it detects as the next error – a misspelling of the word **chair**.

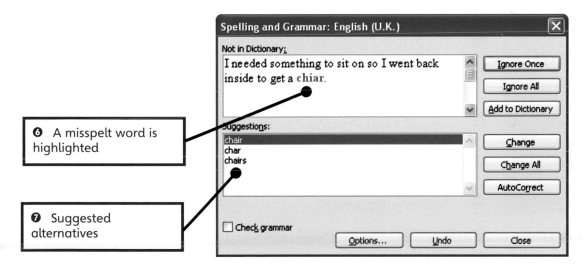

❻ A misspelt word is highlighted

❼ Suggested alternatives

Figure 3.78 Finding a misspelt word

7 The checker provides some suggestions that it 'thinks' might be the word you meant to type. Select the correct word (if it is there), and then click the **Change** button. The spellchecker moves on to what it detects as the next error – it does not recognise the word **sunlounger**.

8 If you decide that this is a valid word, you have three options.

◉ To ignore it for this occurrence only – click the **Ignore once** button.

⊙ To ignore it for every occurrence in the document – click the **Ignore All** button. This might be a good choice for this example because the word appears several times more.

⊙ To add the word to Word's dictionary so that it won't be detected as a spelling mistake in any future occurrences in this or any other documents – click the **Add to Dictionary** button. This might also be a valid option for **sunlounger**.

9 The spellchecker will tell you when it has finished.

10 Now read through the document. There is one error that the spellchecker interpreted as being correct. At the end of the first paragraph, change **sown** to **mown**.

11 Save and close the document.

Preview a document (3.6.2.3)

Before you print a document, preview it to see how it will look when printed. Check the layout. You might find it needs formatting (e.g. making the font smaller or changing the width of the margins) to prevent it from printing on unnecessary pages – it is annoying (and wasteful) to find that the last line of a document has printed on its own on a new page!

1 Open **A day in the garden (final for printing).doc**.

2 Click **Print Preview** on the **File** menu.

3 Look at the page carefully, asking yourself if there is anything you could do to make the document look better, for example change the margins, change the formatting and/or font size etc.

4 Cancel **Print Preview** by clicking the **Close** button (or pressing **Esc** on the keyboard).

5 Make the changes if you have any, and **Print Preview** it again.

6 Save the document.

Printing parts or several copies of a document (3.6.2.4)

It is likely that at some time you will want to print several copies of the same document, or perhaps only selected pages of a multi-page document. Word lets you do this easily.

1 Open **A day in the garden (final for printing).doc** if is not open already.

2 Click **Print...** on the **File** menu to display the **Print** dialogue box.

⊙ To singly print a specified page.

If the insertion point is in the page you want to print, click the **Current page** radio button to select it, and then click the **OK** button. Otherwise, click the **Pages** radio button to select it, and then type the page number in the text box.

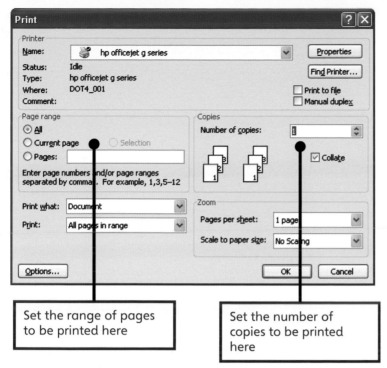

Set the range of pages to be printed here

Set the number of copies to be printed here

Figure 3.79 The **Print** dialogue box

- To singly print a range of pages, click the **Pages** radio button to select it, and then type the pages in the text box.
- To print multiple copies of a document, select or type a number in the **Number of copies:** box.
- ③ Close the document.

Test your understanding

① What is the difference between landscape and portrait orientation?

② What is a header or footer used for?

③ How can you apply automatic page numbering to a document?

④ Name two key features of the spellchecker.

⑤ Why should you thoroughly check a document even when you have spell checked it?

⑥ Why should you preview a document before printing?

⑦ What features does the print option offer?

You can find the answers to the questions on the CD-ROM saved as **Answers to TYU questions 3.6**. How did you do? Go back over anything that you are unsure about.

This module explains how to use a computer spreadsheet program. First you will learn how to create spreadsheets and enter data so that the spreadsheet can calculate results for you. Then you will learn more advanced techniques to help you present information and customise the program. By the end of this module you will be able to use the spreadsheet's powerful tools to carry out everyday tasks associated with storing and working with numerical information.

The step-by-step instructions are written for Microsoft Office Excel 2003. The tasks at the end of each lesson can be used with any spreadsheet software.

MODULE 4.
spreadsheets

Learning objectives

By working through this lesson you will learn:
- ◉ how to open and close Microsoft Excel, and a spreadsheet
- ◉ how to create a spreadsheet based on the default template
- ◉ how to select cells, and edit and delete cell content
- ◉ how to insert text, numbers and dates
- ◉ about formulas
- ◉ about cell referencing
- ◉ how to save and print a spreadsheet.

Open and close a spreadsheet

Spreadsheets help you work with data. In 'the old days', people carried out complex calculations using pen and paper. Bookkeepers worked out companies' profits. Engineers designed bridges or engines. They used sheets of paper the size of large newspapers. The paper had gridlines printed on it to make rows and columns to make it easy for people to set out their work. People spread the paper out so they could see all their calculations. These were the original 'spread sheets'. Now they all use computer spreadsheet programs, such as Microsoft Excel. We can use the same programs for everyday tasks. For instance, many people use spreadsheets for their family or club accounts. Others use them to produce invoices for their businesses, or to create budgets for their property improvements.

Open Microsoft Excel (4.I.I.I)

The first task is to open the program. As with any application installed on a computer, there are many ways to do this.

❶ Click the **Start** button ❙start❙ on the Taskbar.
❷ Click **All Programs**.
❸ Click **Microsoft Office**.
❹ Click **Microsoft Office Excel 2003**.

Excel will open with a blank spreadsheet displayed.

How about...?

Alternatively, if it is there, you can double-click directly on the **Excel** icon on the Desktop or on the Start menu.

Open a spreadsheet (4.1.1.1)

❶ Click **Open...** on the **File** menu to display the **Open** dialogue box.

❷ Navigate to the spreadsheet file **Travel Agency 1.xls** on the CD-ROM.

❸ Open the file in the usual Windows fashion (see Module 2, page 77).

Your screen will look similar to this.

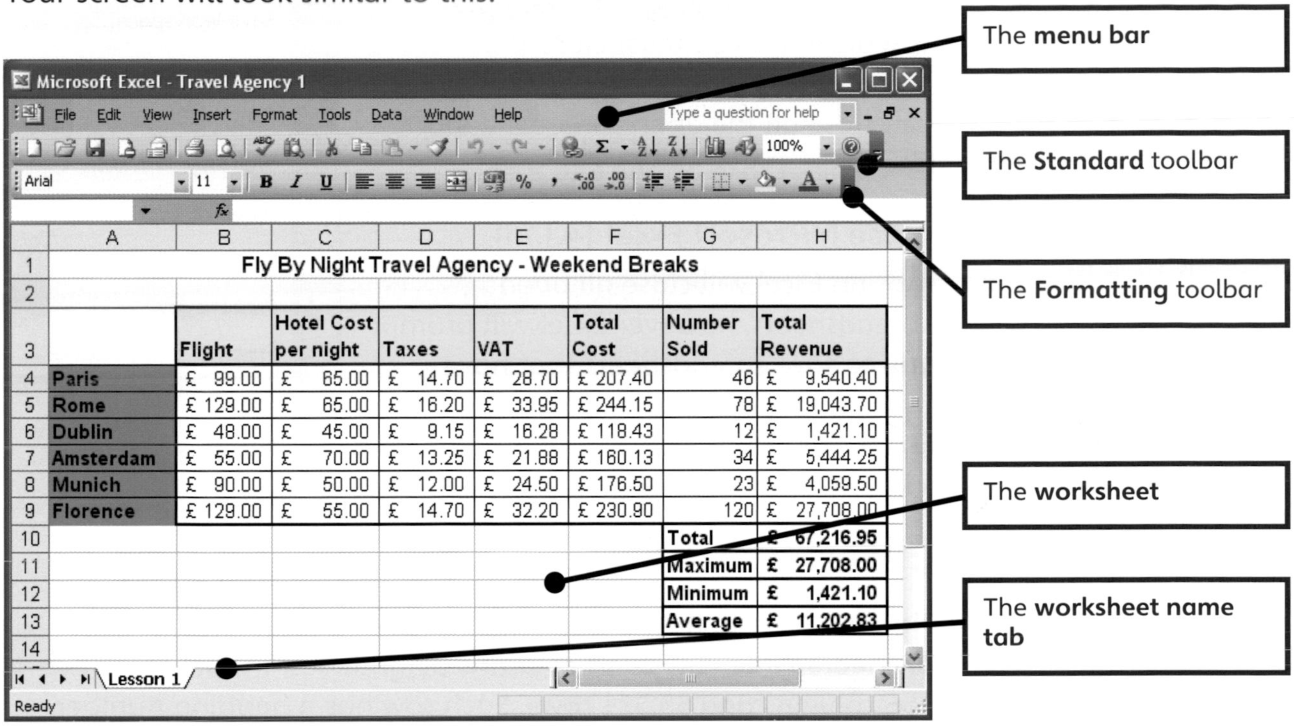

The **menu bar**

The **Standard** toolbar

The **Formatting** toolbar

The **worksheet**

The **worksheet name** tab

Figure 4.1 The **Travel Agency 1** sample spreadsheet

This spreadsheet contains the sales details for a travel agency. They are selling weekend breaks and are using this spreadsheet to record the sales.

Now take a few minutes to look at some of the key features of this spreadsheet. Like most **Windows** programs it has a **menu bar** and **toolbars**. The toolbars contain **buttons** with pictures on them called **icons**. You might be familiar with these from other modules. You enter data into a **worksheet**. It is divided by gridlines into rows and columns. Spreadsheets are made up of one or more worksheets, and are sometimes called **workbooks**. Each worksheet has a name which is shown on a **tab** at the bottom.

The travel agent has entered some information. She has only entered the cost of flights and hotels, and the number of breaks sold. The spreadsheet has calculated taxes, VAT and the cost of each break, the total revenue for each city break, the overall revenue and the average, highest and lowest revenues. Isn't that

Tip!

If your toolbars don't look exactly like these, you can reset them. Click **Customize...** on the **Tools** menu, then use the **Reset...** button on the **Toolbars** tab to reset them.

Note

Excel refers to a spreadsheet as a **worksheet**. An Excel file can hold a number of worksheets in a **workbook**.

useful? And the program never gets its sums wrong! You will learn how to enter the data and formulas to do this on page 223, and how to format them on page 208.

Close a spreadsheet (4.1.1.1)

Closing a spreadsheet will leave Excel open. When working with multiple spreadsheets you must close the spreadsheets individually as closing Excel will close all the open spreadsheets.

◉ Click **Close** on the **File** menu.

Close Microsoft Excel (4.1.1.1)

Closing Excel will close all open spreadsheets, however Excel will prompt you to save spreadsheets that have unsaved work in them.

◉ Click **Exit** on the **File** menu.

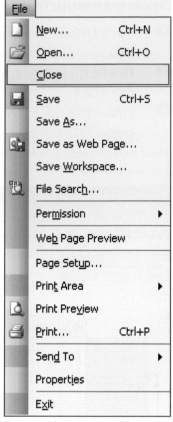

Figure 4.2 Closing a spreadsheet

Entering data

Figure 4.1 shows that a worksheet is divided up into **rows** and **columns** by gridlines. In fact there are 256 columns and 65,536 rows. Each row has a heading number, and each column has a heading letter(s).

Rows and columns are made up of **cells**. When you use a spreadsheet you enter data into cells.

Create a spreadsheet based on the default template (4.1.1.2)

Every spreadsheet has default settings for things like fonts, currency format, text size and paper size. These are stored in a special file called a **template**.

As you have seen on page 188, when you open Excel, a new blank spreadsheet is created automatically. This is based on the default template, but you need to learn how to do this yourself.

❶ Open Excel and close the spreadsheet that opens.

❷ Click **New...** on the **File** menu. The **New Workbook** Task pane appears on the right-hand side of the screen.

❸ Click **Blank Workbook** to create a spreadsheet based on the default template.

Figure 4.3 **New Workbook** Task pane

Save a spreadsheet under another name (4.1.1.3)

You save your spreadsheets so you can use them again.

> ### *Note*
>
> Your tutor may have already allocated a folder for you to store your ECDL work. If not, create a subfolder for this module – **My ECDL Spreadsheet Folder** – in your **My Documents** folder. This module refers to this subfolder for convenience, but you will need to substitute the subfolder name allocated to you if it is different.

Excel has given your new spreadsheet a name – probably **Book 2** (**Book 1** was the spreadsheet that opened, and you closed, when you first started Excel). Now save your spreadsheet with a different name, and in a specified location, as follows.

❶ Click **Save As...** on the **File** menu to open the **Save As** dialogue box.

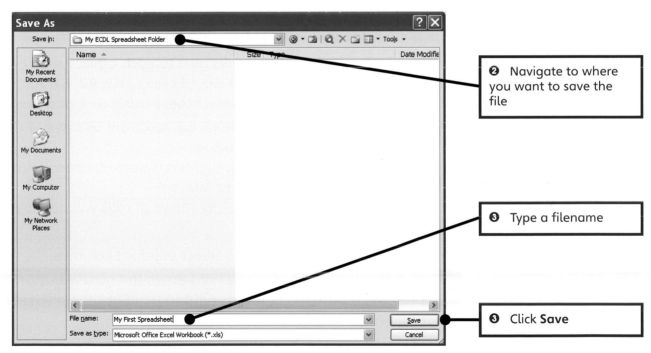

Figure 4.4 The **Save As** dialogue box

❷ Navigate to where you are going to store your spreadsheet in the usual Windows fashion (see Module 2, page 66).

❸ Give your spreadsheet the name **My First Spreadsheet** and click the **Save** button.

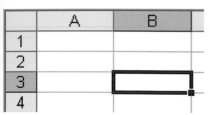
Figure 4.5 A selected cell

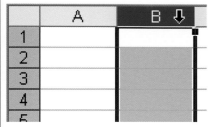
Figure 4.6 A selected column

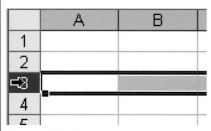
Figure 4.7 A selected row

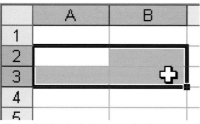
Figure 4.8 A selected range of cells

Click to select the entire worksheet

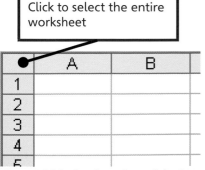
Figure 4.9 Selecting the entire worksheet

Select a cell (4.2.1.4)

When entering data into a spreadsheet you will need to select a single cell. When formatting cells (see page 208) you may need to select multiple cells.

1 Click in the cell you want to select.

2 The selected cell will be displayed with a thick black border. The row number and column letter will be highlighted.
In Figure 4.5 the selected cell is referred to as cell **B3** (i.e. column B row 3 – you can think of a cell reference as the cell's address).

Select single and multiple cells (4.2.1.4, 4.3.1.1–2)

You can select an entire column of a spreadsheet in one click.

◉ Click the letter of the column you want to select.

The selected column will be highlighted and displayed with a thick black border (see column B in Figure 4.6).

You can select an entire row using a similar technique.

◉ Click the number of the row you want to select.

The selected row will be highlighted and displayed with a thick black border (see row 3 in Figure 4.7).

A range of cells is any group of cells next to each other. These are referenced using a colon so A2:B3 would select cells A2, B2, A3 and B3 (see Figure 4.8). You can select these using click and drag.

1 Click in the top-left cell in the range you want to select. Don't let go of the mouse button.

2 Drag the mouse until the highlighted (selected) area covers the range of cells you want to select.

3 Let go of the mouse button. The range of cells will now be selected.

You can use a similar technique to select adjacent columns.

1 Click the column header and hold down the mouse button.

2 Drag the mouse to the left or right to highlight the adjacent columns you want.

3 Let go of the mouse button.

You select adjacent rows in the same way by clicking and dragging the mouse over the row headers.

You can select the whole worksheet with just one click. This is very useful if you need to copy and paste the contents of a worksheet to a new worksheet in the same, or a different, spreadsheet.

◉ Click the blank grey column/row heading at the top-left corner of the spreadsheet (between A and 1, see Figure 4.9).

The whole worksheet will be highlighted.

Cells don't need to be next to each other to be selected at the same time. This is very useful when you format a spreadsheet.

❶ Click in cell **B2**.

❷ Press and hold **Control (Ctrl)**. This lets the computer know that other cells are to be included in the selection.

❸ Now click cell **B4** and release the mouse button.

The non-adjacent selected cells are highlighted but without the thick border. You can use the same technique to select non-adjacent columns or rows. Again, these don't need to be next to each other in order to be selected.

❶ Select column B.

❷ Click and hold the mouse button, and drag to select column C. Let go of the mouse button.

❸ Press **Control** and select column E.

❹ Keep **Control** pressed and select row 3.

❺ Release **Control** and click anywhere on the spreadsheet to deselect the cells (except, of course, the one you have just clicked).

Enter text (4.2.1.3)

❶ Select cell **A1** (the top left-hand cell) by clicking in it.

❷ Type your name, but don't press **Enter** yet.

Your name has appeared in two places: in the **Formula bar** and in cell A1. The Formula bar always shows what is in the selected cell. The cell reference (A1 in this case) appears in the **Name box** to the left of the Formula bar.

Tip!

Screen tips appear if you rest your pointer over a screen feature such as a toolbar button. See if you can identify **Undo** and **Redo** – you will use these a lot (see page 194).

The **Name box** showing the selected cell reference

The selected cell

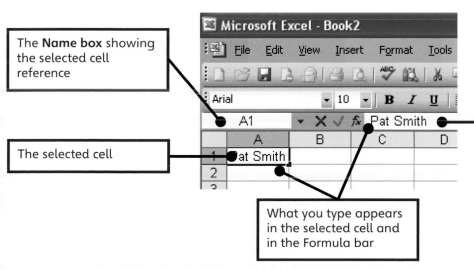

The **Formula bar**

What you type appears in the selected cell and in the Formula bar

Figure 4.10 The selected cell reference and Formula bar

How about...?

Alternatively, click in the **Formula bar** to place the insertion point and type.

③   Press **Enter**.

Cell **A2** is now selected – the cell reference in the **Name box** has changed, and cell **A2** now has a black border.

④   Now click in any other cell. This will select it. Again, the **Name box** shows the reference of the new cell selected.

⑤   Click in the **Name box** and type **AI** in it.

⑥   Press **Enter**. This will select cell **AI**.

⑦   Select **A2** by any method.

⑧   Type **zzz** in this new cell.

⑨   Press **Escape (Esc)**. What you typed has not been saved. Excel only saves what you type in a cell when you press **Enter** or select another cell.

Undo and Redo (4.2.2.2)

Undo and **Redo** are very useful tools.

❶   With **A2** selected type **zzz** again and press **Enter**.

❷   Click the **Undo** button you found earlier. This undoes your last action (**zzz** is removed).

❸   Click the **Redo** button, and your last action is restored (**zzz** is replaced).

❹   Now click **Undo** twice. Your last two actions are undone (both **zzz** and your name are removed).

❺   Click **Redo** once to restore your name to cell **AI**.

Delete cell content (4.2.3.4)

❶   Type **My spreadsheet** in cell **A2** and press **Enter**.

❷   Select **A2** again. Press **Delete (Del)** to delete the cell's contents.

❸   Select **Undo**, this time from the **Edit** menu rather than the **Standard** toolbar button, to undo the delete action.

You can also delete the contents of a range of cells when they are selected.

❶   Select the whole of column A.

❷   Right-click and select **Clear Contents** from the shortcut menu.

❸   Undo the change.

Edit the contents of a cell (4.2.2.I)

You have seen that you can type text directly into a cell or into the **Formula bar**. You can edit (change) existing text similarly.

◉   Select the cell and then click in the **Formula bar** to place the insertion point (a blinking vertical line) in the bar. Or

◉   Double-click in a cell to place the insertion point.

Having set the insertion point, type, backspace or delete as you require.

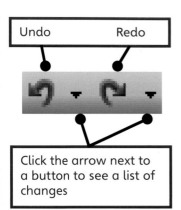

Figure 4.II The **Undo** and **Redo** buttons

Click the arrow next to a button to see a list of changes

How about...?

You can undo your actions by pressing **Ctrl+Z**. You can redo your actions by pressing **Ctrl+Y**.

How about...?

Alternatively use **Ctrl+-** (hyphen) to delete.

Ctrl+X will delete (or 'cut') the contents of a cell(s) and put a copy on the **Office clipboard** for pasting to a new location later.

Warning!

Be careful not to overwrite cell contents when you are just trying to change them.

Modify column widths (4.3.1.4)

❶ Type column A of this table into a spreadsheet.

	A	B
1	My First Spreadsheet	
2	Height in centimetres	182
3	Height in inches	71.7
4	Date of birth	03/07/1953
5	Number of children	2
6		
7		
8	Created by	David Longworth
9	On	16/04/2008

Some of your entries will be too wide for column A. Excel lets you change the width of a cell to an imprecise width, to a precise width or to an optimum width (where the width is adjusted so that it exactly contains the content of the cell in the column with the longest entry).

To set an optimum width column.

❷ Select column A.

❸ Select **Column** from the **Format** menu, and then **AutoFit Selection**.

Column A is widened to fit the longest entry in any cell in column A.

Note

Row heights are adjusted in similar ways to the methods described for changing column width.

Entering numerical data (4.2.1.3)

So far you have entered only text. However, the real power of spreadsheets becomes apparent when they are used to manipulate numbers. There are two more important data types – numeric (numbers) and date.

◉ Type the column B data (exactly as shown in the table above) into your spreadsheet. Use your own name – you don't need to be truthful about your date of birth!

Note

If a cell already has content, the new text you type will overwrite it.

How about...?

To set an imprecise column width, place the mouse pointer over the border between the column headers, so that it changes to a double-headed arrow ✛ . Click the mouse button and drag the border to the left or right as required.

How about...?

To set the column width precisely, select **Format**, **Column**, **Width...** and type the width you want (in character numbers) in the **Column Width** dialogue box.

How about...?

Alternatively, double-click the right boundary of the column header to autofit content.

	A	B	C
1	My First Spreadsheet		
2	Height in centimetres	182	
3	Height in inches	71.7	
4	Date of birth	03/07/1953	
5	Number of children	2	
6			
7			
8	Created by	David Longworth	
9	On	16/04/2008	
10			
11			

Figure 4.12 Sample spreadsheet

Your spreadsheet should look similar to this. If it isn't exactly the same, don't worry! It's good news because you can practise the deleting and editing techniques you have just learned.

Basic printing (4.7.2.5)

You will learn more about printing later in this module (see page 249). For now, to give you a printout of your first spreadsheet, click the **Print** button 🖨 on the **Standard** toolbar. Your spreadsheet will print on the default printer connected to your computer.

Save a spreadsheet (4.1.1.3)

You should protect against losing your work by frequently saving your spreadsheets. You have already saved your new spreadsheet with a new name, so all you need to do now is re-save it to update the stored file and keep the same name.

◉ Click **Save** on the **File** menu.

Save a spreadsheet as a different file type (4.1.1.4)

Sometimes you might want to save a file so it can be used with a different program that uses a different file type. In this case, use **Save As** to save the file, and select the appropriate file type.

❶ Click **Save As...** on the **File** menu to open the **Save As** dialogue box.

❷ Click the arrow on the right-hand side of the **Save as type:** list box to reveal a list of different file types available in Excel.

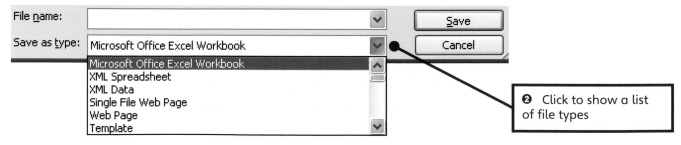

File name:

Save as type: Microsoft Office Excel Workbook

| Microsoft Office Excel Workbook |
| XML Spreadsheet |
| XML Data |
| Single File Web Page |
| Web Page |
| Template |

Save

Cancel

❷ Click to show a list of file types

Figure 4.13 Some file formats available in Excel

Those you need to know about are explained in the table below.

File type	Description	File extension
Microsoft Excel (version number)	Saving a spreadsheet for a previous version of Microsoft Excel	*.xls
Text (Tab delimited)	Text file, often used in word-processing programs	*.txt
Web Page	Can be opened in a web browser	*.htm, *.html
Template	Using a spreadsheet as a basis for new spreadsheets	*.xlt
CSV (Comma delimited)	Often used to export spreadsheet data into other programs	*.csv
DIF (Data Interchange Format)	Another format used to export spreadsheet data into other programs	*.dif
WK4 (I-2-3)	An example of a software specfic file extension – a file to be opened with Lotus I-2-3 (release 4)	*.wk4

❸ Select **Text (Tab delimited)** and click the **Save** button.
If you see a message warning that some features may not be saved, simply click **OK**.
The spreadsheet has been saved as **My First Spreadsheet.txt**.
❹ Close your spreadsheet.

Using formulas

Good practice in spreadsheets (4.2.1.1–2, 4.4.1.1)

When you create a spreadsheet, you need to think carefully about what you want to do with the data you enter into it. You can use a spreadsheet to sort data, provide information, perform calculations and present data graphically – but only if the data is ordered logically and consistently.

Below are some important rules to follow when creating a spreadsheet.

◉ A cell in a spreadsheet should contain only one piece of data. For example, a list of client addresses should consist of a number of cells, one containing the building number, one containing the street name, one containing the town name, one containing the county and one containing the postcode. This will let you sort the clients by addresses in a number of different ways.

◉ You should avoid leaving blank rows or columns in the main body of a list. Whenever data of the same type (e.g. date of purchase) is listed, it should be kept together to make sure that the relationship is clear.

Note

If you are familiar with Microsoft Word, you could open the tab delimited file you've just saved. It may look strange, but it is in a format that can be opened by many different types of program.

- You should leave a blank row or column before a cell calculating a grand total, or make the total stand out by using a contrasting format. This makes the presentation clearer, and it also helps to avoid introducing errors into calculations.

- You should make sure that cells bordering lists are left blank. This makes it clear that anything outside the list is not related to the content of the list.

- When using formulas for calculations, always use cell references rather than entering numbers into the formula. For example, if your spreadsheet listed an item's price, the cost of shipping and a total cost, you could use a formula that added the item's price to the cost of shipping to produce the total cost. This means that, if either price changed, you could update the total cost automatically.

Introduction to formulas

1. Open **Travel Agency 1.xls**.
2. Select cell **H4**.

Excel uses formulas to work out calculations on the contents of cells.

The formula entered into cell H4

	A	B	C	D	E	F	G	H
1				Fly By Night Travel Agency - Weekend Breaks				
2								
3		Flight	Hotel Cost per night	Taxes	VAT	Total Cost	Number Sold	Total Revenue
4	Paris	£ 99.00	£ 65.00	£ 14.70	£ 28.70	£ 207.40	46	£ 9,540.40
5	Rome	£ 129.00	£ 65.00	£ 16.20	£ 33.95	£ 244.15	78	£ 19,043.70
6	Dublin	£ 48.00	£ 45.00	£ 9.15	£ 16.28	£ 118.43	12	£ 1,421.10
7	Amsterdam	£ 55.00	£ 70.00	£ 13.25	£ 21.88	£ 160.13	34	£ 5,444.25
8	Munich	£ 90.00	£ 50.00	£ 12.00	£ 24.50	£ 176.50	23	£ 4,059.50
9	Florence	£ 129.00	£ 55.00	£ 14.70	£ 32.20	£ 230.90	120	£ 27,708.00
10							Total	£ 67,216.95
11							Maximum	£ 27,708.00
12							Minimum	£ 1,421.10
13							Average	£ 11,202.83
14								

Figure 4.14 A formula in a cell

Although the cell shows **£9,540.40**, the formula bar shows **=G4*F4**.

=G4*F4 is a formula using cell references. It means multiply the contents of cell **G4** by the contents of cell **F4** and display the result. A formula in Excel always begins with an equal sign (=).

Warning!

The = sign is very important. It tells Excel to treat what follows it as something to be calculated. Excel will not calculate the expression if you miss out the = sign.

③ Select **H5** and then **H6** to see how the spreadsheet is used so that data on the same row is related, and the cells in each column hold similar data.

④ Change the cost of the **Paris Hotel Cost per night (C4)** to **£165.00** and press **Enter**.

The contents of cells **E4**, **F4**, **H4**, **H10** and **H13** all change because they are all affected (directly or indirectly) by the the content of cell C4. Whenever you change a value in a cell all the cells which reference it in a formula are changed.

⑤ Close the spreadsheet without saving it.

Creating formulas (4.4.1.2)

① Create a new spreadsheet and save it as **My Travel Agency. xls**. Then enter the data shown here.

	A	B	C	D	E	F
1	Fly By Night Travel Agency – Weekend Breaks					
2						
3		Flight Cost	Hotel Cost	Total Cost	Number Sold	Total Revenue
4	Paris	99	65		46	
5	Rome	129	65		78	
6	Dublin	48	45		12	
7	Amsterdam	55	70		34	
8	Munich	90	50		23	
9	Florence	129	55		120	
10						
11				Total		
12				Average		

② Save your work now – you've just done too much to risk losing it!

③ The **Total Cost** is worked out by adding the **Flight Cost** and the **Hotel Cost**. Type **=99+65** for the Paris break, and press Enter. Excel displays the result of the sum.

=99+65 is a **formula**, but unlike the one you met at the bottom of the previous page, this one calculates the result directly using the values you typed. If you change the costs, the result in cell D4 is not updated.

Tip!

It is good practice to use cell references as the operands in a formula. This means that any changes in the figures involved in the calculation are automatically taken into account. This can avoid duplicated work at best, and inaccuracies at worst.

The equals sign tells Excel that what follows is to be evaluated. Following the equal sign are the elements to be calculated (called the **operands**) separated by calculation **operators**. The operands can be cell references or numbers, so here **99** and **65** are the operands and **+** is the operator.

In this course you will use the following arithmetic operators:

+ (add)
- (subtract)
* (multiply)
/ (divide)

❹ Select cell D4. The cell shows the result of the calculation. The Formula bar shows the formula you typed in the cell.

❺ Type **=B5+C5** in **D5**. Press Enter to see the result for the total cost of a break in Rome.

Now imagine there are price increases in flights to Paris and Rome.

❻ Change the Paris flight cost to 120 and the Rome flight cost to 140.

The total cost for Paris remains unchanged, but the total cost for Rome is recalculated instantly because its formula references the value in B5. You should always use cell references rather than values whenever you can so that you can make use of Excel's automatic recalculations.

❼ Edit the formula in **D4** so that it uses cells **B4** and **C4** instead of using values.

❽ Enter formulas to calculate the remainder of the **Total Cost** column.

The total revenue is the total cost multiplied by the number sold. In other words, for each row, the result in column **F** is the number in column **D** multiplied by the number in column **E**.

Tip!

(4.7.2.1) Always check the result of a formula by using simple sample data – this is particularly important when you are using complex formulas in which you could easily make a mistake.

Note

D4 should be =B4+C4, and F4 should be =D4*E4.

Do it!

Work out the formula for the **Total Revenue** from the Paris trips. Type it into **F4** and enter it.

If the result is **8510** you got it right. If it shows **D4*E4** you forgot the = sign. If it shows a different number you need to check your formulas, including **D4**.

❾ Save and close the spreadsheet.

Prove it!

Explain in words what the formula in cell **F4** and the formula in cell **E5** do in the sample spreadsheet **Travel Agency 1.xls**.

Tip!

An error code (text preceded by the # symbol) will appear if you make certain errors. See page 225 to find out what the errors mean.

Prove it!

Check your understanding of how formulas work by matching these answers to their formulas.

Answers

7	7	7	7	8	9	10	28	32

a) ((2 * 3) + 1) * 4 = ?
b) (1 + 2) * 3 = ?
c) (2 * 3) + 1 = ?
d) 2 * (3 + 1) * 4 = ?
e) 2 * (3 + 1) = ?
f) 2 * 3 + 1 = ?
g) 1 + 2 * 3 = ?
h) 2 * 3 + 1 * 4 = ?
i) 1 + (2 * 3) = ?

Note

You can find the answers to these questions, and the answer to the **Prove it!** on page 200 on the CD-ROM saved as **Prove it Answers 4.1 Pages 200–1** in the **Answers** folder.

Relative and absolute cell referencing

Using the fill handle to copy formulas (4.2.3.2)

Spreadsheets may contain many repeated formulas that are similar, like the sums you entered in the Travel agency exercise. Imagine how long it would take to type them all if there were 500 entries, and mistakes would inevitably happen! Excel provides a very important and powerful technique to make repeatedly entering similar formulas more efficient and reliable. It is the **fill handle**. The fill handle will copy a formula while changing the cell references appropriately!

1 Open spreadsheet **Fill handle.xls**.

2 Save it as **My fill handle.xls**.

3 Select cell **H4**. Look closely at the black border. You will see a small square in the bottom-right corner. This is the **fill handle**.

4 Place the mouse pointer on the fill handle. It will change to a large black plus sign.

5 Hold the left mouse button down and drag the fill handle to the bottom of cell **H9**. A border around the cells will show the ones you are filling as you move the mouse.

6 Let go of the mouse button. Excel copies the formulas, changing the row numbers in each formula as it goes.

7 Select **H4** again and look at the formula. It is =G4*F4.

8 Select **H5**. The formula has been filled as =G5*F5.

9 Look at cells H6 to H9. All the formulas have been changed to include the relevant row number. This is called **relative cell referencing**.

Warning!

Formulas calculate values in a specific order. Anything in brackets is calculated first, then all the multiplications and divisions, and finally the additions and subtractions. If you have operators with the same level of importance, for example if a formula contains both an addition and a subtraction operator, Excel evaluates the operators from left to right. Always use brackets to control the order in which your formula is computed.

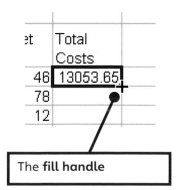

The **fill handle**

Relative cell referencing (4.4.1.4)

Relative cell referencing lets Excel change formulas when formulas are copied to other cells. In the example, Excel has created the formulas as **the cell two columns to the left** multiplied by **the cell one column to the left**. When you copy like this, the new formula is created by using the same operators, with the operands in the same position relative to the result cell.

❶ Select cell **E4**, and use the fill handle to copy the formula to cells **E4** to **E9**.

❷ Select cell **F4**, and use the fill handle to copy the formula to cells **F4** to **F9**. (Incidently, notice how the total costs have been updated now that this column has been filled in.)

❸ Save the spreadsheet.

Absolute cell referencing (4.4.1.4)

There is a problem associated with relative cell referencing. Suppose you always want to use the same cell in the formula rather than change the reference as you did with relative referencing. In this case you do not want Excel to change the formula.

◉ Select cell **E4** and look at the formula.

The **Flight Cost** is added to two nights' **Hotel Cost**, then multiplied by the **VAT rate** (0.175 or 17.5%). Imagine if the VAT rate changed – you would have to go back and change every cell in which it was used.

In a case such as this, the VAT rate should be included in a cell on its own so the formulas that use it will always use the correct value whenever the cell's content are changed. If this cell is referenced using relative referencing, then, when the cell is copied, the reference will become invalid. In these cases you should use **absolute cell references** that fix the reference to the cell you want without changing it.

❶ Edit and enter the formula in cell **E4** to read =(B4+(2*C4))*B13.

❷ Use the fill handle to copy E4 into cells E5 to E9.

The value in E4 is correct, but the other values are now 0.

❸ Select cell **E5**. The formula is =(B5+(2*C5))*B14 because Excel has used relative cell referencing on all the operands. There isn't a value in cell **B14**, so we want **B13** to be fixed.

❹ Select **E4** again and edit the formula to read =(B4+(2*C4))*$B$13. The dollar sign $ tells Excel to use **absolute cell referencing**.

❺ Use the fill handle to drag this formula into cells E5 to E9.

6   Look at the new formulas. **$B$13** has been copied to every row, and the cells now show the correct values.

Do it!

Use absolute cell referencing to replace the **5% Flight Tax** and **15% Hotel Tax** in cell **D4** with the values in cells **B11** and **B12**, respectively, and then replace the formulas in cells **D5** to **D9** using the fill handle.

Remember to check the results using simple sample numbers.

You can have more than two operands and one operator in a cell. For example, the total target sales are the sum of all the values in G4 to G9.

7   Enter **Total** in cell **F11**.

8   Enter **=G4+G5+G6+G7+G8+G9** in cell **G11**.

When you enter a formula it can be easier to select the cells you want rather than type their reference.

The average target sales is the total target sales divided by the number of destinations, 6.

9   Enter **Average** in cell **F12**.

10   Select cell **G12**. Type = and then click cell **G11**.

11   Complete the formula by typing **/6** and press **Enter**.

The result **52.1667** is displayed (the number of 6s might be different). If it isn't, go back through the spreadsheet to find and correct the error.

12   Save and close the spreadsheet.

You have already seen that the fill handle is very clever at copying formulas. It is equally clever at copying text or data!

Using the fill handle to copy series and text (4.2.3.2)

Built-in series

1   Create a new spreadsheet based on the default template.

2   Enter **Monday** in cell B2.

3   Select cell **B2** again, and drag the fill handle one cell to the right. **Tuesday** appears in cell **C2**.

4   Select **C2**, and drag the fill handle several cells to the right. The days of the week appear in the correct order in the cells you have dragged over. As you drag a screen tip appears showing you the text that will appear in each cell.

Excel has recognised **Monday** as the first entry of a series. It enters the next in the series as you drag the fill handle. When it reaches the end, it starts again.

How about...?

Alternatively, you can use the **SUM** function (see page 223) to add together several cells.

Tip!

You can view the finished spreadsheet **My fill handle.xls** on the CD-ROM.

Tip!

Sometimes you will want to display a spreadsheet with the formulas visible in all the cells, rather than have to view each individually in the Formula bar.

To do this, press **Ctrl+`** (a grave accent) to toggle between the two different views.

Do it!

Excel recognises other series as well as days of the week. It even recognises abbreviations. Use the fill handle to try out some of these.

Months (e.g. January and Jan)

Dates (e.g. 1/1/08)

Quarters (e.g. Q1 is sometimes used by accountants to mean the first quarter)

Anything followed by a number (e.g. Product 1)

Try some ideas of your own and see if Excel recognises them as a series.

Copying general text and creating a series

1. Type **Red** in any cell.
2. Drag the fill handle down a few cells. The text **Red** is copied.
3. Overwrite the text in the second cell with **Green**.
4. Overwrite the text in the third cell with **Blue**.
5. Select the first three cells, and drag the fill handle down over the existing cells containing **Red**. The series **Red Green Blue** is copied repeatedly.

Test your understanding

You can find the answers to the questions on the CD-ROM saved as **Answers to TYU questions 4.1**. How did you do? Go back over anything that you are unsure about.

1. By what name does Excel refer to a spreadsheet?
2. In which pane do you click **Blank workbook** to create a new spreadsheet?
3. What is the difference between **Save** and **Save As**?
4. Where are your spreadsheets stored?
5. What other places might you open files from or store them to?
6. List the operations you need to do to save a spreadsheet as a web page.
7. Describe the difference between **relative** and **absolute cell referencing**.
8. A spreadsheet has 2 in a cell and 4 in an adjacent cell. You select both and use the fill handle to copy the series. What do the next three cells contain?

Prove it!

Exercise 1

1. Create a new spreadsheet using the default template.
2. Save it as **Invoice formatting exercise.xls**.
3. Type the invoice below. Use arithmetic formulas for the entries in bold. Use the fill handle to enter the Item References and to copy the formulas.

   - Complete the **VAT** column by entering a formula for **Number × Unit cost × Vat rate**, and using absolute cell referencing for the VAT rate.

   - Complete the Cost column by entering a formula for **(Number × Unit cost) + VAT**.

   - Complete the **Total** by adding together the **Cost** on each of the lines.

	A	B	C	D	E	F	G	H
1	Invoice	Number	10023				<Your name>	
2		Date					Odd Jobs Company	
3	Mr B Jones						61 Hardy Street	
4	26 Birtles Road						Anytown	
5	Anytown						SG66 H93	
6	SG66 4QJ							
7								
8	Item Ref	Description			Number	Unit cost	VAT	Cost
9	ELI018	Paving slabs			66	7.4	**85.47**	**573.87**
10	**ELI019**	Mallet			1	3.5	**0.6125**	**4.1125**
11	**ELI020**	Cement			3	4.2	**2.205**	**14.805**
12	**ELI021**	Sand			12	2.2	**4.62**	**31.02**
13		Labour			32	15	**84**	**564**
14								
15								
16								
17							Total	**1187.88**
18								
19	VAT Number		VAT rate	17.5%				
20	999 88 777							
21								
22	Invoice to be settled within 28 days							

4. Save your file when you have finished.
5. Save your file as a web page (*.htm).
6. Close the spreadsheet.

Income is calculated by multiplying the **Price per cup** by the number of **Cups sold**.

Cost per cup is calculated by adding the **Materials Cost per cup** and the **Other Costs per cup**.

Total Costs is calculated by multiplying the **Cost Per Cup** by the number of **Cups sold**.

Profit is calculated by subtracting the **Total Costs** from the **Income**.

Prove it!

Exercise 2

In this exercise, a coffee shop owner analyses the profit on a small range of decaffeinated coffee.

1. Open the file **Coffee Shop exercise.xls**.
2. Save it as **My Coffee Shop exercise.xls**.
3. Use formulas to fill in the **Income**, **Cost per cup**, **Total Costs** and **Profit** columns. Don't forget to use the fill handle.
4. Provide a total for these four columns.
5. Save and close the spreadsheet.

Use **Coffee Shop exercise – completed.xls** to see the completed spreadsheet. Look at the formulas to see how the numbers were calculated.

Prove it!

Exercise 3

Probably by now you will have thought of ways in which you can use spreadsheets. Have a chat with your tutor or a friend about them. Decide on one use, then take some time to create a first draft of a spreadsheet that will be useful to you.

Formatting

Learning objectives

By working through this lesson you will learn how to:
- ◉ work with more than one spreadsheet
- ◉ align cell contents
- ◉ apply borders
- ◉ copy formatting
- ◉ apply text wrapping
- ◉ modify column width and row height
- ◉ format text with font, size, colour, and emphasis
- ◉ use number styles – currency, percentages
- ◉ format dates.

Working with more than one spreadsheet

Switching between open spreadsheets (4.1.1.5)

You will often find that you need to work with more than one spreadsheet or worksheet open at the same time.

1 Open the file **Formatted Travel Agency.xls**.
2 Open the file **Unformatted Travel Agency.xls**. You do this in exactly the same way even though you have one spreadsheet open already.

It is possible to show the open spreadsheets at the same time on the screen, but this usually means that the working area is small and you will find yourself continually scrolling to show the part of the spreadsheet you want at any particular time. The simplest, and quickest, way is to use the Windows Taskbar which displays the open spreadsheets.

3 Click the Taskbar buttons labelled with your spreadsheet names to switch between them.

Figure 4.15 Taskbar buttons showing two open spreadsheets

How about...?

Alternatively, press **Alt+Tab** or **Ctrl+F6** to step through open spreadsheets, or click the filename on the **Window** menu.

Formatting cells

Your spreadsheets will look better, and be easier to understand if you format them with colour, font effects and borders so that the important information really stands out. Many of the formatting features are found in the **Format Cells** dialogue box. The **Formatting** toolbar often provides a shortcut.

⦿   Display **Unformatted Travel Agency.xls** and save it as **My Formatted Travel Agency.xls**.

Some of the cells in column **E** are showing **####**. This means that a number is too big to fit in the cell width. You need to make the column wider.

Format cell contents: font, font size, bold, italic, underline, font colour (4.5.2.1–3)

Note

Choose a different font if Verdana is not in the list.

❶   Select cell **A1**.

❷   Click **Cells...** on the **Format** menu to display the **Format Cells** dialogue box.

❸   Click the **Font** tab.

❹   In the **Font:** section, choose **Verdana**.

❺   In the **Size:** section, select **14**.

❻   In the **Font Style:** section, choose **Bold Italic**.

❼   In the **Underline:** section, click the arrow and click **Double**.

❽   In the **Color:** section, click the arrow and choose **Blue** from the palette that is displayed.

❾   Click **OK** to apply the selections.

❿   Save the spreadsheet.

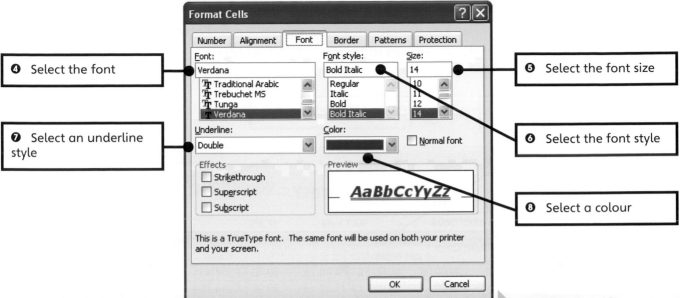

Figure 4.16 The **Format Cells** dialogue box

④ Select the font

⑦ Select an underline style

⑤ Select the font size

⑥ Select the font style

⑧ Select a colour

How about...?

Alternatively, use **Ctrl+1** (one) to open the **Format Cells** dialogue box.

How about...?

Alternatively, you can apply the formatting described by using the **Formatting** toolbar. (Note that only single underlining is available on the toolbar in its default configuration.)

Verdana ▾ 14 ▾ **B** *I* <u>U</u>

Click the arrow on the **Font color** button **A** ▾ on the **Formatting** toolbar to display the **Color:** palette.

Also, the keyboard shortcuts **Ctrl+B**, **Ctrl+I** and **Ctrl+U** apply bold, italic and underline formatting, respectively.

Cell background colour (4.5.2.3)

❶ Select cells **A4** to **A9** and open the **Format Cells** dialogue box.

❷ Select the **Patterns** tab.

❸ Select **Green** from the **Color:** palette.

❹ Click **OK** to apply the changes.

Tip!

You do not need to display the colour palette each time you want to apply colour to text or as a background using the **Formatting** toolbar. The last used colour is displayed on the button and is applied when you click it.

Do it!

❶ Format the following cells as text **Arial**, size **11**, **bold**, Underline: **none**, and Color: **Automatic**:
   A2 to **A9**   **B2** to **H3**   **G10** to **H10**   **D11**

❷ Format cells **D3** and **E3** as **red underlined**.

❸ Apply a **Yellow** background to cells **B3** to **H3**.

❹ Adjust the column widths as necessary so the text is clearly visible.

❺ Save the spreadsheet.

How about...?

Alternatively, use the **Fill Color** button ◇ ▾ on the **Formatting** toolbar.

Align cell contents (4.5.3.2)

The key alignment features applied to **Formatted Travel Agency. xls** are shown in the next screenshot.

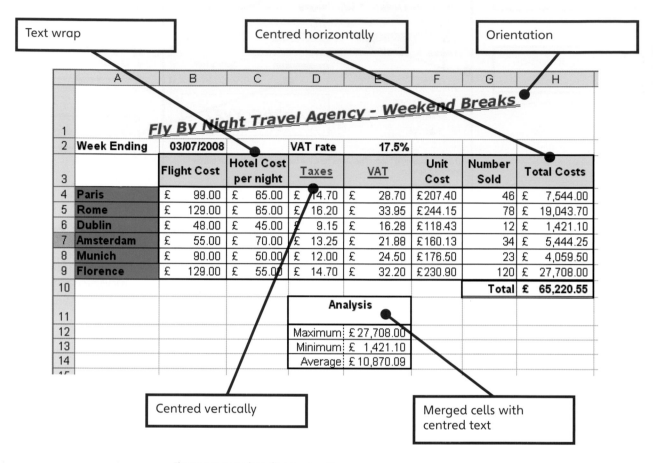

Figure 4.17 Some key alignment options

You need to learn how to align cell contents horizontally, to the left, right or centre of a cell; and vertically to the top, bottom or centre of a cell; as well as changing the text orientation (slope).

1. Check you are still working in **My Formatted Travel Agency. xls**.
2. Select cells **B3** to **H3**.
3. Select the **Alignment** tab on the **Format Cells** dialogue box.
4. Click the arrow on the right-hand side of the **Horizontal:** list box and select **Center**.
5. Select **Center** in the **Vertical:** list box.
6. Click **OK** to apply the changes, and save your spreadsheet.

Do it!

Practise selecting some of the other alignments available in these list boxes to see what effect they have. When you have finished, leave the text aligned centrally both horizontally and vertically.

How about...?

Alternatively, you can align text horizontally, left, centre and right, respectively, by clicking these buttons on the **Formatting** toolbar.

Note that you cannot apply vertical alignment using the **Formatting** toolbar in its default configuration.

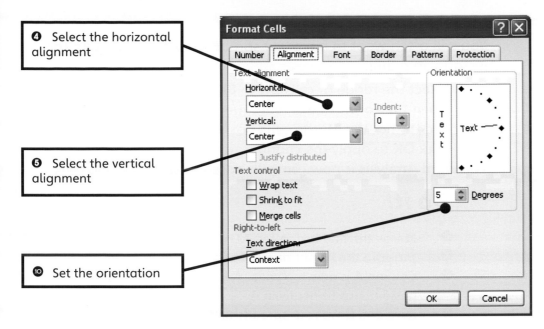

❹ Select the horizontal alignment

❺ Select the vertical alignment

❿ Set the orientation

Figure 4.18 The **Format Cells** alignment options

❼ Select cell **A1**.

❽ Open the **Format cells** dialogue box on the **Alignment** tab.

❾ Set the horizontal and vertical text alignment to **Center**.

❿ Set the orientation to **5 degrees**.

⑪ Click **OK** to apply the changes, and save your spreadsheet.

Do not worry that the heading is not completely visible at this stage.

Apply text wrapping (4.5.3.1)

Although you adjusted the width of columns B to H so that the text in row 3 fitted, the spreadsheet would look better if these columns were narrower. To keep the text visible it will have to spread over two lines. This is called text wrapping.

❶ Select cell **C3** and open the **Format Cells** dialogue box on the **Alignment** tab.

❷ Click to tick **Wrap text** box in the **Text Control** section.

❸ Click **OK** to apply the changes.

❹ Drag the right border of the column **C** header until the text in cell **C3** is neatly positioned on two lines.

> ## *Note*
>
> Note that you cannot apply text wrapping from the **Formatting** toolbar.

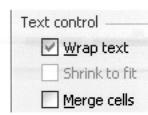

Figure 4.19 Selecting **Wrap text**

Do it!

Select cell range **F3** to **G3** and apply text wrap. Adjust the widths of columns **F** and **G** so the text in **F3** and **G3** is on two lines. Save the spreadsheet.

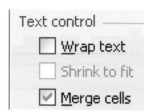

Figure 4.20 Selecting **Merge cells**

Merge and centre (4.5.3.3)

You will often want to have text spread across several cells, for instance in a title.

1 Select the range of cells **DII** to **EII**.

2 Open the **Format Cells** dialogue box on the **Alignment** tab.

3 Click to tick the **Merge cells** box in the **Text Control** section.

4 Click **OK** to apply the changes, and save the spreadsheet.

The word **Analysis** is now centrally spread across the two cells.

How about...?

Alternatively, you can merge cells by first selecting the range of cells and then clicking the **Merge and Center** button on the **Formatting** toolbar.

Do it!

1 Merge the title text in cell **AI** across cells **AI** to **HI**.

2 Increase the height of row **I** so the text is clearly visible.

3 Column **A** is now too wide. Adjust its width so the destinations fit neatly in it.

4 Save and close your spreadsheet.

Formatting numbers (4.5.1.1)

When a cell holds a number, Excel stores the number and a format to display the number. You will now learn how to apply the more common numerical formats.

Format cells as currency (4.5.1.2)

Currency values have two decimal places. Excel rounds the displayed value up or down appropriately, but the stored value is unaffected.

1 Select cells **B4** to **B9**.

2 Open the **Format Cells** dialogue box on the **Number** tab.

3 Click **Currency** in the **Category:** section.

4 Check that the currency symbol in the **Symbol:** list box is correct for your country. If it is not, click on the arrow on the right-hand side of the list box and select the desired currency symbol.

5 Click on **OK** to confirm your settings, and save the spreadsheet.

You will format the other cells as currency by copying the formatting (see page 215).

How about...?

Alternatively, if you know that your desired currency symbol is set as the default, you can select the cells and click on the **Currency** button on the **Formatting** toolbar.

Format cells as dates (4.5.1.2)

Excel stores a date as the number of days since I January 1900! This helps Excel make calculations based on dates, however it displays the dates in a number of different formats that we can recognise.

1 Select cell **B2**. Note that it shows 39 632.

2 Open the **Format Cells** dialogue box on the **Number** tab.

Tip!

Use the **Text** category for phone numbers. Phone numbers start with a 0 – Excel will not display a leading zero (0) if the cell category is **Number**.

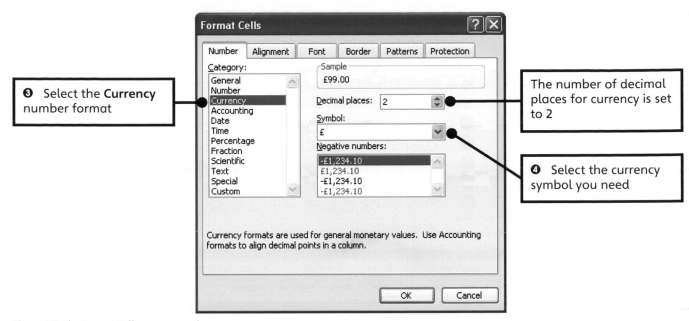

❸ Select the Currency number format

The number of decimal places for currency is set to 2

❹ Select the currency symbol you need

Figure 4.21 The **Format Cells** currency options

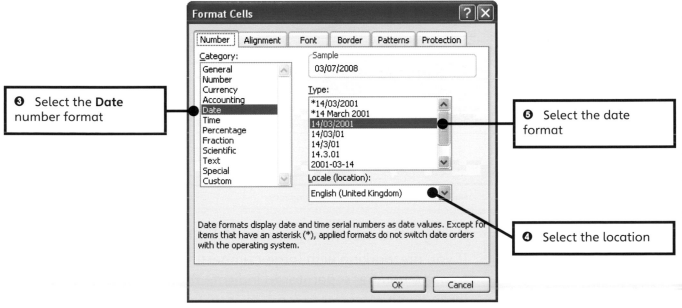

❸ Select the Date number format

❺ Select the date format

❹ Select the location

Figure 4.22 The **Format Cells** date options

❸ Click **Date** in the **Category:** section.

❹ Select the relevant country from the **Locale (location):** list. This will change the available options in the **Type:** section so that the language and display of the date are matched to the customs of the country.

❺ Select the date format **14/03/2001**.

❻ Click on **OK** to confirm your settings, and save the spreadsheet.

The date shown is 03/07/2008. This is 39 632 days after 1 January 1900!

How about...?

Alternatively, you can use the **Increase Decimal** or **Decrease Decimal** buttons ⁺⁰₀₀ ⁰₀.₀ on the **Formatting** toolbar to increase or decrease the number of decimal places in a selected cell or range.

Specify decimal places (4.5.1.1)

Specifying the number of decimal places for numbers is a way of controlling the detail and readability of information displayed in your spreadsheet. Excel rounds the displayed value up or down appropriately, but the stored value is unaffected.

① Select cell **E14**. It shows more decimal places than are useful.
② Open the **Format Cells** dialogue box on the **Number** tab.
③ Click **Number** in the **Category:** section.
④ Enter **2** in the **Decimal places:** box.
⑤ Click on **OK** to confirm your settings, and save the spreadsheet.

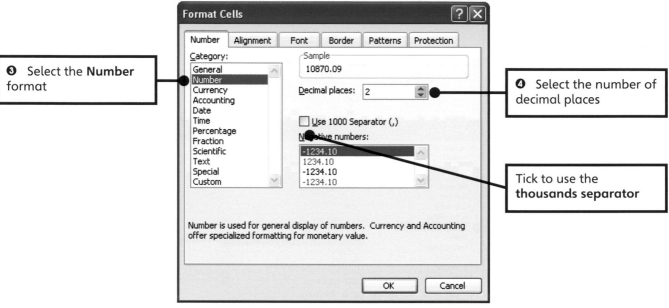

❸ Select the **Number** format

❹ Select the number of decimal places

Tick to use the **thousands separator**

Figure 4.23 The **Format Cells** number options

How about...?

Alternatively, you can use the **Comma Style** button 🔸 on the **Formatting** toolbar to apply a comma number separator style.

Using a thousands separator (4.5.1.1)

If you are working with large numbers, you may also find it useful to use a number separator to indicate thousands. This makes large numbers easier to read, by inserting commas, for example 10000000000 becomes 10,000,000,000.

① To use a comma separator, click to place a tick in the box next to **Use 1000 Separator (,)**.
② Set all the cells in the range **C4** to **H9** and cells **H10**, **E12** and **E13** to use the thousands separator.
③ Click on **OK** to confirm your settings, and save the spreadsheet.

Percentages (4.5.1.3)

When a cell is formatted as a percentage, the displayed value is multiplied by 100 and the % sign added. The stored value is unaffected.

1 Select cell **E2**.

2 Open the **Format Cells** dialogue box on the **Number** tab.

3 Click **Percentage** in the **Category:** section.

4 Set the **Decimal places:** box to **I**.

5 Click on **OK** to confirm your settings, and save the spreadsheet.

How about...?

Alternatively, click the **Percent Style** button % on the **Formatting** toolbar to display the cell value as a percentage.

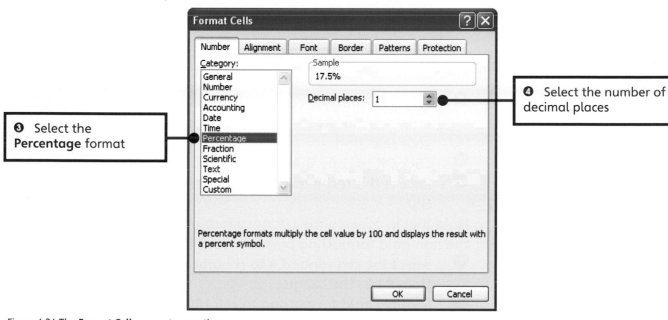

3 Select the **Percentage** format

4 Select the number of decimal places

Figure 4.24 The **Format Cells** percentage options

Copy formatting (4.5.2.4)

So far you have applied formatting to cells by using the **Format Cells** dialogue box features or by using some of the buttons on the **Formatting** toolbar. However, once you have decided upon a format for a cell, or range of cells, you can copy the format to other cells. This will enable you to apply consistent formatting without running the risk of slight differences, thereby making the spreadsheet look more professional.

1 Select cell **B4**.

2 Click **Copy** on the **Edit** menu. The cell's contents and formats will be placed on the **Office Clipboard**.

The cell will now be surrounded by an animated marquee border to show it has been copied.

3 Select cell **EI2**.

4 Click **Paste Special...** on the **Edit** menu to display the **Paste Special** dialogue box.

How about...?

Alternatively, use **Ctrl+C** to copy.

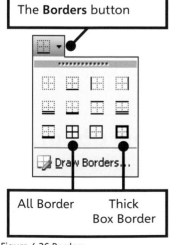
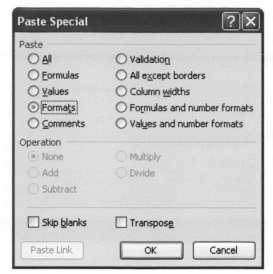

Figure 4.25 The **Paste Special** dialogue box

⑤ Select **Formats** by clicking the radio button. This means that only the formats (and not the cell contents) will be copied to your selection.

⑥ Click **OK** to copy the formats.

⑦ Repeat this technique to copy the format to cells **E13**, **E14** and **H10**.

Note that in copying the currency format from cell **B4** to cell **H10** the non-bold formatting present in cell B4 was also copied.

⑧ Select the cell range **C4** to **H9** and **Paste Special** the format from **B4** to the range.

⑨ Reapply bold formatting to cell **H10**.

⑩ Save the spreadsheet.

Apply borders (4.5.3.4)

Using different borders is a very effective way of highlighting and separating information on a spreadsheet. Key techniques include:

◉ separating cells of data with thin borders

◉ surrounding a block of data with a thicker border

◉ placing a thicker border above a total

◉ placing a double underline under a total.

The techniques described below can be used for single cells or selected ranges of cells.

❶ Open **My Formatted Travel Agency.xls** (if you have closed it).

❷ Select the cell range **B3** to **H9**.

❸ Click the arrow on the **Borders** button on the **Formatting** toolbar.

❹ Click the **All Borders** button to place a border around each cell in the range.

The **Borders** button

All Border

Thick Box Border

Figure 4.26 Borders

⑤ Select the range **B3** to **H9** again.

⑥ Click the arrow on the **Borders** button again and select the **Thick Box Border** to place a thick line around the range of selected cells.

⑦ Select the cell range **B3** to **H3** and repeat step 6 to draw a thick border around the yellow cells.

⑧ Save the spreadsheet.

Do it!

Use the **Borders** button on the **Formatting** toolbar to apply a thick border around the destinations (green formatted cells) and to apply thin lines between each destination cell.

You can apply more complex borders using the **Format Cells** dialogue box.

① Select the cell range **G10** to **H10**.

② Open the **Format Cells** dialogue box on the **Borders** tab.

③ You will see in the **Border** section that the top border is shown as a thick line. This is because you have already applied this border in step 6 above.

④ Click the left and right sides of the **Border** section representation of the cells to apply the thick style.

⑤ Select a thin line in the **Style:** box, and click in the centre of the **Border** section representation (between the words **Text**) to show it in place.

⑥ Select **red** from the **Color:** palette, and click the double line style.

⑦ Click on the bottom edge of the **Border** section representation to show it in place.

Tip!

The **Format Cells** dialogue box includes some preset borders that mean you do not have to select each line individually.

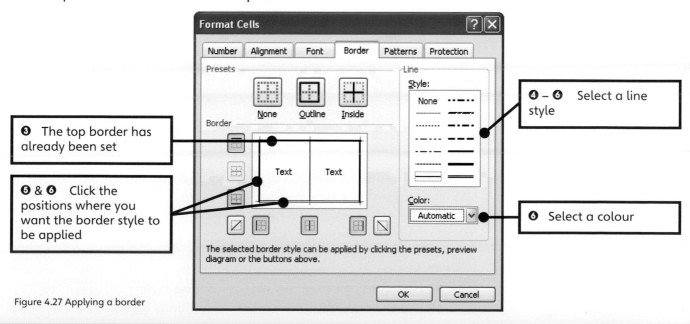

❸ The top border has already been set

❺ & ❻ Click the positions where you want the border style to be applied

❹ – ❻ Select a line style

❻ Select a colour

Figure 4.27 Applying a border

⑧ The **Format Cells** dialogue box should look like that shown in Figure 4.27.

⑨ Click **OK**, and save your spreadsheet.

Do it!

Use the techniques described above to apply the following borders.

◉ A thick blue border around the **Analysis** data (cells DII to EI4).

◉ A thick blue line around the merged cells containing the word **Analysis** (cells DII/EII).

◉ A dashed blue line between the analysis subtitles and the figures.

Save and close the spreadsheet.

Prove it!

Exercise I

❶ Create a new spreadsheet.

❷ Save it as **My Ice Cream Exercise.xls**.

❸ Enter **Ice Cream Sales** in cell **AI**. Underline it and make it bold.

❹ Merge and centre **AI** across the range of cells **AI:EI**.

❺ Format the merged cell to use the **Comic Sans MS** font, size **I6**.

❻ Adjust the height of row **2** to approximately twice the standard row height.

❼ Enter the following data in the range of cells **B3:D6**.

Flavour	Price	Number sold
Vanilla	0.50	I238
Strawberry	0.50	845
Chocolate	0.70	770

❽ Format all the cells in row **3** to be bold and centred. Use the **Times New Roman** font, size **I4**.

❾ Format cells in the range **B4:B6** in italics. Use the **Times New Roman** font, size **I4**.

❿ Format cells in the range **C4:D6** as **Arial** font, size **II**.

⑪ Format the prices as **currency**.

⑫ Format the numbers sold as **comma style**.

⑬ Optimally adjust the widths of columns **B** to **D**.

14   Enter your name in cell **A2**.

15   Save and print your spreadsheet.

Check your answer against the example spreadsheet **Ice Cream exercise – completed.xls**. If yours looks different, you should go back over the module and check out where you have gone wrong.

Prove it!

Exercise 2

1   Open the answer file **Formatted Invoice.xls**.

2   Print this spreadsheet, then close it.

3   Open the spreadsheet **Invoice Formatting exercise.xls**. Save it as **My Invoice Formatting exercise.xls**.

4   Format it as shown in the printout you have just created.

5   If you are stuck go back to the answer file to check what formatting has been applied.

6   Save the file when you are finished.

Prove it!

Exercise 3

1   Open the answer file **Formatted Coffee Shop.xls**.

2   Print this spreadsheet, then close it.

3   Open the spreadsheet **Coffee Shop Formatting exercise. xls**. Save it as **My Coffee Shop Formatting exercise.xls**.

4   Format it as shown in the printout you have just created.

5   If you are stuck go back to the answer file to check what formatting has been applied.

6   Save the file when you are finished.

Do not worry if you feel you will never remember it all. The more you practise, the more you will remember. Don't forget to use Excel's help feature (see page 222) if you are stuck.

Getting Excel to work for you

Learning objectives

By working through this lesson you will learn how to:
- display and hide toolbars
- use the magnification tools
- set a default location for your files
- make Excel record you as the creator of new spreadsheets
- use Excel's Help function.

In this lesson, you will learn how you can customise Excel to suit your way of working with it. You will learn the options for how your screen looks, different ways to save your work, and some important options for printing your work. You will work with the spreadsheets you have already created, and others provided for you on the CD-ROM.

Display and hide toolbars (4.1.2.4)

Figure 4.28 Part of the toolbar list

You have already met and used two of Excel's toolbars: the **Standard** toolbar and the **Formatting** toolbar. However, there are many more that are hidden either until you use an option that requires them, or until you choose to display them. You can display, hide, move and modify toolbars to suit how you like to work. For ECDL you only need to know how to display and hide a toolbar.

❶ Open **Excel**.

❷ Click **Toolbars** on the **View** menu to display list of toolbars installed on your version of Excel.

❸ Click a toolbar name on the list to tick/untick it. (A tick means the toolbar is displayed.)

Set basic options and preferences (4.1.2.1)

You can modify the way Excel works to make it more efficient for you.

Set the default folder to open and save spreadsheets

You can set Excel to always save the spreadsheets you create in a defined folder. When you open a spreadsheet you've saved, Excel will automatically go to this location to retrieve the file.

❶ Select **Options...** on the **Tools** menu to display the **Options** dialogue box.

❷ Select the **General** tab.

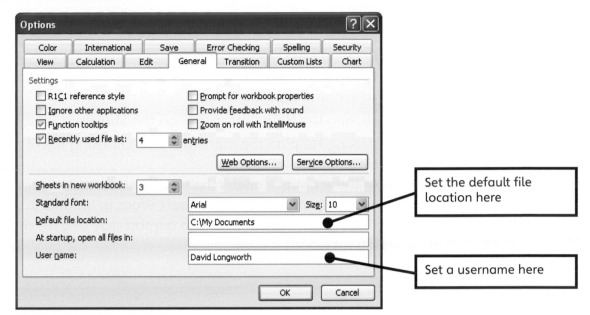

Figure 4.29 The **General** options dialogue box

Set the default file location here

Set a username here

❸ Type your preferred default file location into the **Default file location:** text box. (See Module 2, page 61, for more on files and folders.)

The example shows the default as the My Documents folder on the computer's hard disk (C: drive)

Set a username

The username is saved with your spreadsheet. It can be used to identify who created the file and can make searching for a file easier.

❹ Type your name or other identifier into **User name:** text box.

The Zoom tool (4.1.2.3)

Excel provides a magnification feature called **Zoom**, just like other Microsoft Office programs. You can use it to magnify a spreadsheet on the screen, or to zoom out so you see more of it in the window.

❶ Open **Travel Agency 2.xls**. This spreadsheet contains analysis that extends beyond the window area.

❷ Use the horizontal scroll bar to confirm this.

❸ Click **Zoom...** on the **View** menu.

❹ Click the **200%** magnification radio button, and then **OK**.

You have zoomed into the window so each cell now looks bigger. The zoom only applies to what you see on the screen. If you printed this spreadsheet it would not have changed size.

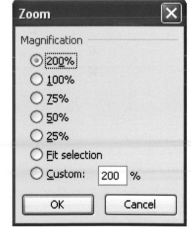

Figure 4.30 The **Zoom** dialogue box

How about...?

Alternatively, you can use the **Zoom** box on the Standard toolbar.

100%

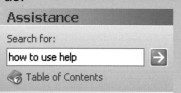
The Help system (4.1.2.2)

Excel provides help in the same way as other Microsoft Office programs.

You can access the Excel Help system by:

- pressing the **F1** key
- typing in the **Type a question for help** box at the top of the screen and pressing **Return**
- clicking the **Help** button ⓒ on the **Standard** toolbar
- clicking **Help** on the menu bar and choosing **Microsoft Excel Help**.

Each of these options opens the **Help** Task pane. Use this in the same way as explained for Microsoft Word in Module 3, page 128. Using the table of contents is also a good way of getting to know more about what Excel can do.

Prove it!

Use the techniques described above to do the following.

1. Create a new spreadsheet and save it as **Customise Screen exercise.xls**.
2. Set the default font to **Tahoma**, size **12**.
3. Check that the default folder is set to your module folder.
4. Check that you have entered your name as the username.
5. Type your name in cell **A1**, and the date in cell **A2**.
6. Type =5*5 in cell **A3**.
7. Set the magnification factor to **140%**.
8. Display the **Borders** and the **Chart** toolbars.
9. Display the **Help** page relating to **displaying gridlines**.
10. Use the Windows print screen feature (see Module 2, page 96) to copy an image of the screen. Paste it into cell **B1**.
11. Print this spreadsheet for your portfolio.
12. Save and close the spreadsheet.

Using functions

Learning objectives

By working through this lesson you will learn how to:
- ◉   use some of Excel's built-in functions
- ◉   recognise some of Excel's standard error codes.

You have already worked with formulas involving the arithmetic operators +, -, * and / (see pages 197 to 201). Spreadsheets also use **functions** in formulas. They are one of the most powerful tools that Excel provides. When you enter a function in a formula Excel will carry out a series of calculations, sometimes very complicated. For instance, you can use the **SUM** function to add up the values of all the cells in a range. You can use the **AVERAGE** function to find the average value of a range of cells.

Some functions (4.4.2.1)

A function is like a built-in formula. It takes data and calculates results from it. **SUM** is one of the simplest and most often used functions in Excel. It can be used to add up the values in a range of cells.

Imagine you want to add up all the numbers in a range of cells **C4** to **C504**. On page 203 you learned how to do this using the + operator. The formula would be very long: **=C4+C5+C6+...** all the way to **...+C504**. It would be very tedious to type and would be prone to typing errors. Instead you can use the expression **=SUM(C4:C504)**, which means sum (add up) all the contents of the cells in the range **C4** to **C504**.

This is a typical function: it has a name – SUM, an opening bracket, then a series of values, and finishes with a closing bracket. Each of the values in the series (in this case, the contents of cells C4 to C504) is called an **argument**.

1.   Open **Travel Agency I.xls** that you worked with before.
2.   Select cell **F4** and look at the formula. It uses the + operator.
3.   Select cell **F5**. Here the travel agent has been more efficient and used the **SUM** function.
4.   Now find the cells containing the Average (HI3), the Maximum (HII) and the Minimum (HI2) values. The formulas

use the **AVERAGE**, the **MAX** and the **MIN** functions, respectively. Each has a similar format to the **SUM** function: the **function name** followed by a range as the **argument**.

❺ Close the spreadsheet.

Here is a summary of the functions you need to know, and the format they take.

Function	Description	Format
SUM	Calculates the sum of the contents of the selected cells	SUM(FirstCell:LastCell)
AVERAGE	Calculates the mean value of the contents of the selected cells	AVERAGE(FirstCell:LastCell)
MIN	Displays the lowest content in the selected cells	MIN(FirstCell:LastCell)
MAX	Displays the highest content in the selected cells	MAX(FirstCell:LastCell)
COUNT	(I) Counts the number of cells that contain **numbers**, and (2) counts particular numbers within an argument in the selected range	(I) COUNT(FirstCell:LastCell) (2) COUNT(FirstCell:LastCell, Number)
COUNTA	(I) Counts the number of cells that contain **data** in a range, and (2) counts the number of instances of a particular value appearing in the selected cells	(I) COUNTA(FirstCell:LastCell) (2) COUNTA(FirstCell:LastCell, Value)
ROUND	Rounds a number to a specified number of digits	ROUND(Cell, NumberOfDigits)

How about...?

Alternatively, you can use the **AutoSum** button Σ on the **Standard** toolbar to apply often-used functions. Click the arrow on the button and select which function to use. The AutoSum button saves you even more typing as it 'decides' which arguments you want to use. However, carefully check what it has used in case it has chosen incorrectly!

Tip!

After you type the opening bracket, Excel provides a prompt for you to help you remember the arguments.

Do it!

❶ Open **Ice Cream Sales.xls** and save it as **My Ice Cream Sales.xls**.

❷ Enter the following text in the cells shown: **Total** (B8), **Maximum** (B9), **Minimum** (BI0), **Average** (BII), **Count** (BI2).

❸ Enter the total sold in cell D8 as **=SUM(D4:D6)**.

❹ Enter the total income and the average, maximum, and minimum number sold and income in the relevant cells.

❺ Enter the total number of flavours sold in cell **DI2** as **=COUNTA(B4:B6)**.

❻ Save the spreadsheet.

❼ Use **Ice Cream Sales – completed.xls** to look at the formulas if you get stuck.

Standard error codes (4.4.1.3)

It is likely that at some time you will make an error using formulas. When you do, Excel will help you by showing special error codes which tell you more about the mistake you have made. Error codes are preceded with the # symbol.

❶   Open **Films.xls**.

❷   Select **B55**.

You will see the text **#NAME?** indicating an error.

❸   Look in the Formula bar. The function has been entered incorrectly as **COUN**. Excel doesn't recognise it.

❹   Correct the formula to **=COUNT(B5:B54)** so that the cell displays the number of films in the spreadsheet.

❺   Close the spreadsheet without saving it.

Common error codes are:

Tip!

If an error code is displayed, you can rest the mouse pointer over the 🛈 icon to see a screen tip giving the reason for the error. Click the icon and select **Help on this error** to see how to correct it.

Error code	Meaning	Likely cause
#NAME?	Excel doesn't recognise the text used in a formula	A misspelling
#REF	A cell reference is invalid	A cell referred to in the formula has been deleted or pasted over
#DIV/0!	A number is divided by 0	A formula references a cell that is blank or contains zero

The IF function (4.4.2.2)

The **IF** function tests a condition and returns an answer of **True** or **False**.

The general format is **=IF(Test,"value if test is true","value if test is false")**, so as an example, in the **Films.xls** spreadsheet you could check if each film was an Oscar winner or not, and generate a result of **Yes** or **No** in an appropriate cell. For Dr No, the cell to be tested is **D5**. The function would be written:

$$=IF(D5>0,\text{"Yes"},\text{"No"})$$

That is, the result would be **No** because the Oscars cell for Dr No is blank.

The > (greater than) symbol is a logical operator. Here are three logical operators that Excel uses.

=   **equal to**

>   **greater than**

<   **less than**

Warning!

The quote signs " and " are important. They tell Excel that these parts of the argument are text.

Note

The returned answers of true and false do not have to be text. For example, you could instruct Excel to return the results of calculations dependent on the outcome of the text.

Do it!

❶ Open **Films – error corrected.xls** and save it as **My Oscar Films.xls**.

❷ Type and enter **Oscar Winner?** in cell **H4**.

❸ Type and enter **=IF(D5,"Yes","No")** in cell **H5**.

Note the quick prompt that Excel provides for the structure of the function when you type the opening bracket.

❹ Use the fill handle to copy the formula to cells **H6** to **H54**.

❺ Save and close the spreadsheet.

If you need to, check your work against the finished spreadsheet **Oscar Films – completed.xls**.

Prove it!

Exercise I

❶ Open **Formatting and Functions exercise.xls**. Save it as **My Formatting and Functions exercise.xls**. Save your work frequently during this exercise.

❷ Format the data as follows.

◉ Title row – **merged** and **centred** across columns **A** to **D**, **Times New Roman** font, **14 point**, **bold**, **black** text with **yellow** background.

◉ Second row: row height **50**.

◉ Column headings: **Times New Roman, 12 point, bold, centred, black** text, **sky blue** background.

◉ Data rows: **Arial, 11 point**.

◉ Title data: **left justified, AutoFit** width.

◉ Year data: **centred**, width **10**.

◉ **Receipts** and **Budget** data: **right justified, currency, no decimal places, AutoFit** width.

◉ Totals row: **Arial 12 point, white** text, **red** background, **italics, underlined**.

❸ Use a function to compute the **total Receipts** and **Budgets**.

❹ Enter **Profit** in **E3**. The **Profit** is the **Receipts** minus the **Budget**. Use an expression to compute the **Profit** for **Gladiator** in **E4**.

❺ Enter **Percentage Profit** in **F3**. The **Percentage Profit** is the **Profit** divided by the **Budget** with **Percent** style formatting applied. Use an expression and formatting to compute this for **Gladiator** in **F4**. Use **two** decimal places.

❻ Use the fill handle to copy these expressions, with relative cell referencing, to the rest of the films.

❼ Use the fill handle to copy the function in **D12** to **E12**.

❽ Enter **Average** in **B14**.

9　Use a function in row I4 to identify the **average Receipts, Budget, Profit** and **Percentage Profit**, placing each value in the appropriate column.

10　Enter **Highest** in BI5.

11　Use a function in row I5 to identify the **highest Receipts, Budget, Profit** and **Percentage Profit**, placing each value in the appropriate column.

12　Enter **Lowest** in BI6.

13　Use a function in row I6 to identify the **lowest Receipts, Budget, Profit** and **Percentage Profit**, placing each value in the appropriate column.

14　As a check of your work, in cell **FI** add together the **average Receipts** and **highest Budget**. Divide by the **lowest profit** and multiply by the **average Percentage profit**. Show the result to **four** decimal places. (The result should be **40.1087**.)

15　Print your work and save it.

You can see the completed spreadsheet in **Formatting and Functions exercise – completed.xls.**

Prove it!

Exercise 2

1　Open **Formatted Invoice.xls**. Save it as **My Formatted Invoice with Functions.xls**. Save your work frequently during this exercise.

2　Add cells that show the number of different types of item sold (with an appropriate heading) and a subtotal for the **VAT** (again, with a heading).

3　Check your work thoroughly.

4　Format the new information so that it is easily identifiable.

5　Print and save your spreadsheet.

You can see an example of the completed spreadsheet in **Formatted Invoice with Functions – completed.xls.**

You have seen how to enter data into cells, and edit it. This section builds on these skills. You will learn how to search for content and replace existing content, how to sort and copy cells, how to insert copy and delete cells, rows, columns and worksheets.

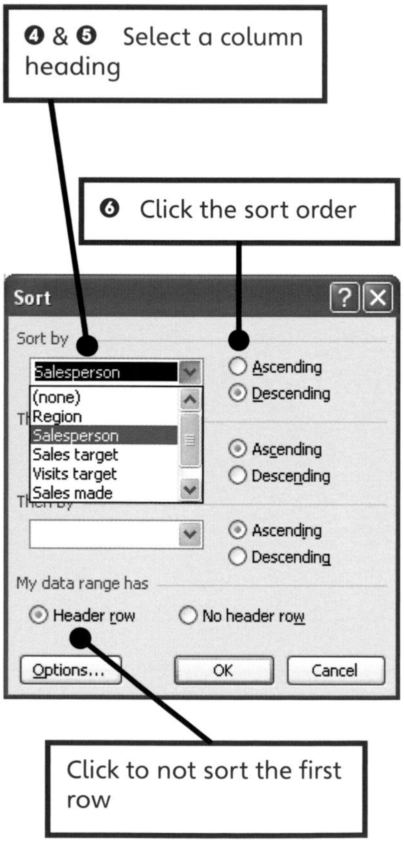

❹ & ❺ Select a column heading

❻ Click the sort order

Click to not sort the first row

Figure 4.3l The **Sort** dialogue box

Sort a cell range by one criterion (4.2.2.5)

It is often useful to sort spreadsheets so data provides more information. You need to learn how to sort into **alphabetical** or **numerical** order, in either **ascending** (lowest first) or **descending** (highest first) order.

❶　Open **Widget Co.xls** and save it as **My Widget Co.xls**.

❷　Select cell **B6** to **G33**.

❸　Click **Sort...** on the **Data** menu to display the **Sort** dialogue box.

❹　Click the arrow on the right-hand side of the **Sort by** list box to display the column headings.

Excel has suggested that you have a header row because the first row of the range has a different format. This will not be included in the sort. Note that you can override this in the **My data range has** section.

❺　Click **Salesperson**.

❻　Click the **Descending** radio button in the **Sort by** section. This controls the sort order.

❼ Click **OK** to apply the sort.

Excel sorts the list into alphabetical order of first name because the column contains text, and descending order because the **Descending** button was clicked.

Do it!

❶ Select a data cell in column **D**.

❷ Click the **Sort Ascending** button on the **Standard** toolbar.

The data is sorted numerically on column D with the lowest sales target at the top.

Find and replace

Search for specific content (4.2.2.3)

Excel provides a way to find specific content. This is very useful in large spreadsheets.

❶ If it is not still open, open **Widget Co.xls**.

❷ Click **Find...** on the **Edit** menu to display the **Find and Replace** dialogue box.

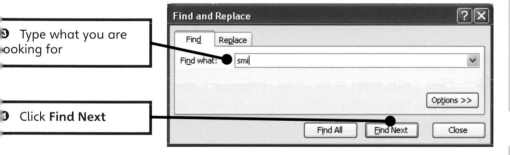

Type what you are looking for

Click **Find Next**

Figure 4.32 The **Find** dialogue box

❸ Type **smi** in the **Find what:** box.

❹ Click **Find Next**. Excel finds the **smi** in **Brian Smith**.

❺ Click **Find Next** again. Excel finds **Pat Smith**.

❻ Click **Find Next** again. Excel can not find any more occurrences of **smi**, so it starts to search again at the beginning, and finds **Brian Smith** again.

Search and replace (4.2.2.4)

Now suppose the managing director of Widget Co has pointed out that the **East** and **West** regions should be called **Eastern** and **Western**, respectively. You can use the **Search and Replace** feature to change the regions automatically.

❶ If you have closed the **Find and Replace** dialogue box, then click **Replace...** on the **Edit** menu to open it on the **Replace** tab. If the dialogue box is still open, click the **Replace** tab.

Note

Click the **Ascending** radio button to sort from A to Z.

How about...?

Alternatively, select a cell in the column you want to sort, and click the **Sort Ascending** button 🔼 or **Sort Descending** button 🔽 on the **Standard** toolbar.

Tip!

You should always select the range of cells that you want to sort. If you don't the results may not be what you want! Sorts that go wrong are the most common way of really messing up your spreadsheets.

Tip!

Click the **Options >>** button to reveal some features you can select to narrow your search.

How about...?

Press **Ctrl+F** to Find.
Press **Ctrl+H** to Replace.

②   Type **East** in the **Find what:** box.

③   Type **Eastern** in the **Replace with:** box.

④   Click **Find Next** to find the first occurrence of **East**.

⑤   Click **Replace**.

You could continue checking each potential replacement. If you are sure that there are no occurrences of **East** that you don't want to replace, click **Replace All**. Excel replaces all the remaining occurrences.

⑥   Use the same technique to replace all occurrences of **West** with **Western**.

⑦   Save your file as **My Widget Co.xls**.

⑧   You can check your work by opening **Widget Co – completed.xls**.

Managing worksheets

Insert columns (4.3.1.3)

❶   Open **Widget Co – completed.xls** and save it as **Managing My Widget Co.xls**.

❷   Using the technique described on page 228, sort the data into **ascending** order of **Region**. Make sure you don't include the **Totals** line.

❸   Select any cell in column **F**.

❹   Click **Columns** on the **Insert** menu. A new column is inserted to the left of the cell selected. Note that any formatting is copied to it.

❺   Type **Target Sales per Visit** in cell **F6**.

❻   Apply text wrapping so the text fits in the cell.

❼   Type the formula **=D7/E7** in cell **F7**.

❽   Using the fill handle, copy the formula down to **F33**.

Insert rows (4.3.1.3)

❶   Select **B20**, the first row with data for the **Western** region.

❷   Click **Rows** on the **Insert** menu. A new row is inserted above the cell you selected.

❸   Type **Eastern Totals** in cell **B20**, then use the **SUM** function to create the regional totals in columns **D**, **E**, **G** and **H**.

❹   Use the **AVERAGE** function to create a regional average in **F20**. Give the cells **B20** to **H20** a thick **black** border, make the text **bold**, and use a **turquoise** background.

❺   Repeat this technique to insert a row of **Western Totals**, immediately above the current totals.

❻   Save the spreadsheet.

Warning!

Inserting the **Western Totals** shows why you need to be very careful and check your work when using spreadsheets. The fact that spreadsheets update data immediately can work against you on occasions as shown here.

The **Totals** cells in row **36** have been automatically updated to include the two new rows you've just inserted. Obviously, the **Totals** should now show only the sum of the two subtotals.

Correct row **36**.

Move cells or cell range in a worksheet (4.2.3.3)

You can cut and paste to move cells and cell ranges. However, here is a quick method that works well when you are moving cells within the current window.

1. Open **Managing My Widget Co.xls**.
2. Select the cell range **A3** to **B4**.
3. Place the mouse pointer on the border, avoiding the fill handle. When it touches the border it changes to an arrow-headed cross.
4. Hold the mouse key down and drag the cell range to a new position, two columns to the right – cell range **C3** to **D4**.
5. Adjust the column widths if the text doesn't fit.
6. Save the spreadsheet.

Note

(4.2.3.1) You can **copy** the contents of a cell or range to a new location on the open worksheet, on a new worksheet or new spreadsheet.

1. Select the cell or cell range to be copied.
2. Click **Copy** on the **Edit** menu.
3. Select the destination cell or range of cells.
4. Click **Paste** on the **Edit** menu.

See Managing multiple worksheets on page 232 to learn how to switch between open worksheets.

Delete rows and columns (4.3.1.3)

Sometimes you simply want to delete cells' contents, and use the delete key of the keyboard. At other times, you want to remove the row or column altogether.

To delete a row

1. If it is not already open, open **Managing My Widget Co.xls**.
2. Click any cell in the **Totals** row (row **36**).
3. Click **Delete...** on the **Edit** menu.

The **Delete** dialogue box is shown because Excel is unsure if you want to delete just the cell, the row or the column.

4. Check the **Entire row** radio button.
5. Click **OK** to delete the row.

To delete a column

1. Select **Column A** by clicking on the column heading.
2. Click **Delete** on the **Edit** menu. The column is deleted immediately.
3. Save the spreadsheet.

Note

You can move a single cell in exactly the same way (as it is effectively a range of 1).

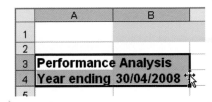

Tip!

Use cut and paste if you are moving a selected cell or range of cells to a new spreadsheet or worksheet.

How about...?

Alternatively, select the cell(s) you want to copy, right-click, and choose **Copy** from the shortcut menu that is displayed.

Warning!

Pasting cut or copied cell(s) contents will overwrite any contents in the destination cell(s).

Note

You cannot move a column that contains a merged cell.

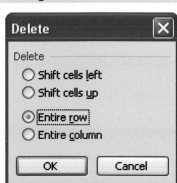

Figure 4.33 Deleting an entire row

Freeze panes (4.3.1.5)

❶ If it is not already open, open **Managing My Widget Co.xls**.

❷ Press **Ctrl+Home** to ensure that cell **A1** is selected and shown on the screen.

❸ Select cell **C7**.

❹ Click **Freeze Panes** on the **Window** menu.

❺ Drag the vertical scrollbar down so that you can see the **Western Totals** row. Everything above row **6** remains stationary.

❻ Drag the horizontal scrollbar to the right. Columns **A** and **B** remain stationary.

❼ To unfreeze panes, click **Unfreeze Panes** on the **Windows** menu.

❽ Save the spreadsheet with the panes frozen.

Managing multiple worksheets

Rename a worksheet (4.3.2.3–4)

When using more than one worksheet, it is good practice to use a meaningful name for each worksheet rather than accept the default name. This will help you navigate between worksheets as you will easily recognise which worksheet is which.

Figure 4.34 Worksheet names

❶ If it is not already open, open **Managing My Widget Co.xls** and save it as **Managing My Widget Co Tabs.xls**.

❷ Look at the tabs at the bottom of the worksheet. They show the worksheet names. The default name for the first worksheet is **Sheet1**.

❸ Double-click the worksheet name **Sheet1**.

❹ When the text appears white on black, type in **East and West**.

❺ Click anywhere in the worksheet to apply the change.

Insert a worksheet (4.3.2.2)

By default, new spreadsheets are created with three blank worksheets. For practice you are going to create a fourth.

❶ Click the **East and West** worksheet tab to make the worksheet the current worksheet, if it is not already selected.

Figure 4.35 The **Insert** menu

② Click **Worksheet** on the **Insert** menu. A new worksheet, **Sheet4**, is created. It is placed immediately to the left of the selected current worksheet as the new current worksheet.

Switch between worksheets (4.3.2.I)

① Click the **Sheet3** worksheet tab to switch to that worksheet.
② Using the technique above, rename it **North and South**.

Copy a worksheet (4.3.2.4)

① Click the **Sheet2** worksheet tab to switch to it.
② Using the technique above, rename it **My Copy**.
③ Click the **East and West** worksheet tab to switch to it.
④ Select all of the worksheet (**Ctrl+A**).
⑤ Click **Copy** on the **Edit** menu.
⑥ Click the **My Copy** worksheet tab to switch to it.
⑦ Select all of the worksheet.
⑧ Click **Paste** on the **Edit** menu.

Move a worksheet (4.3.2.4)

You can reorder the worksheets in a spreadsheet by dragging the worksheet tabs.

① Click the **East and West** worksheet tab to switch to it, and hold down the mouse button.
② Drag the mouse all the way to the left of the worksheet tabs to reposition the **East and West** worksheet tab.
③ Release the mouse button to place the worksheet in the new position.

Delete a worksheet (4.3.2.2)

① Click the **My Copy** worksheet tab to switch to it.
② Click **Delete Sheet** on the **Edit** menu or right-click the tab and select **Delete** on the shortcut menu.

You will see this warning message.

Figure 4.36 Warning message

③ Click **Delete**.
④ Save the spreadsheet.

Tip!

You can move a cell range or selected worksheet to a new worksheet or spreadsheet by clicking **Cut** on the **Edit** menu.

How about...?

Alternatively, select the entire worksheet by clicking the grey column/row heading at the top-left corner of the spreadsheet (between A and I).

	A	B
1		
2		
3		
4		
5		

How about...?

Right-click anywhere in a worksheet to display a shortcut menu from which you can select options to cut or copy the currently selected cells.

Right-click the destination worksheet and select **Paste** from the shortcut menu to place the copied or cut worksheet.

Warning!

When you delete a worksheet you cannot undo it. If you have made a mistake you can only recover by closing the file without saving.

Copy or move a cell range between worksheets

1 Make the **East and West** worksheet the active worksheet.

2 Select the cell range **AI** to **G5**.

3 Click **Copy** on the **Edit** menu.

4 Make the **North and South** worksheet the active worksheet.

5 Select cell **AI**.

6 Click **Paste** on the **Edit** menu.

7 Save **Managing My Widget Co Tabs.xls**.

Managing multiple spreadsheets

1 Open **Managing My Widget Co Tabs.xls** if it is not already open.

2 Use **Save As...** on the **File** menu to save the file as **Managing My Widget Co Tabs 2.xls**.

3 Open **Managing My Widget Co Tabs.xls** again, leaving **Managing My Widget Co Tabs 2.xls** open.

Switch between open spreadsheets

◉ Practise the techniques you've already learned to switch between the two spreadsheets (see page 207).

Display multiple spreadsheets

It is sometimes useful to display two (or more) spreadsheets at the same time so that you can make comparisons or refer to data.

1 Click **Arrange...** on the **Window** menu to show the **Arrange Windows** dialogue box that gives the following options.

◉ **Tiled** – displays all the spreadsheets individually in separate windows.

◉ **Horizontal** – displays the spreadsheets next to each other across the screen.

◉ **Vertical** – displays the spreadsheets next to each other from the top to the bottom of the screen.

Figure 4.37 **Arrange Windows** dialogue box

◉ **Cascade** – displays the spreadsheets one on top of the other with only the Title bars of the covered spreadsheets visible.

2 Click the **Tiled** radio button to select it, and click **OK**.

The two open spreadsheets are displayed next to each other.

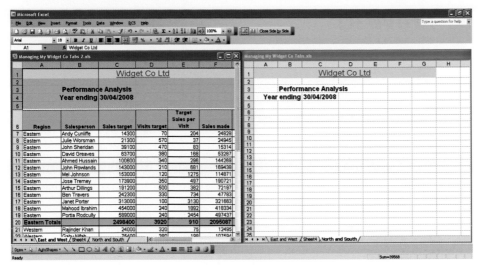

Figure 4.38 Tiled windows

3   Click the Title bar of **Managing My Widget Co Tabs.xls** to make it active.

4   Click the **Minimize** button ☐ on the top right of **Managing My Widget Co Tabs.xls**. The spreadsheet will appear as a button at the bottom of the Excel window and is deactivated. **Managing My Widget Co Tabs 2.xls** becomes the active spreadsheet.

Managing My Widg...

5   Resize the active window by dragging a border until all the spreadsheet content is visible.

6   Right-click the minimised spreadsheet to display the **Restore**, **Maximize** and **Close** buttons. Click the **Restore** button 🗗 .

Copy or move a cell range between open spreadsheets

1   Using the techniques above, display both open spreadsheets.

2   Make **Managing My Widget Co Tabs 2.xls** the active window.

3   Select the cell range **A6** to **G20**.

4   Right-click in the selected range and select **Cut** from the shortcut menu.

5   Make **Managing My Widget Co Tabs.xls** the active window.

6   Click the **North and South** worksheet tab to make it the active worksheet.

7   Right-click in cell **A6** and select **Paste** from the shortcut menu.

8   Adjust the column widths so all the column headings are visible.

9   Save the file.

10   Make **Managing My Widget Co Tabs 2.xls** the active window once again.

11   Close **Managing My Widget Co Tabs 2.xls** without saving any changes.

Tip!

To move or copy a single cell, simply select that cell.

Tip!

Don't forget to frequently save your files.

Prove it!

Create a spreadsheet for Widget Company where every region has its own worksheet.

Exercise 1

1. Create a new spreadsheet and save it as **My multiple spreadsheet exercise**. This is the spreadsheet you will work on in this exercise.
2. Open the two spreadsheets **Managing My Widget Co Tabs** and **Multiple Spreadsheet Exercise** from the course folder.
3. Make **My multiple spreadsheet exercise** the active window.
4. Delete all the worksheets except **Sheet1**.
5. Copy the worksheet **East and West** from **Managing My Widget Co Tabs** to **Sheet1** (of **My multiple spreadsheet exercise**).
6. Rename the worksheet **Eastern**.
7. Change the column widths if necessary to see the data.
8. Delete all data rows except the **East Salespersons**, and the **Totals**.
9. Sort the data by **Sales made**, in **Descending numerical** order. Take care not to move the **Totals** row.
10. Move the **Sales made** column to between the **Sales target** column and the **Visits target** column.
11. Insert a column before the **Sales target** column.
12. Type a heading **Performance** in this column.
13. Enter a formula to calculate the performance (**Sales made** divided by **Sales target**). Format this as a percentage with no decimal places.
14. Copy this formula to the other **Salespersons** rows.
15. Save the file and close it.

Prove it!

Exercise 2

1. Open the saved file **My multiple spreadsheet exercise** from Exercise 1.
2. Insert a row immediately below the headings (i.e. a new row 7).
3. In this new row, type **Created by** followed by your name.
4. Insert a row immediately below this one.
5. In this new row, type **Created on** and today's date.
6. Sort the data by **Performance**, in **Descending numerical** order. (This is a sort without a header row.)
7. Move the cell contents of range **B3** to **D4** to the range **A3** to **C4**.
8. Delete **row 2**.

9   Freeze panes so that the first seven rows and the first two columns are frozen.

10   Adjust the column widths, borders and formatting so your spreadsheet looks like that below.

11   Save the file and close it.

	A	B	C	D	E	F	G	H
1					Widget Co Ltd			
2	Performance Analysis							
3	Year ending		30/04/2008					
4								
5	Region	Salesperson	Performance	Sales target	Sales made	Visits target	Target Sales per Visit	Visits made
6	Created by David Longworth							
7	Created on 3 July 2008							
8	Eastern	Andy Cunliffe	174%	14300	24828	70	204	75
9	Eastern	Ahmed Hussain	143%	100600	144269	340	296	367
10	Eastern	John Rowlands	118%	143000	169438	210	681	200
11	Eastern	Julie Worsman	117%	21300	24945	570	37	298
12	Eastern	Jose Tremey	110%	173900	190721	350	497	262
13	Eastern	Janet Porter	103%	313000	321663	100	3130	119
14	Eastern	Mahood Ibrahim	92%	454000	418334	240	1892	234
15	Eastern	Portia Rodcully	84%	589000	497437	240	2454	227
16	Eastern	David Greaves	84%	63700	53287	380	168	493
17	Eastern	Mel Johnson	75%	153000	114871	120	1275	105
18	Eastern	John Sheridan	39%	39100	15314	470	83	553
19	Eastern	Arthur Dillings	38%	191200	72197	500	382	821
20	Eastern	Ben Travers	20%	242300	47783	330	734	649
21	Totals			2498400	2095087	3920	910	4403
22								

Figure 4.39 Formatted spreadsheet

Prove it!

Exercise 3

1   Open the saved file **My multiple spreadsheet exercise** from Exercise 2.

2   Insert three new worksheets.

3   Copy rows 1 to 4 from the **Eastern** worksheet to each of the new worksheets.

4   Repeat Exercise 1 step 5 to Exercise 2 step 10, to create worksheets for the **Western**, **Northern** and **Southern** regions. Substitute the new region name at Exercise 1 steps 6 and 8. You can reuse the **Eastern** and **Western** data for the **Northern** and **Southern** regions.

5   Insert **two** new worksheets.

6   Copy rows 1 to 4 from the **Eastern** worksheet to each of the new worksheets. Rename them **Scotland** and **Wales**.

7   Copy the data for **Scotland** and **Wales** from **Multiple spreadsheet exercise** to the new worksheets.

8   Copy the worksheet **Analysis** from **Multiple Spreadsheet Exercise**.

9   Use the worksheet tabs to drag them into alphabetical order.

10   In **Analysis**, type your name in cell **A1** and the today's date in cell **B1**.

11   Answer the questions and perform the tasks set in the **Analysis** worksheet.

12   Print each worksheet.

13   Save the file and close it.

Learning objectives

By working through this lesson you will learn:
- ⊙ how to create charts
- ⊙ how to select, move and resize charts
- ⊙ how to change a chart type
- ⊙ how to add colour to a chart
- ⊙ how to add labels to a chart
- ⊙ how to format text on a chart.

Creating charts

Excel provides a means of creating charts to pictorially depict data contained in the worksheets. This helps you present and understand your data. Most people find charts easier to understand than tables of figures.

Create charts (4.6.1.1, 4.6.2.1)

Different charts are useful in different situations. For instance: **bar** or **column** charts show differing amounts; **pie charts** show relative proportions; **line charts** show trends.

To create a column chart.

1 Open **Travel Agency 1.xls** and save it as **My Travel Agency Charts.xls**.

2 Select the range **A3** to **C9** – the destinations, flight and hotel costs.

3 Click **Chart...** on the **Insert** menu to open **step 1** of the **Chart Wizard**.

4 Select **Column** from the **Chart type:** list box.

5 Select the **clustered column** type on the top left of the **Chart sub-type:** section.

6 Click the **Next >** button to move to **step 2** of the **Wizard**.

Here, the Wizard asks you to confirm the cell range.
=Sheet1!$A$3:$C$9 means from **A3** to **C9** in worksheet **Sheet1**.

7 Check that the **Columns** radio button is selected to display the data in columns.

How about...?

Alternatively, click the **Chart Wizard** button [icon] on the **Standard** toolbar.

Tip!

Click and hold the mouse button down on the **Press and Hold to View Sample** button. The wizard shows you what this column chart will look like.

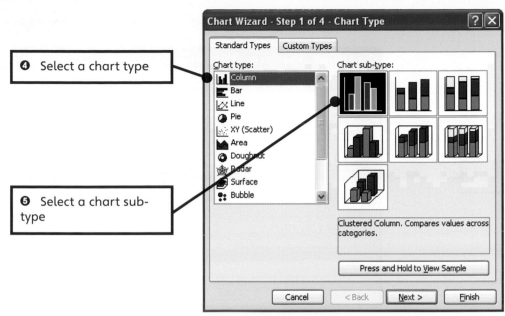

④ Select a chart type

⑤ Select a chart sub-type

Figure 4.40 Step I of the Chart Wizard

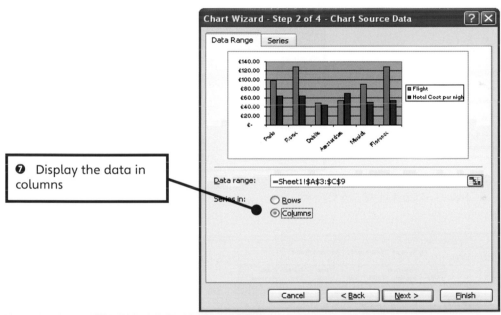

⑦ Display the data in columns

Figure 4.4I Step 2 of the Chart Wizard

⑧ Click the **Next >** button to move to **step 3** of the **Wizard**.

⑨ Select the **Titles** tab on the **Step 3 – Chart Options** dialogue box.

⑩ Type **Costs** in the **Chart title:** text box.

⑪ Click the **Next >** button to move to **step 4** of the **Wizard**.

⑫ Click the **As object in:** radio button, and make sure that the worksheet name **SheetI** is entered.

⑬ Click the **Finish** button. The chart will appear on the worksheet.

⑭ Save the spreadsheet.

Note

Select **As new sheet:** if you want to create the chart on its own without showing the source data.

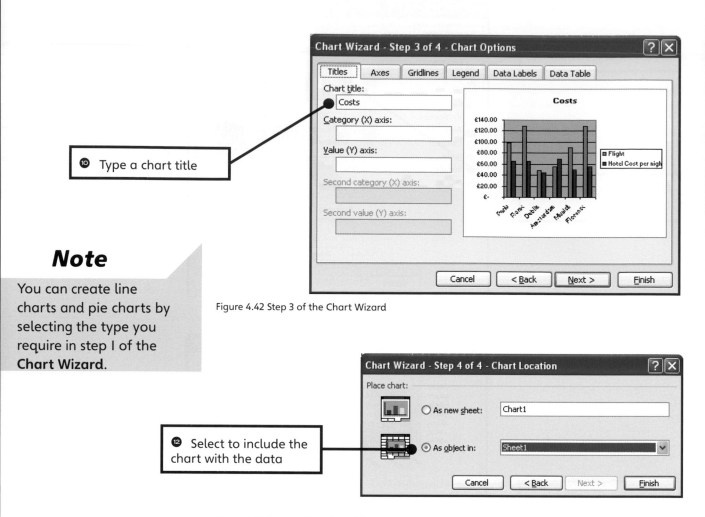

Figure 4.42 Step 3 of the Chart Wizard

⑩ Type a chart title

Note

You can create line charts and pie charts by selecting the type you require in step I of the **Chart Wizard.**

⑫ Select to include the chart with the data

Figure 4.43 Step 4 of the Chart Wizard

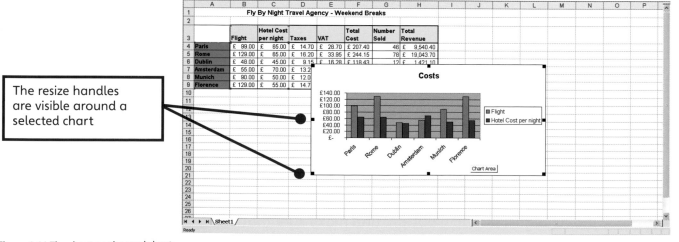

The resize handles are visible around a selected chart

Figure 4.44 The chart on the worksheet

Select, move and resize a chart (4.6.1.2)

The chart is unlikely to be where you want it.

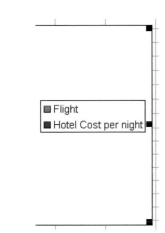

Figure 4.45 The resize handles on the right-hand side of the chart

1 Select the chart by clicking in its white background. Black resize handles appear on the chart border (Figures 4.44 and 4.45).

2 Drag it with the mouse to move it to a new position below the data.

The chart is too small to see clearly. Resize it by dragging a **resize handle**.

3 With the chart selected, position the mouse pointer on the bottom left resize handle.

4 Hold down the left mouse key and drag the left edge of the chart to the left.

Delete a chart (4.6.1.4)

1 Reselect the chart.

2 Press the **Delete** key. The chart is deleted.

3 **Undo** the last action so the chart reappears.

Change a chart type (4.6.1.3)

1 With the chart selected, click the **Chart Wizard** button on the **Standard** toolbar.

2 Select the **stacked column Chart sub-type** (top-middle) on the **Chart Type** dialogue box.

3 Click the **Finish** button.

4 Save the spreadsheet.

You can check your work against the example file **Travel Agency Charts.xls**.

More chart skills

Remove a chart title (4.6.2.1)

1 Click the title on the chart so a border with handles appears.

2 Press the **Delete** key.

Costs

Changing chart colours

It is useful (and fun!) to change the colours on your charts and create some stunning effects. However, be careful! It is not good practice to apply too much colour as it can detract from the content and look unprofessional.

Tip!

Hold down the **Shift** key while dragging a corner resize handle to keep the chart's side lengths in the same proportions.

Note

You can also completely change the type of chart (e.g. column to pie) by right-clicking it, and then selecting **Chart Type...** from the shortcut menu that is displayed. This opens the **Chart Type** dialogue box where you can select the chart type you want.

How about...?

1 Right-click the background area within the selected chart.

2 Click **Chart Options...** on the shortcut menu that appears.

This opens the **Chart Options** dialogue box. The different tabs allow you to add and delete features such as the **Title** and **Legend**.

Change the chart background and legend fill colour (4.6.2.3)

1 Right-click in the background **Chart Area** to display a shortcut menu.

2 Select **Format Chart Area....**

3 Click **lime green** in the **Area** section of the **Format Chart Area** dialogue box.

4 Click **OK** to apply the format.

5 Click the **Legend** area to select it.

6 Right-click it and click **Format Legend...** on the shortcut menu that appears.

7 Click **green** in the **Area** section of the **Format Legend** dialogue box.

8 Click **OK**.

Change a column colour (4.6.2.4)

1 Right-click one of the columns in the **Plot Area** of the chart.

Handles (small square) appear in all related columns.

2 Select **Format Data Series...** from the shortcut menu that has appeared.

3 Select the **Patterns** tab.

4 Click **red** in the **Area** section of the **Format Data Series** dialogue box.

5 Click **OK**.

6 Save the spreadsheet.

Add data labels to a chart (4.6.2.2)

1 Right-click one of the columns as above, and select **Format Data Series...** from the shortcut menu.

2 Click the **Data Labels** tab.

3 Click the **Value box** to tick it.

4 Click **OK**.

The data values are added to the chart – you might need to format them to make them look neat.

Change chart text attributes (4.6.2.5)

1 Right-click the text (e.g. axis, legend, data label etc.) you want to change the attributes (e.g. font, size, colour etc.) of.

2 Select the **Format** option on the shortcut menu (e.g. **Format Axis…, Format Legend…, Format Data Labels…** etc.).

3 Click the **Font** tab on the **Format** dialogue box that appears.

4 Select the attribute(s) you want to change and click **OK**.

5 Save the spreadsheet.

It should ably demonstrate how too much use of colour can complicate a simple chart – remember, the information a chart provides is the important part!

Test your understanding

What type of chart would you use to show:
  a) the proportions of profit that each region contributes to the overall profit of Widget Co Ltd?
  b) the trends in profit for each month from January to September for a travel agency?

Prove it!

You have been using different spreadsheets throughout this module to practise different spreadsheet techniques. Choose one of them and add two charts to it to illustrate part of the data. Add some colour to demonstrate that you can do this, but be careful it does not detract from the information your chart gives.

You can find the answers to the questions on the CD-ROM saved as **Answers to TYU questions 4.6**. How did you do? Go back over anything that you are unsure about.

Learning objectives

By working through this lesson you will learn how to:
- preview what a printout will look like
- change print orientation
- print to different paper sizes
- change worksheet margins
- print to a specified number of pages
- use headers and footers
- print gridlines and row/column headings in pages
- print a range of pages.

Print setup

Excel allows you to control printing just like the other Microsoft Office applications. Techniques you learn for those programs can also be used here.

- Open **Films for Printing.xls** and save it as **My Films for printing.xls**.

Preview a worksheet (4.7.2.4)

You can use **Print Preview** to see how your document will look when it prints. This is very useful, as you will be able to see if the worksheet fits on a page(s) before you print it and waste paper.

1 Click **Print Preview** on the **File** menu.

You will see the first of four pages.

2 Use the **Next** button to see the others.

Change paper orientation and size (4.7.1.2)

1 Click **Setup...** on the **Print Preview** toolbar to show the **Page Setup** dialogue box.

2 Select the **Page** tab.

3 Click the **Landscape** radio button in the **Orientation** section.

4 Check that the **Paper size** is **A4**. If it isn't use the selection arrow to select A4 paper size.

5 Click **OK**.

How about...?

Alternatively, click the **Print Preview** button on the **Standard** toolbar.

How about...?

Alternatively, you can open the **Page Setup** dialogue box at any time from the **File** menu.

Note

If you have opened the **Page Setup** dialogue box from the **File** menu, a **Print Preview** button is present on the box.

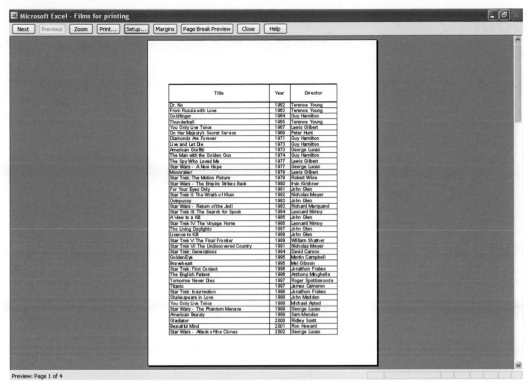

Figure 4.46 The **Print Preview** screen

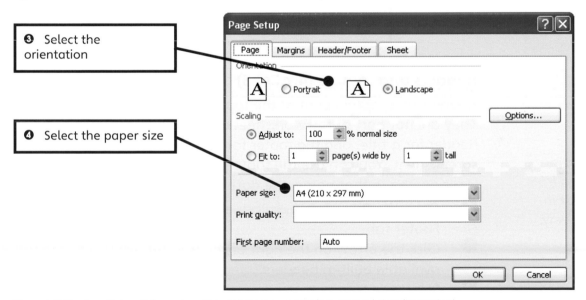

Figure 4.47 The **Page Setup** dialogue box, **Page** tab (as it appears when accessed via **Print Preview**)

Scaling (4.7.1.3)

Scaling allows you to fit the worksheet contents on a specified number of pages. The worksheet itself is unaffected.

❶　Click **Setup...** on the **Print Preview** toolbar.

❷　Select the **Page** tab.

❸　Click the **Fit to:** radio button in the **Scaling** section.

❹　Enter values so the print is **1** page wide by **2** pages tall.

❺　Click **OK**.

Adjust margins (4.7.1.1)

❶   Open the **Page Setup** dialogue box and click the **Margins** tab.

❷   Enter the values shown in Figure 4.48 to set the margins. The grid in the middle of the screen shows the effect of your entries.

❸   Click **OK** to apply the changes.

❷ Set the page margins

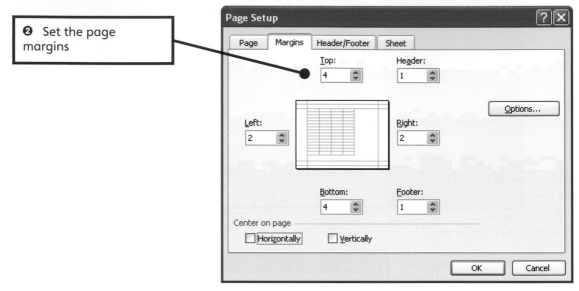

Figure 4.48 The **Page Setup** dialogue box, **Margins** tab

Headers and footers (4.7.1.4–5)

Headers and footers print at the top and bottom of every page. They are not part of the worksheet data. You often use the header for a title, and the footer for information about the spreadsheet. You can use the footer to show the filename and location, the author name, the date and page number.

❶   Open the **Page Setup** dialogue box and click the **Header/Footer** tab.

❷   Click the arrow on the right of the **Header:** list box to see the available built-in headers.

❸   Select the filename you are using. It appears in the header preview box as shown in Figure 4.49 on page 247.

❹   Click the **Custom Footer...** button to show the **Footer** dialogue box (Figure 4.50 on page 247).

❺   Click in the **Left section:** area and type **Page** followed by a space, then click the **Page number** button to add the text **&[Page]**. This is an Excel field that tells the program to add the page number to every page.

❻   Click the **Center section:** and type your name.

❼   Click the **Right section:** and click the **Date** button, then type a comma and a space, and then click the **Time** button.

Note

You can add built-in footer information from the **Footer:** list box in exactly the same way.

Note

You delete header and/or footer information by selecting **(none)** from the drop-down **Header and Footer** lists, or by deleting it from the **Custom** sections of the **Header** or **Footer** dialogue box.

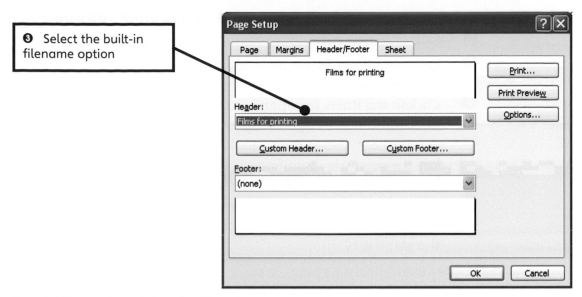

❸ Select the built-in filename option

Figure 4.49 The **Page Setup** dialogue box, **Header/Footer** tab

❽ Click **OK** to apply the changes.
❾ Click **OK** to close the **Page Setup** dialogue box.
❿ **Print Preview** your header and footer.

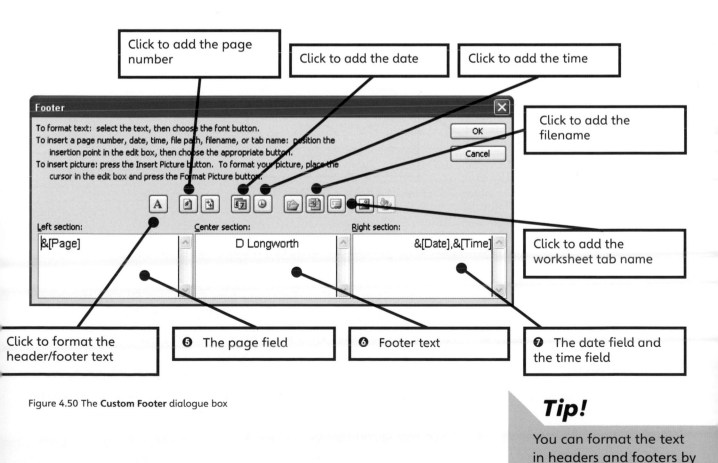

Click to add the page number

Click to add the date

Click to add the time

Click to add the filename

Click to add the worksheet tab name

Click to format the header/footer text

❺ The page field

❻ Footer text

❼ The date field and the time field

Figure 4.50 The **Custom Footer** dialogue box

Tip!

You can format the text in headers and footers by clicking the button on the Custom dialogue box.

Repeat title row(s) on every page of a printed worksheet (4.7.2.3)

Note

This option is unavailable if you open the **Sheet** tab from **Print Preview**.

❶ Open the **Page Setup** dialogue box from the **File** menu, and click the **Sheet** tab.

❷ Click in the **Rows to repeat at top:** box.

❸ Click outside the **Page Setup** dialogue box, in the spreadsheet. Select rows **I** to **4**. When you release the mouse key the rows are identified in the box as **$I:$4**. You can choose to type this value in instead.

❹ Click **Print Preview** to see the effect, and then return to the worksheet. You could choose columns to repeat in exactly the same way.

❷ Set the rows to be repeated

Tick to print gridlines

Tick to print row/column headings

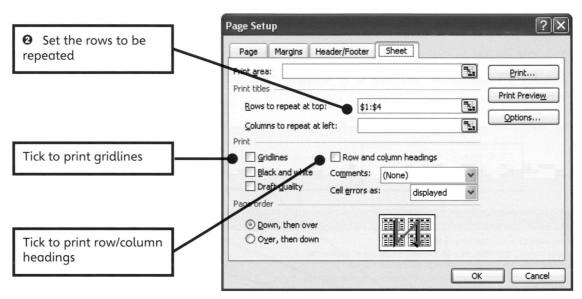

Figure 4.5I The **Page Setup** dialogue box, **Sheet** tab

Add/remove gridlines and row/columns headings from your print (4.7.2.2)

❶ Open the **Page Setup** dialogue box from the **File** menu, and click the **Sheet** tab.

❷ Note the **Gridlines** and **Row and column headings** tick boxes. Tick them to print the features, untick them if you do not want these to appear on your printouts.

❸ Experiment, and use **Print Preview** to see the effects of both. Finish with the boxes unticked.

❹ Save the spreadsheet.

Printing a spreadsheet

You control printing in Excel in the same way as in other Microsoft Office programs. For ECDL you need to know how to print cell range, an entire worksheet, multiple copies of a worksheet, the entire spreadsheet or workbook, and a selected chart.

Checking the spreadsheet (4.7.2.1)

Before printing your spreadsheet, you should always check and correct calculations and text. Make sure that you are satisfied that all calculations are correct, and that there are no spelling mistakes.

Print multiple copies (4.7.2.5)

1 Open **My Films for printing.xls** if it not already open. Close **Print Preview** if it is active.

2 Click **Print...** on the **File** menu to display the **Print** dialogue box.

3 Use the **Print what** section to choose what to print. Click **Active sheet(s)**.

4 Use the **Copies** section to tell Excel to print multiple copies. Enter **2**.

5 Click **OK** to print two copies of the worksheet.

> ### Tip!
>
> Click the **Spelling** button ✔ on the **Standard** toolbar to run the spellchecker. You use this in a similar way to the spellchecker in Microsoft Word (see Module 3, page 182).

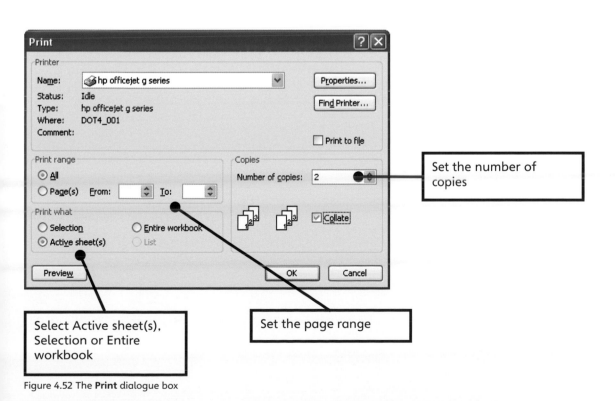

Set the number of copies

Set the page range

Select Active sheet(s), Selection or Entire workbook

Figure 4.52 The **Print** dialogue box

Print a range of cells (4.7.2.5)

1 Select cells **A4** to **D25**.

2 Click **Print...** on the **File** menu to display the **Print** dialogue box.

3 Click **Selection** in the **Print what** section.

4 Click **OK** to print the selected cells.

Print a selected chart (4.7.2.5)

1 Click the line chart below the data to select it.

2 Click **Print...** on the **File** menu to display the **Print** dialogue box.

3 In the **Print what** section, the only option available is **Selected Chart**.

4 Click **OK** to print the selected chart.

Print the entire spreadsheet (4.7.2.5)

This is as straightforward as the other printing options.

1 Open the **Print** dialogue box.

2 Click the **Entire workbook** radio button in the **Print what** section.

3 Click **OK** to print the entire spreadsheet.

4 Close the spreadsheet.

This module shows you how to create a database for storing lists of data such as a 'friends and family' address book. You will learn how to input and present data in different ways and about different types of data and their importance. You will also learn how to sort and filter data to give information, and how the computer uses phrases and instructions to interrogate (query) the database and provide answers to your questions.

These step-by-step instructions and the figures shown are for Microsoft Office Access 2003 and Microsoft Windows XP.

MODULE 5.
using databases

Understanding databases

Learning objectives

By working through this lesson you will learn:
- what a database is and how it is organised
- the difference between data and information
- about database design
- about some common uses of databases
- about relational database fundamentals
- about database operations.

You will use the Microsoft Access 2003 database program in this module. Using Access will provide you with an insight into the power of computing. You will need to take careful note of the instructions as the program relies on rules.

As you work through the step-by-step instructions in this module you will use a database provided for you on the CD-ROM. You will need to copy the files to your hard drive. You will have a chance to practise the techniques covered throughout the module, and to check your understanding at the end of each section.

However, before using Access to create a database, you need to know some basic database concepts to help you realise what you are doing in the step-by-step instructions.

Database concepts

Understand what a database is (5.1.1.1)

A database is simply a computer-held collection of data on a topic that can be interrogated to provide useful information. The collection might be, for example, music CDs (where details such as artist, release date, genre etc. are listed) or a personal contact list (with birthday, address, phone number etc. listed). For these examples, the information the databases might provide could be the number of CDs you have by a particular artist, or how many of your friends have a birthday coming up next month, respectively.

Databases, such as the above examples, can be easily produced as a spreadsheet list, but database software such as Microsoft Access is much more powerful. Websites designed to provide information (such as train timetables) as a result of the answers you give to questions (From? To? When? etc.) usually have an underlying database structure either to store data or to show information.

The stored data can be presented as information in a variety of formats. For example, a database holding many details about particular products could be used to provide reports about sales without having to provide the price of each item, even though both details are in the list. A company might want to produce a sales report showing the top three bestselling products without revealing to its competitors the value of those sales.

Understand the difference between data and information (5.1.1.2)

The data held on a database, in itself, doesn't tell you much. It is simply a list. However, as explained above, when questions are asked about the data, it yields information. The information is provided in an accessible and useful format. For example, a database containing data about stock at a warehouse could give information about stock levels, rate of depletion of certain items, items that will need reordering in the next month etc. – all worked out from the basic lists of items, numbers and dates.

So that useful information can be gained from the data, you need to first identify the key data components. The purpose of the database is to hold comprehensive records so that the data becomes unique in some way to each item.

Item	Stock Code	Warehouse Location	Number in stock	Reorder At	Reorder Number	Reordered On
Screwdriver	ACS 0021	R1	30	10	50	12/5/08
Bucket	ACS 0032	R4	2	1	5	14/4/08
Paintbrush	ACS 004	R1	43	10	50	19/4/08
Ladder	ACS 002	R4	4	1	10	19/4/08
Drill	ACS 030	R2	5	5	2	1/3/08

Figure 5.1 A simple database table of data

Figure 5.1 shows an example list for items held in a database. The list is very simple and does not uniquely describe every item. In reality, so the data can provide useful information, the item description needs to be further categorised with a column for **Type** that holds data such as size of bucket, width of paintbrush etc.

Uses of large-scale databases (5.1.1.4)

There are many examples of large-scale databases. Here are some examples:

◉ Doctors' surgeries and hospitals use databases to hold patients' records. Each record is based on a unique identifier:

the patient's national insurance number. Each time a patient visits the doctor or hospital, the database will be updated with the reasons for their visit and any treatment given.

◉ Airlines use databases to provide information to passengers and to match bookings to flights. Each passenger is given a unique booking reference number, allocated a flight number and then a seat on a plane. Reports could be produced that show which passengers will travel or have travelled on each flight.

◉ Government uses databases to store details such as the electoral register, benefits payments, and tax details.

◉ Bank account details are stored in databases. The database is able to produce reports (bank statements) showing the balance in an account at any one time, the movements of money in and out of the account and any further details such as cheque numbers, standing order payments and cash withdrawals.

Database tables, records and fields (5.1.1.3, 5.1.2.1–2)

A database **table** contains everything related to a single topic (the **subject type**). Data related to another subject type might form part of a database but should be kept in another table. A database therefore might contain several tables.

The data kept on the topic is organised into **fields**. Each field in a table contains only one element of data.

A set of each of the fields makes up a **record**. That is, a record is everything known about a particular item in the table.

Tables, records and fields are best illustrated with an example.

Consider an organisation that keeps data on its customers. It keeps all the related data in database **tables**. The customer contact details are stored in one table in the database (see Figure 5.2). The customers' products and related data on those products are stored in another table. The table for customer contact details should not contain product data, and vice versa.

Every row in the table contains data related to one particular customer. These are the **records**. In the contact details table, this data might be the company name, a contact name, phone number etc. When broken down into unique data, these become the database **fields**. They can be thought of as the columns in a table. Breaking down the data in this way gives you more scope for getting information. For instance, if the whole address was included in one field, it would be much harder to analyse the data to find out how many customers were based in a particular county.

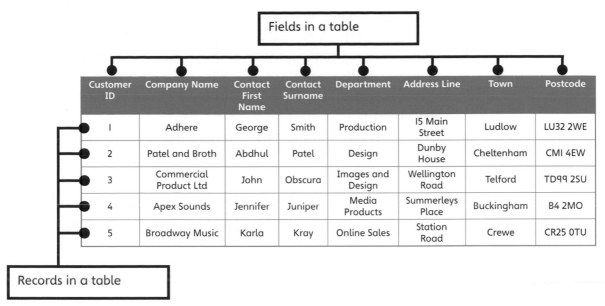

Figure 5.2 An example table structure of a simple database table of data

Data types and field properties (5.1.2.3–4)

When you create a database table, before including the data, it is necessary to define the type of data that each field will contain. The **data type** tells the database software how to use the data thereby affecting how the computer processes and stores it. Each data type has properties that determine the length of the field (size), its format and its default values.

Here are the main data types and their uses in an Access database.

Data type	Use
Text	Small amounts of text, or text and numbers (e.g. postcodes, addresses, telephone numbers)
Memo	Paragraphs of text and numbers
Number	Data that is likely to be used for calculations or sorted
Date/Time	Data that is formatted as a date or a time
Currency	Amounts of money that will be handled correctly by the software (e.g. not rounded up or down)
AutoNumber	A unique number (usually sequential) that is allocated to each record
Yes/No	Data that is either True or False

You will learn how to create a table and specify fields on page 275.

Note

Access does not recognise leading zeros or spaces in a **Number** field, therefore you need to allocate the **Text** field to telephone numbers.

Tip!

Plan your database on paper before creating your database structure on the computer.

Warning!

If you try to make changes to the structure of the database at a later stage when it is being used with 'live' data, you are likely to damage your database. If you do make changes to the structure of any part of the database after entering data, you could also lose your data. (See page 275.)

The primary key (5.1.2.5)

Each record in a database needs to be unique. When a company stores records of its staff, each individual's record can be unique by using a field containing the national insurance number. Without this unique reference, records could be duplicated. If a record is duplicated, the output from a database (e.g. in a report) will be unreliable.

Unfortunately, not all data has a unique identifier, and one will need to be added. This can be as simple as a number that is not repeated. Access provides the option of allocating its own unique identifier to each record. This is called an **AutoNumber** (see page 255). Every record that is entered into the database is given a unique number which remains attached to that record, so if the record is deleted, the number is also deleted and never used again. One or more fields that contain unique data are allocated a **primary key** to identify it or them. Access uses the primary key to locate data and, in particular, to link tables of data together to avoid duplications and allow indexing. You will learn how to define the primary key on page 278.

Indexing (5.1.2.6)

When a database gets large, the time taken to interrogate it for information can increase as it processes the data in more records. This time is decreased (at the expense of increasing the file size) by **indexing** the fields. Access automatically updates the index as data is entered in or deleted from the database.

An index speeds up searching and sorting in a table by using key values. It works like using a bookmark or index in a book. Data is indexed by sections and Access can find data by going to the index (section) and then searching that section rather than the whole database. If your table has a field which has a primary key it is automatically unique and can be found quickly. However, there might be a time where you choose not to have a unique field or you might want to prevent any duplications in a field. Therefore you could change the default settings in the index to prevent duplications. You will learn how to use indexes on page 279.

Relational database fundamentals

Relating tables (5.1.3.1–2)

The previous section has detailed how and where data is stored using tables. Access can handle an almost indefinite amount of data, but, inevitably, this will need a large storage capacity.

Warning!

The **primary key** is automatically indexed. Some fields can't be indexed because of their data type but this does not apply to the data types you will be using.

The data held in the database needs to be manageable. This means that information can be easily and quickly retrieved, that storage space is optimised, and that it is easy to maintain and add data.

A database is more effective when divided up into a number of tables which contain relevant data but also share some common fields with another table or tables. To do this, one unique field in one table is matched with a field in another table. This means that data is not repeated unnecessarily across different tables. Once again, this concept is best explained by using an example.

Imagine you work for a distribution company. The company buys in products from abroad and companies buy from you. In other words you are the 'middle man'.

Think of the information you need to keep.

- Customer details
- Supplier details
- Product details
- Order details
- Delivery details

Here are some suggested fields for providing this information.

- Customer name
- Customer address (several fields)
- Customer phone number
- Customer email
- Supplier name
- Supplier address (several fields)
- Supplier phone number
- Supplier email
- Product name
- Product code
- Product buying cost
- Product selling price
- Product stock
- Which supplier supplies which product
- Order detail
- Order quantity
- Order price
- Which customer ordered which product
- Delivery details (several fields)
- etc.

As you can see, there is a lot of data to be kept. There is also a lot of data that could be duplicated. Therefore it would be easier to manage all this data if it was broken down into several tables.

For example, you could have a table that held customer details, and another table that held order details. By using a unique customer number in a customer details table and a unique order number in an order details table, a relationship between the two tables can be created. Otherwise all the customer details would have to be held in the record for each order.

Referential integrity (5.1.3.3)

Once you have defined a unique field in one table and related it to another unique field in another table, you can ask Access to ensure that the relationship remains valid. This is called **enforcing referential integrity**, and it is important to prevent errors occurring that could affect the information you get from the database. In the example above, enforced referential integrity would prevent a customer being linked to a product that does not exist.

It also prevents deletion of a record from the database that is linked to other tables. For example, a product might become obsolete. However, if it was deleted from the database, it would affect all the records of previous orders for it.

You can enforce referential integrity when you create a relationship between two tables.

This all seems very complicated, so you'll be pleased to hear that this is all you need to know about relational databases for this module. Everything that follows is for single table databases!

Database operation (5.1.4.1–4)

As you can imagine, databases such as those listed on page 253, need to be carefully managed. There may be one user, or many users, entering data and other users retrieving information. Those entering data and those retrieving information could be the same people (e.g. a telesales person may create a new record for a customer, update fields for an existing customer, or retrieve price and availabilty information for a potential customer). Several people may use the database at the same time, as is likely to be the case in a booking system.

In some databases, it is not appropriate for all the users to be able to enter or retrieve data. A database administrator allocates access rights to users so that records can be seen or changed only by authorised people. For example, a hospital porter might be authorised to view a patient's location in a ward, but would not be able to change any personal or medication data.

The database administrator is usually responsible for the seamless recovery of a database in the event of a system failure. Some important databases rely on duplication of systems, so in the event of one system failure, the duplicate system can be used immediately without loss of data and the need for using backups. It is important that the data held and information retrieved is accurate, so databases are designed and maintained by specialists.

Test your understanding

1. Describe what a database is and what it does.
2. What are the parts of a table?
3. a) What are **data types**?
   b) Name **seven** different data types.
   c) What are data type properties?
4. Why is it important to plan your database carefully before creating it on the computer?
5. What is a **record**?
6. What is a **primary key**?
7. What does a database **index** do?
8. What is a **relational database**?
9. What does **referential integrity** mean?

You can find the answers to the questions on the CD-ROM saved as **Answers to TYU questions 5.1**. How did you do? Go back over anything that you are unsure about.

Using a database program

Learning objectives

By working through this lesson you will learn how to:
- ◉ open and close a database program, and a database
- ◉ create a new database
- ◉ display and hide toolbars
- ◉ use the Help function
- ◉ open, save, delete and close database objects
- ◉ navigate and sort records.

How about...?

Alternatively, if it is there, you can double-click directly on the **Access** icon on the Desktop or on the Start menu.

Note

Microsoft Access can be opened by more than one method – as can any other Microsoft Office application.

Existing databases will be shown here on the Task pane

Click to create a new database

How about...?

Alternatively, click the Close icon ⊠ on the top right of the window to close Access.

Working with databases

Open and close a database program (5.2.1.1)

❶ Click the **Start** button 🏁 *start* on the Taskbar.
❷ Click **All Programs**.
❸ Click **Microsoft Office**.
❹ Click **Microsoft Office Access 2003**.

As Access loads you will see an **hourglass** icon ⧗ to let you know that something is happening and you need to wait.

Access looks like this when it first opens.

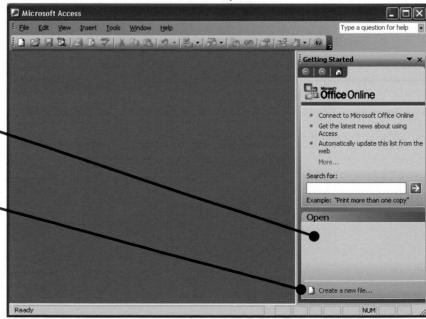

Figure 5.3 The Access opening screen

◉ You can close Access by clicking **Exit** on the **File** menu.

Open and close an existing database (5.2.1.2)

① Open **Access**.

② Click **Open...** on the **File** menu to display the **Open** dialogue box.

③ Navigate to the database file **Client database.mdb** and click the **Open** button.

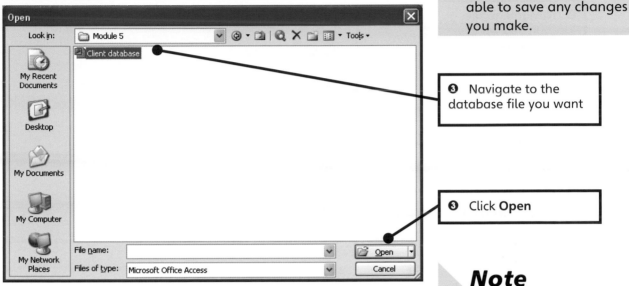

Figure 5.4 The **Open** dialogue box

The database will open showing a window similar to Figure 5.5. This is the **Database Window**. The objects are the tables, queries, forms etc. that make up the database (see page 264). The database might open showing a different selected object.

④ Close the database by clicking the **Close** icon ☒ .

⑤ Close Access.

> **Note**
>
> If you are using the CD-ROM example files directly rather than using saved copies on your computer, you will not be able to save any changes you make.

> **Note**
>
> If you see a warning telling you that the file might be unsafe, do not worry. Click **OK** to continue.

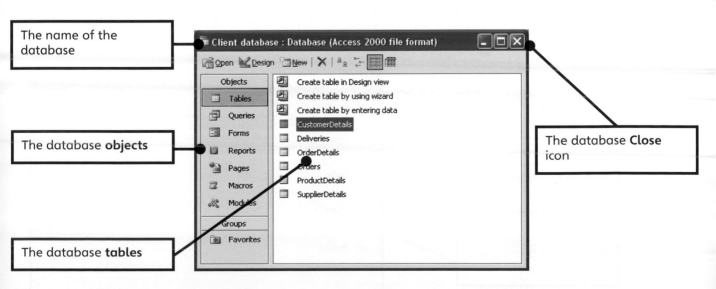

Figure 5.5 The open database displaying the tables

Create a new database (5.2.I.3)

❶ Open Access and click **Create a new file...** on the **Getting Started** Task pane.

❷ Click **Blank database...** on the **New File** Task pane to display the **File New Database** dialogue box.

❸ Navigate to the location you want

❹ Type a filename

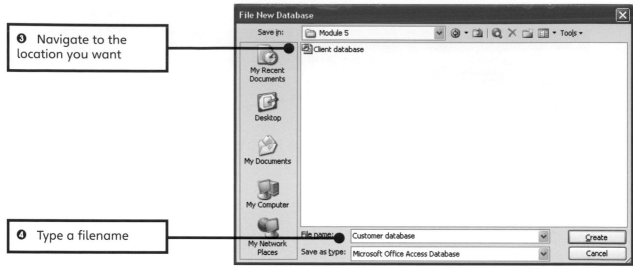

Figure 5.6 The **File New Database** dialogue box

❸ Navigate in the usual Windows fashion (see Module 2) to the location where you want to save your database.

❹ Type the name **Customer database** for your database in the **File name:** text box.

Tip!

When naming a database, use a name that describes what the database is for, such as **Music Collection**, **Friends and Family** etc.

❺ Click the **Create** button.

The **Database Window** is displayed showing the **Tables** options. This is a new database, so all the options are for creating a new table. If you were to click the other object buttons down the left-hand side of the **Database Window**, you would see that only 'create' options are available for queries, forms and reports as well.

❻ Close the database.

The database name appears here

The Tables object is selected

The options that let you create a table

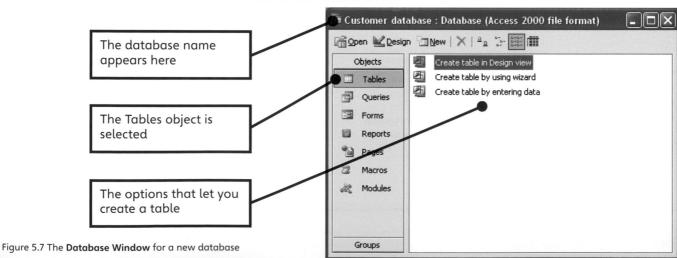

Figure 5.7 The **Database Window** for a new database

Display and hide toolbars (5.2.1.4)

Many of the toolbars in Access are **context sensitive**. This means that they only appear when you are working on the part of a database they are relevant to. For example, when you are working with a table, the toolbar will be either the **Table Datasheet** toolbar if you are working with the data, or the **Table Design** toolbar if you are setting up the fields etc.

As with other Microsoft Office applications, more than one toolbar might be relevant to each feature of the database you are working in. In this case you might want to hide toolbars that are showing, or display those that have been hidden. You can display, hide, move and modify toolbars to suit how you like to work. For ECDL you only need to know how to display and hide a toolbar.

❶   Open **Access**.

❷   Click **Toolbars** on the **View** menu to display list of installed toolbars.

❸   Click a toolbar name on the list to tick/untick it. (A tick means the toolbar is displayed.)

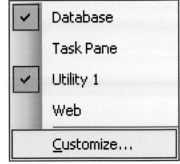

Figure 5.8 Showing toolbars available and displayed for a particular Access feature

Using the Help function (5.2.1.5)

Access provides help in the same way as other Microsoft Office programs.

You can access the Access Help System by:

⦿   pressing the **FI** key

⦿   typing in the **Type a question for help** box at the top of the screen and pressing **Return**

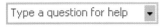

⦿   clicking the **Help** button ⓞ on the **Standard** toolbar

⦿   clicking **Help** on the menu bar and choosing **Microsoft Office Access Help**.

Each of these options opens the **Help** Task pane. Use this in the same way as explained for Microsoft Word in Module 3, page 128. Using the table of contents is also a good way of getting to know more about what Access can do.

Figure 5.9 The **Access Help** Task pane

Tip!

When using a database program, you will work with more than one window (such as tables, queries etc.) open at a time. Each time you open a new window it will be placed in front of any others. You will need to switch between windows by clicking on the window you want.

Common tasks

Database objects

You have already learned that a database uses tables to hold data in records and fields (see page 254). Tables are one type of database **object**. Some other common database objects are **queries**, **forms** and **reports**. You can see the objects that make up a database in the **Database Window** by clicking the object name in the **Object** panel on the window's left-hand side.

The query, form and report objects do not have any effect on the database structure, and are used for inputting, processing and outputting data.

- ◉ A **query** (see page 285) is a means of interrogating the data held in tables. It contains the 'questions' to be asked to get information. There are other ways of getting information (such as **sorts** (page 271) and **filters** (page 282)) but queries have more advanced features and are useful if the 'questions' are likely to be often repeated. The results of a query can be displayed in tables, forms or reports.

- ◉ A **form** (see page 296) provides a structured way of entering or displaying data. It can be thought of as an electronic version of a paper-based form where you write answers to questions. Data can be input to tables by typing it into defined text boxes on the form. Other text boxes can be used to display data from the tables. The user of a form can be prevented from changing the structure of the database.

- ◉ A **report** (see page 303) is a structured means of outputting information gleaned from data in the database and processed according to queries etc.

Open, save and close database objects (5.2.2.1)

Database objects, such as tables, forms, queries and reports, can be opened, worked on, saved and closed individually. You will usually want to save tables because these contain the data which gives the database its point. However, although you will often want to save forms, queries and reports, so that you can use them again, you do not have to. For example, in the Client database, you might want to find out how many customers placed orders in May 2006. You might not want to ask this question again, therefore you wouldn't need to save the query. However, the beauty of queries is that they can provide detailed responses to questions that are asked often, without having to re-create the query every time.

Tip!

When designing a query, as with designing a table, if you plan it first it is more likely to be effective.

1. Open **Client database.mdb**.
2. Click **Tables** (if it is not already highlighted) in the **Database Windows** object list.
3. Select the **OrderDetails** table and click the **Open** button.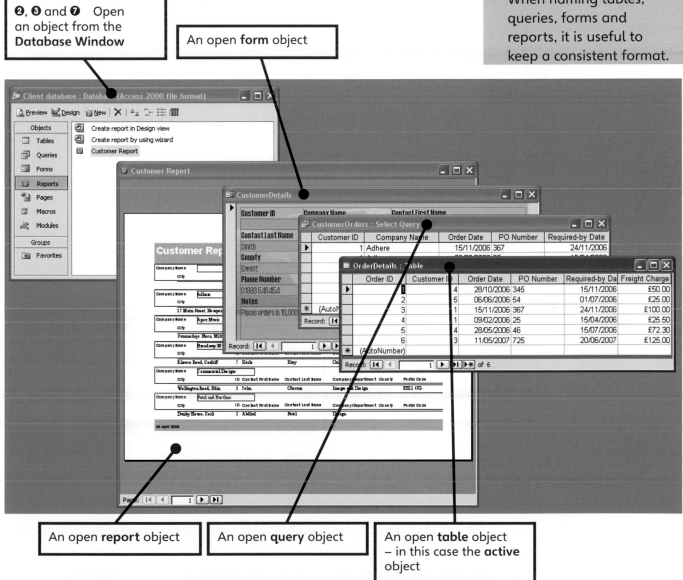
4. Press **FII** to show the **Database Window** again.
5. Click **Queries** in the **Database Windows** object list.
6. Select the **CustomerOrders** query and click the **Open** button.
7. Open the **CustomerDetails** form and **CustomerReport** report in a similar manner.

How about...?

If you select the object (e.g. **OrderDetails**) so it is highlighted, you can press **Enter** on the keyboard to open it. Alternatively, simply double-click the name.

Tip!

When naming tables, queries, forms and reports, it is useful to keep a consistent format.

②, ③ and ⑦ Open an object from the **Database Window**

An open **form** object

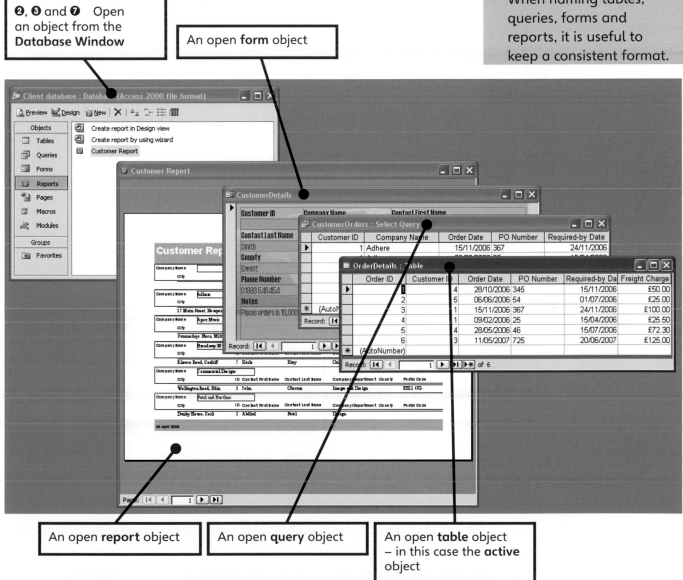

An open **report** object

An open **query** object

An open **table** object – in this case the **active** object

Figure 5.10 Open objects

Whether or not you need to save an object after making changes depends on the object. If you alter the data in a table field, you do not need to save the table when you close it. The data is saved automatically. You only need to save the designs of queries, forms and reports when you change them.

You can save an object as a different type of object, with or without a new name.

❶ Select the object.

❷ Click **Save As...** on the **File** menu to open the **Save As** dialogue box.

❸ Choose a new name and object type, as required.

❸ Type a name and select an object type

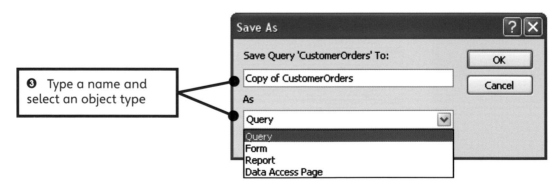

Figure 5.II The **Save As** dialogue box

❹ Close any type of open object by clicking the red-background cross on the top-right corner of the object window.

Switch between view modes (5.2.2.2)

So far you have seen the objects as they appear when you use them. For tables and queries, this is called the **Datasheet View**.

For a form, it is called the **Form View**. A report is usually printed out, so you are shown the **Layout Preview**.

Each of these objects has to be planned.

◉ The fields and data types need to be specified for a table so the database works correctly.

◉ The criteria by which a query interrogates the data in a table(s) need to be defined.

◉ A form needs to be planned so that it looks professional, but also so that data entered is input to the correct fields in a table, and so that output data is correct and appears in the right places.

◉ Similarly, a report needs to be planned so that the information it gives is correct and the printed version of it is easy to understand and looks professional.

Once planned, the object can be designed in the **Design View**.

❶ If you have closed the database, open it again, and open the **OrderDetails** table. If the database is still open, close all the objects except the **OrderDetails** table.

❷ Click the **Design View** button 📐 on the **Table Datasheet** toolbar that is displayed.

The **OrderDetails** design view is displayed, and the **Table Design** toolbar replaces the **Table Datasheet** toolbar.

Warning!

You will get an error if a query or form that is based on a table is open when you try to switch to the table's **Design View**.

Figure 5.12 The Table Design View

Note

You will learn more about the Table Design View on page 275.

③ Click the **Datasheet View** button 🎛 on the **Table Design** toolbar to return to the **OrderDetails** datasheet view.

④ Close the table datasheet view and open the **CustomerDetails** form.

⑤ This time, click the **Design View** button that is on the **Form View** toolbar that is displayed.

The **CustomerDetails** form design view is displayed, and the **Form Design** toolbar replaces the **Form View** toolbar.

Note

You will learn more about the Form Design View on page 296.

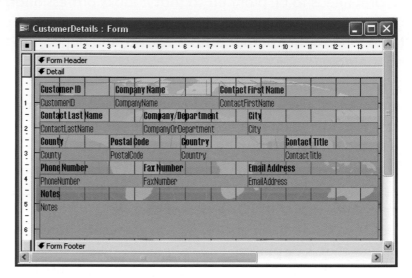

Figure 5.13 The Form Design View

⑥ Click the **Form View** button 📇 on the **Form Design** toolbar to return to the **CustomerDetails** form view.

⑦ Close the form view and open the **CustomerReport** report.

⑧ Now click the **Design View** button that is on the **Print Preview** toolbar that is displayed.

The **CustomerReport** design view is displayed, and the **Report Design** toolbar replaces the **Print Preview** toolbar.

Note

You will learn more about the Report Design View on page 303.

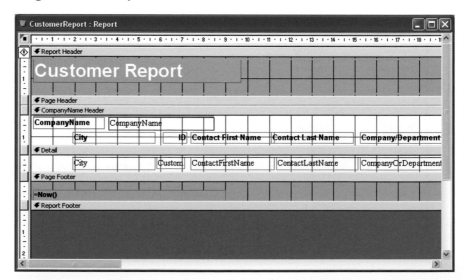

Figure 5.14 The Report Design View

⑨ Click the **Print Preview** button 🔍 on the **Report Design** toolbar to return to the **CustomerReport** report view.

⑩ Close the report view and open the **CustomerOrders** query.

⑪ Finally, click the **Design View** button that is on the **Query Datasheet** toolbar that is displayed.

The **CustomerOrders** query design view is displayed, and the **Query Design** toolbar replaces the **Query Datasheet** toolbar.

How about...?

Alternatively, you can select the object in the **Database Window**, then click the **Design View** button 🔧 Design on the **Database Window** toolbar.

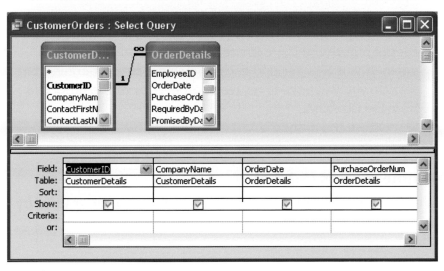

Figure 5.15 The Query Design View

Note

You will learn more about the Query Design View on page 285.

⑫ Click the **Datasheet View** button on the **Query Datasheet** toolbar to return to the **CustomerOrders** query view.

⑬ Close the query view.

⑭ Close the database.

Delete a table, query, form and report (5.2.2.3)

You have already learned (on page 264) that the query, form and report objects are used for processing and/or presenting the data that is held in table objects. Therefore, deleting any query, form or report will not affect the source data in any table. However, if you delete a table, you will lose all the data held in that table. To delete any object.

❶ Close the object, if it is open.

Display the **Database Window**, if it is not already showing.

❷ Click the object in the **Database Window** to highlight it and press the **Delete** key on your keyboard.

How about...?

Alternatively, right-click an object in the **Database Window**. A shortcut menu will give you some options, one of which is **Delete**.

Do it!

There are no records in the **Orders** table of the Client database, so you can delete it.

❶ Open **Client database.mdb**.

❷ Click the **Tables** object on the left-hand side of the **Database Window**.

❸ Delete the **Orders** table.

Access will ask you if you really want to delete the table. This is because **Orders** is part of a relationship, and Access will only allow you to delete a table if you also delete the relationship. For the purpose of this exercise, click **No** so you can practise again. If you click **Yes** and decide you want to start again from scratch, you will have to resave another copy of the database from the CD-ROM.

❹ Close the database.

How about...?

Alternatively, in tables and queries, you can use the arrow keys or tab key on the keyboard to move between records, and between fields within records.

Navigate records (5.2.2.4)

You can navigate between records in a table, query or form by using the record selector.

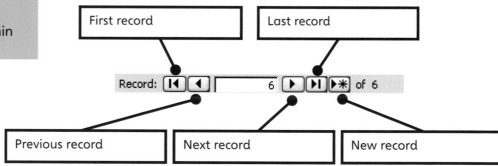

Figure 5.16 The record selector

Do it!

❶ Open **Client database.mdb**.

❷ Open the **OrderDetails** table.

❸ The data entry cursor should be positioned in the **Order ID** field of first record.

❹ Use the **record selector** buttons to move the cursor within the table.

❺ Open the **Customer Details** form and practise using the **record selector** to move through the records in the form.

❻ Close the objects and close the database.

Tip!

To move to a known record, type the record number you want in the box between the **Previous** and **Next** record buttons, then press **Return**.

Sorting records in tables (5.2.2.5)

Records in a table, query or form can be sorted **alphabetically** or **numerically** in **ascending** (up) or **descending** (down) order. For example, you might want to quickly find all companies in a particular county. In a large database, rather than step through each record looking at the county field, it will be quicker to sort all the counties in alphabetical order.

- ◉ **Ascending order** means: alphabetically from A to Z; numerically from zero to highest; and dates from earliest to most recent.

- ◉ **Descending order** means: alphabetically from Z to A; numerically from highest to zero; and dates from most recent to earliest.

1. Open the database and object.
2. Click anywhere in the field you want to sort.
3. Click the **Sort Ascending** button $\begin{smallmatrix}A\\Z\end{smallmatrix}\downarrow$ on the toolbar to sort the records based on ascending order of the selected field, or click the **Sort Descending** button $\begin{smallmatrix}Z\\A\end{smallmatrix}\downarrow$ to sort the records based on descending order of the selected field.

You will be prompted to save the sorted object when you close it. A sort is usually a temporary means of providing information, so saving the reordered object is often unnecessary. You can always re-sort the data if you need the information again.

Note

Sorting records based on a field in a query results table is no different from sorting within a table, except, of course, the query results might only show a subset of the table records, depending on the query.

When you sort records based on a field in a form, you will only see the results of the sort by stepping through the records using the record selector.

Note

The toolbar will be different depending on the selected object. However, the sort buttons appear on them all.

Do it!

1. Open the database **Music relationships.mdb**.
2. Open the table **AlbumTitles**.
3. Click anywhere in the **Release date** (field) column.
4. Click the **Sort Ascending** button to sort by release date.
5. Close the table without saving the changes.

An unsorted table

AlbumID	ArtistID	Album title	Number of tracks	Genre	Running time	Release date	Cost
CP5	CP01	A rush of Blood to t	11	Pop	0	01/11/2002	6.99
JB2	JB01	All the Lost Souls	10	Pop-acoustic ro	0	17/09/2007	8.98
KP1	KR01	Awkward Annie	12	Folk-pop	0	03/09/2007	8.98
AW2	AW01	Back to Back	11	Soul	0	30/10/2006	8.98
KT3	KT01	Drastic Fantastic	11	Folk-pop	0	10/09/2007	7.98
FF4	FF01	Echoes Silence Pa	13	Rock	0	24/09/2007	7.98
KW2	KW01	Graduation	14	Hiphop Rap	0	10/09/2007	8.98
NF1	NF01	Hand Built by Robc	17		0	30/07/2007	7.98
MK2	MK01	Kill to Get Crimson	12	Rock	0	17/09/2007	11.98
HF3	HF01	Once Upon a Time	11	Pop	0	03/09/2007	8.98
P38	P001	The Ultimate Collec	41	Classical	0	13/10/1997	8.97
							0.00

AlbumID	ArtistID	Album title	Number of tracks	Genre	Running time	Release date	Cost
P38	P001	The Ultimate Collec	41	Classical	0	13/10/1997	8.97
CP5	CP01	A rush of Blood to t	11	Pop	0	01/11/2002	6.99
AW2	AW01	Back to Back	11	Soul	0	30/10/2006	8.98
NF1	NF01	Hand Built by Robc	17		0	30/07/2007	7.98
KP1	KR01	Awkward Annie	12	Folk-pop	0	03/09/2007	8.98
HF3	HF01	Once Upon a Time	11	Pop	0	03/09/2007	8.98
KW2	KW01	Graduation	14	Hiphop Rap	0	10/09/2007	8.98
KT3	KT01	Drastic Fantastic	11	Folk-pop	0	10/09/2007	7.98
JB2	JB01	All the Lost Souls	10	Pop-acoustic ro	0	17/09/2007	8.98
MK2	MK01	Kill to Get Crimson	12	Rock	0	17/09/2007	11.98
FF4	FF01	Echoes Silence Pa	13	Rock	0	24/09/2007	7.98

The same table, sorted in ascending date order

Figure 5.17 Sorting a data field

Prove it!

Practise using the sort buttons on different fields within the objects of the **Music relationships** database. Do not save any of your sorted objects.

Test your understanding

① Why is the working area empty when you open Access?

② List the steps to open a database once you are in Access.

③ How do you know which is the active window?

④ How do you show hidden toolbars?

⑤ Can you create a new database without saving it?

⑥ Where can you find out more about a topic or an answer to a question about Access if you have Internet access?

⑦ How do you switch between database windows?

⑧ How do you delete a table, report, form or query?

⑨ How do you sort records in a table?

⑩ The toolbar sort buttons are labelled A–Z and Z–A. How do you sort numerical data?

You can find the answers to the questions on the CD-ROM saved as **Answers to TYU questions 5.2**. How did you do? Go back over anything that you are unsure about.

Tables

Records

The output (information returned) from a database is only as good as the data held in the database. This means that the table design, the records in the tables, and the data in the tables all need to be correct. If the data is wrong, then the information will be wrong.

For example, if you queried a customer database for all the orders placed in February 2008, but the dates had been typed in carelessly and contained errors, then the query results would be useless.

It is also important to keep the data held in the tables up to date (e.g. addresses).

Here are three common reasons for deleting data in a database.
- The product no longer exists.
- The data has been duplicated.
- The data is out of date.

Manipulating records and data in records (5.3.1.1–2)

Data can be amended in, added to or deleted from a table.
1. Navigate to the record which contains the data you want to modify (see page 270).
2. Navigate to the field that contains the data you want to modify by using the keyboard arrow keys or tab key.
3. Click in the field to set the text insertion point and edit the data as required.

If the field is empty, you can type in data directly without having to edit the data already there.

Tip!

If you can see the data you want to edit or delete, you can click it directly to set the text insertion point, without having to step through other fields to get to it.

Note

Remember that a database is simply a repository for data. So long as data is in the correct field, then the order of the records does not matter.

Note

You cannot delete a record if it contains related records in another table in a relationship.

- Delete data in a field by using the **Delete** or **Backspace** key as appropriate. To delete all the data in a field, press **Delete** when the whole field is highlighted.

- To delete a whole record, click the the grey square ▭ to the left of the record. The whole record will be highlighted. Press **Delete**.

- A new record is effectively a new set of fields, so the data can be added in the empty record row marked ✳ at the bottom of the existing data. An **AutoNumber** field will be updated if it has been included in the table. If it is the primary key, the updated number will be the next unused one (see page 256). If a field has been set as primary key, and is not **AutoNumber**, you must add data to that field.

Click a grey box to select a record

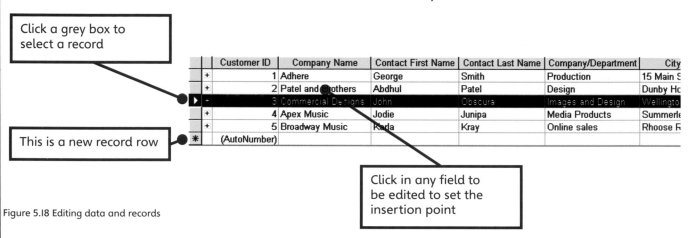

This is a new record row

Click in any field to be edited to set the insertion point

Figure 5.18 Editing data and records

Warning!

If you try to delete data by deleting the contents of each cell only, you will still be left with the record and a series of empty cells. You must delete a whole record or amend the data in a cell and not leave empty records.

Do it!

1. Open **Client database**.
2. Open the **CustomerDetails** table.
3. Place the insertion point in the **Company Name** field of record **2**.
4. Delete **and**, so the new name reads **Patel Brothers**.
5. Add the following data as a new record.

Field name	Data
Company Name	Way out!
Contact First Name	Demetrius
Contact Last Name	Petros
Company/Department	Owner
City	Athens
Country	Greece
Contact Title	Mr
Notes	Add shipping costs and allow 3 weeks for delivery

Table design

You have already learned about the importance of planning when designing a database structure. You need to decide:

- ◉ the type of data to be input into the table
- ◉ the field names (headings) for each column in a table
- ◉ the formatting (properties) for each data type
- ◉ which fields must contain data
- ◉ the rules you need to apply and where to apply them (e.g. no duplicates)
- ◉ any indexes you need
- ◉ which field in each table will be unique in order to assign a primary key.

Changing data types and field properties after data has been entered (5.3.2.4)

It is important to spend time planning the design and structure of a database and the tables within it. It will help avoid wasted time and possibly frustration later! If a database structure is not created properly you might find that data is lost or appears in the wrong format. For example, numbers such as currency or dates will not perform as correctly if the **Text** data type is used. If insufficient storage space has been provided for text, then not all the data can be input. It is usual practice to plan the database and its components (tables, forms, reports and queries) and structure on paper. You should also keep a record of the data types and properties you have used in the design so you can refer to them when designing other tables that might be needed to create a relationship.

Once data has been entered, any design changes can have major consequences that affect how the database works (e.g. links to other tables may be broken if the field size of one is changed, or existing data might be lost if field lengths are altered).

Create a named table and specify fields with their data types and properties (5.3.2.1–2)

Now it's your turn! Up to now you've been learning a lot of database theory and practising by using databases given to you. Now you are going to design your own database.

You are going to create a table to hold records of fitness instructors in the Fitness Centre in your town. You have suggested that information about the fitness instructors can be found much more quickly and accurately if they have a database. They have asked you to design this.

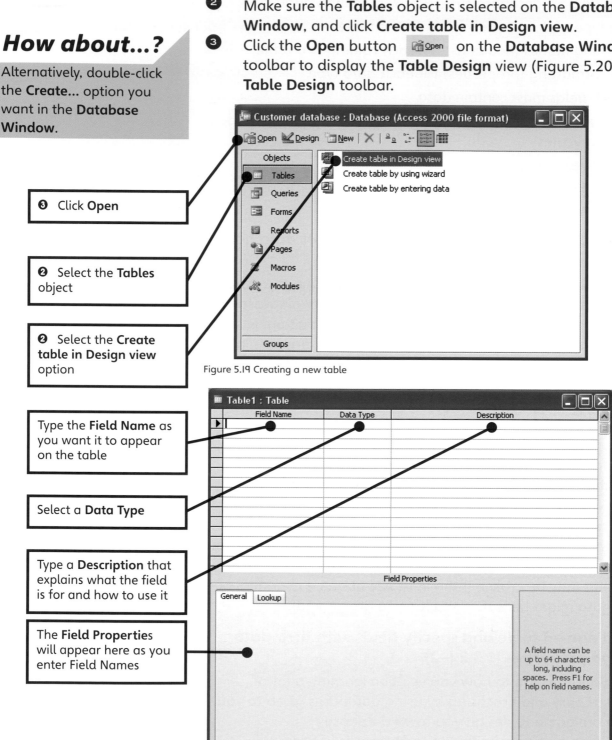

① Open **Access** and create a new database. Save the database as **Fitness records.mdb**. (See page 262 to remind yourself how to create and save a new database.)

② Make sure the **Tables** object is selected on the **Database Window**, and click **Create table in Design view**.

③ Click the **Open** button [🔓 Open] on the **Database Window** toolbar to display the **Table Design** view (Figure 5.20) and **Table Design** toolbar.

How about...?

Alternatively, double-click the **Create...** option you want in the **Database Window**.

❸ Click **Open**

❷ Select the **Tables** object

❷ Select the **Create table in Design view** option

Figure 5.19 Creating a new table

Type the **Field Name** as you want it to appear on the table

Select a **Data Type**

Type a **Description** that explains what the field is for and how to use it

The **Field Properties** will appear here as you enter Field Names

Figure 5.20 The **Table Design** view for a new table

You are going to design a table with the following Field Names and structure.

Field Name	Data Type	Description	Properties
StaffID	Text	Unique reference	Use Field Size 10, required
FirstName	Text	Use title case	Use default
LastName	Text	Use title case	Use default
Fully Qualified	Yes/No	Must identify	Use default, required
Male	Yes/No	Tick box if Yes	Use default
Female	Yes/No	Tick box if Yes	Use default
Date Started	Date/Time	Date started at the centre	Use Medium Date

④ Click in the first **Field Name** box (where the insertion point is flashing), and type **StaffID**.

⑤ Click in the **Data Type** box to the right of the **StaffID** field name.

⑥ Access displays a **Text** data type for you. This is what you want.

⑦ Click in the **Description** box to the right of the **Data Type** box, and type **Unique reference**. Do not move the insertion point out of the **Description** box when you finish typing.

⑧ In the **Field Properties** panel at the bottom of the **Design View**, make sure that the **General tab** is selected.

⑨ The default **Field Size** property is set to **50**. Change this to **10**.

⑩ The default **Required** property is set to **No**. Change this to **Yes**. You can do this either by typing **Yes** in the text box, or by clicking the arrow on the right of the box and selecting **Yes** from the drop-down list.

⑪ Type the next two field names, with their data types and descriptions, into the next two rows of the **Design View**. You do not need to change the properties.

⑫ Type **Fully Qualified** as the **Field Name** in the fourth row of the **Design View**.

⑬ Move the insertion point into the **Data Type** box on its right.

⑭ Click the arrow on the right of the box, and select **Yes/No** from the list.

⑮ Change the field's **Required** property to **Yes**.

Note

You might ask why bother using a **Yes/No** field for both **Male** and **Female** when they are mutually exclusive (e.g. one box will be left blank as the instructor can only be male or female). This is because when you query your database, Access will 'know' that those cells that appear blank are actually indicating **No**.

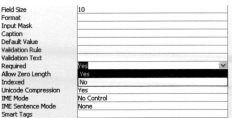

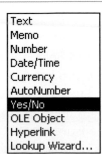

Figure 5.21 Ways to change the default

Setting a primary key (5.3.2.5)

Earlier (on page 256) you learned why a primary key is needed. Here you'll define the **StaffID** field as the primary key as this holds unique data.

❶ Click the **StaffID** field name.

❷ Click the **Primary Key** button on the **Table Design** toolbar.

A key symbol will appear to the left of the **Field Name**.

Adding a new field (5.3.2.7)

You realise that you need another field after **Fully Qualified** to show the number of years each instructor has been fully qualified. This will be a whole number of years, with **0** meaning that the instructor is not fully qualified.

❶ Click the field name **Male**.

❷ Click the **Insert Rows** button on the **Table Design** toolbar.

❸ A new row is inserted between the **Fully Qualified** and the **Male** fields.

❹ Type **Years Qualified** in the new **Field Name** box where the insertion point is flashing.

❺ Select the **Number** data type.

❻ Set the properties as **Integer** field size and **0** decimal places.

❼ Type the description **Enter 0 if not fully qualified**.

Creating validation rules (5.3.2.3)

Validation rules ensure that data typed into a table matches certain criteria. For example, it may be crucial that a membership fee, defined as a **Currency** data type, matches one of two values (perhaps for adult membership and child membership). If a fee which is different from these values is entered into the database, then an error is shown telling the person typing the data what is wrong and how to put it right.

The Fitness Centre opened at the beginning of the Millennium, therefore none of the instructors could have started before the

How about...?

Alternatively, right-click and select **Insert Rows** from the shortcut menu that is displayed.

Note

Important

Setting a **validation rule** is **not** the same as setting a field property as **Required**.

A **validation rule** constrains the data to certain values or formats.

A **required** field (such as those you have set for the **StaffID** and **Fully Qualified** fields in your table) ensures that a field always contains data (i.e. it cannot be left empty).

year 2000. Any date entered that shows a start date earlier than I January 2000 is obviously wrong.

You also think that it is unlikely that an instructor will have been fully qualified for more than 50 years, so you want to prevent anybody typing a number greater than this into the table.

1 Click in the **Date Started** field row.

2 In the **Field Properties** section of the **Design View**, click in the **Validation Rule** box, and type >#31/12/1999#.

This is the Access way of saying that the date must be greater than 31 December 1999. The > symbol means **greater than**. (The < symbol means **less than**.) Dates must be surrounded by the # symbol.

3 Now click in the **Validation Text** box, and type **Cannot be earlier than I January 2000**.

This is the message that will appear if an invalid date is entered.

Format	Medium Date
Input Mask	
Caption	
Default Value	
Validation Rule	>#31/12/1999#
Validation Text	Cannot be earlier than 1 January 2000
Required	No
Indexed	No
IME Mode	No Control
IME Sentence Mode	None
Smart Tags	

Figure 5.22 A **Validation Rule** and **Text** in the Field Properties

Prove it!

Enter the validation rule for the number of years an instructor has been qualified. Enter suitable validation text as an error message. You can check to see if you have set the rule correctly by opening the **Fitness records 2** database on the CD-ROM, and inspecting the table's **Design View**.

Indexing a field (5.3.2.6)

On page 256 you were introduced to the concept of indexing, and learned how it is useful in large databases for speeding up searches.

You use the **Indexed** box in the **Field Properties** section of the **Design View** to set indexing.

Indexing can allow or disallow duplication.

A primary key field, by definition, is unique, so indexing is set automatically as **Yes (No Duplicates)**. The **Yes (Duplicates OK)** index setting might be used to index a field that contains names.

Field Size	50
Format	
Input Mask	
Caption	
Default Value	
Validation Rule	
Validation Text	
Required	No
Allow Zero Length	Yes
Indexed	No
Unicode Compression	No
IME Mode	Yes (Duplicates OK)
IME Sentence Mode	Yes (No Duplicates)
Smart Tags	

Figure 5.23 Setting indexing

Tip!

Use the Help system to find out more about the symbols used in validation rules.

Note

These validation rules are fairly simple examples. Rules can be written that are more complicated. For instance, in the Fitness Centre example, a rule could be written to ensure that the Years Qualified cannot be entered as more than 0 if the Fully Qualified box is unticked.

Note

Examples of other useful validation examples that use the < and > symbols are:

- **<#I/I/2000#** which requires every date to be before I January 2000, and

- **>50** which could be used to ensure that fees being entered are more than a specified amount (in this case £50 if the Data Type is Currency).

① Click in the **LastName** field row.
② In the **Field Properties** section of the **Design View**, click in the **Indexed** box.
③ Click the arrow on the right of the box and select **Yes (Duplicates OK)**.

Saving a table design

You've now spent a lot of time designing your table. You need to save it so you do not lose your work, and so that you can start to enter data into the table.

① Click the **Save** button 🖫 on the **Table Design** toolbar.
② Overwrite the suggested name that Access provides with **FitnessInstructorRecords**, and click **OK**.

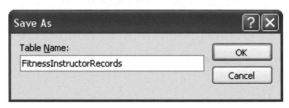

Figure 5.24 Saving a new table

Populating the table with data

You have now designed and saved a new table. Now you are going to enter some data. This is called **populating** the database.

① Click the **Datasheet View** button on the **Table Design** toolbar (as described on page 266).
② Type the following data into the fields so your table looks like this:

StaffID	FirstName	LastName	Fully Qualified	Years Qualified	Male	Female	Date started
FI001	Narinder	Kumur	☑	10	☑	☐	01-Jan-00
FI002	Justin	Stone	☐	0	☑	☐	15-Mar-07
FI003	Jasmine	Grant	☑	5	☐	☑	03-Jul-06
▶			☐	0	☐	☐	

Figure 5.25 Sample data for the Fitness Centre example

Changing table column width (5.3.2.8)

Sometimes you might find that the data does not fit neatly in the columns. You can adjust the width of a column as follows.

① Position the mouse pointer between two field headings so the cursor changes to a double-headed arrow.
② Click and hold down the left mouse button as you drag the mouse to the left or right.
③ Release the mouse button when the column width is correct.

Test your understanding

1. How do you delete a record?
2. Why do you need to delete the whole record instead of deleting data in a field?
3. How do you amend the data in a field?
4. What steps do you need to take when designing a database table?
5. How can you add a field to an existing table?
6. What might be the consequences of changing field sizes in an existing table?
7. How can you change field properties?
8. Why might you need to create a validation rule?
9. a) How do you change the width of a column?
   b) Describe the meaning of field size and explain how it is different from changing column width.
10. Which types of fields should have a primary key assigned to them?
11. When would you assign an index?

You can find the answers to the questions on the CD-ROM saved as **Answers to TYU questions 5.3**. How did you do? Go back over anything that you are unsure about.

Retrieving information

Learning objectives

By working through this lesson you will learn how to:
- ⊙ use the search command
- ⊙ apply a filter to and remove a filter from a table or a form
- ⊙ understand what a query is and how to create one
- ⊙ edit a query
- ⊙ run a query
- ⊙ print the results of a query
- ⊙ add criteria to a query using operators.

Searches and filters

Now comes the really exciting part! You are going to learn how to interrogate your database and really make it work for you.

Finding specific data (5.4.1.1)

Earlier you learned how to navigate a table or form using the record selector and keyboard (see page 270). If you are looking for specific data in a large database, this becomes unrealistic. Access has a **Find** command to speed up searches. It is similar to the **Find** command you might have used in other Microsoft Office applications.

(see page 270)

1. Click the **Find** button 🔍 on the toolbar showing for the table or form, to open the **Find and Replace** dialogue box.
2. Enter what you are looking for in the **Find What:** text box.
3. Select where you want to look for the data from the **Look In:** drop-down list.
4. Click the **Find Next** button to start the search.

Tip!

If you are at a particular record in a table or form, you can set the search to look only before or only after the current record. Set this in the **Search** list box.

Do it!

1. Open Access and the database **Fitness records 2** from the CD-ROM.
2. Open the table **FitnessInstructorRecords**.
3. Click anywhere in the **Last Name** (field) column.
4. Click the **Find Next** button on the **Database** toolbar.
5. Set the following search criteria to look for a record that shows an instructor who started in 2000. You don't know if the date has been entered as **2000** or as **00**, so you need to search any part of the field.   Continues...

How about...?

Alternatively, use **Ctrl+F** to open the **Find and Replace** dialogue box.

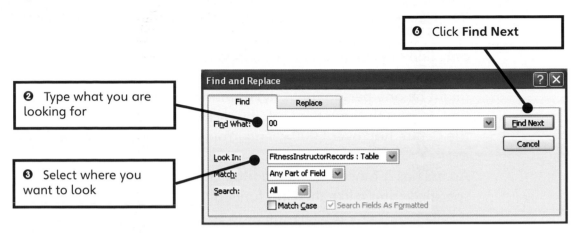

❻ Click **Find Next**

❷ Type what you are looking for

❸ Select where you want to look

Figure 5.26 Finding specific data

- ◉ Find What: **00**
- ◉ Look In: **FitnessInstructorRecords : Table**
- ◉ Match: **Any Part of Field**
- ◉ Search: **All**
- ◉ Match Case: **Unticked**
- ❻ Click **Find Next** a few times and watch the table. The text that matches the **00** criteria is highlighted. Notice that it includes the **00** in the **StaffID** number. If the table was very large, it would waste time to search for every occurrence of 00 even though you are interested only in the date.
- ❼ Click anywhere in the **Date started** column: the column you are interested in.
- ❽ Open the **Find and Replace** dialogue box again. It should show the search criteria you typed above.
- ❾ Change the **Look In:** box to show **Date started**. This restricts the search to this field only.
- ❿ Click **Find Next**. The date **00** is highlighted.
- ⓫ Click **Find Next** again. This time no more occurrences are found.

Prove it!

Open the **ClientRecords** table in the **Fitness records 2** database that is on the CD-ROM.

Practise using the **Find** command to search for:
- ◉ all the clients who pay **£20.00** for extra sessions
- ◉ all the clients who joined the Fitness Centre in **2006**
- ◉ all the clients who joined the Fitness Centre in **November of any year**
- ◉ **Carlene's** record.

Apply and remove a filter to a table or form (5.4.1.2–3)

You can quickly search for specific data (such as words, numbers or dates) using the **Find** command as described, but it will only find one result at a time. Suppose you want to find all the customers who come into a Fitness Centre on Thursdays. There might be one person (unlikely) or many. It would take too much time to step through the table by clicking the **Find Next** button if the Centre had over 1,000 clients. You would have to count them too!

Access has a function called a **filter** that performs a search on specified criteria like the **Find** function, but shows all the matching results together – it filters the data so you see only the data you want. A filter can be used with a table or a form. The results can be saved and printed, but a filter's power is that it is easy to apply for quick, perhaps one-off, searches. A **query** (see page 285) is better for more complicated and often repeated searches.

To apply a filter by selection

1. Open the database table or form you want to filter.
2. Click in a field that contains the data you want to filter for.
3. Click the **Filter By Selection** button ▼ on the toolbar.

The table or form immediately shows only the records that contain the example you selected.

4. Click the **Remove Filter** button ▼ to display the whole table or form once more.

To apply a filter by form

1. Open the database table or form you want to filter.
2. Click the **Filter By Form** button ▼ on the toolbar.
3. Type what you want to filter for in the blank table or form that appears.
4. Click the **Apply Filter** button ▼ .
5. Click the **Remove Filter** button ▼ to display the whole table or form once more.

Tip!

If you cannot see the data you want to filter for, then use the **Find** function to find the first occurrence.

Note

When you click the **Remove Filter** button, it toggles to become the **Apply Filter** button ▼ . You can click this to reapply the filter criterion you originally set.

Tip!

When filtering by form, you can click the arrow on the right-hand side of the field to show a list of the different data items in the field. Select one of them to filter by.

Tip!

The number of records that match a filter criterion are displayed in the record selector.

Do it!

1. Open Access and the database **Fitness records 2** if it is not already open.
2. Open the table **ClientRecords**.
3. Click anywhere in a field containing FI002.
4. Click the **Filter By Selection** button to show only the records with **FI002**.
5. Click the **Remove Filter** button to show the whole table again.

Queries

Extract and analyse (5.4.2.1)

Throughout this module you have been slowly introduced to the database query, learning that it is a tool used to find information from a database. Information can be found from single tables or from related tables. You can even query a query!

If you have a question that you are likely to repeatedly ask, then building a query that can be saved means you can get the answer more quickly and consistently. Each time you want to ask the question you simply run the query. You will get a different answer if the data being used in the query has changed since it was last run. Here is a scenario showing when a query might be used.

Imagine that you run an online secondhand book store. You keep details of all your books on a database. You keep data in fields that tell you, among other things, the title, the author, the publisher, the category, where you have shelved it, the selling price, how much it cost you, date sold etc.

When you sell a book, you update the database accordingly.

Being so well organised, you keep track of the financial side of your business as well. At the end of each week you like to know the number of books that have sold in each category, and how much money each category of book has taken. You also want to know which category of book makes the most profit.

All the data needed to tell you these things is in the database. You use a query as the best way to repeatedly get the information, rather than use searches, filters, and pen and paper each week!

Create, run and save a named single-table query (5.4.2.2/9)

The scenario above is quite complicated, so to demonstrate how to build and run a query you are going to use a simpler requirement: your boss wants a list that shows which instructors are fully qualified.

Before building a
query, write down what
questions you need to
ask, then list the fields
and tables that you will
use.

Selecting the tables to be used in a query

① Open the **Fitness records 2** database.

② Select **Queries**.

③ Select **Create query in Design view**.

④ The **Show Table** dialogue box is displayed.

⑤ Select the **Tables** tab if it is not already selected.

The **Show Table** dialogue box shows all the tables in the
database.

⑥ Select the table **FitnessInstructorRecords** and click the **Add**
button. The table is added to the grey panel at the top of
the **Query Builder** window.

⑦ Click the **Close** button on the **Show Table** dialogue box
when you have added all the tables you require.

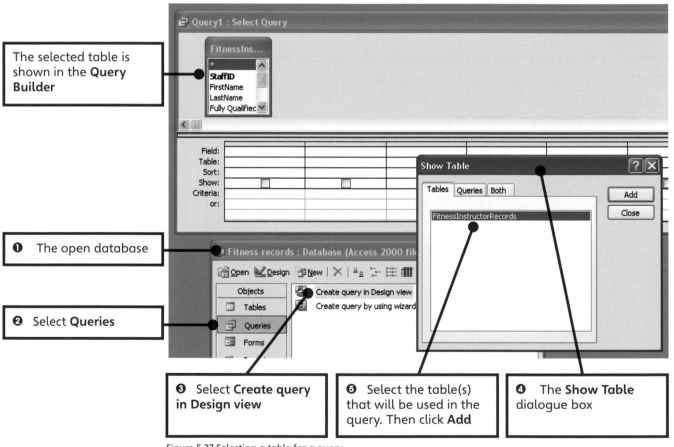

The selected table is
shown in the **Query
Builder**

❶ The open database

❷ Select **Queries**

❸ Select **Create query
in Design view**

❺ Select the table(s)
that will be used in the
query. Then click **Add**

❹ The **Show Table**
dialogue box

Figure 5.27 Selecting a table for a query

Selecting the fields to be used in a query

Note

If more than one table is
listed in the **Show Table**
dialogue box, you will
need to add all the tables
that are relevant to your
query.

◉ Double-click each field name in the table representation in
the **Query Builder**. (Scroll down to make sure you select all
field names.)

The field names are added to the next empty column in the **Field:**
row in the bottom half of the **Query Builder**. The table where
each selected field is located is shown in the **Table:** row.

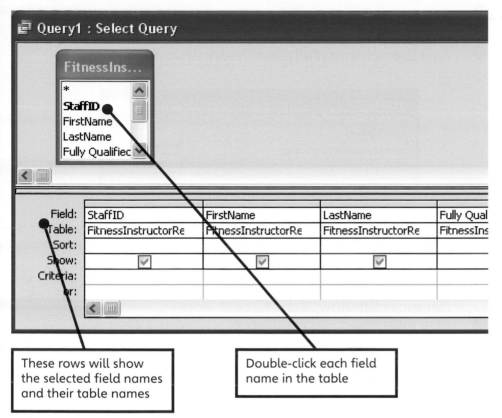

Tip!

To delete a table from the **Query Builder**, click it to select it, then press **Delete**.

These rows will show the selected field names and their table names

Double-click each field name in the table

Figure 5.28 Selecting the fields to be used in a query

How about...?

Alternatively, you can drag and drop the field name into the **Field:** row, or select the field from the drop-down list that appears if you click the arrow on the right-hand side of the **Field:** row boxes.

Setting the query criteria

As explained, it is possible to build queries that involve many complex criteria to produce a result. However, you have been asked to build a simple query that uses only one criterion to give information – the results must only show instructors who are fully qualified.

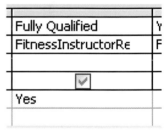

Figure 5.29 Building a simple query

⦿ Type **Yes** in the **Criteria:** row under the field name **Fully Qualified**.

Running and saving a query

Once you have built the query by defining the tables, fields and criteria that will be used, you need to run it to show the results. You could save your query now and then run it from the **Database Window**, or you can run it first to see the results.

Note

You need to type **Yes** as the criterion even though you didn't type **Yes** into the table – you ticked a box instead. This is because the underlying **Data Type** is **Yes/No**.

❶ Click the **Run** button 🔴 on the **Query Design** toolbar. The results are displayed. They show two records meeting the criterion that the instructor is fully qualified.

	StaffID	FirstName	LastName	Fully Qualified	Years Qualified	Male	Female	Date started
	FI001	Narinder	Kumur	☑	10	☑	☐	01-Jan-00
	FI003	Jasmine	Grant	☑	5	☐	☑	03-Jul-06
▶				☐	0	☐	☐	

Figure 5.30 The query results

❷ Click the **Save** button 💾 on the toolbar to show the **Save As** dialogue box.

❸ Type the name **qryFullyQualifiedInstructors** and click **OK**.

Figure 5.31 Saving a query

Print the result of a query (5.6.2.4)

Often you will want a printout of the results of a query.

❶ Open the query **qryFullyQualifiedInstructors** from the **Database Window**, if it is not still open.

❷ Click **Print...** on the **File** menu to display the **Print** dialogue box.

Here you can set:

- the printer you want to print to
- the range of pages or records you want to print
- the number of copies you want to print.

❸ Set the print options you want, and click **OK**.

❹ Close the query.

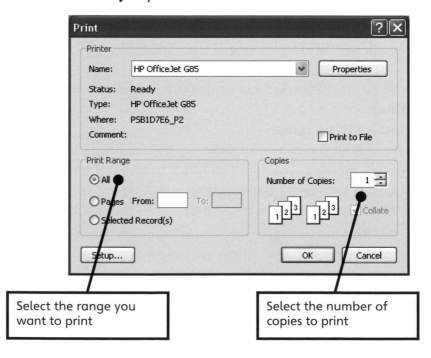

Select the range you want to print

Select the number of copies to print

Figure 5.32 Printing a query

Creating a named two-table query (5.4.2.3)

You can build queries that interrogate two or more tables. This is particularly useful in a relational database in that you can combine data from the tables related to each other.

Your boss now asks you to provide a list of clients the different instructors have on different days of the week. Your boss wants the list sorted by instructors' names.

1 Open the **Fitness records 2** database if it is not already open.

2 Select **Queries**.

3 Select **Create query in Design view**.

4 Add both tables in the **Show Table** dialogue box to the **Query Builder**.

To build a query that meets the requirements you decide that you will need the results to show the following fields.

◉ **FirstName** and **LastName** from the **FitnessInstructorRecords** table.

◉ **FirstName**, **LastName** and **Day of visit** from the **ClientRecords**.

5 Fill the **Field:** and **Table:** rows in the bottom half of the **Query Builder** with these fields and tables, respectively.

6 Your boss has asked for the instructor names to be sorted, so click in the **Sort:** box in the **LastName** column for the **FitnessInstructorRecords** table.

7 Click **Ascending** from the drop-down list that appears when you click the arrow on the right of the box.

Note

The link between the two tables shows they are related and the type of relationship.

A query could be built using two unlinked tables, but the query results would not be based on a relationship between the tables.

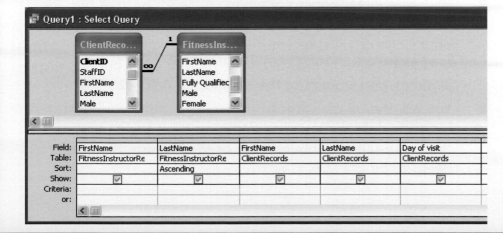

Figure 5.33 A query based on two tables

8 Run the query.

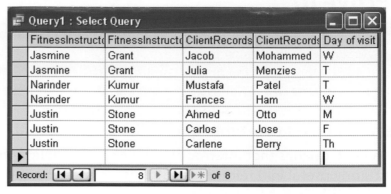

Figure 5.34 The query result from two tables

9 Save as **qryFitnessInstructorsAllocatedToClients** and close it.

Querying with operators (5.4.2.4–5)

Where dates or numbers are stored in a database you can design a query to find all numbers that are equal, smaller, greater or even a mixture such as greater than or equal to.

To give such an instruction requires the use of **operators**. You have already met two operators (< and >) on page 279. One example might be to find all those clients who joined the Fitness Centre in 2006 or since that date. The operators you need to know are on the left.

Operator	Symbol
Equal to	=
Not equal to	<>
Less than	<
Less than or equal to	<=
Greater than	>
Greater than or equal to	>=

So, in the **qryFitnessInstructorsAllocatedToClients** example, if you wanted the results to show every day except for Wednesday, you would include the criterion **<>"W"** in the **Day of visit** column of the **Query Builder**. This could also be achieved using the logical **NOT** operator.

You also need to know two other logical operators: **AND** and **OR**.

⦿ You use the **AND** operator when you want **both** of two (or **all** of more than two) criteria to be satisfied – in other words all the criteria must be satisfied. For example, if you want to find clients who had visited more than 10 times but less than 20 times, you would use the criteria **>10 AND <20**.

⦿ You use the **OR** operator when any one of the criteria stated is matched. In the query example we have been using, to display results for only Tuesday **or** Wednesday, the query needs to be **="T" OR ="W"**.

Note

If you state criteria in more than one field, you are using **AND**. For example, **Yes** in the **Male** field, **>350** in the **Membership fee** field, will only find records that match **both**.

Let's find all the clients who have visited more than **20** times, and who paid more than **£15** per extra session.

❶ Build a query using the **ClientRecords** table of the **Fitness records 2** database, and the **LastName, No of visits used** and **£ per extra session fields** from the table.

The crucial word in this requirement is **and**, so this means that you will need to type the criteria in the appropriate columns of the **Criteria:** row.

❷ Type **>20** as the **No of visits used** criterion.

❸ Type **>15** as the **£ per extra session** criterion.

They are on the same line so the two criteria are ANDed.

Field:	LastName	No of visits used	£ per extra session
Table:	ClientRecords	ClientRecords	ClientRecords
Sort:			
Show:	☑	☑	☑
Criteria:		>20	>15
or:			

Figure 5.35 Building an AND query with 'greater than' operators

❹ Run the query.

❺ Save the query as **qryBigSpenders**.

Prove it!

Your boss now asks you to query the database to find all the clients who are entitled to either 30 or 40 visits. Try building the query two ways. There are two ways to enter the criteria. Try both and compare the results – they should be the same!

By now you should realise how powerful queries are, and how they make databases so useful at providing information.

Wildcard (5.4.2.6)

There is one final technique to help you use queries and searches. It is the use of **wildcards**. A wildcard is a symbol that represents a series of data.

Suppose you want to find out how many clients joined in a particular year, say **2007**. However, the **Date Joined** field does not show only 2007, so you use a wildcard to represent the characters before 2007. This is represented by an asterisk: *. The * represents any character or any number of characters. In this example you would type the criterion *2007 in the **Date Joined** field.

How about...?

Alternatively, the same result for the **OR** operator can be achieved by typing the criteria on separate lines in the field column.

In the example, you would type **T** in the **Criteria:** box of the **Day of visit** column, and **W** in the **or:** box below it in the same column.

Note

When you type letters as a criterion, they need to be in quotes (" "). Access automatically adds these.

Tip!

Where a query uses a number of criteria it is sensible to build the query in stages and test as you go along. It is harder to spot an error if you apply all the criteria at one time.

Warning!

You must replicate (copy) the exact way your data is entered into your database table as the criteria for searching. For example, if you type in **Thursday** when the table shows the data as **Th**, it will not be found. The search uses pattern matching to locate data. It cannot read!

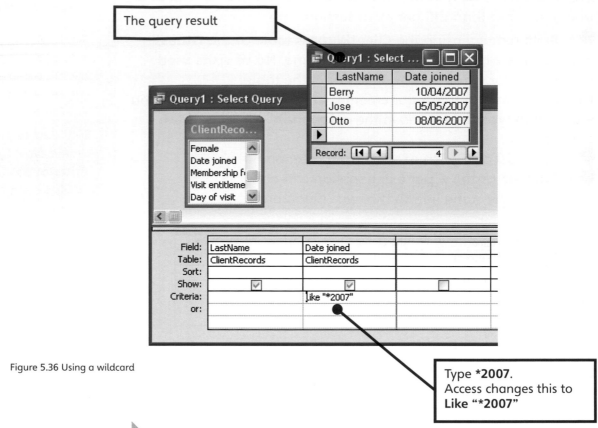

The query result

Type ***2007**.
Access changes this to
Like "*2007"

Figure 5.36 Using a wildcard

Prove it!

Now use the same method to find all the clients who joined in **November**. There is a worked copy of this query on the CD-ROM saved as **qryAllClientsJoinedNov**.

Here are the wildcards you need to know.

Wildcard	Meaning
*	The asterisk is used to replace **all** characters in a continuous **string**, for example where the data all exists in one field: first line of an address where you want to find all the **streets** or a date where you want to find all the **March** dates.
%	The percent symbol is used to locate zero or more characters in that position. For example, if you want to find all staff in an organisation whose names start with **Mc** or end in **th** by inputting into the criteria field **Mc%** or **%th**.
?	The question mark is used to replace **one** character. For example, if you wanted to find **Ahmed** but you weren't sure of the spelling, you could input on the criteria row **a?med** and the query would locate **Ahmed** and any other names where the **h** had not been specified.
_	The underscore is used to find one character at that position. For example, if you wanted to find all the staff in an organisation with the first name of **Jan, Jon, Jen** the criteria would read **J_n**. This would not find any longer names such as **Jenny, Jonathan, Janice**.

Editing query criteria (5.4.2.7)

You can alter (edit) a query and save it as another query. You can change the query criteria and/or change the tables and fields the query is using. This means that if you already have a query that is similar to the new query you want, you can open it, edit it, then save it with a new name. Of course, being able to edit a query is also useful if it doesn't do what you expect and you need to correct any errors.

1 Open the **Fitness records 2** database if it is not already open.

2 Create a query using the **ClientRecords** table that finds the first and last names of clients who have visited **21 or more** times. Also include the **Visit entitlement** field.

3 Save the query as **qryClients21MoreVisits**.

4 Run the query to check the results and close the query.

5 Open the query in **Design View** from the **Database Window**.

6 Click in the **Criteria:** box for the **No of visits used** to place the insertion point.

7 Edit the criteria so that it will now find the clients who have visited **less than 21** times.

8 Run the query to check the results, and use **Save As** to save it as **qryClients21LessVisits**.

9 Click in the **Criteria:** box for the **No of visits used** to place the insertion point.

10 Use the **Backspace** or **Delete** keys to delete the criterion <21.

11 Click in the **Criteria:** box for **Visit entitlement** to place the insertion point.

12 Type >=15 AND <35.

13 Run the query to check the results, and save it as **qryClientsAndVisit**.

Do not close the database.

Editing query fields (5.4.2.8)

Sometimes when you edit a query you might need to do more than edit the criteria. For example, you might have included fields that are not used, or forgotten to include a field that is vital for giving you the correct information. Fields can be added to and removed from a query. They can also be moved so the results show the fields in the order you want them.

Let's suppose that you do not want to show the clients' first names, but you think it might be useful to keep the field in the **Query Builder**. You need to hide the field from the results.

1 Open **qryClientsAndVisit** in the **Design View**.

2 Click the tick box in the **Show:** row of the **FirstName** column to remove the tick.

> **Tip!**
>
> You are starting to collect quite a few queries in your database. Remember to use names that identify what the query does otherwise you might not be able to find it easily without running them first. Some large databases might have many hundreds of queries!

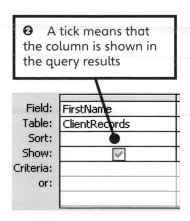

Figure 5.37 Show/hide a field column

How about...?

❶ Alternatively, move the mouse pointer over the thin grey bar at top of the field column until the cursor changes to the small black down-pointing arrow.

❷ Click.

The whole column is selected (it appears black).

❸ Press the **Delete** key.

Tip!

You can remove and move columns in the query results in the same way as in the **Query Builder**. The underlying data table is unaffected.

❸ Run the query. You will see the **FirstName** field is no longer displayed.

Seeing the query result without this field, you decide that you might as well delete it completely from the results.

❹ Open the **Query Builder** again and click anywhere in the **FirstName** column.

❺ Click **Delete Columns** on the **Edit** menu. The field is deleted.

❻ Save the query.

Now you want to add the **Day of visit** field to the **Query Builder**. You do this in exactly the same way as you did when you first added the other fields.

❼ Double-click **Day of visit** in the **ClientRecords** table representation in the top half of the **Query Builder**.

The field is added to the next available column in the **Query Builder**. If you run the query you will see that this is the position it will be in the results. You want to move it so that it appears as the second column (i.e. just to the right of the **LastName** column).

❽ Select the **Day of visit** column as described in **steps I** and **2** of the **How about...?** box on the left.

❾ With the cursor showing as a white left-pointing up arrow, click the top of the selected column and keep the mouse button held down while dragging the mouse to the left.

As you drag a bold vertical line will show you the new position that you have moved the column to.

❿ When the bold line is just to the right of the **LastName** column, release the mouse button. The column will be repositioned.

⓫ Run the query, save it and close the database.

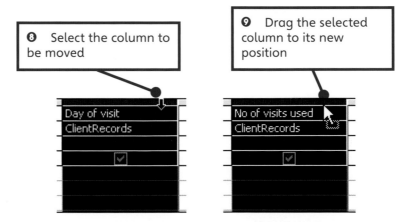

Figure 5.38 Moving a column in the **Query Builder**

Test your understanding

1. Which function can be used to search for a specific word, number or date in a field?
2. a) Which search functions can be saved?
   b) Which search function would you use if you needed to do the same search many times?
3. How do you read the results of a search in a form?
4. How do you know how many records have been found when searching in a form?
5. How do you remove the search function from a table or a form?
6. Describe what a query does.
7. Why go to the bother of designing a query when a filter or the find function will give the information?
8. How can you get information from more than one table at the same time?
9. What is a logical operator? Give some examples.
10. What are criteria?
11. How can an existing query be used to create another query if the two are similar but both required?
12. Why is it important to give queries meaningful names that explain what they actually do?
13. How can an edited query be adapted to include extra or fewer fields?
14. When would a query need to include any fields that are not needed to be seen?
15. What does the term run mean?
16. What would happen to a record if it was deleted in a query result table?

You can find the answers to the questions on the CD-ROM saved as **Answers to TYU questions 5.4**. How did you do? Go back over anything that you are unsure about.

Forms

The purpose of a form (5.5.1.1)

This lesson is entirely about the form object. You were introduced to forms on page 264.

◉ A form provides a structured way of entering data into tables or of displaying information using queries etc. that is more user-friendly than a table.

◉ The user of a form can be prevented from making changes to the underlying table structure. The form can be designed so the user can only enter data into allowed fields. Similarly, only data that is permitted for a particular user might be displayed on the form.

Create and name a form (5.5.1.2)

Each form is made up of a number of elements. The purpose and position of these on a form need to be specifed, so designing a form 'from scratch' is not only time-consuming but can also be quite difficult at first. However, to help you, Access provides a **Wizard** which takes you step by step through the process.

❶ Open the **Fitness records 2** database.
❷ Select the **Forms** object from the **Database Window**.
❸ Open **Create form by using wizard**.
❹ Check the data source to be used in the form in the **Tables/Queries** list box. There is only one table in this database, so you will see **Table: FitnessInstructorRecords**.

You now need to select the fields that will be used on your form.

❺ Click a field you want to use in the **Available Fields:** pane and then click ⟩ to move it across to the **Selected Fields:** pane. Move all the fields across.

Tip!

You can build a form using other objects. For instance, if the form already has queries, and you want to base a form on one of them, you would select one in the **Tables/Queries** list box.

Tip!

You can select all the fields in one go by clicking the ⟩⟩ button.

Note

You can move fields into the **Selected Fields:** pane in any order.

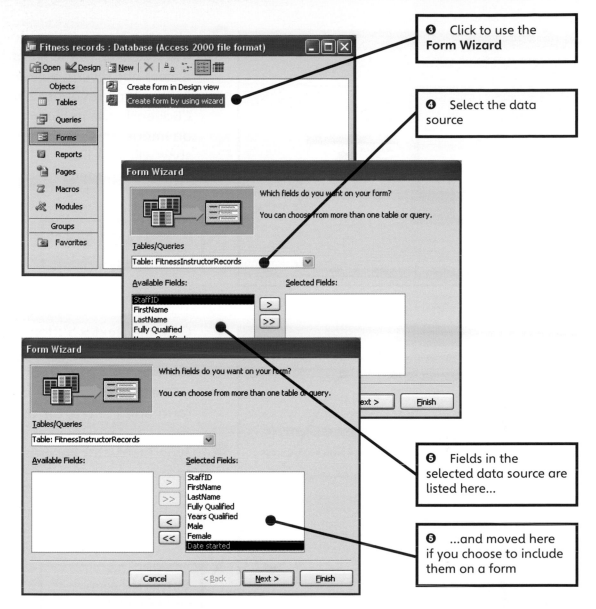

③ Click to use the **Form Wizard**

④ Select the data source

⑤ Fields in the selected data source are listed here...

⑤ ...and moved here if you choose to include them on a form

Figure 5.39 Selecting fields in the **Form Wizard**

⑥ Click the **Next >** button to display the layout step of the wizard.
Access has several built-in form layouts to help you. Click the radio buttons by each layout to see an image of what the finished form will look like.
⑦ Select **Justified**.

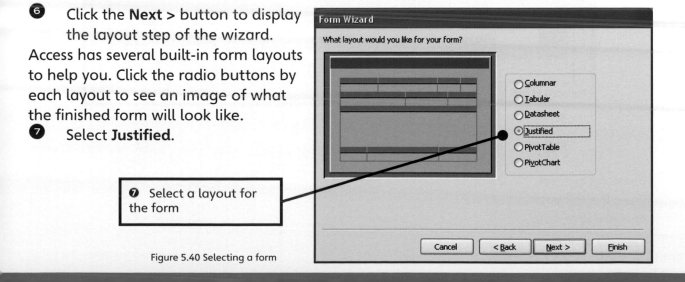

⑦ Select a layout for the form

Figure 5.40 Selecting a form

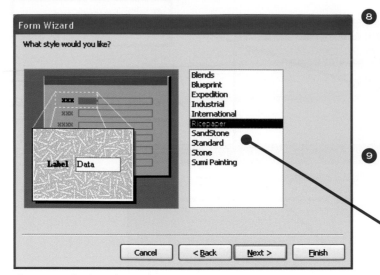

Figure 5.41 Selecting a form style

⑧ Click the **Next >** button to display the style step of the wizard. Access has several built-in styles for the form layout to help you. Click each one in the panel to see an image of what the finished style will look like.

⑨ Select **Ricepaper**.

> ❾ Select a style for the form

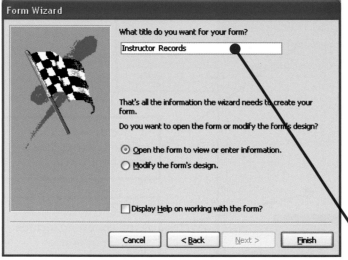

Figure 5.42 Giving the form a title

⑩ Click the **Next >** button to display the final step in the wizard. The name of your report is the name that will appear on the form and the one the user will see.

⑪ Type **Instructor Records** (with a space as it is more user-friendly for a title).

⑫ Click the **Finish** button to view the form you have just created.

> ⑪ Type the name as it will appear on the form

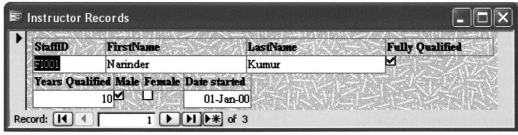

Figure 5.43 The completed form

Tip!

If the headings are not fully visible it is because your columns have not been widened in your table.

Prove it!

The Fitness Centre has asked you to create a form for a member of staff to input data into the client records. They will be only entering personal details and not information about fees. Produce a form based on the **ClientRecords** table with the following fields in the order given:

> **FirstName**
> **LastName**
> **Client notes**
> **Date joined**
> **Male**
> **Female**
> **Day of visit**

Save the form as **Client Personal Details**.

Use a form to insert new records (5.5.I.3) and delete records (5.5.I.4)

A form can be used to edit, delete and add new records. You are going to use the **Client Personal Details** form you have created above to add a new record.

❶   Display the **Client Personal Details** form.

❷   Click the **Insert New Record** button ▶✳ on the **recorder selector**. There are eight existing records. Clicking this button creates an empty ninth record.

❸   Type the following into the appropriate spaces on the form.

◉   FirstName: **Axel**

◉   LastName: **Seraph**

◉   Client notes: **Training for tiddlywink competition**

◉   Date joined: **27/04/08**

◉   Male: **Yes**

◉   Day of visit: **Th**

❹   Click the **record selector** to move on one record, and close the form.

❺   Open the **ClientRecords** table to see the new record.

You are told this record is a hoax and needs to be deleted.

❻   Close the **ClientRecords** table and reopen the **Client Personal Details** form.

❼   Use the record selector to display the new record you've just added.

❽   Click **Delete Record** on the **Edit** menu.

❾   You will be asked if you want to delete the record. Click **Yes**.

How about...?

Alternatively, you can click the **Delete Record** toolbar button ▶✕ .

There are many reasons why the data you type into a form can result in an error message. Some common ones are these.

- The field has an **AutoNumber** data type.
- The field is protected to stop it being changed.
- The field has a validation rule assigned to it which you have broken.

Similarly, if you forget to fill in a field that has the **Required** property, you will be prompted to do so.

Use a form to enter, modify and delete data in a record (5.5.1.5)

In the same way as you created a new record and added data in the previous section, you can use a form to change existing records. You can modify existing data, add new data that has become available into empty fields, or delete the data already there. As you can imagine, it is usual for a database to have some protection so that accidents or malicious acts cannot compromise the usefulness of the data.

1. Open the form you need.
2. Navigate to the records that show the data you want to add or modify.
3. Click in the box containing the data to set the insertion point.
4. Either:

- edit the data currently in the box
- delete the data currently in the box, or
- type new data in an empty box.

Prove it!

Open the **Instructor Records** form you created earlier. **Jasmine Grant** has just got married. Change her surname to **Walker**.

Form headers and footers (5.5.1.6)

Form headers and footers are similar to headers and footers on documents and spreadsheets in that the text they hold appears on every record of the screen form. For example, it is particularly helpful to have a header that shows a clear title.

Headers and footers can only be modified in the form's **Design View**, so they cannot be accidentally deleted by the user of the form.

1. Open the **Fitness records 2** database if it is not already open.
2. Open the **Instructor Records** form in **Design View**.
3. If they are not already showing, drag the borders of the **Form Design View** window so the header and footer bars are clearly visible.
4. Drag the header and footer borders to reveal the header and footer areas.

Form headers/footers appear on screen.

Page headers/footers appear on printed forms.

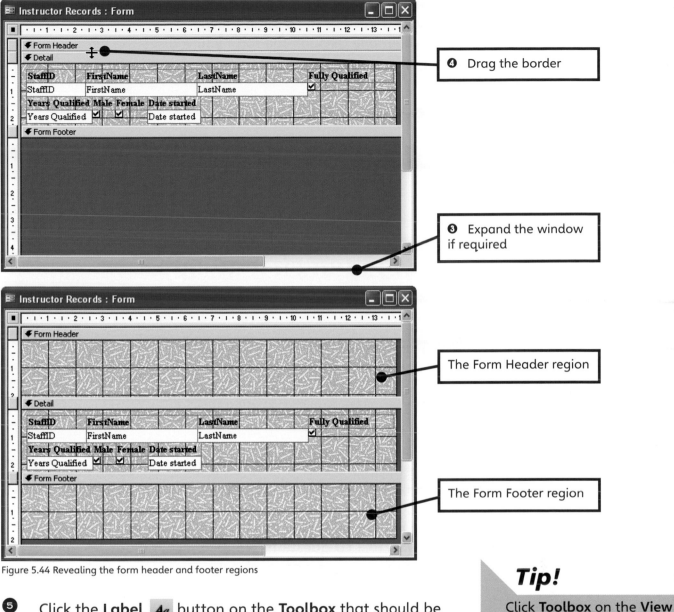

Figure 5.44 Revealing the form header and footer regions

❹ Drag the border

❸ Expand the window if required

The Form Header region

The Form Footer region

Tip!

Click **Toolbox** on the **View** menu if the **Toolbox** is hidden.

❺ Click the **Label** 𝐀𝒶 button on the **Toolbox** that should be showing.

❻ Click in the top left of the **Form Header** area and drag out a text box.

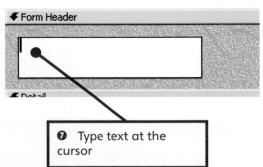

❻ Drag out a text box

❼ Type text at the cursor

Figure 5.45 Creating a header text box

7 Type **Fitness Instructor Records** in the label box.

8 Save and close the **Design View**.

When you move through the form you will see the header and footer on every record.

Prove it!

Follow the steps above to place the form footer **Fitness is our game!** at the bottom of the screen form.

Test your understanding

1. How can a record be deleted in a form?
2. How can records be added to a form?
3. How can records be amended in a form?
4. What is the quickest way to move between records in a form?
5. What is a form header?
6. How can a form header be modified?

You can find the answers to the questions on the CD-ROM saved as **Answers to TYU questions 5.5**. How did you do? Go back over anything that you are unsure about.

Reports

The purpose of a report (5.6.l.l)

This lesson is entirely about the report object. You were introduced to reports on page 264. Here you will learn how to create a report from a table and from a query and give your reports suitable names.

Reports are for displaying output information only. Records are not amended, added or deleted in reports. In other words, a report exists to present data either from the data contained in a table or from the results of a query. Reports are usually printed out. They can be particularly useful as the information can be presented in different ways easily using a wizard. For example, numbers can be calculated or field names can be presented in a different order or grouped together.

Create a named report and arrange fields and headings (5.6.l.2–3)

① Open the **Fitness records 2** database.

② Click the **Reports** object on the **Database Window**, and select **Create report by using wizard** to display the first step of the **Report Wizard**.

③ Select **Table: ClientRecords** in the **Tables/Queries** list box if it is not already showing.

④ Move the following fields from **Available Fields:** to the **Selected Fields:** pane: **LastName, Membership fee, Day of visit, No of visits used, £ per extra session**. Click **Next >** when you have finished.

Tip!

A report can also be based on a query. If this is the case, select the query in the **Tables/Queries** list box.

Note

You can select fields in any order to determine how they appear in the end report.

Note

You will give the report a name at the end of the wizard steps.

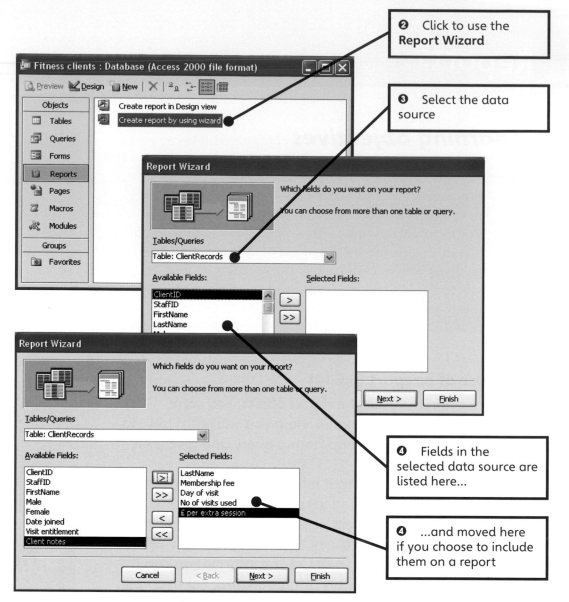

Figure 5.46 Selecting fields in the **Report Wizard**

The order in which fields appear in the final report is determined by the order you select them in step 4.

Step 2 of the Report Wizard lets you choose the grouping of the fields. When creating a report you can present your field headings in any order you need. You might be asked to put the client or a company name first or alternatively to produce a report by product and then list the clients who have purchased each of the products in different sections. This is called **grouping**. You might want to present the product in alphabetical order and also list the clients who have purchased the product in alphabetical order or maybe order of date of purchase. If you change your mind about the order in which the groups appear, you can move them up and down by clicking the **Priority** arrow.

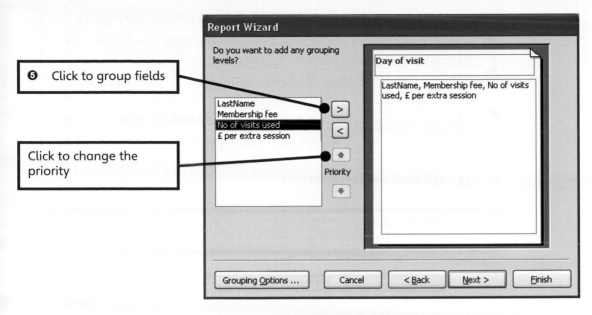

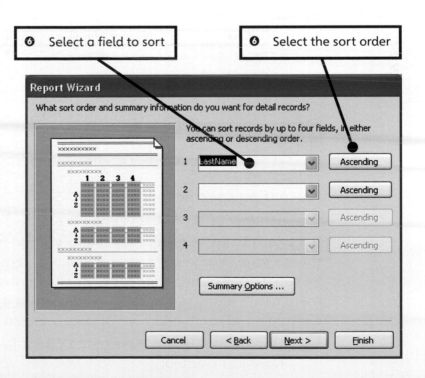

Figure 5.47 Grouping fields

⑤ Select **Day of visit** and then click $\boxed{>}$ so it appears as a group heading, then click **Next >**.

The wizard takes you to step 3 where you can sort records in order.

⑥ Select **LastName** from the drop-down list number I. This will sort the field in **Ascending** order, then click **Next >**.

> ## Tip!
> Click the **Ascending** button to change it to **Descending** to sort the fields in descending order.

Figure 5.48 Sorting fields

Step 4 of the wizard lets you choose a layout for your report.

⑦ Select the **Outline I** layout and **Landscape** orientation by clicking the relevant radio buttons, then click **Next >**.

⑧ Select the **Bold** style from the next step of the wizard, then click **Next >**.

⑨ In the final wizard window, type the name **Client Records** as the report name. Make sure **Preview the report** is selected, and click **Finish**.

The report preview is displayed.

Client Records

Day of visit	F			

LastName		Membership fee	No of visits used	£ per extra session
Jose		275.00	8	£20.00

Day of visit	M			

LastName		Membership fee	No of visits used	£ per extra session
Otto		425.00	15	£17.50

Day of visit	T			

LastName		Membership fee	No of visits used	£ per extra session
Menzies		350.00	21	£20.00
Patel		300.00	6	£32.50

Day of visit	Th			

LastName		Membership fee	No of visits used	£ per extra session
Berry		475.00	16	£15.00
Saffri		375.00	1	£12.50

Day of visit	W			

LastName		Membership fee	No of visits used	£ per extra session
Ham		200.00	39	£7.50
Mohammed		350.00	32	£20.00

28 April 2008   Page 1 of 1

Figure 5.49 The final report showing clients sorted by Day of Visit

Presenting specific fields (5.6.1.4–5)

The manager of the Fitness Centre is pleased with your report but wants to know how many clients visit on each day, and what the average charge per extra session is on each day. He says that he can work it out on the report you have given him, because there aren't many clients, but he thinks that it would be too time-consuming when the number of clients increases.

① Display the **Design View** of the **Client Records** report you have just created.

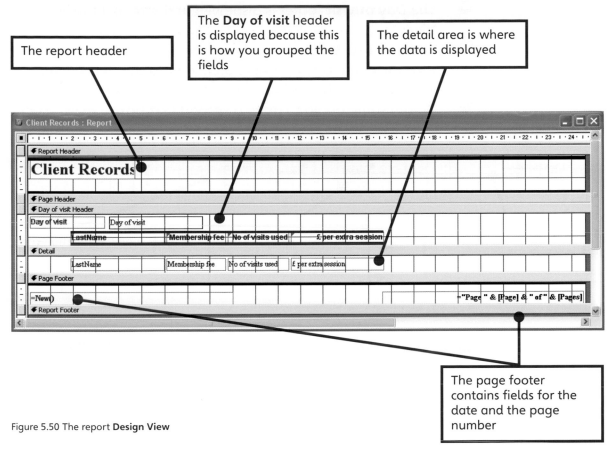

The report header

The **Day of visit** header is displayed because this is how you grouped the fields

The detail area is where the data is displayed

The page footer contains fields for the date and the page number

Figure 5.50 The report **Design View**

❷ Click the **Sorting and Grouping** button on the toolbar to display the **Sorting and Grouping** dialogue box.

❸ The requirement is to find the statistics by day of the week, so click **Day of visit** in the **Field/Expression** column.

❹ Change the **Group Footer** to **Yes** in the **Group Properties** panel. Close the box by clicking the cross.

Warning!

The **Day of visit** and **Detail** areas of the report contain fields that relate to the table in which the data is held. It is possible to add, move, edit and delete these fields, but unless you do it correctly, the report results accuracy could be compromised.

Tip!

You can edit the text and fields in headers and footers.

❸ Select the field to be grouped

❹ Select Yes to display a group footer

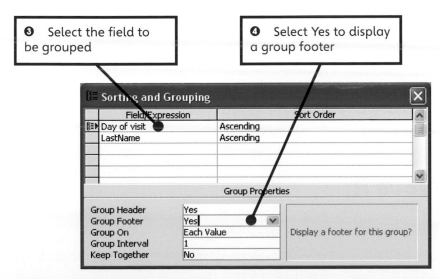

Figure 5.5I Setting a group footer

⑤ The **Day of visit** footer is displayed in the report **Design View**.

⑥ Click the **Text Box** button abl on the **Toolbox**, and draw a text box in the **Day of visit** footer. You do this in a similar way to adding a text box onto a form (see page 301).

⑦ Do the same again to draw a second text box.

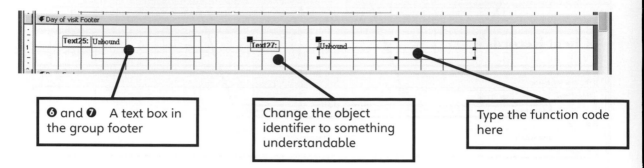

❻ and ❼ A text box in the group footer

Change the object identifier to something understandable

Type the function code here

Figure 5.52 Adding text boxes to a group footer

Each box you draw will appear in two parts. The first will have a label (e.g. **Text25:** – although the number part is likely to be different on your report since it depends on the number of objects already created). The second part will contain the word **Unbound**.

⑧ Click the left-hand **Text25:** (or similar) label to select it. Click in it again to place the insertion point in the text. Replace the text with **No of Visitors**.

⑨ Click out of the box, and then click it again to reselect it. Place the cursor over the large black square at the top left side, and drag the box so it is clear of the box containing the text **Unbound**.

⑩ Click the **Unbound** box to select it and then click in it again to place the insertion point.

⑪ Type **=Count([LastName])**. This counts the number of items (in this case: visitors) in each group (in this case: day of the week).

⑫ Switch to **Print Preview**.

You will see the new information after each day of the week group. Do not worry about the layout at this stage.

Note

As well as the **Count** and **Average** functions that you have used here, you can use **Sum**, **Min** and **Max** on fields with a **Number** data type, to display the total, minimum and maximum values, respectively.

Prove it!

Edit the second label and text box that you added to the report so that the label reads **Average charge**.

Copy and paste **=Count([LastName])** into the new text box and edit it so it reads **=Avg([£ per extra session])**.

Your finished report will look something like that in Figure 5.53.

Client Records

Day of visit	F			
	LastName	Membership fee	No of visits used	£ per extra session
	Jose	275.00	8	£20.00
No of Visitors	1	Average charge		20
Day of visit	M			
	LastName	Membership fee	No of visits used	£ per extra session
	Otto	425.00	15	£17.50
No of Visitors	1	Average charge		17.5
Day of visit	T			
	LastName	Membership fee	No of visits used	£ per extra session
	Menzies	350.00	21	£20.00
	Patel	300.00	6	£32.50
No of Visitors	2	Average charge		26.25

28 April 2008   Page 1 of 2

Figure 5.53 Report with grouped summary data

Exporting (5.6.1.6)

You can export data from Access in other formats so that it can be used in other applications. As you learn how to use spreadsheet, word-processing and other applications you will find this useful, particularly if you are asked to produce a report that uses files that were created in different programs.

Suppose you need to export the **Music** database **CDList** table to an Excel 2003 spreadsheet.

1. Open the **CDList** table in the **Music** database.
2. Click **Export...** on the **File** menu to display the **Export Table** dialogue box.
3. Select the location of where you want to export the file, in the usual Windows fashion.
4. Type the filename **Music Spreadsheet**.
5. Select **Microsoft Excel 97-2003** from the drop-down **Save as type:** list.
6. Click the **Export All** button.

The table is converted into the correct format.

7. Open Excel, navigate to where you exported the table to, and open it.

> **Tip!**
>
> When you first view the report, the grouped summary data may not appear neat and exactly where you want it. Practise moving and formatting the text boxes in **Design View**.

> **Note**
>
> **Export** means to send a file from one application to another so that it can be used in the new application.

> **Note**
>
> You can export query results as well as tables. Access can export in many file formats. As well as different versions of Excel spreadsheets, common formats include **Text** and **XML**.

① Which data source objects can be used to create a report?

② What steps would you need to take to change the order of the field names and headings in a report layout?

③ What does grouping mean in the creation of a report?

④ What calculations can be automatically presented in a report, and how?

⑤ Which data types must be used to create calculations?

⑥ What is the main benefit to using a report to calculate a sum?

⑦ What are the main benefits of using headers and footers in a report?

You can find the answers to the questions on the CD-ROM saved as **Answers to TYU questions 5.6**. How did you do? Go back over anything that you are unsure about.

Printing

Learning objectives

By working through this lesson you will learn how to:
- change the orientation and paper size of printed output
- print a page, selected records and complete tables
- print in form layout
- print a report.

As with all Microsoft Office applications you can be selective in what you print from an Access database. Access lets you print:

- records or complete tables
- query outputs
- forms
- reports.

For each of the above you can select the number of copies you print, the orientation of the printed output, page size, and exactly what you print of the object.

Orientation and paper size (5.6.2.I)

When you print a table, form, query output or report, you may find that there are more fields across a page than will fit onto a portrait layout. Therefore, in order to read the records more easily, you might want to change the layout of the paper to landscape. This is really easy. You do not have to do anything to the printer but change the settings in Access.

1. Open the **Fitness records 2** database.
2. Open the **FitnessInstructorRecords** table.
3. Click **Page Setup...** on the **File** menu to display the **Page Setup** dialogue box.
4. Click the **Page** tab.
5. Click the **Landscape** radio button to set the **Orientation**.

It is likely that your printer uses **A4** paper.

6. Check the paper size is correct. Select the correct size from the **Size** drop-down list if you need to.

> **Tip!**
>
> If you have forgotten what the orientation options mean, look at the images on the **Page Setup** dialogue box to remind you.

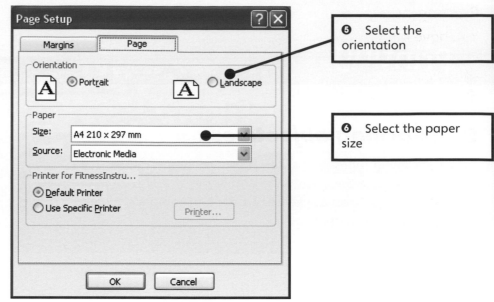

❺ Select the
orientation

❻ Select the paper
size

Figure 5.54 Page setup

Print a page or selected record(s) from a table (5.6.2.2)

Once you have set the page so that the table data neatly fits, you
might then decide that you only want to print selected pages or
selected records from the table.

❶ Click **Print...** on the **File** menu to open the **Print** dialogue
box.

The default printer for your computer should be displayed.

❷ The **Print** dialogue box gives you three **Print Range** options.
Select the one you want by clicking the button.

◉ **All:** This prints the whole table or query.

◉ **Pages:** Type the numbers of the pages you want to print.

◉ **Selected Record(s):** Select the records you want to print by
clicking the row header on the left of the record to highlight
it. Selecting this option then prints the selected records only.

❸ Click **OK** to print.

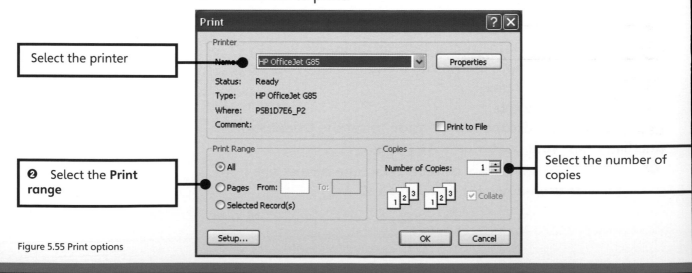

Select the printer

❷ Select the **Print
range**

Select the number of
copies

Figure 5.55 Print options

Printing query results, forms and reports (5.6.2.3/5)

You have already look at printing query results on page 288. Printing a form or report is very similar to printing a table.

1. Open the form or report.
2. Click **Print...** on the **File** menu to open the **Print** dialogue box.
3. Select the page range, and click **OK**.

Tip!

Always **Print Preview** a form before printing. It is likely that you will have to alter the layout so that it looks neat on a page.

Prove it!

Use the sample databases on the CD-ROM to practise using the different print options for tables, query results, forms and reports, to see how they work. **Important:** remember to use **Print Preview** to see what the printout will look like before you print.

Note

The nature of a report means that you cannot print individual records.

Test your understanding

1. What do landscape and portrait mean in terms of printing?
2. Which menu option do you use in order to change the orientation of the page?
3. How do you set the page size of a printout?
4. Explain how to print
   a) a specified page, and
   b) a selected record in table format.
5. How can you select which records in a report to print without printing the whole report?
6. What are the steps to print all records in a form?
7. How is the result of a query printed?
8. How can you print preview a report?

You can find the answers to the questions on the CD-ROM saved as **Answers to TYU questions 5.7**. How did you do? Go back over anything that you are unsure about.

This module explains how to use a computer presentation program. Throughout, you will practise and learn how to create presentations that include graphics and animation. You will also learn how to view and print your slides in different ways. By the end of this module, you will be able to use the presentation software's powerful tools to really grab your audience's attention.

The step-by-step instructions are written for Microsoft Office PowerPoint 2003. The tasks at the end of each lesson can be used with any presentation software.

This training, which has been approved by the ECDL Foundation, includes exercise items intended to assist Candidates in their training for an ECDL Certification Programme. These exercises are not ECDL Foundation certification tests. For information about authorised ECDL Test Centres in different national territories, please refer to the ECDL Foundation website at www.ecdl.org

MODULE 6.
presentation

Getting started

Learning objectives

By working through this lesson you will learn:
- how to open and close Microsoft PowerPoint
- how to use PowerPoint's Help system
- how to create a new presentation using built-in slide layouts
- how to add and format text
- how to align text
- about different view modes.

Note

PowerPoint uses the word slide for each page created, even if you are creating paper printouts or overhead transparencies.

How about...?

Alternatively, if it is there, you can double-click directly on the **PowerPoint** icon on the Desktop or on the Start menu.

How about...?

Alternatively, if the **Getting Started** Task pane is showing, click **Create a new presentation...** to show the **New Presentation** Task pane.

From prehistoric cave paintings to overhead projectors, people have always used visual aids to help them explain themselves. Today, presentation software can help you to present information and ideas effectively and with originality. Applications such as Microsoft PowerPoint let you create, organise and design slides and handouts. Presentations might be on transparencies, 35 mm slides or as automated presentations on a computer.

Opening PowerPoint (6.I.I.I)

As with any Microsoft Office application, there are several ways to open PowerPoint. The following will work for any loaded program.

1. Click the **Start** button ![start] on the Taskbar.
2. Click **All Programs**.
3. Click **Microsoft Office**.
4. Click **Microsoft Office PowerPoint 2003**.

PowerPoint will open with a blank presentation displayed (Figure 6.I on page 3I7).

Create a new presentation based on the default template (6.I.I.2)

1. Click **New...** on the **File** menu to display the **New Presentation** Task pane.
2. Click **Blank Presentation** to show the **Slide Layout** Task pane (Figure 6.2 on page 3I7).

PowerPoint has highlighted the top-left **Text Layout** slide image – it is for the **Title Slide** template. This is the default template on which your new presentation will be based. You will see how to change from the default template on page 333.

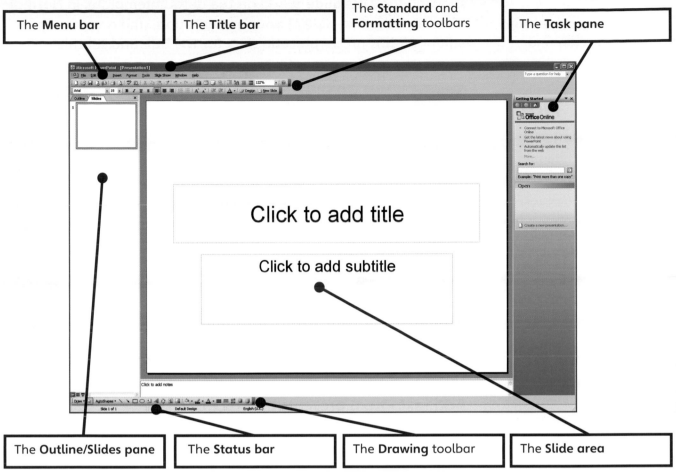

The **Menu bar** | The **Title bar** | The **Standard** and **Formatting** toolbars | The **Task pane**

The **Outline/Slides pane** | The **Status bar** | The **Drawing** toolbar | The **Slide area**

Figure 6.I The PowerPoint opening screen

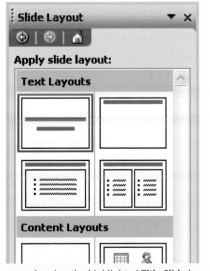

Figure 6.2 Part of the **Slide Layout** Task pane showing the highlighted **Title Slide** layout

Tip!

If you need more working space on your screen, click the cross **x** to close the Task pane.

Tip!

There are many slide layouts. Rest the mouse pointer over a layout to see its name. Scroll down so that you can see all the layouts you can use.

Placeholders around the title and subtitle with instructions on how to use them

The **Slide area** is the working area of PowerPoint, and this is showing the **Title Slide** based on the default template, in **Normal View**. It is the first slide of your presentation, and is ready for editing. It has preset **placeholders** for the title and subtitle in which you can type your text.

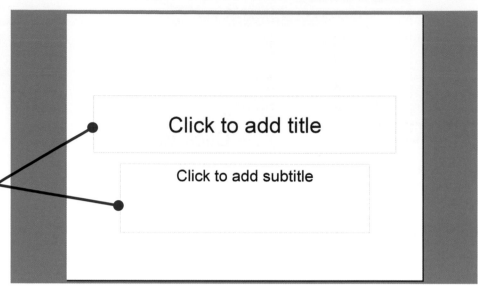

Figure 6.3 Placeholders

Add text into a presentation (6.3.1.2)

① Click in the top placeholder and type **Using Presentations**.
② Click in the bottom placeholder and type **Learning to Pass ECDL Module 6**.

Saving your presentation (6.1.1.3)

You have just created your first PowerPoint slide. It might not look very exciting at the moment but you can format it later to be more eye-catching. However, it will be the basis for your presentation and so you need to save your work.

You should use the folder allocated to you for saving files. If you have not been told which folder to use, create your own (refer to Module 2, page 63, to remind yourself of how to do this).

① Click **Save As...** on the **File** menu to display the **Save As** dialogue box.
② Navigate in the usual Windows fashion to the location where you want to save your presentation file.

PowerPoint will have given your presentation a name (such as Presentation1). You should always give a file a name that tells you something about its content so you can easily recognise it again.

③ Type **My First Presentation** in the **File name:** text box.
④ Click the **Save** button.

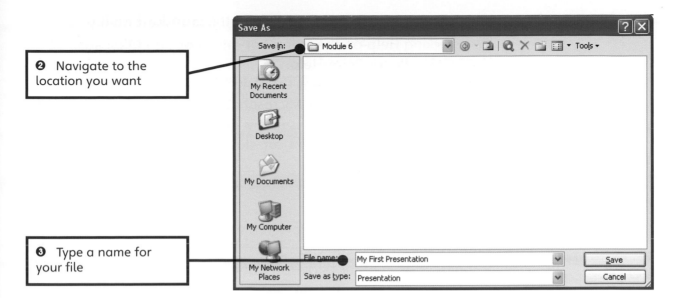

❷ Navigate to the location you want

❸ Type a name for your file

Figure 6.4 Saving a presentation

Close a presentation and PowerPoint (6.1.1.1)

❶ Click **Close** on the **File** menu to close the presentation.
❷ Click **Exit** on the **File** menu to close PowerPoint.

Toolbars (6.1.2.4)

As with all Microsoft Office applications, you can use the built-in toolbars to do common tasks. Like Microsoft Word and Excel, PowerPoint displays the **Standard** and the **Formatting** toolbars by default (Figure 6.1). These are the toolbars that you are likely to use most often. However, there are many more that are hidden either until you use an option that requires them, or until you choose to display them. You can display, hide, move and modify toolbars to suit how you like to work. For ECDL you only need to know how to display and hide toolbars.

❶ Open **PowerPoint**.
❷ Click **Toolbars** on the **View** menu to display the list of toolbars installed on your version of PowerPoint.
❸ Click a toolbar name on the list to tick/untick it. (A tick means the toolbar is displayed.)

Getting help (6.1.2.2)

PowerPoint provides help in the same way as other Microsoft Office programs.
You can access the PowerPoint Help system by:

◉ pressing the **F1** key
◉ typing in the **Type a question for help** box at the top of the screen and pressing **Return**

Type a question for help ▾

How about...?

Alternatively, close PowerPoint by clicking the **Close** button ☒ on the Title bar. Close a presentation by clicking the **Close window** button ☒ in the active window.

Tip!

Rest the mouse cursor over a toolbar button or other feature to see a screen tip telling you what the feature is.

Tip!

The **Help** Task pane **Table of Contents** is often a good way of finding out what the application can do.

Assistance
Search for:
how to use help ⇥
🔹 Table of Contents

- ◉ clicking the **Help** button 🔘 on the **Standard** toolbar
- ◉ clicking **Help** on the menu bar and choosing **Microsoft Office PowerPoint Help**.

Each of these options opens the **Help** Task pane. Use this in the same way as explained for Microsoft Word in Module 3, page 128. Using the table of contents is also a good way of getting to know more about what PowerPoint can do.

Formatting text

The default text format in PowerPoint is based on a **master slide**. However, you can change text formatting using the same techniques as in other Microsoft Office 2003 programs.

Open an exisiting presentation (6.1.1.1)

1. Open PowerPoint.
2. Click **Open...** on the **File** menu to display the **Open** dialogue box.
3. If you need to, navigate to where your file **My First Presentation** is stored.
4. Select the file and click the **Open** button.

Changing font and font size (6.3.2.1)

1. Click the title text **Using Presentations**. The text insertion point will show as a flashing vertical line and the placeholder border will be revealed.
2. Select the title text so that it is highlighted (white on black).
3. Click **Font...** on the **Format** menu to display the **Font** dialogue box.

Note

You will learn more about master slides on page 336.

Note

The **Open** dialogue box will display the location that has been set as the preferred location to save to (see page 338).

How about...?

Alternatively, once you have located the file you need, double-click it.

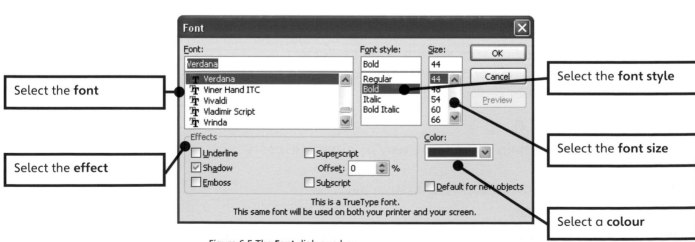

Figure 6.5 The **Font** dialogue box

④ Scroll through the fonts listed in the **Font:** section and click **Verdana**.

⑤ Scroll through the **Size:** section and click **44**.

⑥ Click **OK** to view the changes and save your work.

Changing font styles, effects and colours (6.3.2.2–3)

① Reselect the title text if it isn't highlighted already.

② Reopen the **Font** dialogue box.

③ Click **Bold** in the **Font style:** box.

④ Click the **Shadow** tick box in the **Effects** section to select it.

⑤ Click the arrow on the right of the **Color:** box. Click a blue colour if it is showing as a small square. Otherwise, click **More colors...** to display the **Colors** palette. Click a blue colour and then the **OK** button.

⑥ Click **OK** on the **Font** dialogue box to apply the changes. The title text should look similar to this.

Using Presentations

⑦ Save your work.

Prove it!

Repeat the processes to format the subtitle as **Verdana**, size **20**, **underlined**, **bold**, **italic**, and a **pale blue** colour. Save your work.

Changing case (6.3.2.4)

① Reselect the subtitle text if it isn't already highlighted.

② Click **Change Case...** on the **Format** menu to display the **Change Case** dialogue box.

③ Click the **UPPERCASE** radio button to select it.

④ Click **OK** and save your work.

Use Undo and Redo commands (6.3.1.6)

Undo cancels the last command (i.e. it restores the presentation to how it was before the last command). You can undo several commands in succession. **Redo** repeats the command, and is useful if you accidently undo something you want back. These commands are on the **Standard** toolbar.

① Click the **Undo** button. The last action you took is cancelled, and the upper case is removed.

② Click the **Redo** button. The upper case is reapplied.

Note

Choose another font if you do not have **Verdana** on your computer.

How about...?

Alternatively, type the size directly in the **Size:** box.

How about...?

As is usual in Microsoft Office applications, most of the formatting commands described here are available on the **Formatting** toolbar for accessibility. If you are unfamiliar with the toolbar, rest the mouse cursor over a feature to reveal a screen tip that explains its purpose.

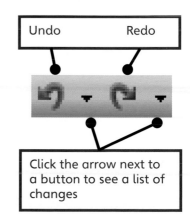

Undo   Redo

Click the arrow next to a button to see a list of changes

Figure 6.6 The **Undo** and **Redo** buttons

How about...?

Ctrl+Z = Undo

Ctrl+Y = Redo

Test your understanding

You can find the answers to the questions on the CD-ROM saved as **Answers to TYU questions 6.1**. How did you do? Go back over anything that you are unsure about.

1. What is presentation software used for?
2. A word-processed document consists of a number of pages. A presentation consists of a number of what?
3. What is this toolbar button used for: **A ▾** ?
4. What is the **Save In:** box used for in the **Save As** dialogue box?

Prove it!

Exercise 1

You are the secretary of a gardening club. You want to use a presentation to help you report what the club has done through the year.

1. Create a presentation using the default template.
2. Apply a **Title Slide** layout to the first slide.
3. Give the presentation the title **Green Fingers Gardening Club** formatted as **48 pt, bold, Bradley Hand ITC** font, in **dark green** text with a **light green** background.
4. Give the presentation the subtitle **The Committee's Annual Report** formatted as **40 pt, bold, italic, Bradley Hand ITC** font, in **blue** text with a **light green** background.
5. Save the presentation as **Garden Club Presentation**.

Prove it!

Exercise 2

Imagine you have succeeded in getting an interview for your dream job! You have been asked to make a presentation to explain why you are perfect for the position.

1. Create a presentation with the default title slide.
2. Use the job name or description as the title.
3. Use your name as the subtitle.
4. Format it in any way that you think will help to impress the interviewers.
5. Save the presentation in your module folder as **Interview Presentation**.

Adding content

Learning objectives

By working through this lesson you will learn how to:
- ◉ add slides to presentations
- ◉ add, move and align text and graphics
- ◉ include bullet and numbered lists
- ◉ spellcheck text on slides
- ◉ apply a design template
- ◉ print slides.

You're now going to build your presentation by adding further slides that follow in sequence from the title slide you've already created.

❶ Open PowerPoint.

❷ Open the presentation **My First Presentation**.

❸ Save the file as **Added Content**.

❹ Click **New Slide** on the **Insert** menu to place a new slide immediately after the title slide.

By default, PowerPoint has chosen the **Title and Text** slide which is automatically laid out for a title (in the top placeholder) and a bullet list (in the bottom placeholder).

Prove it!

Insert two more **Title and Text** (the default) slides so you have a total of four slides showing in the **Slides** pane.

Choose a different slide layout (6.2.2.I)

❶ Click **slide 2** on the **Slides** pane to highlight it. The slide in the working area will change to the second slide of the four.

❷ Click **Task Pane** on the **View** menu to display the Task pane (if it is not showing).

❸ Change the Task pane view to **Slide Layout** (if it is not showing).

❹ Click the **Title, Text and Clip Art** layout in the **Other Layouts** section. This applies the layout to the current slide.

The new slide has three placeholders instead of two.

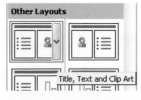

Tip!

An example copy of the title page is on the CD-ROM.

How about...?

Alternatively, insert a new slide by clicking the **New Slide** button on the **Formatting** toolbar.

Tip!

You can find out which slide layout a slide is using by looking at the **Slide Layout** Task pane. The layout in use is surrounded by a blue border.

Note

Slides in your presentation are visible, in order, in the **Slides** pane on the left of the PowerPoint screen.

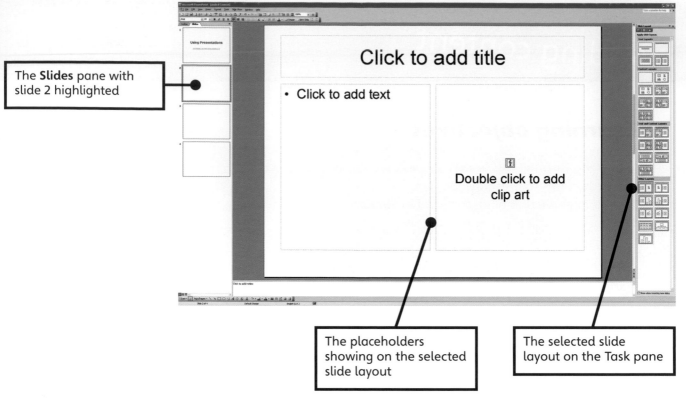

The **Slides** pane with slide 2 highlighted

The placeholders showing on the selected slide layout

The selected slide layout on the Task pane

Figure 6.7 A new slide in position

You are going to add the slide content to the different placeholders.

- Top placeholder: This is for the slide title. You learned on page 318 how to add text directly into a placeholder. This time you are going to add text in the **Outline** view.
- Left placeholder: This has been formatted as a bullet list.
- Right placeholder: This has been formatted for a clip art image.

Slide titles (6.2.1.2)

Throughout the different modules in this book, you have learned that it is good practice to give files easily recognisable names when you save them. It is similarly important that you give slide titles names that are unique and meaningful. There are two good reasons for this.

- You will be able to quickly distinguish one slide from another when you list them in the **Outline** view (see below).
- When you give the presentation, you will instantly know what the slide is about. If two slides have the same title, or the slide title is unclear, you might be confused when you give the presentation – and then you won't look professional!

Adding text in the Outline pane (6.3.1.2)

The panel on the left of the PowerPoint screen is currently showing the **Slides** view.

❶   Click the **Outline** tab to show the presentation content as a list.

❷   **Slide 2** should still be selected so this will appear highlighted in the **Outline** view. If it isn't, click the second slide in the list to select it and place the text insertion point.

❸   Type **A List and a Picture**. The words will appear in the **Outline** pane and on the slide.

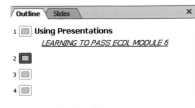

Figure 6.8 The **Outline** pane

Adding text (6.3.1.1)

So far you have added a presentation title and subtitle to the first slide in your presentation, and a title to the second slide. Now you are going to add text to the second slide to summarise what the slide is about.

A slide is in a presentation to get the important points over to the audience. The audience might be a group who have come to listen to you give a sales pitch for a new product you've designed, or it might be one person who is watching a series of adverts on a screen while waiting in a queue at a shop. Whatever the reason, the audience will not read line after line of text, so it is good practice to use short phrases and lists. The audience will better remember a few well-chosen points than paragraphs of detail. If you are presenting the slides as a talk, the list items will help prompt you so you can expand on the content as you speak.

The slide layout you have applied to slide 2 has already been configured for a bullet list in the left-hand placeholder. You are going to add a list of some of the world's continents.

❶   Click in the left placeholder of slide 2 where it says **Click to add text**.

❷   Type **Continents** and press the **Return** key.

❸   The text insertion point moves down to start a new bullet list item. Type **Africa** and press **Return**.

❹   Type the following exactly as shown as each new bullet item: **America, Antartica, Asia, Europe**. Press **Return** after each.

❺   Save your work.

Using the spellchecker (6.6.2.1)

At best, spelling mistakes will spoil your presentation. Worse still, they will make you look unprofessional. Always check your spelling!

❶   Display the first slide.

❷   Click **Spelling...** on the **Tools** menu to display the **Spelling** dialogue box.

Note

You can choose whether or not your spelling is checked as you type.

❶   Click **Options...** on the **Tools** menu to display the **Options** dialogue box.

❷   Click the **Spelling and Style** tab.

❸   Click the **Check spelling as you type** tick box. A tick in the box means the option is set.

Note

The incorrect spelling of **Antarctica** is deliberate.

How about...?

Alternatively, click the **Spelling** button on the Standard toolbar, or press **F7** to check spelling.

The spellchecker will go through all the spelling mistakes and repeated words in the presentation. It immediately finds the spelling mistake **Antartica**.

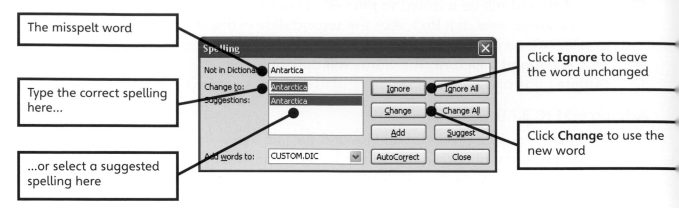

The misspelt word

Type the correct spelling here...

...or select a suggested spelling here

Click **Ignore** to leave the word unchanged

Click **Change** to use the new word

Figure 6.9 The spellchecker

Tip!

If the spellchecker finds a repeated word, you will be given the option to delete it.

Tip!

Use the **Decrease Indent** button to remove an indent from a bulleted list.

❸ In this case, the suggested spelling is the one you want to use. It is highlighted, so click the **Change** button.

❹ If the spellchecker finds further mistakes, it will automatically move on to them. There are no other errors, so click **OK**.

❺ Save your work.

Indenting bulleted text (6.3.3.1)

The word **Continents** is really a heading for the continent names listed below. You need to indent the names.

❶ Click the word **Africa**.

❷ Indent this text by clicking the **Increase Indent** button on the **Formatting** toolbar.

The text is indented. The text format and bullet format change too.

❸ Repeat for the remaining four continent names.

❹ Save your work.

A List and a Picture

- Continents
  - Africa
  - America
  - Antarctica
  - Asia
  - Europe

Double click to add clip art

Your slide 2 will look something like that in Figure 6.10. Do not worry if the bullet points and style are different as these will depend on how PowerPoint has been set up on your computer.

Figure 6.10 The **text** placeholder with the bulleted list

Change the bullet style (6.3.3.3)

1. Click the word **Continents** and, holding down the mouse button, drag the mouse to highlight the list. Release the mouse button.
2. Click **Bullets and Numbering...** on the **Format** menu to display the **Bullets and Numbering** dialogue box.

The **Bulleted** tab should be selected. If it isn't, click it now.

3. Click the square bullet option.
4. Click **OK**. The bullets on the highlighted list will change to squares.
5. Click away from the list to deselect it, and save your work.

How about...?

Alternatively, click the **Numbering** or the **Bullets** button 🔢 ☰ on the **Formatting** toolbar to apply a list format to text.

When clicked, the list wil be formatted with the last used list style.

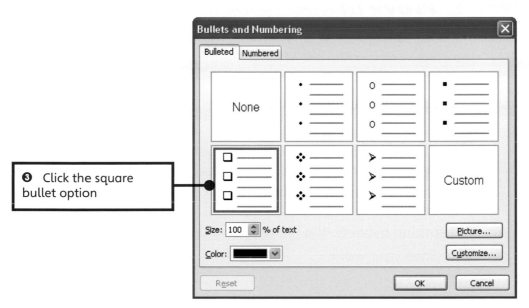

❸ Click the square bullet option

Figure 6.11 The **Bullets and Numbering** dialogue box

Note

A **numbered list** is similar to a **bulleted list** except, as its name suggests, it is made up of list items numbered in sequential order. It is good practice to use a numbered list where the list items comprise a series of instructions that need to be followed in order, like the step-by-step instructions used in this book. The list of continents used in the example are better listed with bullet points as the order they appear in does not matter.

To change a list to a numbered list.

1. Select the list items.
2. Open the **Bullets and Numbering** dialogue box.
3. Click the **Numbered** tab, and choose the number style.
4. Click **OK**.

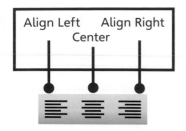

Align Left   Align Right
Center

Figure 6.I2 The text alignment toolbar buttons

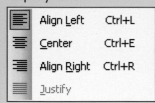
Aligning text in a text frame (6.3.2.5)

Imagine you are unhappy with the way the slide looks. You think that the top bullet item **Continents** is really a heading for the list items below and doesn't need to be bulleted itself.

❶ Click the word **Continents**.

❷ Click the highlighted **Bullets** button 📇 on the toolbar to remove the bullets format.

❸ The word **Continents** is currently aligned to the left of the placeholder. Click the **Center** align button on the **Formatting** toolbar to centre it within the placeholder.

Prove it!

Decrease the indent on the country names bulleted list so they are aligned at the left of the placeholder.

Changing line spacing (6.3.3.2)

❶ Click the word **Africa**.

❷ Click **Line Spacing...** on the **Format** menu to open the **Line Spacing** dialogue box.

❸ Increase the **Before paragraph** spacing to **0.5 lines** and click **OK**.

The spacing between the heading and the first list item is increased.

❹ Save your work.

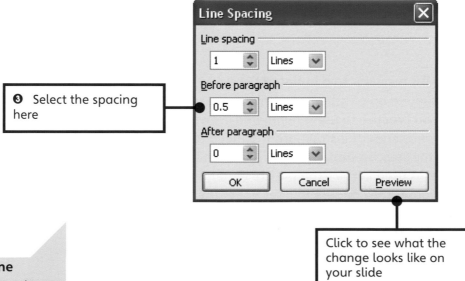

❸ Select the spacing here

Click to see what the change looks like on your slide

Figure 6.I3 The **Line Spacing** dialogue box

Editing and moving text (6.3.1.3–4)

It is likely that you will want to revise your slides as your presentation develops. Here, you will insert **Australia** into the list.

1 Click **America** and move the text insertion point to the end of the word.

2 Press **Return** to create a new line. You will see that PowerPoint is prepared to create a bullet for you.

3 Type **Australia**.

This is in the wrong position alphabetically.

4 Select the word **Australia** by double-clicking it.

5 Click **Cut** on the **Edit** menu, and then press the **Backspace** key twice to remove the bullet point. The whole line will disappear.

6 Click the word **Asia**, and move the insertion point to immediately after the last letter.

7 Press **Return**.

8 Click **Paste** on the **Edit** menu to place the new text.

9 Save your work.

Prove it!

Use the techniques you have learned so far to create slide 3 of your presentation. Here is the slide 3 content you want:

Title: Population I

Bullet list:

- Africa
  - 20.4% of land mass
  - 14.0% of population
- America
  - 28.4% of land mass
  - 14.0% of population
- Antarctica
  - 13.0% of land mass
  - no permanent population

Copying and deleting text (6.3.1.4–5)

1 Select the text **Population I** on **slide 3**.

2 Click **Copy** on the **Edit** menu.

3 Select **slide 4** on the **Outline** pane, and click in the title placeholder.

4 Click **Paste** on the **Edit** menu. The selected text is copied to the new location.

5 Return to **slide 3**, and select all the list text.

6 Copy and paste it into the text placeholder on **slide 4**.

Note

To edit text, simply click the text you want to edit so the insertion point is set. You use the **Backspace** and **Delete** keys to remove text, and type new text on the keyboard.

Note

You can copy or cut text and graphical objects in one presentation, and then paste it into another open presentation.

(6.1.1.5) You can switch between open presentations by clicking the respective Taskbar button on your desktop, clicking the presentation filename on the **Window** menu, or pressing **Ctrl+F6** to cycle through open presentations.

How about...?

Alternatively, click the **Cut**, **Copy** or **Paste** buttons ✂ 📋 📋 on the **Standard** toolbar.

Inserting a picture (6.5.1.1)

1. Select **slide 2**.
2. Double-click in the clip art placeholder to display the **Select Picture** dialogue box.
3. Type **world** in the **Search Text:** box and click **Go**.
4. Scroll down to find a picture you like. Click to select it, then click **OK**.

Slide 2 will now look something like this.

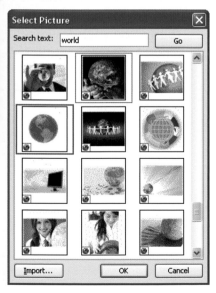

Figure 6.14 Selecting a picture

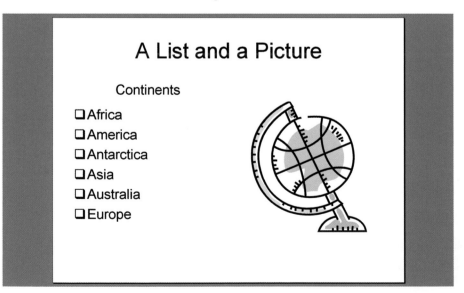

Figure 6.15 Slide 2 of the example presentation

The picture is too large and in the wrong place, so now you are going to resize and move it, then copy to your other slides.

Selecting and deleting a graphical object (6.5.1.2/4)

As with text, you need to select an object such as an image before you can work with it.

- ◉ Click the image. Small circles, called **handles**, appear around it.
- ◉ To delete a graphical object, first select it, then press **Delete**.

Resizing a graphical object (6.5.1.4)

❶ Select the image on **slide 2** by clicking it.

❷ Rest the mouse cursor over the handle on the top right corner. A two-headed arrow appears.

❸ Click and hold the mouse button while you drag the corner to the left to reduce the image size.

❹ When it is about a third of the original size, release the mouse button.

Rotating and flipping a graphical object (6.5.1.5)

❶ Select the object.

❷ Click the **Draw** button on the **Drawing** toolbar.

❸ Click **Rotate and Flip** on the menu.

❹ Choose an option from the displayed menu.

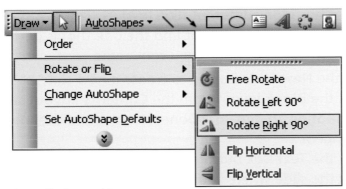

Figure 6.17 Rotating or flipping an object

Copying and moving a graphical object (6.5.1.3)

❶ Click the image and keep the mouse button held down while you drag the image to a new location in the bottom right-hand corner of the slide.

❷ Check that the image is still selected, and right-click it.

❸ Select **Copy** from the shortcut menu that appears.

❹ Display **slide 3**.

❺ Right-click to display the shortcut menu again, and click **Paste**.

❻ The image is pasted on the slide. Move it to the bottom right-hand corner if you need to.

❼ Repeat steps 4 to 6 to copy the image on to **slide 4**.

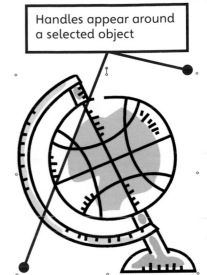

Handles appear around a selected object

Figure 6.16 A selected image

Tip!

Resize a graphical object using the corner handles to keep the image proportions the same.

How about...?

Alternatively, you can also right-click the object and select **Format Picture...**, or double-click the picture. Both these will display the **Format Picture** dialogue box where you can use the **Size** tab to type in **Height** and **Width** values.

Note

The techniques described here will work with any object: photo, chart, image etc.

How about...?

Alternatively, click the **Cut**, **Copy** or **Paste** buttons ✂ 📋 📋 on the **Standard** toolbar.

Aligning a graphical object relative to a slide (6.5.1.6)

① Click the graphical image on **slide 4**. You want to align it on the slide.

② Click the **Draw** button on the **Drawing** toolbar.

③ Click **Align or Distribute** from the menu.

④ Make sure that **Relative to Slide** is ticked.

⑤ Click an **Align** option from the menu to place the image.

Magnifying a slide (6.1.2.3)

Sometimes you want to zoom in on a slide, for instance if you are working with small images. PowerPoint provides a tool to do this.

① Click **Zoom...** on the **View** menu to display the **Zoom** dialogue box.

② Select a **Zoom to** option and click **OK**.

How about...?

Alternatively, you can use the **Zoom** box on the **Standard** toolbar.

Tip!

Select **Fit** to optimally fit the whole of the slide in the slide area.

Prove it!

Save your work, then practise some of the techniques explained above for working with graphical objects. There is no need to save your work when you've finished (unless you want to).

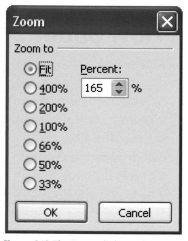

Figure 6.18 The **Zoom** dialogue box

Tip!

(6.2.2.4) You can apply any new slide layout to a new slide.

Adding text into a text box (6.5.2.2)

PowerPoint has many different slide layouts (Figure 6.19 on page 333), but sometimes you cannot find the one that is perfect for your task. When this happens you can create your own layout.

① Use the **New Slide** button to create a new slide.

② Click the **Blank** layout from the **Contents Layout** section of the **Slide Layout** Task pane. Notice the placeholders disappear.

③ Click the **Text Box** button 🖅 on the **Drawing** toolbar.

④ Click the slide where you want the top left of the box to be.

⑤ Type **qqqqq**.

The box will expand sideways until you stop typing.

⑥ Continue typing **wwwww eeeee rrrrr ttttt yyyyy uuuuu iiiii ooooo ppppp aaaaa sssss ddddd fffff**.

The text box goes beyond the slide edge. It will not create a new line until you press **Return**.

⑦ Now create another text box, but this time drag the cross hairs about a third of the way across the slide.

This fixes the width of the text box, so the text will wrap round to a new line when you reach the right border of the text box. The text box will expand downwards as you type.

⑧ Repeat the typing above to see this.

Using a colour scheme (6.2.2.3)

Your presentation will be more effective if the slides have a consistent colour scheme. This is because too much change of colour can detract from the content of the slides.

① Click **Slide Design...** on the **Format** menu to display the **Slide Design** Task pane.

② Click **Color Schemes**.

You will see a number of colour schemes provided. Experiment with these.

You can apply the colour scheme to all the slides in your presentation, or just to selected slides.

③ As you pass your mouse cursor over the colour schemes, an arrow will appear on the right side of the scheme. Click the arrow on the colour scheme you want; a shortcut menu will appear.

④ Click **Apply to All Slides** or **Apply to Selected Slides**.

Applying a design template (6.2.2.2, 6.6.1.4)

One of PowerPoint's most powerful features is its library of design templates. These provide the backgrounds that make presentations look so good!

① Click **Slide Design...** on the **Format** menu to display the **Slide Design** Task pane.

② Click **Design Templates**.

③ Experiment with these design templates. Finally, apply **Orbit**, from the **Available for Use** section, to all the slides.

Note

You may find that **Orbit** is not present on your copy of PowerPoint. If so, choose another template.

④ Save your work.

⑤ Close the presentation and exit PowerPoint.

Figure 6.19 The **Slide Design** colour schemes

Tip!

Apply the colour scheme to all the slides by clicking the scheme image directly without showing the shortcut menu.

Tip!

Select the slides you want in the **Slides** pane before applying selective colour schemes.

Tip!

Handouts look best with a white or very pale background, while on-screen presentations look best with a dark background.

Figure 6.20 The **Slide Design** design templates

Test your understanding

You can find the answers to the questions on the CD-ROM saved as **Answers to TYU questions 6.2**. How did you do? Go back over anything that you are unsure about.

1. What keyboard shortcut will display or hide the Task pane?
2. How does PowerPoint indicate that a word may be misspelt?
3. On a graphic, what is the difference between the corner resize handles and those in the middle of each slide?
4. What colour backgrounds are best for slides displayed on a screen?

Prove it!

Exercise I

1. Open the file **Garden Club Presentation** that you started at the end of the last chapter.
2. Add a second slide, using the **Title, Text and Clip Art** slide layout.
3. Give it the title **Agenda**.
4. Create a numbered indented list as follows:

   1 Pests
   2 Last year's prizes
         Best vegetables
         Best flowers
         Best greenhouse
   3 Treasurer's report
   4 Your committee
   5 Next year's trips
   6 Any other business

5. Insert a clip art image relating to gardening.
6. Add a third slide using the **Title and Text** slide layout.
7. Add the title **Pests**.
8. Create a bulleted list, using square bullets, as follows.

   - Whitefly or Greenfly?
   - The rise of the Harlequin Ladybird.
   - Problems with Vine Weevils.

9. Add the **Maple** design template to all slides.
10. Change the colour scheme to a **pale** background, and change the title text colour to **black**.
11. Save your work.

Prove it!

Exercise 2

1. Open the file **Interview Presentation** that you started at the end of the last section.
2. Add two more slides. Use one to highlight four things in your career to date that give you the experience for the job. Use the next to identify your personal characteristics that mean you are perfect for it.
3. Add an image to each slide.
4. Select an appropriate design template.
5. Select a colour scheme suitable for displaying on a screen, and apply to all slides.
6. Save your work.
7. Close the file and exit PowerPoint.

Getting PowerPoint to work for you

Learning objectives

By working through this lesson you will learn:
- ◉ how to use PowerPoint's master slides
- ◉ how to set user preferences
- ◉ how to use different view modes.

PowerPoint has several features that will help you create your presentations. A master slide gives your presentation a common look and feel. Setting user preferences will set default locations for your files, and note you as their creator.

Using master slides

A **master slide** lets you keep the look of a presentation consistent. It provides default settings for things like a colour scheme, a design template, bullets and text fonts, colour and size. You can also add objects such as slide numbers and graphics. They will appear automatically on all slides based on the master slide.

Applying a master slide

1. Open PowerPoint.
2. Open the presentation **Using a Master Slide** on the CD-ROM.
3. Save the file as **My Master Slide**.
4. Select **Master** from the **View** menu, and then click **Slide Master**.

The **master slide** appears, together with its toolbar (Figure 6.21 on page 337). Your presentation will be based on the content, format and positions of items on the master slide.

Entering text into a footer (6.2.3.2)

1. Click **Header and Footer...** on the **View** menu to display the **Header and Footer** dialogue box (Figure 6.22 on page 337).
2. Tick the **Footer** tick box, and type your name in the text box.
3. Click the **Apply to All** button.

The footer on the master slide will not change. To see the footer in place, you will need to close the master file.

4. Click **Close Master View** on the **Slide Master View** toolbox.
5. Have a look at the slides to see the footer on all of them.

Note

A company or organisation will use a master slide that ensures the corporate colours, fonts, logo etc. appear correctly whenever an employee gives a presentation.

Note

If you have opened the **Header and Footer** dialogue box from the master slide, you will only be able to apply any changes to **all the slides**.

If you want to apply, for example, a footer to **a specific slide**, you need to open the **Header and Footer** dialogue box with the slide you want selected, and not the master slide.

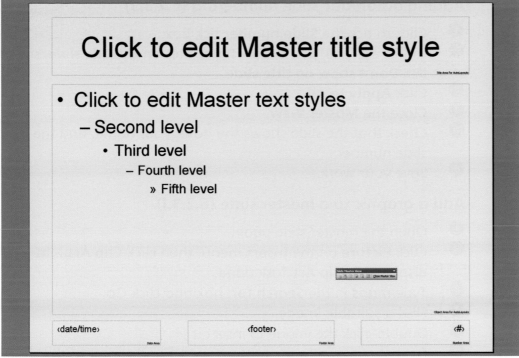

Figure 6.21 An example master slide

Adding a date to footer (6.2.3.3)

① Open the master slide and **Header and Footer** dialogue box again.

② Tick the **Date and time** tick box to include it on the slides.

You now have two choices. First, to include a date that updates automatically from your computer's system clock. Second, to include a fixed date that does not change once you have typed it.

③ Click the **Fixed** radio button.

④ Type the date (e.g. 03 July 2008) in the text box.

Do not apply the changes for the moment.

Select features to appear in the footer

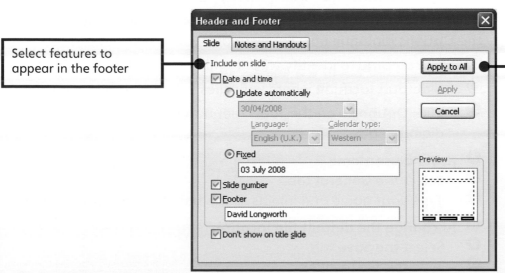

Clicking here will apply the feature to all the slides (except, in this case, the title slide). The **Apply** button will be available if you are using a selected slide

Figure 6.22 Applying footer features

Adding automatic slide numbering (6.2.3.3)

① Click to tick the **Slide number** tick box.

② In this exercise, don't show the footer on the title slide, so tick **Don't show on title slide**.

③ Click **Apply to All**.

④ Close the **Master View**.

⑤ Check that the slide shows the date, your name, and the slide number.

⑥ Save your work.

Add a graphic to a master slide (6.2.3.1)

① Open the master slide again.

② Click **Picture** on the **Insert** menu, then click **Clip Art...** to display the **Clip Art** Task pane.

③ Type **maps** in the **Search for:** box and click **Go**.

④ Find a suitable image.

⑤ Double-click the image to insert it.

⑥ Drag the image to the bottom right-hand corner of the slide.

⑦ Close the **Master View**.

⑧ Check that the clip art appears on all the slides.

⑨ Save your work.

To delete an image on a master slide, simply open the master slide, select the image and press the **Delete** key.

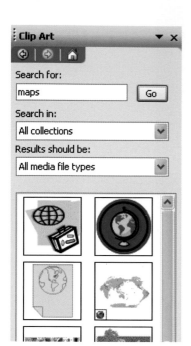

Figure 6.23 Searching for clip art

Note

Once you have chosen a default location for saving files, PowerPoint will automatically display that location when you come to open files.

Warning!

File locations need to be presented in a specific and accurate way. Refer to Module 2, page 61.

Setting user preferences

You can set some options in PowerPoint so that you can use it more efficiently.

The Options dialogue box (6.1.2.1)

Like other Microsoft Office applications you set user preferences in the **Options** dialogue box. For example, you might want to set:

◉ a **username** to identify who the file belongs to

◉ a **default location** where your files will always be saved.

① Click **Options...** on the **Tools** menu to display the **Options** dialogue box.

Ⓐ **To set a username**

② Select the **General** tab.

③ Type your name and initials in the **User Information** section.

Ⓑ **To change the default file location**

② Select the **Save** tab.

③ Type the file location.

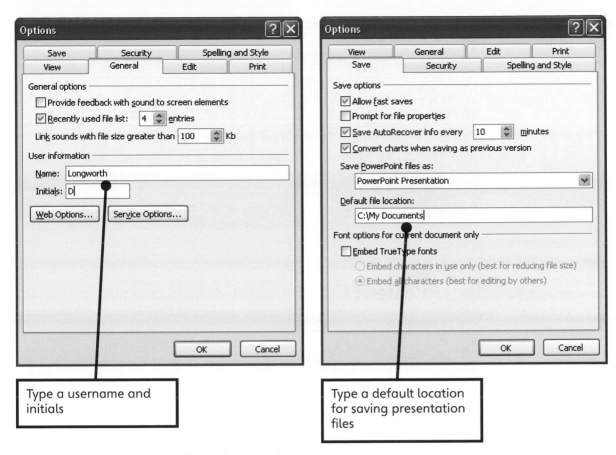

Type a username and initials

Type a default location for saving presentation files

Figure 6.24 Two tabs on the **Options** dialogue box

Test your understanding

① Why are master slides used?

② Describe the differences between using a master slide footer and a footer on individual slides.

③ How do you delete an image that is on a master slide?

④ Why might you want to add a username to a file?

You can find the answers to the questions on the CD-ROM saved as **Answers to TYU questions 6.3**. How did you do? Go back over anything that you are unsure about.

Prove it!

Exercise I

1. Open your file **Garden Club Presentation**.
2. Edit the master slide to show a fixed date (today's will do), automatic slide numbers, and the text **Green Fingers Gardening Club**, on all the slides.
3. Find a piece of clip art relevant to gardening.
4. Insert it on the master slide making sure that it does not obscure any text features on any slide.
5. Save your work.

Prove it!

Exercise 2

1. Open your presentation **Interview Presentation**.
2. Edit the master slide to show the current date automatically, your name in the footer and automatic slide numbering on all slides except the title slide.
3. Save your work.

Drawing

A presentation is unlikely to be comprised solely of text. You've already learned how to add images to slides to illustrate the content, but sometimes you will want to add simple lines and shapes as well.

You can find all the drawing tools on the **Drawing** toolbar.

1. Open PowerPoint.
2. Create a new presentation and save it as **My Presentation Graphics**.
3. On the title slide, type the title and subtitle:
   Title: **Presentation Graphics**
   Subtitle: **Adding and Manipulating Lines and Shapes**
4. Check that the **Drawing** toolbar is shown. If not, display it (see page 319).
5. Take a few moments to identify the buttons.

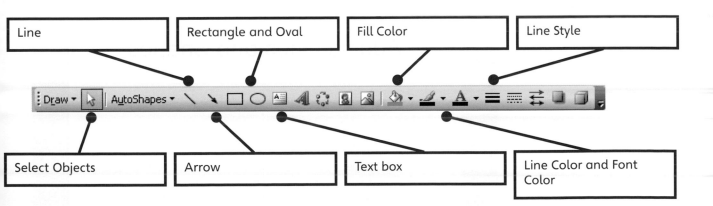

Figure 6.25 The **Drawing** toolbar

6. Add a new slide to the presentation and apply the **Title Only** slide layout.

Tip!

Having drawn a shape, you can set its properties as the default that will be applied to all other shapes you draw. This keeps your slides looking consistent.

① Click the shape to select it.

② Click the **Draw** button and select **Set AutoShape Defaults** from the menu that appears.

Drawing shapes and lines (6.5.2.I)

You are going to draw some shapes on the slide. Don't worry about getting these shapes lined up exactly.

① Type **Adding Lines and Shapes** in the title placeholder.

② Click the **Rectangle** button 🔲 on the **Drawing** toolbar. The mouse pointer changes to cross hairs.

③ Click in the top left of the slide, then, holding down the mouse button, drag down and right. Release the button when you have drawn the shape.

④ Repeat steps 2 and 3, but this time press the **Shift** key as you drag out the rectangle on the bottom left of the slide. This 'forces' the rectangle into a square shape.

Prove it!

Now draw an oval and a circle on the right-hand side of the slide. Use the **Oval** button ◯ on the **Drawing** toolbar. Use the **Shift** key to 'force' the oval into a circle as you drag it out.

Tip!

If you want to accurately draw a vertical or horizontal line, hold down the **Shift** key as you drag out a line.

⑤ Click the **Line** button ＼ on the **Drawing** toolbar, click in the top middle of the slide and drag out a vertical line to separate the rectangle/square from the oval/circle.

⑥ Draw a horizontal line separating the top two images from the bottom two.

⑦ Add text boxes (see page 332) labelling each shape.

Your slide will look similar to this.

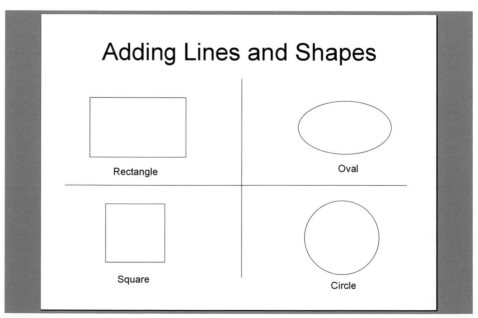

Figure 6.26 Example slide with drawn shapes

⑧ Create a new slide, similar to slide 2, with the title **Adding Arrows**.

⑨ Click the **Arrow** button 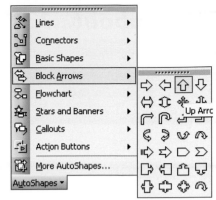 on the **Drawing** toolbar and drag a vertical line downwards in the left half of the slide. An arrowhead will appear when you release the mouse button.

⑩ Click the **AutoShapes** button AutoShapes ▾ on the **Drawing** toolbar.

⑪ Select **Block Arrows** and choose an upward pointing arrow style.

⑫ Drag out the arrow.

⑬ Add text boxes labelling each arrow as shown below.

Figure 6.27 Selecting **AutoShapes**

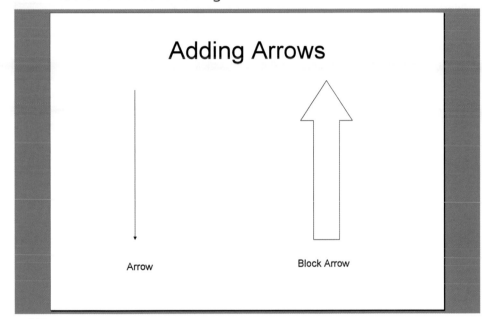

Figure 6.28 Example slide with drawn arrows

Adding text to shapes (6.5.2.2)

You can add text to shapes such as block arrows, rectangles, squares, ovals and circles.

❶ Click **slide 2** on the **Slides** pane to select it, then right-click the oval to show a shortcut menu.

❷ Select **Add Text** and type **My added text**. PowerPoint aligns the text centrally in the shape.

Copying and moving a slide (6.2.2.5)

❶ Click **slide 2** on the **Slides** pane to select it, then right-click it to show a shortcut menu.

❷ Click **Copy**.

❸ Click **Paste**. A copy of **slide 2** is positioned as **slide 3**.

❹ Drag and drop **slide 3** so it is positioned after **slide 4**. The slides are renumbered.

❺ Click **slide 4** to select it, if it isn't already.

Tip!

The **AutoShapes** palette contains many other useful shapes. Try some out to practise drawing.

Tip!

If you want to draw several images of the same shape, double-click the **Drawing** toolbar button to keep it selected.

Note

You can use the **Cut** and **Paste** options to move a slide without making a copy.

How about...?

Alternatively, click the **Cut, Copy** or **Paste** buttons ✂ 📋 📋 on the **Standard** toolbar to move and copy slides in a presentation.

Format shapes (6.5.2.3)

❶ Delete the text from the oval.

❷ Select the square by clicking its border. The handles appear to show it is selected.

❸ Click **AutoShape...** on the **Format** menu to display the **Format AutoShape** dialogue box.

❹ Click the **Colors and Lines** tab.

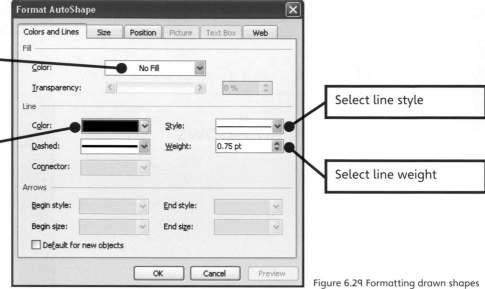

Select fill colour

Select line colour

Select line style

Select line weight

Figure 6.29 Formatting drawn shapes

Figure 6.30 Selecting a fill colour

To change fill colour

❶ Click the arrow to the right of the **Color:** selection box in the **Fill** section of the dialogue box.

❷ Select the **light blue** colour from the palette.

❸ Click **OK**.

To change line colour, weight and style

❶ Click the horizontal line to select it.

❷ Open the **Format Autoshape** dialogue box.

❸ Click the arrow to the right of the **Color:** selection box in the **Line** section of the dialogue box.

❹ Select the **red** colour from the palette.

❺ Click the arrow to the right of the **Style:** selection box and select a double line style.

❻ Select a **3 pt** weight in the **Weight:** box.

❼ Click **OK**.

❽ Apply similar formatting to the vertical line.

Applying shadow (6.5.2.5)

❶ Click the square to select it again.

❷ Click the **Shadow Style** button 🔲 on the **Drawing** toolbar to display a palette of different shadows.

❸ Click **Shadow Style 6** to apply it.

Your slide will look similar to Figure 6.31 on page 345.

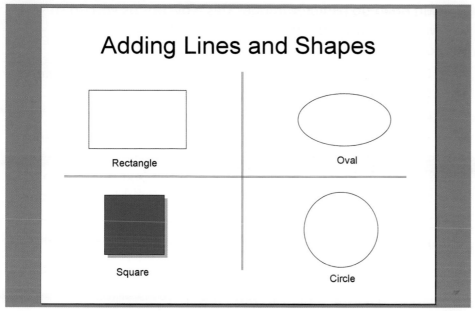

Figure 6.31 Formatted lines

Formatting arrows (6.5.2.4)

1 Create a copy of **slide 3** and position it as **slide 5**.

2 Open the **Format Autoshape** dialogue box.

3 Select the **Oval** arrowhead from the **Begin style:** selection box in the **Arrows** section of the dialogue box.

4 Select the **Oval** arrowhead from the **End style:** selection box in the **Arrows** section of the dialogue box.

5 Click **OK**.

6 Save your work.

Ordering graphic images (6.5.2.7)

1 Create a new slide with a **Title Only** layout.

2 Give it the title **Graphic Layout**.

3 Draw an oval in the centre of the slide, and fill it with a pale colour.

4 Draw a circle over the oval so it overlaps, and fill it with a darker colour.

5 Draw a square over the other objects so it extends beyond them, and fill it with a contrasting colour.

6 Draw a text box and type **The Logo Co**.

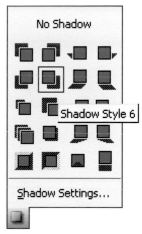

Figure 6.32 Adding shadow

The image will look similar to this. The shapes are layered in the order that you created them. The oval is at the bottom, and is partially obscured by the circle. The square is partially obscuring the shapes underneath it.

Figure 6.33 Ordering

You can build up complex images this way, but as you do so you will want to reorder the layers.

Suppose you want the oval at the front.

❶ Right-click the oval to select it and display a shortcut menu.

❷ Click **Order**, then click **Bring to Front**.

This has hidden the text.

❸ Right-click the oval again, click **Order**, and then click **Send Backward**.

The oval is positioned one layer back and the text box is visible.

Now suppose you want the circle to be in the middle. This is one layer forward of where it is now.

❹ Right-click the circle to select it and display the shortcut menu again.

❺ Click **Order**, then click **Bring Forward**.

The design will look similar to this.

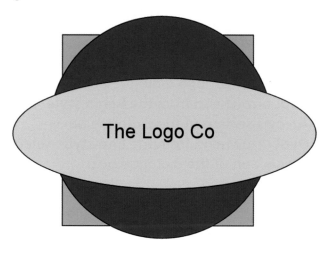

Grouping objects (6.5.2.6)

Now suppose you are happy with the design, but it is in the wrong place on the slide. You have already learned that you can select an object then drag it to a new position, but if you do this to your design, your carefully positioned shapes will be separated. You need to **group** the shapes so you can drag them all together in one go.

❶ Press and hold the **Shift** key while clicking each part of the image in turn to select them.

❷ Release the **Shift** key and right-click the selected objects.

❸ Click **Grouping**, then **Group** on the shortcut menu.

The individually selected parts of the image are grouped as one object. You can now move, copy etc. the group image as you need to.

To ungroup an object, right-click it and select **Grouping, Ungroup**.

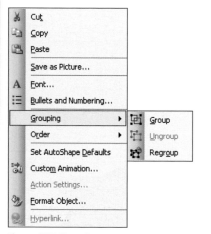

Figure 6.34 Grouping

How about...?

Alternatively, click the slide and drag a frame over the objects to select them all.

Prove it!

Exercise 1

1. Create a new slide in your file.
2. Use the techniques you have just learned to re-create this noughts and crosses game.
3. Align the grid for the game with the centre and middle of the slide.
4. Include the text box.
5. Save your file.

Noughts and Crosses

Win with three adjacent symbols

Prove it!

Exercise 2

1. Open your file **Garden Club Presentation**.
2. Select **slide 3**, **Pests**.
3. Use the **"No" Symbol** (an **AutoShape** basic shape) and a piece of clip art to create this graphic.
4. The **"No" Symbol** is **red** and in front of the pest.
5. Adjust the size of the pest so it fits in the **"No" Symbol** as shown.
6. Group the two graphics so they form a single object.
7. Resize and position the graphic so it fits neatly between the last line of text and the footer.
8. Align the graphic with the centre of the slide.
9. Save your file.

Prove it!

Exercise 3

1. Open the presentation **Interview Presentation**.
2. Add lines, shapes, and images to your slides, to enhance the meaning of the text. Be creative and enjoy yourself, but remember too much embellishment can detract from the message you are trying to convey.
3. Save your file.

Learning objectives

By working through this lesson you will learn:
- how to use tables on slides
- how to create charts and graphs
- how to format charts and graphs
- how to create and modify organisation charts.

Tables

Sometimes a table can be an effective way of presenting information. A table is usually used for numerical data which can be assessed more easily than a list. In this lesson, you will add a table to present the population information you met earlier in a different way.

1. Open PowerPoint.
2. Open the file **Tables and Charts**, and save it as **My Tables and Charts**.
3. Insert a new slide and give it the **Title and Table** slide layout.
4. Move the slide so it is the last in the presentation.
5. Type **Table of Population and Land Mass** as the slide title.
6. Double-click in the table placeholder to display the **Insert Table** dialogue box.
7. Enter **3** columns and **7** rows.
8. Click **OK** to create the table.

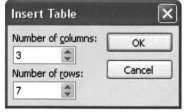

Figure 6.35 Selecting the number of rows and columns

Entering and editing text into a table slide (6.3.4.1)

1. Click in a cell to place the text insertion point.
2. Type in the details shown in the table on the next page. If you make a mistake, click in the relevant cell and use the **Backspace** or **Delete** keys to delete, then retype the data.
3. Format the table as shown: use the buttons on the **Formatting** toolbar that you are used to.

The following will help you select cells if you need to.

Selecting cells in a table (6.3.4.2)

- Double-click in a cell to select it.
- Press **Tab** on the keyboard to select the next cell.

Note

You do not have to apply colour to the rows unless you want to.

Tip!

Use the keyboard arrow keys to move between table cells.

- Press **Shift+Tab** on the keyboard to select the previous cell.
- Select a cell and hold down the mouse button as you drag to select groups of cells.
- To select a column, move the cursor just above the top border of a column so the pointer is a down-facing arrow, then click.
- Click in any cell and press **Ctrl+A** to select the whole table.

Continents	Population (%)
Africa	14
America	14
Asia	60
Australia	1
Antarctica	0
Europe	12

Deleting and adding a row/column (6.3.4.3)

The rows should be in alphabetical order.

Land mass (%)
20
28
13
29
6
7

1. Right-click in the **Antarctica** row, and click **Delete Rows** on the shortcut menu.
2. Right-click in the **Asia** row, and click **Insert Rows** on the shortcut menu. A blank row is inserted above the one you clicked.
3. Re-enter the **Antarctica** data and format it.
4. Right-click the **Population** column with the black down-arrow showing (as described above), and click **Insert Columns**. A blank column is inserted to the left of the selected column.
5. Type in and format the **Land mass** data shown.

Modifying column width and row height (6.3.4.4)

The table would look better if the number columns were narrower.

1. Move the mouse cursor over the column border between the **Land mass** and the **Population** columns. At the boundary, it will change to a double-headed arrow ⁌‖⁍ .
2. When this happens, click and hold the mouse button as you drag the border to the left. Drag it so that the **(%)** text just appears on a new line.
3. Do the same for the **Population** column.

Tip!

You can delete a column by first selecting it, and then selecting **Delete Columns** on the shortcut menu.

Tip!

You can change row heights by dragging the row borders.

Charts and graphs

You have seen how tables can make lists of figures more accessible. In a similar way, charts and graphs make it easier to compare and understand data in tables. For most people, a graph or chart is the best way to communicate numerical information. In this section, you will see how to record the basic data, and then present it in a series of charts.

Input data to create a chart (6.4.1.1)

1. Insert a new **Title and Chart** slide after the current last slide in your presentation.
2. Click in the **Title** placeholder and type **Population Chart**.
3. Double-click in the **Chart** placeholder. PowerPoint will display an example datasheet and bar graph.
4. Enter the population data you used for the table into the datasheet.
5. Delete the second and third columns that you do not need by clicking the grey column headers and pressing the **Delete** key.
6. As you type the chart is updated with the new text and figures. When you have finished, it will look like this.

> **Tip!**
>
> You can drag the datasheet boundaries and column boundaries to widen them.

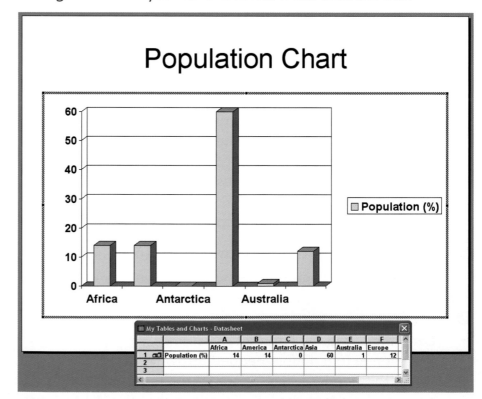

Figure 6.36 Adding data to a chart datasheet

7. Click anywhere outside the datasheet to see the slide.

Select a chart and change the chart type (6.4.1.2–3)

❶ Click the chart to select it.

❷ Now double-click it so a grey border appears around it.

❸ Right-click one of the bars, and click **Chart Type…** on the shortcut menu to open the **Chart Type** dialogue box.

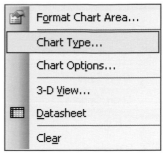

Figure 6.37 Opening the **Chart Type** dialogue box

❹ Select the chart type

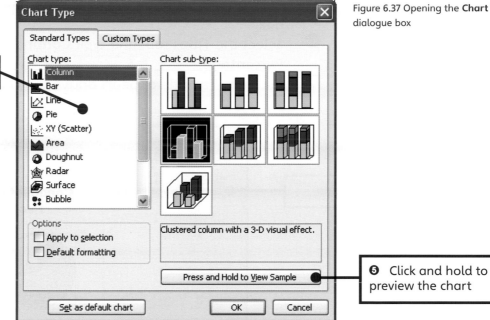

❺ Click and hold to preview the chart

Figure 6.38 Selecting a chart type

❹ Click **Line** in the **Chart type:** section.

❺ Click and hold the **Press and Hold to View Sample** button. A line graph could be drawn but it is not very meaningful as we have not got continuous data.

❻ Release the button.

❼ Click **Pie** in the **Chart type:** section, and preview it. A pie chart could be drawn and would be good to show the relative size of the populations.

❽ Keep the default pie chart format and click **OK**.

The slide will look similar to Figure 6.39. You need to format it so it is more useful.

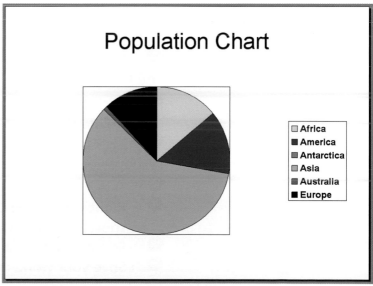

Figure 6.39 A pie chart of the population data

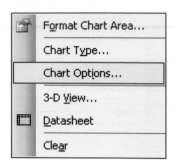

Figure 6.40 Opening the **Chart Options** dialogue box

The chart title (6.4.1.4)

You need to give the chart a title.

① Double-click the chart to select it.

② Move the mouse around the selected area, including the white spaces. Take note of the screen tips telling you what the different parts of the chart are called.

③ Right-click the **Chart Area** to display a shortcut menu.

④ Click **Chart Options...** to display the **Chart Options** dialogue box.

⑤ Select the **Titles** tab, and type **Continent Population Percentages**.

⑥ Click **OK**. The title appears above the chart.

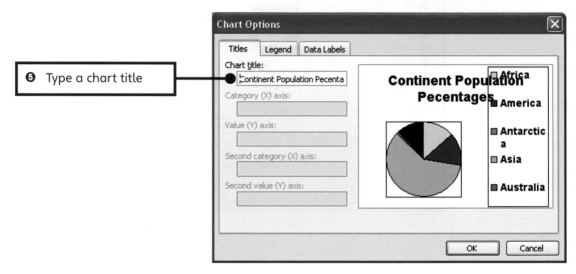

Figure 6.41 Adding a chart title

This title looks rather long.

⑦ Select the chart by double-clicking it.

The **Chart Title** text box is highlighted along with the chart.

⑧ Click to place the insertion point in the **Chart Title** box. Delete the word **Continent**.

⑨ Click anywhere ouside the text box to complete the edit.

Perhaps you don't need both a slide title and a chart title.

⑩ Select the chart again.

⑪ Right-click in the **Chart Title** text box, and click **Clear** on the shortcut menu. The **Chart Title** is removed.

⑫ Edit the **Slide title** to be **Population Percentages**.

⑬ Save your work.

Adding data labels (6.4.1.5)

Although you can see on the pie chart the relative proportions for the different populations, it would be useful if you could also display the actual percentages in figures.

① Select the chart.

② Right-click in one of the sectors and select **Format Data Series...** from the shortcut menu to display the **Format Data Series** dialogue box.

③ Click the **Data Labels** tab, and click the **Percentage** tick box to select it.

④ Click **OK** to display the percentages.

⑤ Save your work.

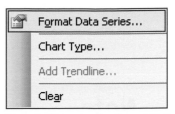

Figure 6.42 Opening the **Format Data Series** dialogue box

Tip!

On a line graph or bar chart, you would tick **Value** to display the number that is in the datasheet.

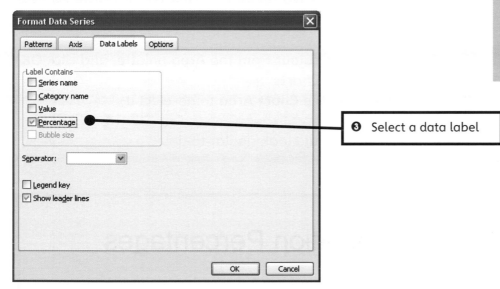

③ Select a data label

Figure 6.43 Adding data labels

Changing the background colour (6.4.1.6)

The chart could benefit from some colour changes to the sectors and to the background.

① Select the chart.

② Right-click in the **Chart Area** and select **Format Chart Area...** from the shortcut menu to display the **Format Chart Area** dialogue box.

③ Click the **Patterns** tab, and choose a **light blue** colour from the **Area** palette of colours. Click **OK**.

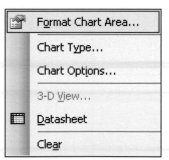

Figure 6.44 Opening the **Format Chart Area** dialogue box

Note

PowerPoint provides a large range of colours and fill effects for formatting charts. Use them carefully and sparingly, and remember the purpose of each slide is to put over information effectively to the audience. Too much formatting can detract from the slide content!

4. Right-click in the **Plot Area** of the chart and select **Format Plot Area...** from the shortcut menu to display the **Format Plot Area** dialogue box.
5. Click **None** in the **Border** area, then click **OK** to remove the border around the pie chart.

Note

You can use all these formatting techniques on different types of graph and chart.

Change the sector colour (6.4.1.7)

Finally, to finish the pie chart slide, you are going to change the colour of the black sector which doesn't look right with the other colours.

1. With the chart selected, click the **Series** area of the pie chart circle, then click the **black** sector so only it is selected.
2. Right-click the selected sector and click **Format Data Point...** from the shortcut menu to display the **Format Data Point** dialogue box.
3. Choose a **mauve** colour from the **Area** palette, and click **OK** to apply it to the **Chart**.
4. Click away from the **Chart Area** to deselect it.
5. Save your work.

Your finished chart should look similar to this.

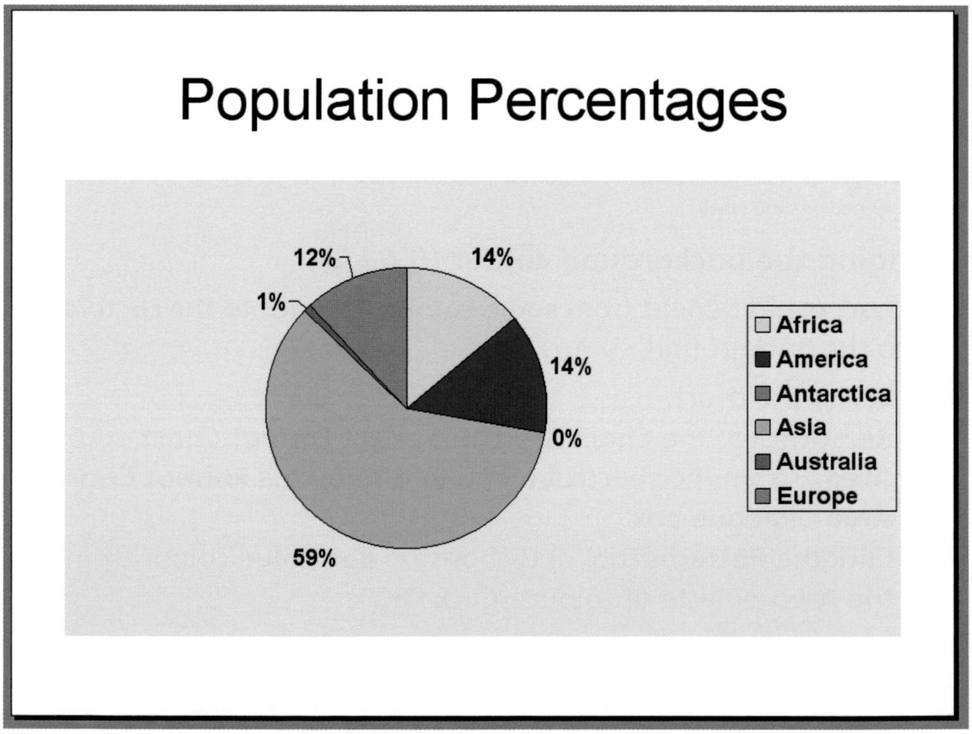

Figure 6.45 The finished example chart

Organisation charts

Create an organisation chart (6.4.2.1)

① Insert a new **Title and Diagram or Organization Chart** slide after the current last slide in your presentation.

② Click in the **Title** placeholder and type **An Organisation Chart**.

③ Double-click in the **Chart** placeholder. PowerPoint will display the **Diagram Gallery**. The **Organization Chart** is selected. Click **OK**.

PowerPoint creates an organisation chart for you. Note that the **Organization Chart** toolbar is displayed automatically.

Tip!

Read the description on the dialogue box when you click a diagram type.

Figure 6.46 The **Diagram Gallery**

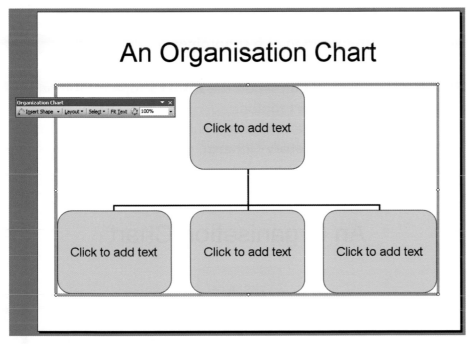

Figure 6.47 The organisation chart and toolbar

④ Click in each placeholder in turn and type in the names and roles shown below. Press **Return** to create new lines as required. Use the **Italic** button on the **Formatting** toolbar where needed.

Tip!

To format the chart, right-click any part of the chart and select **Format Organization Chart...** or **Format AutoShape...**

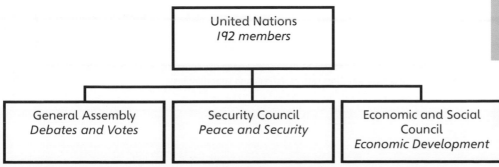

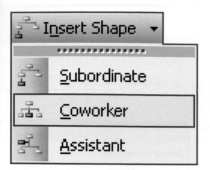

Figure 6.48 Adding a coworker

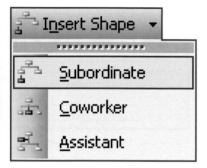

Figure 6.49 Adding a subordinate

Add and remove coworkers and subordinates (6.4.2.3)

Add coworkers

There are three more principal branches in the United Nations. Add one of these now.

➊ Select the **Economic and Social Council** box by clicking the border.

➋ Click the selection arrow on the **Insert Shape** button on the **Organization Chart** toolbar.

➌ Select **Coworker**. A new box is created. Complete it as follows. Type **Secretariat**, press **Return** for a new line then type **Works for other principal branches**.

Add subordinates

The Secretary-General of the United Nations is the head of the Secretariat and is the spokesman and leader of the United Nations. Add this position as a subordinate.

➊ Select the **Secretariat** box.

➋ Click the selection arrow on the **Insert Shape** button on the **Organization Chart** toolbar.

➌ Select **Subordinate**. A new box is created. Complete it as follows. Type **Secretary-General**, press **Return** for a new line then type **Ban Ki-moon**.

Tip!

If the text doesn't fit neatly in the boxes, click **Fit Text** on the **Organization Chart** toolbar.

Tip!

Use the **Zoom** function if the text is too small to read easily.

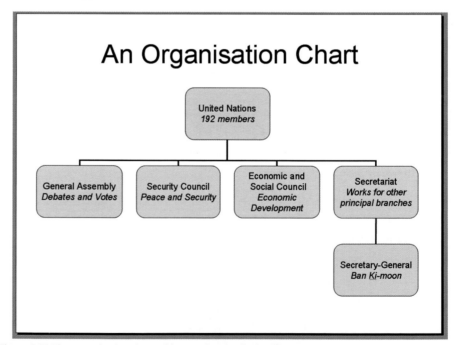

Figure 6.50 The organisation chart with coworkers and subordinates

Prove it!

1. Create two new coworkers under the **United Nations** box as follows:

International Court of Justice *Legal Matters*	Trusteeship Council *(Suspended)*

2. Create a new subordinate under the **Secretary-General** box as follows:

Dept of Peace-keeping Operations

> ### *Tip!*
> Don't forget to use the spellchecker.

The **Trusteeship Council** has no functions at the moment and is suspended. Delete it from the chart.

4. Select the **Trusteeship Council** box and press **Delete**.

Change the hierarchical structure of a chart (6.4.2.2)

Now imagine that the **Dept of Peace-keeping Operations** is transferred to the **Security Council**. You can change the structure of the chart easily.

1. Select the **Dept of Peace-keeping Operations** box and drag it over the **Security Council** box.
2. Release the mouse button. The box moves to the new position.
3. Save your file.

> ### *Tip!*
> If you are moving a box that has subordinates, don't forget to select all the group before dragging it to its new position.

The organisation chart now looks like this.

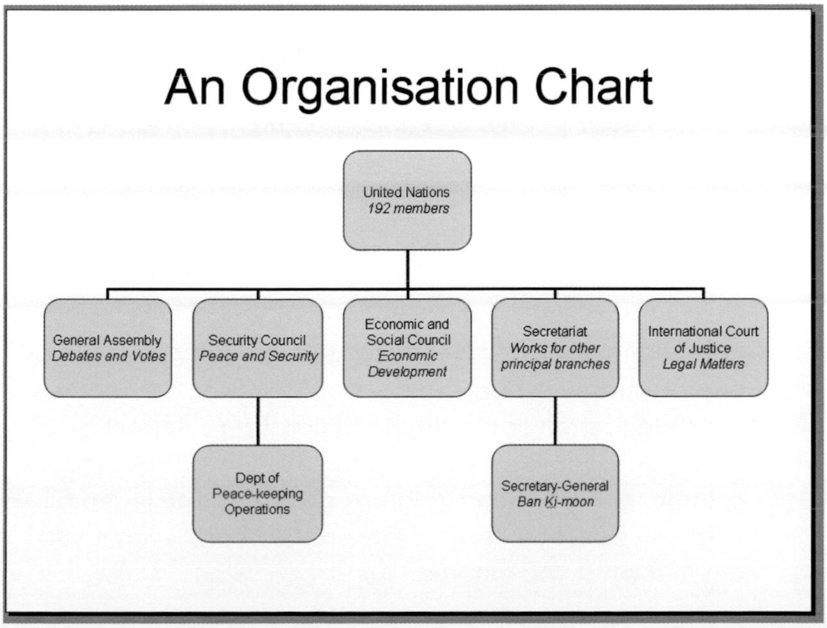

An Organisation Chart
United Nations
192 members
General Assembly
Debates and Votes
Security Council
Peace and Security
Economic and Social Council
Economic Development
Secretariat
Works for other principal branches
International Court of Justice
Legal Matters
Dept of Peace-keeping Operations
Secretary-General
Ban Ki-moon

Figure 6.51 The completed organisation chart

You can find the answers to the questions on the CD-ROM saved as **Answers to TYU questions 6.5**. How did you do? Go back over anything that you are unsure about.

1. Why do you need to check your spelling in a presentation?
2. Imagine you are going to give a presentation to the Board of Directors about your department's performance. What kind of graph should you use:
   a) to show expected sales, month by month
   b) to show the proportions of your sales from each region you work in
   c) to compare last year's income to this year's income?

Prove it!

Exercise I

1. Open your file **Garden Club Presentation**.
2. Create a new **slide 4**, with a **Title and Table** layout. Give it the title **Prizes**.
3. Create this table, and format it as shown.

Category	Winner	Prize
Best Flower Garden	Hasim Arfan	Johnson vase
Best Vegetable Garden	Bernie Coughlin	£75 voucher
Best Greenhouse	Beata Zywicky	£50 voucher

4. Create a new **slide 5**, with a **Title and Chart** layout. Give it the title **Treasurer's Report**.
5. Create this data set:

	Subs	Fees Paid	Prizes	Equip. Bought	Pest Control	Misc.
Income	879					
Expenditure		85	125	410	150	75

6. Create a **bar chart** with a chart title **Income and Expenditure 2008**. Show the data values, and colour the bars **red** for expenditure and **blue** for income.
7. Copy **slide 5** to a new **slide 6**.
8. On **slide 6**, change the title to **Expenditure Report**.
9. In the data set, delete the **Income** row, the **Subs**criptions column, and any other columns shown on the legend. (Any column you typed in will show on the chart, even if you deleted what you entered.)

10   Change the chart type to a **pie chart** that shows the data values as **percentages**.

11   Create a new **slide 7**, with a **Title and Diagram or Organization Chart** layout. Give it the title **Your Committee**.

12   Create this organisation chart:

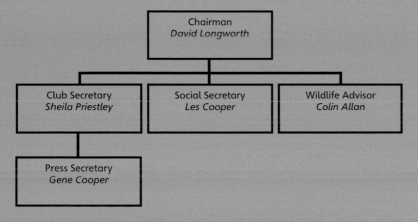

13   Change the committee structure so **Gene** works for **Les**.

14   Save your file.

Presentation

Learning objectives

By working through this lesson you will learn:

- ● how to use different views
- ● how to use slide transitions
- ● how to hide a slide
- ● how to animate slides
- ● how to print and save presentations in different ways.

Normal View

Slide Show

Slide Sorter View

Figure 6.52 PowerPoint presentation view buttons

Tip!

You can drag the pane borders to change their size.

Slide views (6.2.1.1/3, 6.2.2.6)

❶ Load PowerPoint.

❷ Open the file **Delivering Presentations** and save it as **Delivering My Presentations**.

PowerPoint provides three main views for you to use as you develop and show your presentation. You will find the three presentation view buttons in the bottom left of the PowerPoint window.

Normal View

Throughout this module you have been working in the **Normal View**. It consists of three panes: the **Outline/Slides pane**, the **Slide Area** and **Notes**. The **Slide Area** display slides one at a time. You use this view while developing slides because this is where you edit slides to add text and graphics etc. The **Outline/Slides pane** gives an overview of the slides.

Slide Sorter View

Use the **Slide Sorter View** to organise or rearrange slides. The screen looks like this.

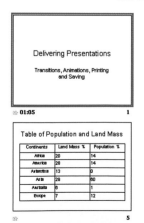

☆ 01:05   1

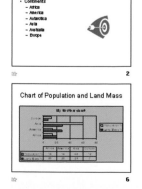

☆   2

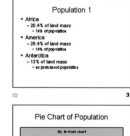

☆   3

☆   4

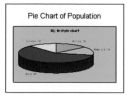

Figure 6.53 The Slide Sorter View

In **Slide Sorter View** you can:

- use select and drag, and cut or copy and paste to rearrange the presentation order of your slides
- position the pointer between two slides then click the **New Slide** button to create a new slide in that position
- delete a selected slide with the **Delete** key.

Slide Show

This is the presentation in action! It shows your slides one at a time on the full screen. Simply click the mouse button to move forward through the slides. Try it now.

Transition effects (6.6.1.1)

Transition effects are ways that the slides change from one to the next. You can even apply timings so the slides change automatically after a set time. Used carefully they can be used effectively to hold the audience's attention. It is easiest to apply them from **Slide Sorter View**.

Note

PowerPoint has many built-in transition effects, some of them fun to use. However, use them sparingly and carefully! Always keep in mind the purpose of your presentation and the audience. For instance, the example file demonstrates some of the many transitions available, but imagine how annoying it would be if they were all used in a real-life presentation (especially the drum roll every time a slide appears!).

1. Display the **Slide Sorter View**.
2. Click **slide 2** to select it.
3. Click **Slide Transition...** on the **Slide Show** menu to display the **Slide Transition** Task pane.
4. Select **Blinds Horizontal**. The transition is previewed in the **Slide Sorter** pane.
5. Click the **Play** button at the bottom of the pane to see the transition again.
6. In the **Modify transition** section, select **Slow** in the **Speed:** selection box and **Drum Roll** in the **Sound:** selection box.
7. In the **Advance slide** section, tick the box to advance **On mouse click**.
8. Click the **Apply to All Slides** button.
9. Click the **Slide Show** button to see and hear the effects on a full screen.

Tip!

Use the **Zoom** function to view the thumbnails more clearly.

Note

(6.6.2.4) The Slide Show starts from the currently selected slide. Press **Home** to return to the first slide. Press **Esc** to exit the show.

Figure 6.54 The Slide Transition pane

Tip!

Select **No Transition** to remove a transition effect.

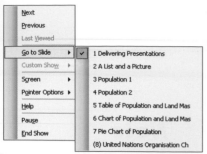

Figure 6.55 The **Go to Slide** menu options

Tip!

It is good practice to use unique slide titles because it helps you navigate round your presentation.

How about...?

Alternatively, use the navigation buttons on the slide.

How about...?

Alternatively, you can right-click the slide and use the shortcut menu to hide/show a slide.

How about...?

Alternatively, you can hide/show a slide by selecting it in the **Slides** pane.

Navigating a Slide Show (6.6.2.5)

❶ Go to **Slide Show View**.

❷ Right-click anywhere on the slide to display a shortcut menu.

❸ Take a moment to see the options, then select **Go to Slide** and select the first slide.

❹ Click a slide to move to the next one, or use the shortcut menu.

Hide a slide (6.6.1.5)

Hide a slide if you don't want to display it, but want to keep it in the file for future use.

❶ Select **slide 8** in the **Slide Sorter View**.

❷ Click **Hide Slide** on the **Slide Show** menu.

The slide number now has a line through it, showing it is hidden.

❸ Run the **Slide Show** and check that **slide 8** is no longer displayed.

❹ Press **Esc** to return.

❺ Repeat step 2 to show the slide again.

Figure 6.56 A hidden slide

Using animation (6.6.1.2)

In this section you will learn how to animate elements of your slides to create some attention-grabbing effects. Again, be careful about over-doing the use of animations – they can enhance a presentation if used appropriately, but they can also detract from it.

Animations are different from slide transitions. They are effects that happen on a slide, rather than effects that happen as one slide changes to another.

❶ Show the **Slide Sorter View**.

❷ Click **slide 5** to select it.

❸ Click **Animation Schemes...** on the **Slide Show** menu to display the **Slide Design** Task pane showing **Animation Schemes**.

❹ Click **Bounce** in the **Exciting** section and watch the effect.

Animating slide elements

You can add animations to different slide elements using the **Normal View**.

❶ Show the **Normal View** and show **slide I**.

❷ Click **Custom Animation...** on the **Slide Show** menu. The **Custom Animation** Task pane appears.

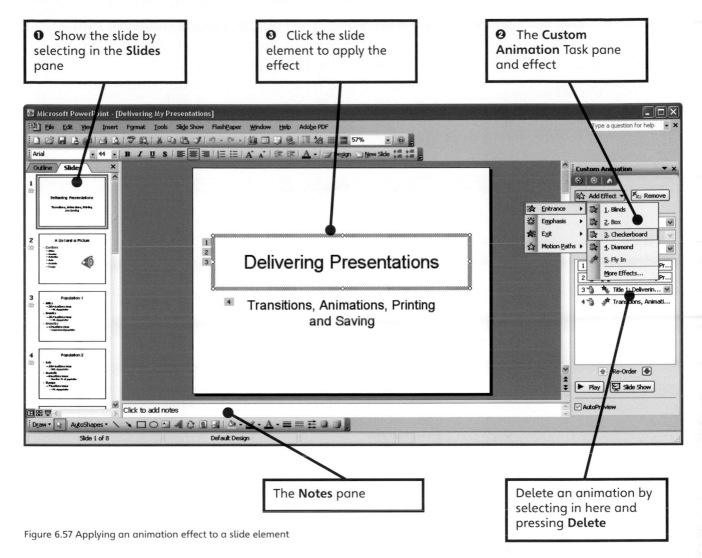

❶ Show the slide by selecting in the **Slides** pane

❸ Click the slide element to apply the effect

❷ The **Custom Animation** Task pane and effect

The **Notes** pane

Delete an animation by selecting in here and pressing **Delete**

Figure 6.57 Applying an animation effect to a slide element

❸ Click the slide title to select it.
❹ Click the **Add Effect** button.
❺ Select **Checkerboard** from the **Entrance** menu item, and watch the effect.

To remove an animation

The animations are listed in the Task pane. You can remove animations here.

◉ Click the third animation to select it, and press **Delete**.

Adding notes for the presenter (6.6.1.3)

To help you give your presentation, you can add notes. They are not visible in Slide Show View. You usually print them as your speaking notes when giving the presentation, and they can remind you of important things you need to say which you might forget in the 'excitement' of the talk.

The **Notes** pane is located at the bottom of the **Normal View** screen (Figure 6.57).

Tip!

Use the **Modify** section of the Task pane to alter how the animation effect is applied to the slide element.

Tip!

Change the size of the **Notes** pane by dragging the border between it and the **Slide** area. If it isn't visible on your slide, drag up the bottom border.

❶ Select **slide 5** and type **Point out to the audience that not only Antarctica but Australia too has a very sparse population** into the Notes pane.

❷ Select **slide 6** and type the note **Australia and Antarctica omitted because their population is so low**.

❸ Select **slide 7** and type the note **Australia and Antarctica do not figure on here because their population is so low**.

❹ Save your work.

Slide setup (6.6.1.4, 6.6.2.2)

Occasionally you might need to display your presentation in a specific format.

❶ Click **Page Setup...** on the **File** menu to display the **Page Setup** dialogue box.

❷ Use the options to change slides and paper orientation, and to set **paper size**.

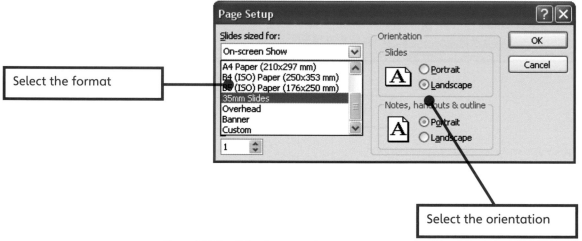

Select the format

Select the orientation

Figure 6.58 Specifying the page setup

Printing your presentation (6.6.2.3)

You can print slides in several different views.

◉ One slide per page.

◉ One slide per page, with notes.

◉ Handouts.

◉ The Outline View.

❶ Click **Print...** on the **File** menu to display the **Print** dialogue box.

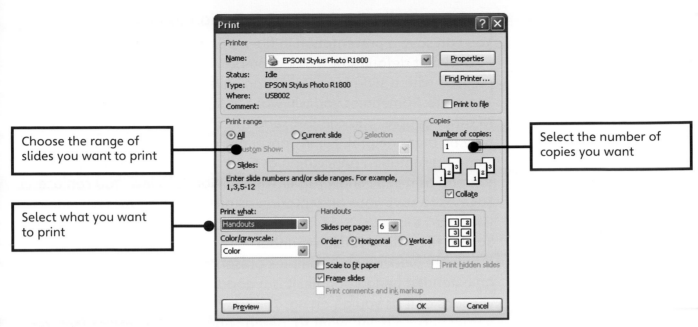

On the left of the figure:
Choose the range of slides you want to print

Select what you want to print

On the right of the figure:
Select the number of copies you want

Figure 6.59 The **Print** dialogue box

Printing all the slides

❶ Click the **All** radio button in the **Print range** section.

❷ Enter **I** in the **Number of copies:** selection box.

❸ Select **Slides** in the **Print what:** selection box.

❹ Select **Color** in the **Color/grayscale:** selection box.

❺ Click to tick the box to **Print hidden slides**.

❻ Click **OK**.

Print notes

❶ Click the **Slides** radio button in the **Print range** section.

❷ Enter **5-7** to print those slides with notes.

❸ Enter **I** in the **Number of copies:** selection box.

❹ Select **Notes** in the **Print what:** selection box.

❺ Select **Grayscale** in the **Color/grayscale:** selection box.

❻ Click to untick the box to **Print hidden slides**.

❼ Click **OK**.

Print handouts

The audience will probably want a handout of all your slides.

❶ Click the **All** radio button in the **Print** range section.

❷ Enter **2** in the **Number of copies:** selection box. (In reality you would normally print one set per audience member.)

❸ Select **Handouts** in the **Print what:** selection box.

❹ Select **6 Slides per page** and **Horizontal Order** in the **Handouts** section.

❺ Select **Grayscale** in the **Color/grayscale:** selection box.

❻ Click to untick the box to **Print hidden slides**.

❼ Click **OK**.

Saving and distributing a presentation (6.1.1.4)

You can save a presentation in file types other than the PowerPoint default (.ppt). For example, if you are particularly pleased with a slide format you can save it as a Slide Design Template. Sometimes you will want to send your presentation files to other people. You can just send the file as it is, but other ways may be more helpful. For instance, not everybody will use the same presentation application as you, or you may want the file to open as a Slide Show rather than in Normal View. You can use Save As to save your presentation as different file types to enable you to do this.

Save a file with a version number

If you are working on a complex presentation, perhaps over an extended period of time, it is a good idea to save different versions of it as you go along. This way you can go back to an earlier version if you want to, perhaps because it contains features you particularly like.

Identifying different versions of a file is as simple as saving it with its name plus a version identifier (e.g. Version 1 or v4 etc.).

❶ Follow the same procedure for saving a file with a new name that you learned on page 318.

❷ Leave the existing filename the same, but add the version number after the name (e.g. version 1).

❸ Click **OK**.

Save a file as a Design Template

❶ Follow the same procedure for saving a file with a new name that you learned on page 318.

❷ Click the **Save as type:** selection arrow and scroll down to find the **Design Template** type and click it.

❸ The template will be shown in the **Slide Design** Task pane.

Figure 6.60 Saving as a Design Template

Save for other applications

Rich Text Format is a format that can be opened by most applications. Unfortunately it does not save graphics or animations. Save as **Outline/RTF** format to save the text only.

Note

You can choose to save a PowerPoint presentation in many other formats. Useful ones are as another version of PowerPoint, as a Slide Show, and as a specific image type.

Test your understanding

You can find the answers to the questions on the CD-ROM saved as **Answers to TYU questions 6.6.** How did you do? Go back over anything that you are unsure about.

1. Describe **two** activities best done in **Normal View**.
2. Describe **two** activities best done in **Slide Sorter View**.
3. How do you apply different transitions to two slides?
4. How do you print the notes pages in landscape format?
5. Describe **three** advantages of saving different versions of your file.
6. What file type would you use if you didn't want people to be able to change your presentation?

Prove it!

Exercise I

1. Open your file **Garden Club Presentation**.
2. Add the following text to notes pages.

Slide I **Welcome, meeting to last less than one hour**
Slide 2 **Sasha Vargacz can provide advice on organic methods of pest control**
Slide 4 **Remember to commiserate with unlucky losers about last year's weather**
Slide 5 **There is no need to increase subscriptions this year**

3. Apply these transitions.

To all slides: **Cover Right-Up, Speed Fast, Advance On Mouse Click.**
To **slides 5** and **6**: **Box Out, Speed Medium, Advance On Mouse Click.**

4. Apply these animation schemes.

Fade in all to **slides I** and **7**.
On **slide 2**, the title **Entrance** with **Faded Zoom**.
On **slide 2**, the list **Entrance** with **Dissolve In** at **Medium** speed so each line appears separately, and turns **dark red** when you move to the next line.
On **slide 3**, the graphic to appear first, with **Spin Emphasis**.
On **slide 3**, the title with a **Scribble Motion Path**, to imitate how a ladybird might fly round the screen.
On **slide 3**, the list **Entrance** with **Random Effects**.
On **slide 4**, the title with a **Grow and turn exit**.
On **slide 5**, the bar graph to **Fly in from the right**, with a **Very Slow** speed.
On **slide 6**, the pie chart with a **Pinwheel Entrance**.

Continues...

⑤ Automate the presentation by setting **slides 1** to **4, 6** and **7** to advance automatically after **6 seconds**, and **slide 5** to advance after **12 seconds**.

⑥ Save your file:

    a) as a **slideshow**

    b) as a set of **Portable Network Graphics** images in a folder

    c) as a **Design Template**.

⑦ Change the colour scheme to one with a **white** background.

⑧ Print:

    a) **all** slides in **Notes** page format

    b) **all** slides, **2 to a page**

    c) **handouts, 6 to a page**, omitting **slide 4**.

Prove it!

Exercise 2

① Open the presentation **Interview Presentation**.

② Add **Exciting** transitions to every slide.

③ Add **Exciting** animations to every element of every slide.

④ Automate the presentation to advance slides after suitable lengths of time.

⑤ Remove these animations and transitions.

⑥ Add the actual transitions and animations that you will use in your interview.

⑦ Create notes pages to help you when presenting in your interview.

⑧ Save your work.

⑨ Create a version suitable for printing.

⑩ Save it as another file.

⑪ Print a set of notes pages for yourself.

⑫ Print two sets of handouts, 3 slides per page, for your interviewers.

This module covers the Internet. You will learn about Microsoft Internet Explorer and how to use it to go to web pages and search for information, and how to use the Address bar, the History list and Favorites which make it easy to revisit websites. You will learn about safety and privacy concerns, and how to subscribe to feeds and podcasts. You will also find out how to use the Internet for email communication.

MODULE 7.
web browsing and communication

Web browsing

Learning objectives

By working through this lesson you will learn:
- the difference between the Internet and the World Wide Web
- some key Internet jargon
- about Web addresses.

The Net and the Web (7.1.1.1–2)

The **Internet** consists of millions of computers, of all shapes and sizes, in tens of thousands of computer networks throughout the world. They are joined through a mixture of special high-speed cables, microwave links and ordinary public and private telephone lines. The Internet itself does not actually do anything – it is simply the hardware, software, data and the connections that join it all together. It can be used in several ways. The most important are the **World Wide Web** and **email**.

The World Wide Web is the simplest and most used way of organising and looking at the information held on the Internet. It consists of billions of pages, held in millions of computers, joined together by hyperlinks (often shortened to links) and viewed through a web browser, such as **Microsoft Internet Explorer**. Some pages are simple text, but most also have images. Some have videos or sound that you can enjoy online; others have links to files (programs, documents, pictures or multimedia) that you can download onto your computer. Some pages work interactively; some are places where people can meet and 'chat' by typing or talking.

Internet terms (7.1.1.3)

The terminology of the Net is full of TLA: Three Letter Acronyms. Here are the first three that you need to know.

- **ISP – Internet Service Provider**. A company which offers access to the Internet to businesses and individuals. Your phone line connects you to an ISP, and they connect into the main highways of the Internet. ISPs also usually provide email addresses and 'web space' in which people can set up their own websites.
- **URL – Uniform Resource Locator**. This is an Internet address. Every website, web page, file and person connected to the Internet has a URL.
- **WWW – World Wide Web**. Often referred to as 'the Web' as it is much faster to say than 'www'.

Web addresses (7.1.1.4)

Every document, file and web page on the Internet has an URL (Uniform Resource Locator). It tells you the name of the file, the computer (and perhaps which folder) it is stored on, and the organisation that owns it. The URL of a web page is often referred to as its address.

A web page URL may be a simple name:

http://www.cnet.com

This is the entrance to (or home page of) the CNET website. The letters http:// tell you that it is a **hyperlinked** web address; the letters www are how web addresses usually start; cnet.com is the domain name (see below).

Web page names often end in html or htm, which shows that they are written in **HyperText Mark-up Language** (**HTML**).

Some web pages are part of a larger website and are linked to the home page. Here is an example:

http://www.classiccrimefiction.com/hardboiled-slang.htm

This page is about hardboiled slang, in the Classic Crime Fiction website.

Some URLs are even more complex:

http://www.bbc.co.uk/bbc7/listenagain/thursday/

This takes us to the **thursday** area in the **/bbc7/listenagain/ thursday** directory at **www.bbc.co.uk**.

On some websites, web pages are generated as they are needed by a program which draws on a database of information.

For example, this URL takes you to the Further Education and Vocational section of Pearson Education's website.

http://www.heinemann.co.uk/FEAndVocational/ ITAndOfficeTechnology/ECDL/ECDL.aspx

Domain names

Every computer site on the Internet has its own unique domain name. This is made up of two or more parts, separated by dots, for example:

virgin.co.uk

The first part of the address identifies the organisation, and is usually related to its name. The other parts of the address follow certain conventions.

The next part identifies the nature of the organisation. Some common ones are:

Identifier	Organsiation	
com	commercial	(USA and international)
co	commercial	(outside the USA)
edu	educational	(USA)
ac	academic	(outside the USA)
net	network provider	
gov	government department	
org	non-commercial organisation	

At the right-hand end there may be a country code. This is not present for US-based and international organisations. Examples are:

Code	Country	Code	Country	Code	Country
au	Australia	ca	Canada	de	Germany
es	Spain	fi	Finland	fr	France
hk	Hong Kong	ie	Ireland	it	Italy
jp	Japan	nz	New Zealand	uk	United Kingdom

Test your understanding

1. a) How do you get onto the Internet?
    b) If you are connected at home:
       i) who is your ISP?
       ii) what is the URL of their website?
    c) If you are connected through an organisation, what is the URL of their website?

Keep a record of these URLs safe. We will use them later.

2. What do these URLs tell you about the organisations that run them?
    a) www.bristol.ac.uk
    b) www.treasury.gov.au
    c) www.microsoft.com

Viewing websites

Learning objectives

By working through this lesson you will learn:

- about Microsoft Internet Explorer and how to adjust its display
- how to browse the Web
- how to move between web pages
- how to go directly to a place on the Web
- how to use the Address bar list
- about tabs and windows.

The browser (7.1.1.3/5, 7.2.1.1)

To view web pages on the World Wide Web you need a **browser**. This is a program which can display the pages and handle hypertext links (or hyperlinks). These allow you to jump from one page to another, which may be on the same computer or on one far away. The hyperlinks are attached to images or words, and are activated by clicking them.

Microsoft Internet Explorer (IE) is the browser supplied with Windows. In this book we will be using Internet Explorer 7.0, the latest version at the time of writing. If you have an earlier version of Internet Explorer, upgrade to 7.0 now. Look for the upgrade link when you get to the Windows website (see page 376).

Starting Internet Explorer

❶ Click the **Start** button.

❷ Click **Internet Explorer** at the top left of the **Start** menu.

How about...?

You can also start **Internet Explorer** by clicking the **Internet Explorer** icon on the **Desktop** or in the **Quick Launch** taskbar.

Windows Internet Explorer 7

Upgrade with Confidence — Internet Explorer 7

Install Windows Internet Explorer 7 today

Figure 7.1 Upgrade to Internet Explorer 7

❷ Click **Internet Explorer**

Quick Launch icon

❶ Click the **Start** button

Figure 7.2 Starting Internet Explorer

Note

Internet Explorer is not the only browser. Netscape Navigator, Mozilla Firefox and Opera are all good alternatives that provide different levels of security against hackers, however some web pages can only be displayed correctly in Internet Explorer. (Making a web page suitable for all browsers can take a lot of hard work – it is simpler to just produce one for Internet Explorer, which is the browser used by 95 per cent of people.)

The Internet Explorer screen

The main part of the window is to display the web pages. Above this are the control elements.

◉ The **Menu bar** is one way to access the commands. You can also reach them through the Command bar.

◉ The **Address** shows you where you are. You can type a URL here to open a page. Up to 20 URLs are stored and can be selected from here, for easy revisiting.

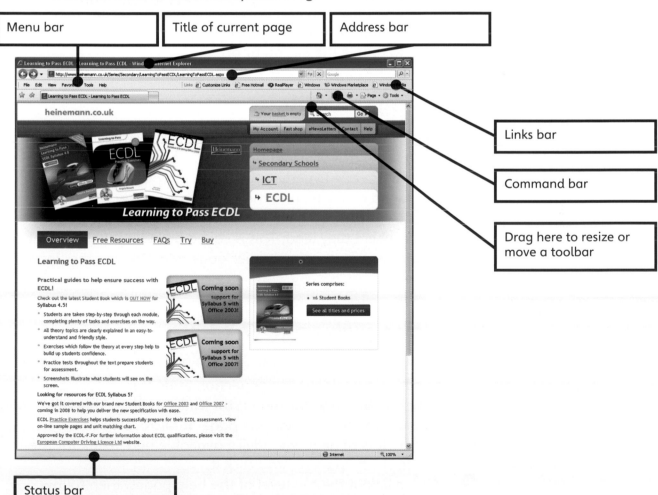

Menu bar

Title of current page

Address bar

Links bar

Command bar

Drag here to resize or move a toolbar

Status bar

Figure 7.3 Parts of the Internet Explorer screen

Figure 7.4 The Internet Explorer toolbar shortcuts

◉ The **Links** offer an easy way to connect to selected places. Initially, the hyperlinks stored here connect to pages on Microsoft's site, but you can replace them or add your own.

◉ The **Status bar** shows how much of an incoming file has been loaded. It can be turned off if you don't want it.

You can also open a pane on the left of the window when you want to use your **Favorites**, the **History list** or **RSS feeds**. We'll come back to these later.

Adjusting the Internet Explorer display (7.2.2.6)

If you are not using a toolbar, you can turn it off to give you more space on the screen for the web page display.

To control the toolbars

❶ Right-click any one of the toolbars.

The Menu bar, Links and Status bar are listed. A tick ✔ by a name shows that the bar is displayed.

❷ Click to toggle the tick on or off.

Browsing the Web

The Web consists of over 20 billion pages in around half a billion sites. There is no overall organisation to it, but the people who create websites write hyperlinks between the pages so that you can get around their site, and they often have other links to pages on other sites. Once you get into the Web, you can follow these links to see where they lead. This is called **browsing**. If you want, you can easily go back to an earlier page and pick up other leads from there.

Display a web page (7.2.1.3)

❶ If you are not already online, go online now. You may need to activate a telephone connection to do this.

❷ Click the **Windows** button on the **Links** toolbar. This will connect you to the Windows page at Microsoft's site.

❸ There's lots of help and advice available here. Look for the link to the help pages and click it.

❹ Click a link at the top level of the help pages, then follow the links down to find some help on a topic that interests you.

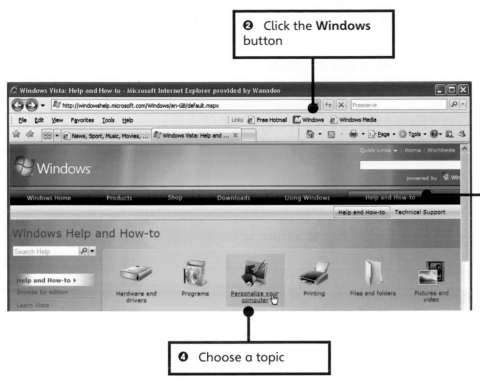

❷ Click the **Windows** button

❸ The **Help** page tab

❹ Choose a topic

Figure 7.5 Displaying a web page

Back and forwards again (7.2.3.2)

The browser keeps track of where you have been. This makes it easy for you to go back to pages that you have visited. The simplest way to move between pages that you have visited recently is to use the buttons in the top left corner of the screen.

⦿ Click the **Back** button to go to the page you were on before the current page. Click again to go back further.

Back   Forward

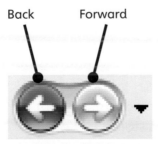

Figure 7.6 The Internet Explorer Back and Forward buttons

⦿ Click the **Forward** button to revisit a page after you have gone back.

Or

⦿ Click the down arrow to open a list of recent pages, then click a page name.

Note

Important (7.2.3.1)

Hyperlinks are very easy to spot. When you point to some text or an image which has a hyperlink attached to it, the pointer will turn into a hand 🖑. The text will become underlined, or if the link is on an image, this will become outlined in blue. Click the link and the browser will go to that page. This may be on the same website, or on another site, perhaps on the other side of the world.

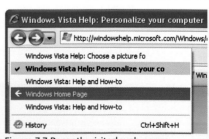

Figure 7.7 Recently visited web pages

Go directly to a page (7.2.1.2)

If you know the URL of a web page, you can go directly to the page by typing it into the **Address bar**. Try it by going to Yahoo!, which is a search engine that offers a good place to start browsing. Yahoo! and other search engines offer all sorts of services and activities that may interest you. The URL of the UK site is uk.yahoo.com

❶ Click in the **Address bar**.

❷ Type the URL in the text box.

❸ Click → or press **Enter** on the keyboard.

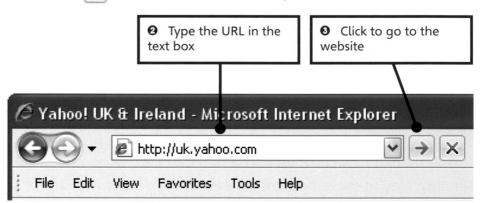

Figure 7.8 Going directly to web page

Using the Address bar list (7.2.3.4)

Internet Explorer stores the URLs that you type into the Address bar. If you want to go back to a place, sometime in the future, you can pick the URL from the Address bar (see Figure 7.9 on page 379).

❶ Click the down arrow on the right of the bar to display a drop-down list of stored URLs.

❷ Scroll through, if necessary.

❸ Click the URL you want.

Tabs and windows (7.2.1.3)

When you click a link or type an address, the new page will normally replace the current one. If you like, you can keep that page and open the next one in a new window or in a new tab.

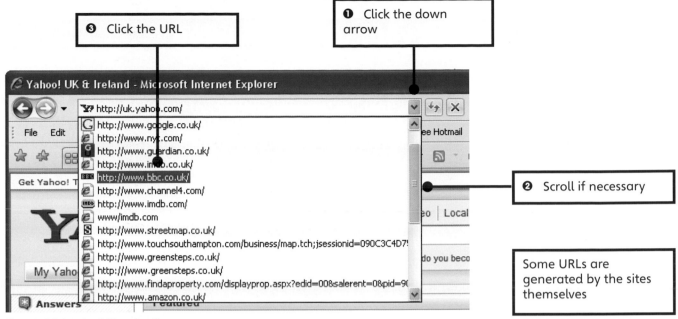

❷ Scroll if necessary

Some URLs are generated by the sites themselves

Figure 7.9 Using the Address bar list

Look above the page display area, to the left of the **Command bar**, and you will see a tab with the name of the page on it. You can have several pages open at the same time, and switch between them by clicking on their tabs.

To open a page in a new tab

◉ If you are following a link to the page, right-click it and select **Open in New Tab**.

Or

◉ If you are going to type in the address, click the **New Tab** button to the right of the existing tabs, to open a new blank page, then enter the address as normal.

To switch between tabs

◉ Click the tab you want.

Click the tabs to switch between open web pages

Figure 7.10 Opening a new tab

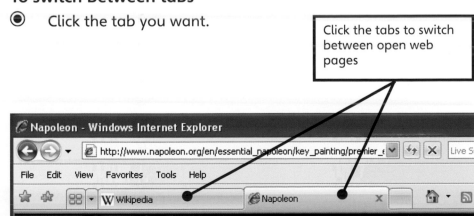

Figure 7.11 Using tabs

Test your understanding

1. Turn on the Links bar and go to each of its linked sites in turn.

2. Use the Address bar to go to these sites:
   www.pearson.co.uk (our home site)
   www.ecdl.com (to find more about this qualification)
   www.imdb.com (if you like films, you'll love this site)
   www.bbc.co.uk/music/news (for the latest music news)

3. In the Exercises on page 373, you found out the URLs of your ISP and/or organisation. Visit them now.

4. a) Go to these three sites, each in a new tab:
   news.bbc.co.uk
   news.sky.com
   uk.msn.com – and then click its News button
   b) Click between the three tabs to see how they cover different stories.
   c) Close two of the tabs when you have finished.

Better browsing

Using the History list (7.2.3.4)

As you browse, each page is recorded in the **History list**. This can be displayed in the **Explorer bar** whenever you need it. (The Explorer bar is a separate pane on the left of the screen. Internet Explorer also refers to this as the **Favorites Center** – and we will come back to this shortly.) The links are grouped into folders by site and/or when they were visited.

You may be able to use the History list to revisit pages even when you are not online. Internet Explorer doesn't just store a link to pages, it stores the text and images from that page – if it can. This does not always work. Some pages are produced by programs which draw information from a database – most online stores display their products this way.

1 Click the **Tools** button, point to **Toolbars** then select **History**.

Or

2 Open the **View** menu (if the menu bar is displayed), point to **Explorer bar** and select **History**.

3 Click a day to open its list.

4 Click a website's folder to display a list of pages.

5 Select the page you want.

6 Open other days or websites as required.

Figure 7.12 The History list (on the left-hand side of the screen)

Figure 7.13 Delete History item

⑦ If the History list is getting crowded, making it difficult to find places, you can remove any unwanted sites. Right-click the website name and select **Delete**. Click **Yes** when prompted to confirm.

⑧ When you have finished, click the cross button **X** at the top right of the **Explorer bar** to close it.

Do it!

Use the **History list** to revisit some of the places you have visited so far. Remove any that you don't think are worth keeping.

Favorites (7.2.4.1–2)

Some good places are easy to find; others you discover after a long and painful search or by sheer chance. If you want to return to a page in future, add it to your **Favorites**. This stores the title and URL in a file and puts the title on the **Favorites list**.

◉ You must have the page open to be able to add it to the Favorites.

◉ If the **Favorites list** is opened from the menu bar, it drops down the screen and closes after you have chosen.

◉ The **Favorites Center**, in the **Explorer bar**, normally closes after you have chosen a page, but can be pinned open.

◉ You can store a **Favorite** in a folder as you create it.

To add a page to your Favorites

① Click 🌟 or open the **Favorites** menu.
② Select **Add to Favorites...**
③ Edit the title if necessary.
④ To store it in a folder, select one from the **Create in** list.
⑤ Click **Add**.

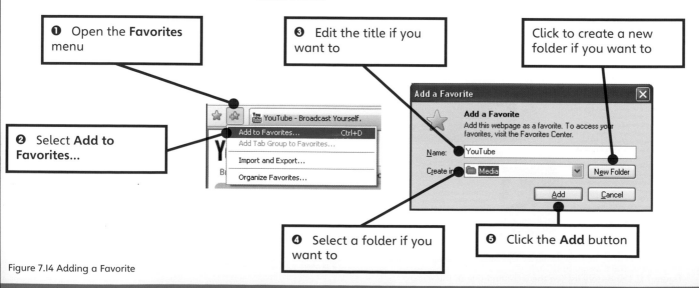

❶ Open the **Favorites** menu

❸ Edit the title if you want to

Click to create a new folder if you want to

❷ Select **Add to Favorites...**

❹ Select a folder if you want to

❺ Click the **Add** button

Figure 7.14 Adding a Favorite

To revisit a Favorite (7.2.4.2)

❶ Click the ⭐ button to open the **Favorites Center**.

❷ If you want to keep the Center open while you browse for your favourite website, click the ⬕ button at the top right to pin it in place.

❸ If necessary, click a folder's name to open it.

❹ Pick a page.

❺ If you have pinned the Center open, click **X** when you have finished to close it.

Note

In other browsers, stored links are called bookmarks, instead of Favorites.

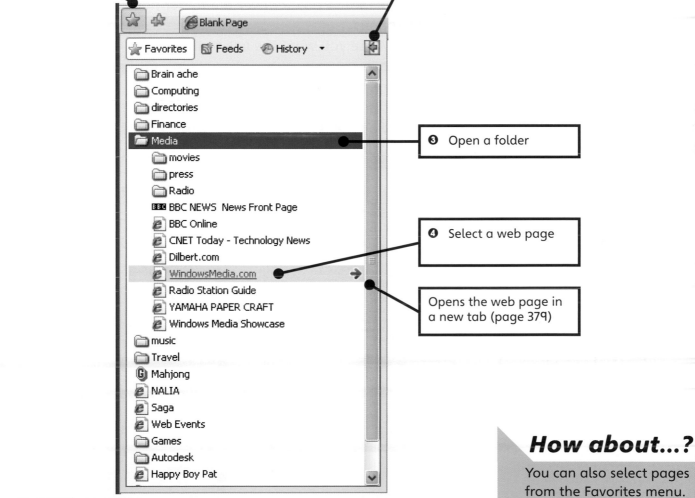

❶ Open the **Favorites Center**

❷ Pin the **Favorites Center** in place

❸ Open a folder

❹ Select a web page

Opens the web page in a new tab (page 379)

Figure 7.15 The Favorites list

How about...?

You can also select pages from the Favorites menu.

Do it!

Add at least three pages to your Favorites list – if you don't really want them, you can remove them later. Go back to the pages by using their entries in the list.

Organising Favorites (7.2.4.4)

When your Favorites list gets so long that you can't find things quickly, it is time to organise it by moving related items into suitable folders. This is easily done. First you need to create some folders, then the Favorites can be moved into them.

How about...?

You can also organise your Favorites through a dialogue box. Open the **Favorites** menu and select **Organize Favorites** to do this.

❶ Open the **Favorites Center**, and pin it into place.
❷ Right-click any item and select **Create New Folder**.
❸ Give the new folder a name.

To move a link into a folder

❹ Select the link.
❺ Drag it over to the folder and drop it in.

Or

❻ Hover the mouse pointer over the folder name for a moment until it opens.
❼ Decide where you want the link to fit into the list, and drop it into place.

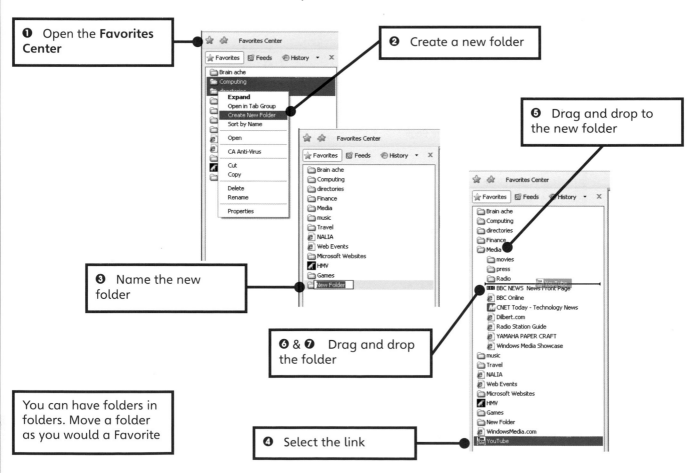

❶ Open the **Favorites Center**

❷ Create a new folder

❺ Drag and drop to the new folder

❸ Name the new folder

❻ & ❼ Drag and drop the folder

You can have folders in folders. Move a folder as you would a Favorite

❹ Select the link

Figure 7.16 Organising Favorites

Delete a Favorite (7.2.4.3)

Unwanted Favorites, or folders, can be easily deleted.
Right-click it in the **Favorites Center**, and select **Delete**.

Do it!

Create at least three folders to store Favorites. Look at the links
that are already there. Move some them into the new folders,
and delete any that you don't want.

Figure 7.17 Deleting Favorites

Control downloading (7.2.1.4–5)

When you connect to a website and start to download a page,
it doesn't always come in quickly. Sometimes this is because the
site is very busy, with lots of people all trying to use it at once.
Sometimes it is because there is a hold-up somewhere along the
line between you and the site. The Internet is interconnected,
which means that there are lots of different ways to get to places.
So, if one way doesn't seem to be working, ask the browser to try
another.

❶   Click the **Stop** download button ☒ .
❷   Click the **Refresh** button ↻ . Internet Explorer will then
     start to download the page again, and it will almost
     certainly take a different route through the connections.

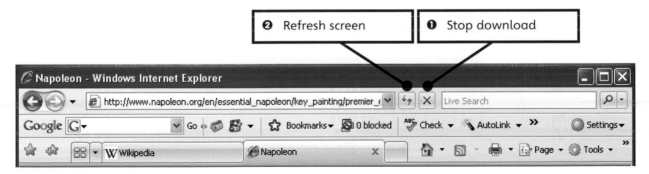

Figure 7.18 Controlling downloads

Tip!

If the page doesn't
download any faster
when you use **Refresh**,
there is probably trouble
at the website. Try again
later.

Getting help (7.2.I.6)

If you need more help on any aspect of Internet Explorer, check its Help pages. Almost everything is covered, though maybe in more detail than you might want! There are three ways to find help: browse through the contents; use the index; or search for key words.

To browse for help

1 Click the **Help** button.

Or

2 Open the **Help** menu.
3 Select **Contents and Index**.
4 Switch to the **Content** tab, if it is not on top.
5 Click 📖 to open a 'book' of topics.
6 Click 📄 to display a Help page.
7 On a Help page, click ➕ for more on a subtopic.
8 Click **Related Topics** then click a title to go to a related page.

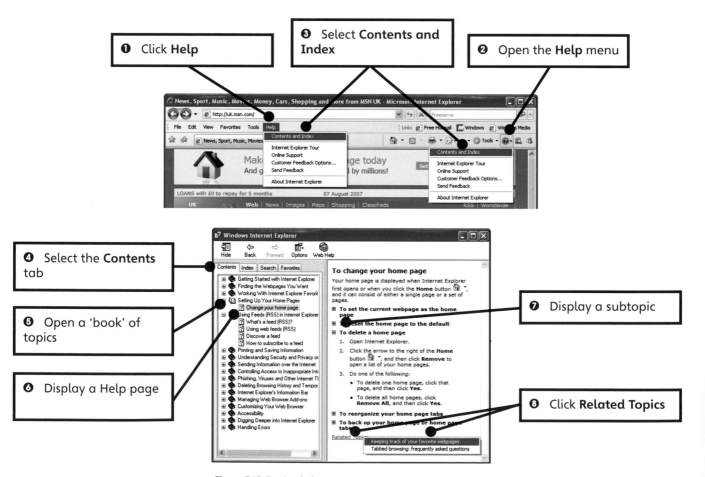

Figure 7.I9 Getting help

Searching for help

If you are clear and specific in defining your key words, a search can be the quickest way to find the help you want. Your search key words are normally highlighted in the Help page displays. This can be useful, especially when you are looking for less common topics as it will direct you to the relevant part of the page. On the other hand, the highlighting can make the text harder to read. With this in mind, Internet Explorer gives you the option of turning the highlight off.

1. Open the **Help** menu and select **Contents and Index**.
2. Switch to the **Search** tab.
3. Type one or more words to describe what you are looking for.
4. Click **List Topics**.
5. Select an entry from the list.
6. Click **Display**.

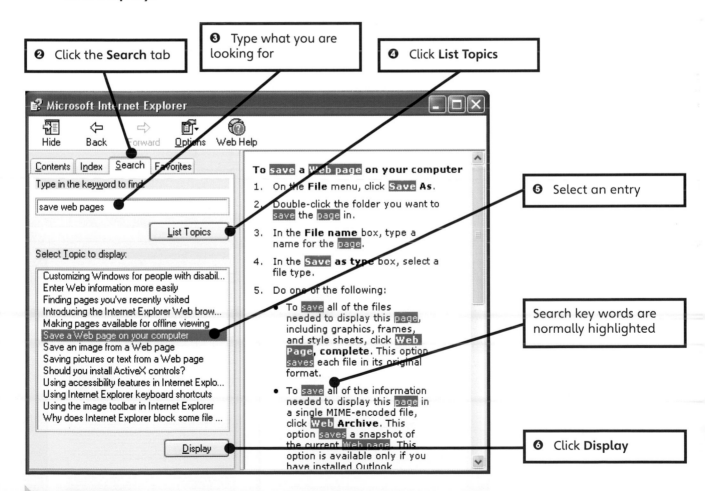

Figure 7.20 Searching for help

Do it!

Use the Help system to find out about the help that is available online at Microsoft's site, and how to access it.

Previewing a web page (7.4.2.2)

Web pages are normally designed to be seen on a screen, not on paper. Before printing anything it is usually a good idea to use the **Print Preview** facility to see how it will look on paper, and how many pages it will take. It is surprising how often there is a last page with nothing relevant on it.

1 Click the **Print** button.

Or

2 Open the **File** menu.

3 Select **Print Preview...**

4 Web pages have to be reformatted for printing. They can be printed with the paper upright (portrait) or sideways (landscape). Click the buttons to see which layout works best.

5 You can adjust the type size, if you like – perhaps to make the page more readable. Open the size list and set the percentage.

6 Scroll through and decide which pages you want to print.

7 Click ⌷ . In the **Print** dialogue box, you can choose which pages to print, and how many copies.

Figure 7.21 Select **Print Preview**

4 Select **Portrait** or **Landscape**

5 Change the print size

7 Click **Print**

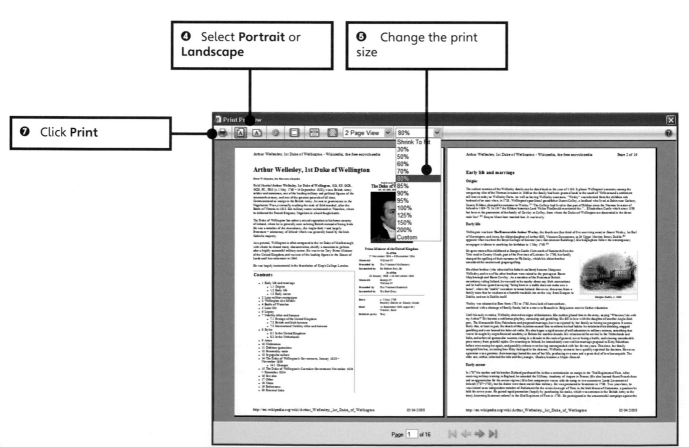

Figure 7.22 Print Preview

Changing the page setup (7.4.2.I)

You can change how the page will be printed on paper. The options here include the orientation of the paper or size of margins, and adding headers or footers if required.

❶ Open the **File** menu and select **Page Setup...**

❷ In the **Paper** area, check the **Size:** and **Source:** – these rarely need changing.

❸ If you want to add text to appear at the top or bottom of each page, type it in the **Header** and **Footer** text boxes.

❹ If the web page will fit better on a landscape format, change the **Orientation**.

❺ If you want to adjust the margins, type in new values.

❻ If you have a choice of printers, click the **Printer...** button and select one.

❼ Click **OK**.

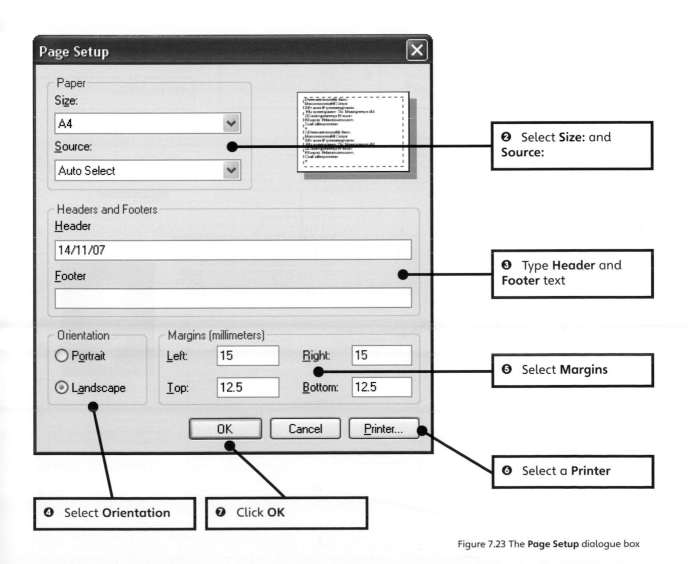

Figure 7.23 The **Page Setup** dialogue box

Printing a web page (7.4.2.3)

If you just want one copy of the whole page printed by the default printer, just click 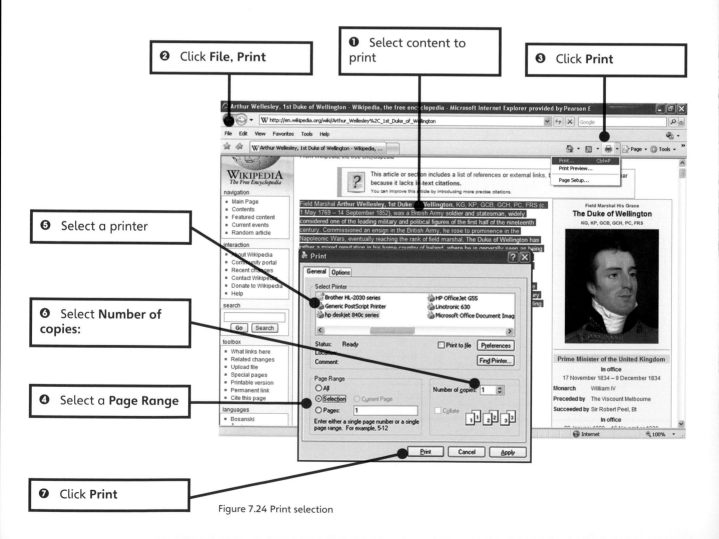.

To print only part of the page.

① Select the part of the page you want to print.

② Open the **File** menu and select **Print**.

Or

③ Click the arrow beside the Print icon on the **Command bar** and select **Print...**

Either way opens the **Print** dialogue box where you can specify what to print, and how.

④ Select **Page Range: All, Selection**, or **Pages** giving the number or range (e.g. **2-4**).

⑤ If you have several printers, select one.

⑥ Set the **Number of copies:** to print if more than one.

⑦ Click **Print**.

② Click **File, Print**

① Select content to print

③ Click **Print**

⑤ Select a printer

⑥ Select **Number of copies:**

④ Select a **Page Range**

⑦ Click **Print**

Figure 7.24 Print selection

Saving a web page (7.4.1.1/3)

Page files are erased from the **History** list after a while. If you want to keep pages for long-term reference, save them on disk. They can be saved in four formats.

⦿ **Webpage, complete** saves the page as a htm file, and saves any pictures, sounds and other content in a folder. This has the same name as the page with **_files** added.

⦿ **Web Archive, single file** also saves the text and other content, but packed into a single file.

⦿ **Webpage, HTML only** saves the text and HTML tags.

⦿ **Text File** saves only the text.

❶ Click **Save As...** on the **File** menu.

Or

❷ On the **Command bar**, click **Page** and select **Save As...**
❸ Navigate to the folder where you want to save to.
❹ Edit the filename, if required.
❺ Set the **Save as type**.
❻ Click **Save**.

Note

You can save an image on a web page by right-clicking it and selecting **Save Picture As...** from the shortcut menu that appears. Use the **Save Picture** dialogue box to save the image.

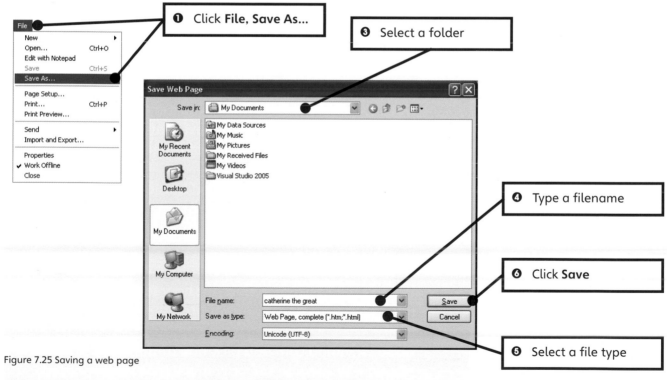

❶ Click File, Save As...
❸ Select a folder
❹ Type a filename
❻ Click Save
❺ Select a file type

Figure 7.25 Saving a web page

Copying from a web page (7.4.1.3)

You can copy data from a web page, and paste it into a document (e.g. into a Word file) on your PC.
To copy text.

❶ Select the text.

How about...?

Alternatively, right-click the selected text and click **Copy** on the shortcut menu that is displayed.

Do it!

Find out what the CIA knows! Go to the Central Intelligence Agency website at www.cia.gov. Select the **World Factbook** link. Pick a country and save the page information about it, complete with its pictures.

② Click **Copy** on the **Edit** menu.

③ Switch to the document you want to copy to.

④ Paste the copied text in the document and format it as necessary.

You can copy images in a similar way. They can be pasted into Word documents or into a graphics software file.

There are two ways to copy a Web address, depending upon where they are.

◉ To copy the URL in the Address bar, right-click it and select **Copy** from the shortcut menu.

◉ To copy a link from a web page, right-click it and select **Copy Shortcut** from the shortcut menu.

The address can then be pasted into any text document or into an email to send to someone.

Test your understanding

① Use your History list to revisit some of the sites you have visited in the last few days. Pick three that you will not want to visit again and delete their entries from the list.

② Pick **three** sites in your History list that you might want to revisit regularly. Go to each of them in turn and add them to your Favorites.

③ Create a Favorites folder named Music. Add links to your favourite music sites. Here are some to start you off:

www.apple.com/iTunes

www.mtv.co.uk

www.bbc.co.uk/music

④ Use the Help system to find out how to switch between full screen view and a normal browser window. Print the topic.

⑤ Go to uk.yahoo.com and pick one of the news stories. Use Print Preview to see how it will look when printed. Print the first page only. Pick a second story and print its first four paragraphs.

⑥ Visit the Darwin Awards website at www.darwinawards.com. Pick an interesting story and save it as a web page, complete. Pick a second and save it as text only.

Setting browser options

You can control many aspects of Internet Explorer's display and how it works by using the Internet Options dialogue box.

The home page (7.2.2.1)

The **home page** of a website is the topmost one – the page that people see when they first arrive at the site. This is different from the home page in Internet Explorer, which is the one you choose for the browser to go to when it first starts. It might be your favourite search engine or directory, or where you go to get the latest news, or anywhere else you like. It can be left blank if there is no particular place that you want to start at.

❶ Click the **Tools** button on the **Command bar** (or open the **Tools** menu) and select **Internet Options**.

The default will probably be Microsoft's or your ISP's website

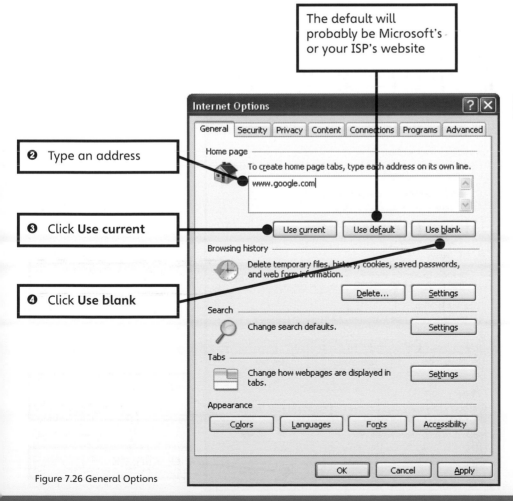

❷ Type an address

❸ Click **Use current**

❹ Click **Use blank**

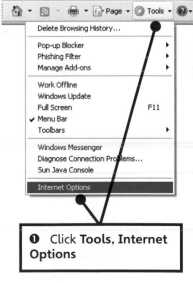

❶ Click **Tools, Internet Options**

Figure 7.26 General Options

Note

(7.2.3.3) You can return to your home page at any time by clicking the **Home** button 🏠 ▾ on the Command bar.

❷ Type the address of the page you want to use as the home page. (You can set more than one page as your home page. Each home page will open on a different tab in the browser.)

Or

❸ Click **Use current** to set the current page.

Or

❹ Click **Use blank** if you don't want a home page.

❺ Click **OK** (or click **Apply** if you want to keep the dialogue box open while you change other options).

Tip!

Clicking the **Delete...** button in the **Browsing history** area clears other files that Internet Explorer places on your hard disk.

The History settings (7.2.2.2/5)

You can keep pages in your **History** list as long as you like, but the longer you keep them, the more there will be in the list, and the more there are in the list, the longer it takes to find the one you want. Try different settings – a week to 10 days should be long enough.

Internet Explorer stores the files of the pages that you visit, so that they can be displayed faster if you go back to them. You can set the amount of disk space that is available for storage.

❶ Open the **Tools** menu and select **Internet Options**.

❷ In the **Browsing history** area, click the **Settings** button.

❸ Set the amount of space to use for storing files.

❹ Set the number of days to keep pages.

❺ Click **OK**, then **OK** again to close the **Options** dialogue box.

Note

(7.2.2.5) Internet Explorer 'caches' (i.e. saves onto your disks) the text and images from the web pages that you visit, so that if you go back to them the pages are displayed much faster. If you need to free up disk space, you can clear these files.

❶ Click **Internet Options** on the **Tools** menu.

❷ Click **Delete** in the **Browsing history** area of the **General** tab.

❸ Click the **Delete files...** button in the **Temporary Internet Files** area of the **Delete Browsing History** window that appears.

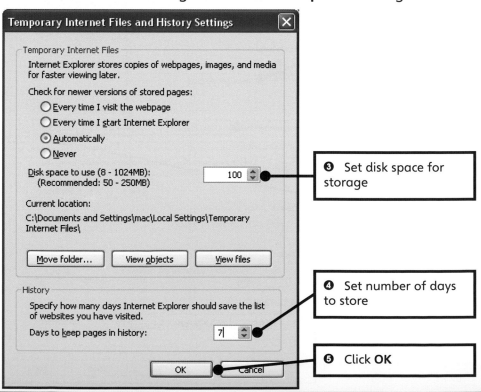

Figure 7.27 History settings

Displaying images

If you have a dial-up connection to the Internet, browsing can be slow and frustrating. What slows it down most are the multimedia files. Text downloads very quickly. Pictures, audio and video files are sometimes essential but often merely decorative. You can turn them off to speed up your browsing. Instead of the image, you will then see this icon ![icon]. Point to it, and you should get a label telling you about the image. Right-click it and select **Show the picture** if you want to see it.

To control image loading

❶ Open the **Internet Options** panel and go to the **Advanced** tab.

❷ Scroll down the **Settings** box to the **Multimedia** section.

❸ Click the check box to turn the **Show pictures**, and other multimedia options, on or off as required.

❹ Click **Apply** or **OK** to save and close the panel.

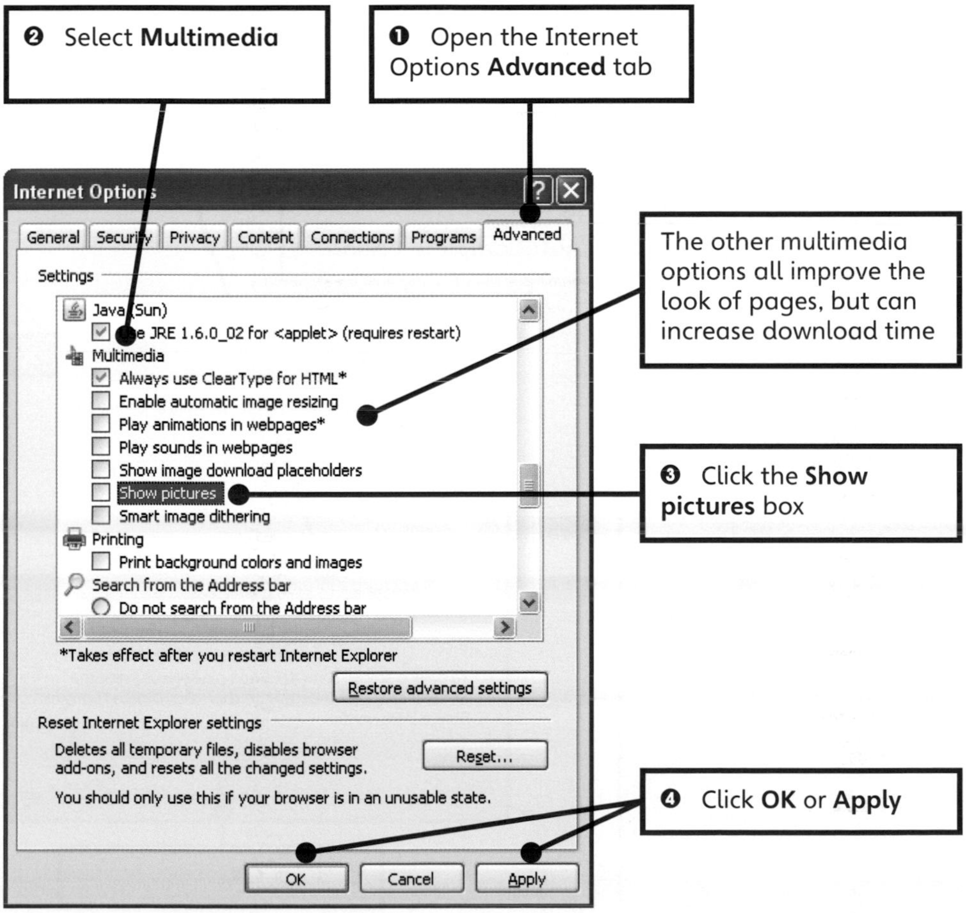

Tip!

Pictures often contain links. If you cannot see them, you may not be able to navigate to some websites. If you need to see the pictures it can be quicker to turn on **Show pictures** and reload the page than to click and load each separately.

❷ Select **Multimedia**

❶ Open the Internet Options **Advanced** tab

Internet Options

General | Security | Privacy | Content | Connections | Programs | Advanced

Settings

- Java (Sun)
  - ☑ e JRE 1.6.0_02 for <applet> (requires restart)
- Multimedia
  - ☑ Always use ClearType for HTML*
  - ☐ Enable automatic image resizing
  - ☐ Play animations in webpages*
  - ☐ Play sounds in webpages
  - ☐ Show image download placeholders
  - ☐ Show pictures
  - ☐ Smart image dithering
- Printing
  - ☐ Print background colors and images
- Search from the Address bar
  - ○ Do not search from the Address bar

*Takes effect after you restart Internet Explorer

[Restore advanced settings]

Reset Internet Explorer settings

Deletes all temporary files, disables browser add-ons, and resets all the changed settings.

[Reset...]

You should only use this if your browser is in an unusable state.

[OK] [Cancel] [Apply]

The other multimedia options all improve the look of pages, but can increase download time

❸ Click the **Show pictures** box

❹ Click **OK** or **Apply**

Figure 7.28 Advanced options

AutoComplete

Internet Explorer likes to save your work! The **AutoComplete** feature offers to complete things for you as you start to type, suggesting words that you have typed previously and that began in the same way. It can complete:

- addresses, when you type them into the Address bar
- data entered into forms (e.g. your name, address and similar details)
- usernames and passwords.

You can decide which of these can be completed for you.

❶ Open the **Tools** menu and select **Internet Options**.
❷ Go to the **Content** tab.
❸ In the **AutoComplete** area, click **Settings**.
❹ Tick the boxes for the items that you want to be AutoCompleted.
❺ Click **OK** to close the **AutoComplete Settings** dialogue box.
❻ Click **OK** to close the **Internet Options** dialogue box.

Do it!

Explore the options. Change those that you know already how you would like them to be. Leave the rest at their defaults, and come back to them later after you have spent more time browsing.

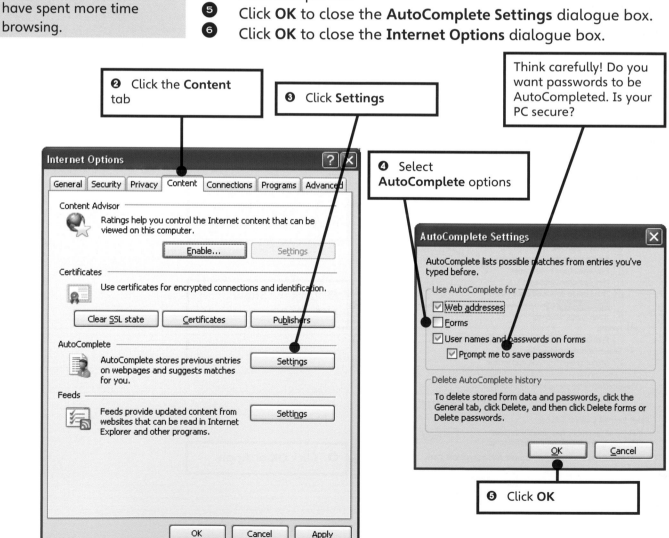

❷ Click the **Content** tab

❸ Click **Settings**

Think carefully! Do you want passwords to be AutoCompleted. Is your PC secure?

❹ Select **AutoComplete** options

❺ Click **OK**

Figure 7.29 Content options

Safety online

Controlling active content

Many web pages have active content, that is they contain multimedia files or applets (small applications) written in Java, ActiveX or other interactive languages. These should not be able to affect your hard disks or access your data, but some hackers have found a way round the restrictions. Active content makes browsing more interesting, and if you stick to major reputable websites, it should not cause problems.

1 Open the **Internet Options** dialogue box and go to the **Security** tab.

2 Pick the **Internet** zone.

Initially the Internet zone (i.e. all websites) should be set to Medium or High. Use the Custom option to fine-tune the settings later, when you have more experience.

3 Select **Medium** or **High** security.

Or

4 Click **Custom level...**

5 Tell Internet Explorer how to deal with each type.

6 Click **OK**.

Learning objectives

By working through this lesson you will learn:

- ◉ how to control active content in web pages
- ◉ about protecting your privacy
- ◉ how to control pop-ups
- ◉ about security online
- ◉ how to set up parental controls.

❶ Click the **Security** tab

❷ Select the **Internet** zone

❸ Select the security level

❹ Select **Custom level...**

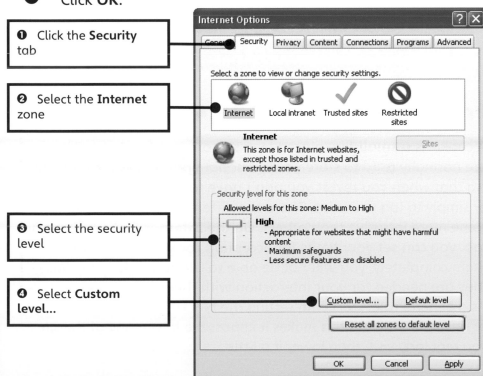

Figure 7.30a Picking an **Internet** zone

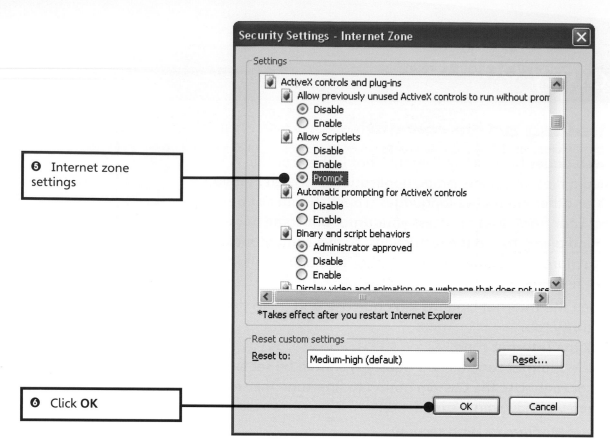

⑤ Internet zone settings

⑥ Click **OK**

Figure 7.30b The **Internet** zone settings

Do it!

Set the security level for Internet sites to Medium-high, then use the **Custom level** feature to set the **Software channel permissions** to High safety.

Privacy and cookies (7.2.2.4)

A cookie is a **small** file, placed by a site on your hard disk. They are normally used to store your personal preferences for that site (so that when you revisit you don't have to set preferences again) or simply to log your visit. There are different sorts of cookies, some more intrusive than others. On the **Internet Options Privacy** tab, you can set your limits for accepting cookies. If you block them completely, you will not be able to use some sites, because they are needed for your interaction with them.

As a general rule, start with setting the blocking level Medium-high or above. If you find this makes it impossible to use any of the sites you regularly visit, then lower it a little.

1. Open the **Tools** menu and select **Internet Options**.
2. Go to the **Privacy** tab.
3. Drag the slider to set the level.
4. Click **OK**.

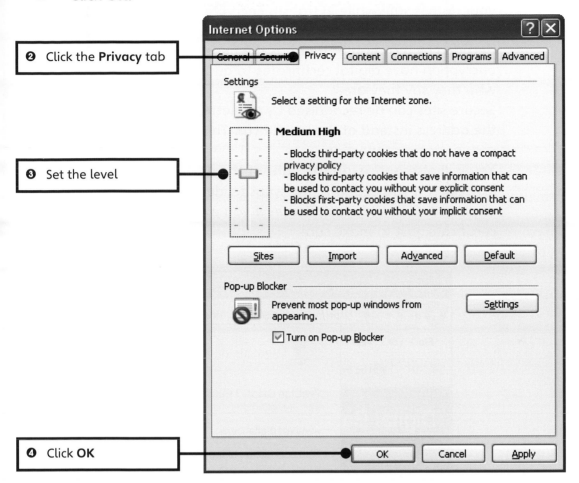

❷ Click the **Privacy** tab

❸ Set the level

❹ Click **OK**

Figure 7.3I Controlling cookies

Controlling pop-ups (7.2.2.3)

Pop-ups are windows that open automatically while you are
browsing a page, normally to display advertisements. They can
be very irritating. Fortunately Internet Explorer, like all modern
browsers, has a pop-up blocker. You will find this on the **Privacy**
tab, along with the cookie control. Make sure this is turned on.
Very occasionally you will meet a site that uses pop-ups to carry
extra information or images that you will want. When this happens,
click the bar that appears at the top of the window when a pop-up
is blocked. At the prompt, allow the pop-up to open.

Security online (7.1.2.1–2)

When banking or shopping online, or when sending sensitive or valuable information to a website, you need to be sure that your data is safe while in transit. Encryption ensures this. If a site uses encryption, data is encoded before sending and can only be decoded by a computer that has the necessary key. Sites that use encryption have digital certificates to guarantee that they are who they say they are.

Secure sites can be recognised by the letters **https** at the start of the address instead of the usual **http**. This tells you that the site uses a secure connection.

You will also notice, on the right of the address bar, the lock icon 🔒 . If you click this, the website identification will be displayed. Click **View certificates** if you want to examine its digital certificate, just to make sure.

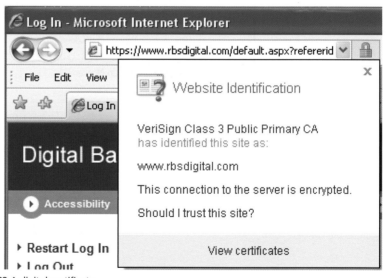

Figure 7.32 A digital certificate

Parental controls (7.1.2.7–9)

Parents and teachers can control the sites that children can visit by turning on **Content Advisor**. This works through a system of ratings, and initially uses those set by the Internet Content Rating Association (ICRA), which rates sites on language, nudity, sex, violence and other types of content. You can set what level of each of these is acceptable and only sites within those limits will then be accessible.

There is a problem: the system is voluntary and many perfectly safe sites do not have an ICRA rating. If a site is unrated, you can either allow free access or control access through a password.

❶ Open the **Internet Options** dialogue box and switch to the **Content** tab.

❷ In the **Content Advisor** area, select **Enable...**

❸ On the **Ratings** tab, select each category in turn and adjust the slider to set the limits – the description will change as you move the slider to show what is permitted.

❹ Switch to the **General** tab.

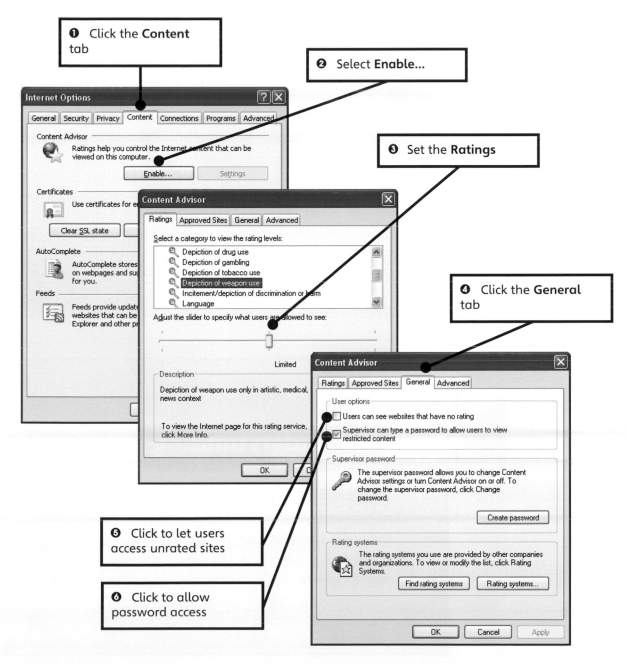

❶ Click the **Content** tab

❷ Select **Enable...**

❸ Set the **Ratings**

❹ Click the **General** tab

❺ Click to let users access unrated sites

❻ Click to allow password access

Figure 7.33 Content Advisor

Note

Parental controls can also be applied to computer games. The Entertainment Software Ratings Board rates games in the same way that the ICRA rates websites. The Xbox 360, Wii and Playstation games consoles all have a facility for parents to control the types of games that can be played. Windows Vista, though not XP, also allows parents to limit when and for how long children can use the PC.

⑤ In the **User options**, if you want to allow access to unrated sites, tick the check box.

⑥ If you want to allow those who know the password access to restricted sites, tick the check box.

⑦ Click **OK**.

⑧ The first time that you use **Content Advisor**, you will be asked to enter a password, and a hint, to help you remember it. (If you forget it, you'll have to reinstall Internet Explorer if you ever want to change the Content Advisor!)

Warning!

For some people, one of the advantages of virtual communities is that you can hide your real name, age, sex, height, weight etc. so that other people can relate to the person inside – the 'real you' – rather than to your appearance. The other side of this is that you cannot be sure what sort of person you are talking to. It is dangerous to give out personal data to those that you do not really know. If you have upload photos or videos to networking or video-sharing sites, remember that if you post them in a public area, anybody can see them.

Do not let yourself be pressured into saying or doing anything that you do not want to do. There are, unfortunately, some bullies and other unpleasant people online – as there are in the real world.

Test your understanding

① Set up **two** alternative home pages. One should be to the site of your organisation or ISP. Make the other one to Yahoo! (uk.yahoo.com) or MSN (uk.msn.com).

② Set your History to store data for only five days.

③ Make sure that the Local intranet and Trusted sites security levels are set to the Default levels.

④ Turn on AutoComplete for forms.

RSS feeds (7.1.1.7)

RSS for stands Rich or RDF Site Summary, but is often referred to as Really Simple Syndication. It is a way for websites to share headlines and stories with other sites, and to bring them to your desktop. An RSS feed is a source of these headlines. Many sites, especially those of news organisations, offer feeds. If they do, the **Feeds** button will change from 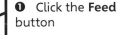 to . To set up a link to the feed, you need to subscribe.

❶ Click the **Feed** button.

❷ You will be taken to the **Feeds** page, where you will see a '**Subscribe to this feed**' link. Click it.

❸ Edit the name, if necessary.

❹ If you want to store it in a special folder, select it from the **Create in** list, or click **New folder** to create one.

❺ Click **Subscribe**.

Learning objectives

By working through this lesson you will learn:
◉ about RSS feeds and how to subscribe to them
◉ about podcasts and downloading them.

❶ Click the **Feed** button

❸ Edit the name if needed

❹ Change the folder

❺ Click **Subscribe**

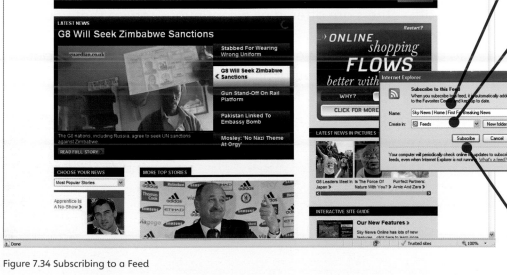

Figure 7.34 Subscribing to a Feed

Figure 7.35 Listing Feeds

To use your Feeds links

❶ Click the ⭐ button to open the **Favorites Center**.

❷ Click **Feeds**.

❸ Click a Feed to get the latest RSS headlines from that source.

Do it!

Subscribe to at least two feeds. Here are some sites that offer them:

www.bbc.co.uk

www.cnn.com

www.telegraph.co.uk

www.guardian.co.uk

www.msn.com

Podcasts (7.1.1.8)

Podcasts are audio recordings downloaded from the Internet that are designed to be listened to on a variety of MP3 players or on your PC. Some radio stations offer podcasts of news reports or other programmes for people who missed the broadcast; bands and singers sometimes release recordings as podcasts; broadcasters and comics produce podcasts alongside or instead of traditional broadcasts. But podcasting is not just for the professional. Anyone can create a podcast – it is only a matter of having a microphone and suitable recording software on your PC, and having something to say (or sing or play). Some podcasts are one-offs; others are offered as a continuous service that you can subscribe to, like feeds.

To download, manage and listen to podcasts you need special software. There are several alternatives (all of them free) including Apple iTunes, My Yahoo! and Google Reader.

Searching the Web

Introduction (7.1.1.6/7.3.2.1)

The Web is vast – it comprises literally billions of pages – so there is no single index or contents list for it, but there are search engines. These are websites that scan the Web, building up a database of page titles, key words and other relevant data, and offering a search facility so that you can find Web pages that meet your search criteria.

There are several different search engine sites, and they vary in the way they collect and hold data. None of them can give 100 per cent complete coverage because pages are added and changed constantly. If you don't find what you want at one, it may be worth trying another. The search techniques are similar for all the engines.

Google

Google is widely accepted as the best search engine. It has a phenomenally large database: over 15 billion pages at the time of writing. The searches are fast: over 800,000 results in a few tenths of a second in the example below.

To run a search using Google, type in one or more words to define what you are looking for, for example **classical harp sheet music**. The search engine will look first for sites that match all four words, then for those that match any two or any single word. When it presents the results, they are in order of 'relevance', which is calculated in a complex, but effective way. This brings to the top of the result list those sites:

◉ that best match your words (because the words feature in the page's key words, title, headings and text)

◉ that other people have found to be the most valuable (as shown by the number of links to their pages and the number of visitors they get).

As a general rule, if you do not find good sites among the first 20 results of a Google search, it's because there are not any out there or because your search was badly defined. A single word will rarely be enough to focus a search properly. Search for 'music' and you'll get over two billion results, covering every conceivable type.

Learning objectives

By working through this lesson you will learn:

◉ how to run a simple search

◉ about advanced searches

◉ how to search for information

◉ about downloading files

◉ how to fill in forms on the Web.

Note

Internet Explorer has a search facility built into it. Type your search words into the box at the top right and they will be passed to a search engine and the results displayed. The default search engine it uses may have been set by whoever supplied your PC or your Internet connection, but you can change it.

Other search engines

There are several other search engines worth trying, including these.

- AltaVista (www.altavista.com). A bare-bones search site, like Google, and equally fast and efficient. After searching the Web for something, you can click the tabs along the top to find images, audio or video clips or news reports for the same key words.
- Excite (www.excite.co.uk). This search engine has lots to offer as well as a search facility. It runs a simple search, with a UK focus.
- MSN Search (search.msn.com). Part of Microsoft Network. This is the default search site used by Internet Explorer, if no one has changed it.

Simple searches (7.3.2.2–3)

If you enter a single word, then the engines will find pages containing that word. If you enter two or more words, what they find depends on how you enter the words.

- Most search engines will search for pages that contain any of the words, for example **Beijing Peking** will find pages referring to the capital of China, however it was spelt.
  This can produce a lot of results. Searching for **graphics conversion software** will find all pages containing the word **graphics**, plus those containing **conversion** and those with **software** – and there will be millions.
- If the words are enclosed in double quotes (" "), most engines will search for that exact phrase. Look for **"greenhouse effect"** and you should find stuff on global warming, and not get pages on gardening!

1. Go to **Google** at **www.google.com** or **www.google.co.uk**.
2. Type one or more key words.
3. If you want to restrict the search to UK pages, click the option button.
4. Click **Google Search** or press **Enter**.
5. When the results appear, click a link.

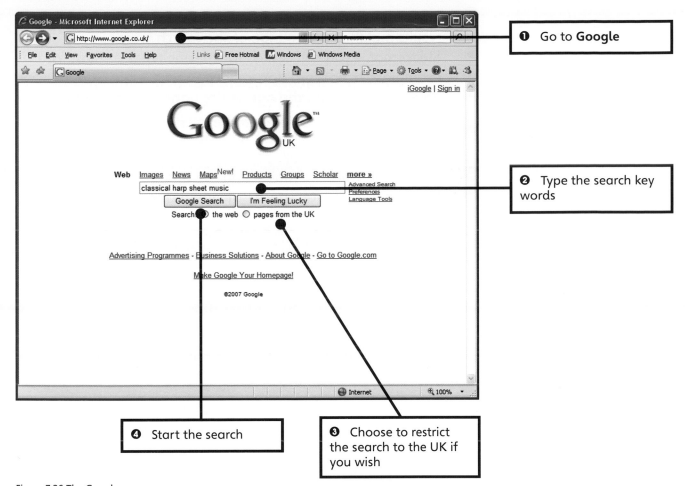

❶ Go to Google

❷ Type the search key words

❹ Start the search

❸ Choose to restrict the search to the UK if you wish

Figure 7.36 The Google screen

Advanced searches (7.3.2.3)

If a simple search produces too many or too few results, you could try an advanced search. With this you can combine different criteria, defining which words must be included on a page, which must not be there and which can be there. You can do this in many search engines by using the words **AND** and **NOT**, or the symbols '+' (AND) and '-' (NOT) in your search words, for example:

lion AND tiger   or   **lion + tiger**

looks for pages which have both big cats.

lion NOT tiger   or   **lion - tiger**

looks for pages with lion, but where tigers are not mentioned. You can define this kind of search in Google, and set up other requirements on the **Advanced Search** page. Among other things, you can restrict a search by:

- language – this doesn't usually make much difference, as results match the language of the search words
- file format – you can search for specific types of files, for example PDF or Word documents.
- date – set a limit to the age of the pages, from 24 hours to a year.

1 Go to **Google** and click the **Advanced Search** link to the right of the **Search** box.

2 Type in the words to look for, in the appropriate boxes.

3 If it would be useful, specify the language, file format, date and other features.

This advanced search in Figure 7.37 is the same as using the expression

reenactment somerset OR devon "civil war" - sealed knot

though it also sets language and date criteria.

Note

If you are very specific in your search, you may find exactly what you want or nothing at all.

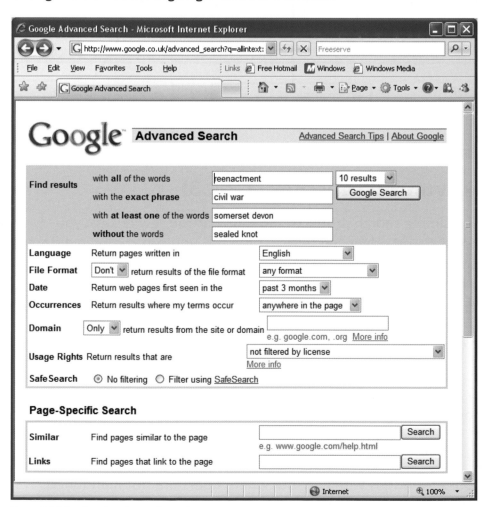

Figure 7.37 The Google Advanced Search screen

Do it!

Use Google to search for pages about:
- ⊙   your favourite singer/actor
- ⊙   the sports team that you support
- ⊙   a historical figure
- ⊙   somewhere you would like to go to on holiday.

Searching for knowledge (7.3.2.4)

A search using a search engine will generally find most things on the Web, but for some types of things you may be better searching elsewhere.

- ⊙   If you want information, try **Wikipedia (www.wikipedia. org)**. This is an encyclopedia that is being created by volunteers. Anyone can join Wikipedia and write or edit entries, though it does help if you are an expert or have first-hand knowledge. To use Wikipedia, just go to the site, pick your language and type in what you want to know about. Once you are into the site, you can pick a new topic by typing in the Search box or click any words in blue to read their entries.

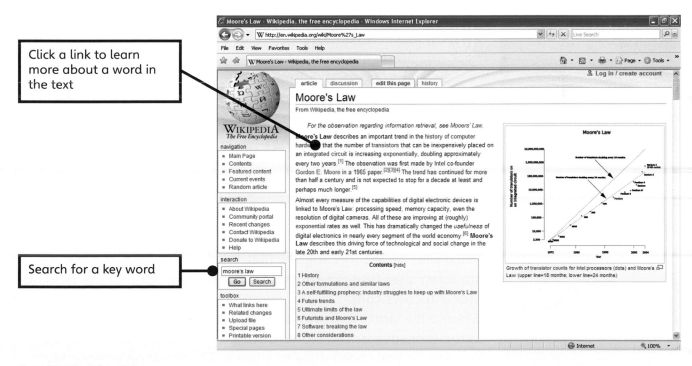

Click a link to learn more about a word in the text

Search for a key word

Figure 7.38 The Wikipedia screen

- For definitions of words, try **Dictionary.com (dictionary. reference.com)**. To use this site, type in the word, then select **Dictionary**, **Thesaurus**, **Encyclopedia** or **All Reference**. The definitions or other entries will be displayed.

Downloading files (7.4.1.2)

There is a lot of software for downloading from the Web. It falls into five categories.

- **Freeware** is there for the taking. People give software away from goodwill or to promote their commercial products. Just because it is free does not mean it is no good. Some excellent programs, including the Linux operating system, are freeware!
- **Shareware** can be tried for free, but you must pay (usually £20–£40) for continued use. There are some excellent shareware products.
- Demos give you a taste of what a program can do, but prevent you from doing some key tasks, such as saving or printing.
- Full-feature, full-price software can also be downloaded, rather than bought on disc in the stores. Sometimes it is supplied as 'try-before-you buy'. You can use it for perhaps a month before it locks up, and can only be unlocked by paying for it.
- Updates and replacement files are offered by most software and hardware firms. Many programs check their home site regularly to see if updates or 'bug-fixes' are available. If the software doesn't do it automatically you can visit the sites yourself. If the drivers (the controlling software) for peripherals become corrupted or you attach an old printer or other device to a new PC, the manufacturer's site will normally have replacement files for download in its support area.

Download sites

Many sites have some specific files for downloading, but there are a few sites that are centres for downloads. One of the leading sites is **tucows.com**.

When a file starts to download, you will be asked if you want to run it or save it. You want to save it. Click **Save**, then select a location on your hard drive to store it. The **Desktop** or your **My Documents** folder would be a good place.

Warning!

Danger: Malware! (7.1.2.4–6)
You must take care when downloading. Software can be infected with viruses or other **malware** – hidden programs that can damage your computer in a variety of ways. They can destroy files, take over your email and send spam or viruses through your account, steal your credit card details, and more. Software from established, big-name manufacturers will be safe, and those from established download sites will also have been checked. Be very wary of anything from any other sources. For real security, install a virus checker, and check all downloaded files. (See Modules 1 and 2 for more on malware, viruses and firewalls.)

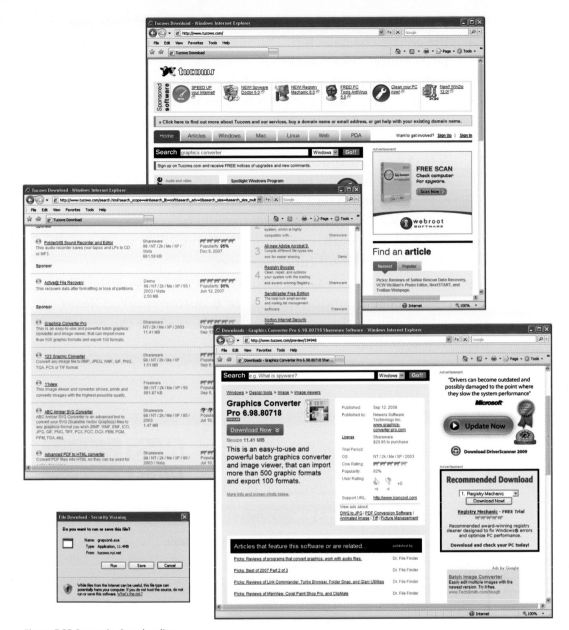

Figure 7.39 Stages in downloading

A downloaded file is often an executable installation program.
Double-click it to install the software on your PC.

Forms on the Web (7.3.1.1–2)

As you browse the Web you will often meet pages where you
need to make choices or give information. This is often done
through forms which gather details in several ways, including these.

◉ **Tick boxes** are used where there are several options, and
you can use as many as you like at the same time. A tick in a
box shows that the option has been selected.

- **Radio buttons** are used for either/or options. Only one of the set can be selected. The selected option is shown by a black blob in the middle.
- A **drop-down list** is a slot with a down-arrow button at its right-hand side. Click the button to display a list, then click an item to select it. Some list boxes allow you to select several, by holding down the **Control** key as you click.
- A **text box** is a space where you can type any text, for example this might be your name or other details, or the number of items you want to buy.

At the bottom of a form there will usually be a button marked **Submit**, **Send**, **Calculate** or similar. Click this when you have filled in the form to send it off for processing.

If you want to clear away the information you have entered, to start again, or to abandon it, look for a button marked **Reset** or similar. Click this to clear all the text fields, and set the options back to the defaults.

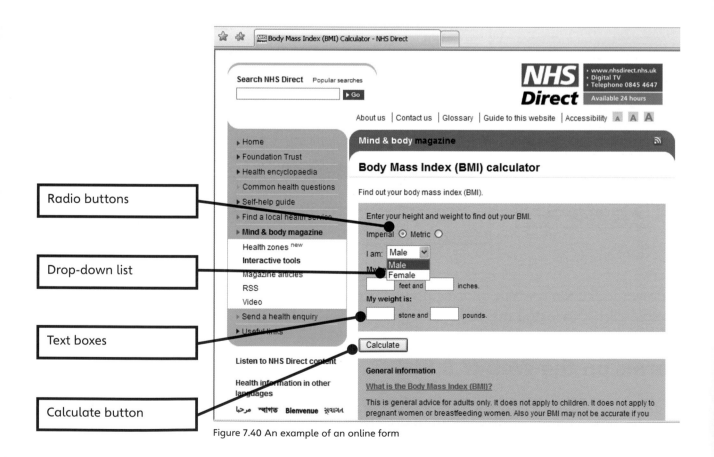

Figure 7.40 An example of an online form

Test your understanding

1. Use Google to find the website of a magazine or newspaper that you read. If it offers an RSS feed, subscribe to it. If it doesn't, try another magazine or newspaper until you find one that does. In a couple of weeks, if you find that you are not reading the feed, unsubscribe – there's no point in wasting bandwidth on unused downloads.

2. Use MSN's search engine to find podcasts from a comedian who makes you laugh. If regular podcasts are available, subscribe. You can unsubscribe later if you choose.

3. Search for exactly the same things at Google, Excite and AltaVista. How many of the same links are present in the first 10 results from each search engine?

4. Go to Microsoft's website (www.microsoft.com) and click the Downloads link. Find the Clip Art area and download one or more clips that you may find useful. Pick the clips, then click the Download now link (you may have to look carefully for it). If your security settings don't allow ActiveX control to run, you will see a message. Follow the instructions to complete the download.

Electronic mail

Learning objectives

By working through this lesson you will learn:

- about email addresses
- about the Outlook Express screen and its display options
- how to adjust the Header pane headings
- about the Send options
- how to read messages
- how to reply to or forward a message
- how to print a message
- about the Help system.

Introduction (7.5.1.1/7.5.3.1)

Emails are messages sent across the Internet. A basic email message is plain text – more like a memo than letter – but the messages can be formatted, and they can have pictures and other files attached to them. Communicating using emails is efficient, cheap, reliable and flexible. A message can be easily copied to other users; and when you receive a message, you can attach your reply to it and send it back, or forward it on to someone else. The email is at best delivered to the recipient almost instantaneously, but at worst it will be there within a few hours. Any delays are because not all of the computers that handle emails are constantly in touch with each other. With a standard email, the message is delivered to the recipient's mailboxes at their service providers, or to the mail computer on their network. It is read when the recipient logs on to their mailbox and downloads the message onto their computer. In addition to ISPs, email services are also offered by web-based companies, such as Hotmail. Here messages stay on the computer at the website, and users read them and write new messages by logging onto the site. The big advantage of web-based email is that you can access your mail from any computer that is connected to the Internet, while standard email can only normally be managed from your own computer.

Limitations (7.5.3.3)

Most email services, standard and web-based, set some restrictions on use, though they may be so loose that you are not aware of them. There is often a limit on the size of a file which can be attached to a message, but this may be 10 MB or higher. There may be a limit to the total quantity of data that you can send by email in any one month. There may also be a limit on the total storage space. One last, crucial restriction is that anti-virus systems may prevent certain types of files being sent or received. Find out the restrictions on your service.

Email addresses (7.5.1.2)

Assuming that you have an email account with your ISP (giving you an address), all you need to send an email is the recipient's email address – and something to say! Let's start with the addresses.

The standard pattern for an email address is:

person@domain

The domain might be that of an ISP, like AOL, or a business like Pearson Education, or a school or other organisation. Some households have their own domains. The person may be the person's real name or some variation of it (perhaps with an identifying number after it) or it can be a made-up name.

Some examples of email addresses are:

johnsmith12345@aol.com
(using an IS Provider, in this case AOL)

jksmith@microstuff.com
(through a company, in this case Microstuff)

Johnny@TheSmithsat42.org.uk
(a household's own domain)

Do it!

Make sure that you know your own email address before going any further.

Outlook Express (7.6.1.1)

Microsoft Outlook Express is the email and news application that comes with Internet Explorer. It is basically a simple piece of software, designed to do one job, that is to handle messages sent through the email system, and it does it well.

❶ Start **Outlook Express** from the **Start** menu or a **Desktop** icon.

❷ Explore the screen and identify the elements labelled on the screenshot.

❸ If you want to close Outlook Express when you have finished, click **Exit** on the **File** menu or click the **Close** button.

Note

Web mail (7.5.3.1)
If you have your email account through college or work, you may only be able to send and receive emails when you are in college or at work. If your email account is with a dial-up or broadband provider, you will only be able to use it when you can connect to them, which normally means when you are at home. There is a more flexible alternative. Several websites offer a free or low-cost web-based email service. With these, your mailbox is stored online at the website. As long as you can get online, through any computer anywhere in the world, you can send and receive emails. The techniques for handling an email are almost exactly the same as with a standard ISP-based email. Yahoo!, MSN Hotmail and Google are three leading web-mail providers.

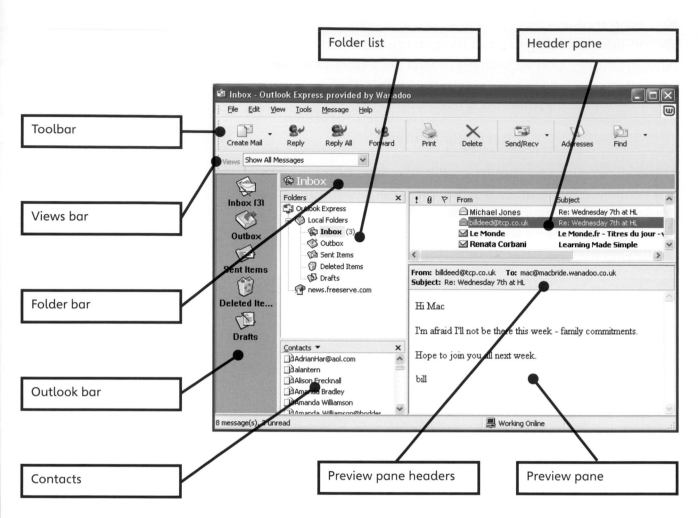

Figure 7.4I The Outlook Express screen

Labels (clockwise from top): Folder list, Header pane, Toolbar, Views bar, Folder bar, Outlook bar, Contacts, Preview pane headers, Preview pane

Mail accounts

To get email, you need an email account and Outlook Express needs to know about it. There's a wizard to help you set it up. This will run automatically the first time that you use the software, or it can be run at any point to add a new account.

Before you start, get this information from your mail service provider:

◉ your **username** and **password**
◉ your **email address**, for example JoSmith@mynet.co.uk
◉ the names of the provider's incoming and outgoing mail servers – these may or may not be the same.

❶ Open the **Tools** menu and select **Accounts...**
❷ In the **Internet Accounts** dialogue box, click **Add** and select **Mail...**

Tip!

Outlook Express can also handle newsgroups. These used to be important as places where people could meet and discuss shared interests, but they have been largely replaced by chat rooms and blogs. They are not covered by the ECDL syllabus.

③ Work through the wizard, giving your name, email address and the server details at the prompts.

④ Click **Next >** after completing each stage.

⑤ Back at the dialogue box, click **Close**.

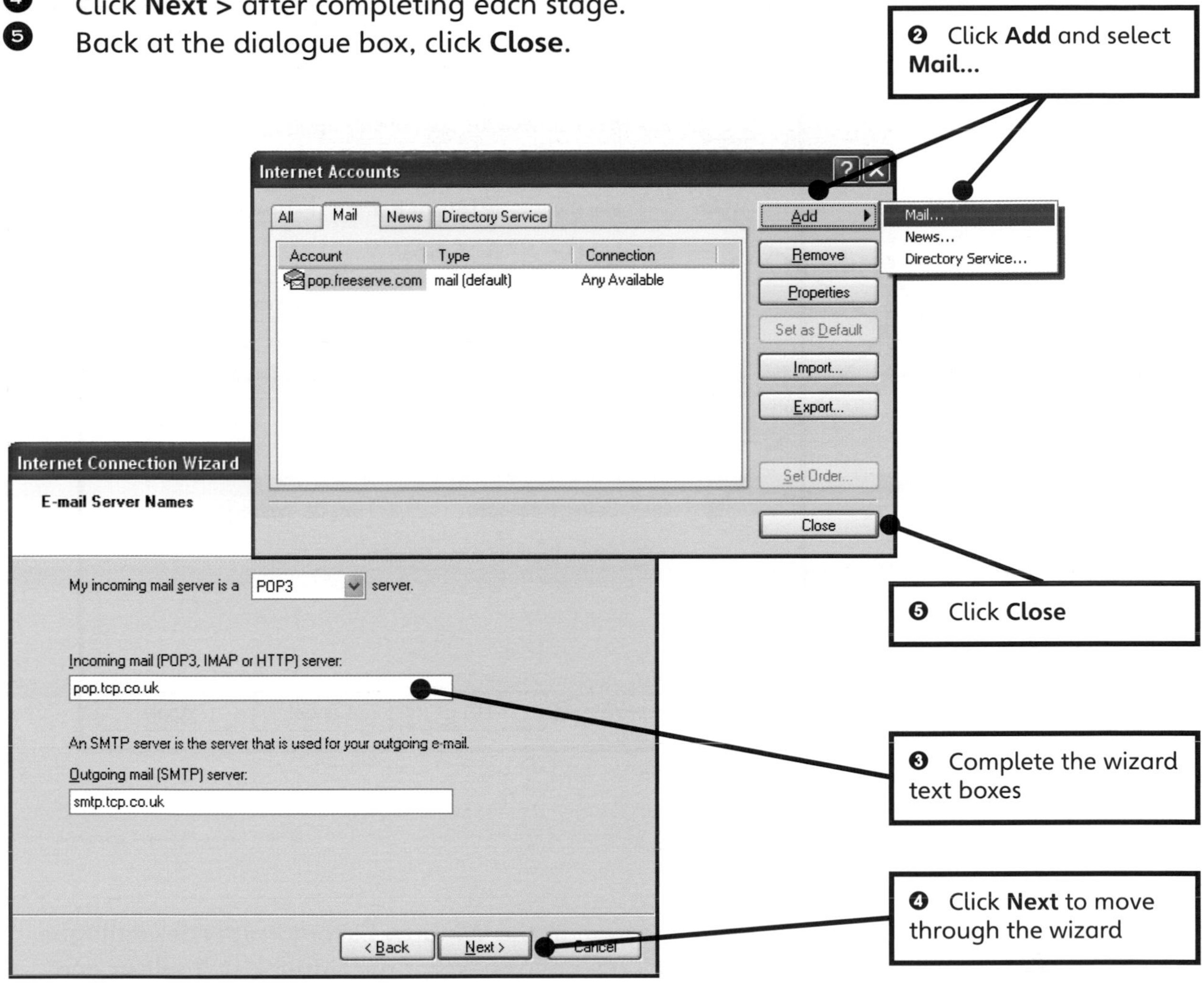

❷ Click **Add** and select **Mail...**

Internet Accounts

| All | Mail | News | Directory Service |

Account	Type	Connection
pop.freeserve.com	mail (default)	Any Available

Add ▶
Mail...
News...
Directory Service...

Remove
Properties
Set as Default
Import...
Export...
Set Order...
Close

Internet Connection Wizard

E-mail Server Names

My incoming mail server is a [POP3 ▾] server.

Incoming mail (POP3, IMAP or HTTP) server:
pop.tcp.co.uk

An SMTP server is the server that is used for your outgoing e-mail.
Outgoing mail (SMTP) server:
smtp.tcp.co.uk

< Back   Next >   Cancel

❺ Click **Close**

❸ Complete the wizard text boxes

❹ Click **Next** to move through the wizard

Figure 7.42 Setting up an account

Display options (7.6.3.5)

The only fixed parts of the window are the Header pane and the menu bar. All the rest are optional. As the **Folder** and **Outlook bars** do the same job, turn one off. If the **Preview Pane** is turned off, a new window will open to display a message when you click it to read it.

① Open the **View** menu, select **Layout...**
② Set the screen layout options.
③ Click **OK**.

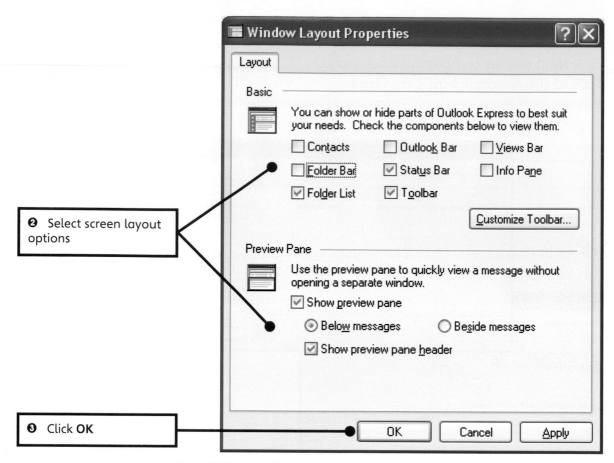

❷ Select screen layout options

❸ Click **OK**

Figure 7.43 Layout options

Tip!

If you get a lot of spam emails (i.e. unsolicited emails), turn off the Preview Pane. This makes them easier to ignore! You just want to delete them, not read them.

Do it!

Simplify your layout. In the **Window Layout Properties** dialogue box, turn off all the options except the **Folder List**, **Toolbar** and **Status Bar**.

The Header pane headings (7.6.3.1)

The **Header pane** shows some details of the message stored in the selected folder. Normally it will show who sent the message, its subject, when it was sent, its priority and whether it has an attachment. You can change this, and include more, or less, information about the messages.

❶ Open the **View** menu and select **Columns...**

❷ Click an item in the list to include it in the header display. Clear the ticks from the items you do not want.

❸ If you want to adjust the position of a column, select it and click the **Move** buttons – up to move left, down to move right.

❹ Click **OK**.

⑤ If you want to change the width of a column, you can do this in the **Columns** dialogue box, but it is simpler to do it directly. Point to the right-hand edge of a column's heading. The cursor will change to a double-headed arrow. Click the dividing line between the headers and drag it to set the width.

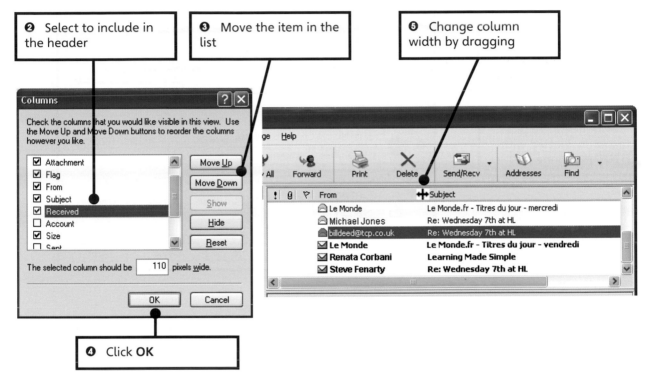

❷ Select to include in the header

❸ Move the item in the list

❺ Change column width by dragging

❹ Click **OK**

Figure 7.44 Displaying columns

The Send options (7.6.3.2)

There are options that you can set to suit the way Outlook Express handles email. The ones that you should look at first are on the **Send** tab of the **Options** dialogue box. Start with 'Include message in reply'. When you reply to someone, their text can be copied into your message. This can be useful for business emails, but you wouldn't normally do this for messages between friends. Included text can be edited or deleted before you send your reply.

❶ Open the **Tools** menu and select **Options...**
❷ Click the **Send** tab to bring it to the front.
❸ Click the **Include message in reply** tick box to set or clear the tick to suit your way of working.
❹ Explore the other options on this and the other tabs, and set any where you are clear about what they do. Leave the rest at their default settings.
❺ Click **OK**.

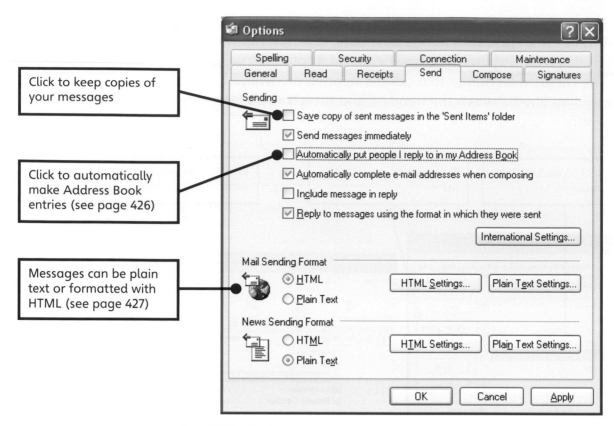

Click to keep copies of your messages

Click to automatically make Address Book entries (see page 426)

Messages can be plain text or formatted with HTML (see page 427)

Figure 7.45 Send options

Reading messages (7.6.1.1)

Incoming messages are downloaded from your mailbox at your service provider and stored in the **Inbox**. The Header pane shows their basic details – who they are from, the subject and so on. When a header is selected here, its message is displayed in the **Preview Pane**, if this is present.

❶ If the **Preview Pane** is not open, use **View**, **Layout...** to turn it on.

❷ Check that the **Inbox** is selected in the **Folders** pane.

❸ Click **Send/Recv** to pick up your email.

❹ Click a header to display its message in the Preview Pane.

Or

❺ Double-click the header line to open a new window to display the message.

How about...?

Alternatively, click **Close** on the **File** menu to close the message window.

If you opened the message in a new window, click ⊠ to close the window after you have read it. If you used the Preview Pane, you can't actually close the message. Just select another one when you have finished reading it.

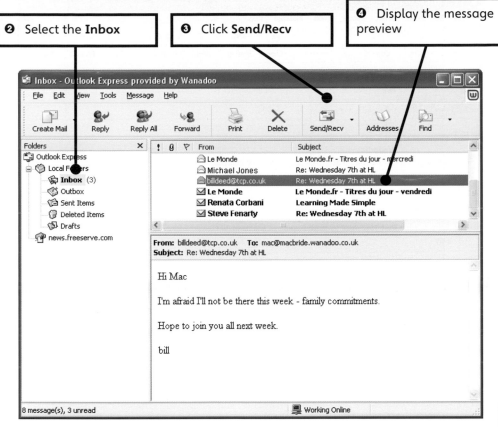

❷ Select the **Inbox**
❸ Click **Send/Recv**
❹ Display the message preview

Figure 7.46 The Inbox

Do it!

Read your email. Even if you have only just set up your account for the first time, there should be at least one message in your Inbox – a welcome greeting from your service provider or perhaps from Microsoft!

Replying to a message (7.6.2.1)

When you reply to an incoming message, the system will open a message window and copy the sender's address into the **To:** box, and the subject originally chosen into the **Subject:** box (see Figure 7.47 on page 422).

If the **Include message in reply** option is turned on, the original text is copied below the new message area with a > symbol or line at the left-hand side of each line. This can be very handy if you want to respond to the mail point by point. You can insert your text between the lines, and any unwanted lines can be deleted.

Note

Working offline

If you connect to the Internet through a dial-up line, you pay for the time that you are online. Consequently, it makes sense to compose your messages 'offline' then send them all at the same time. After sending, Outlook Express will automatically download any incoming messages, and you can then disconnect the phone line and read the messages offline. If you have a broadband connection, there are no time charges, so you can stay permanently online, and send messages immediately.

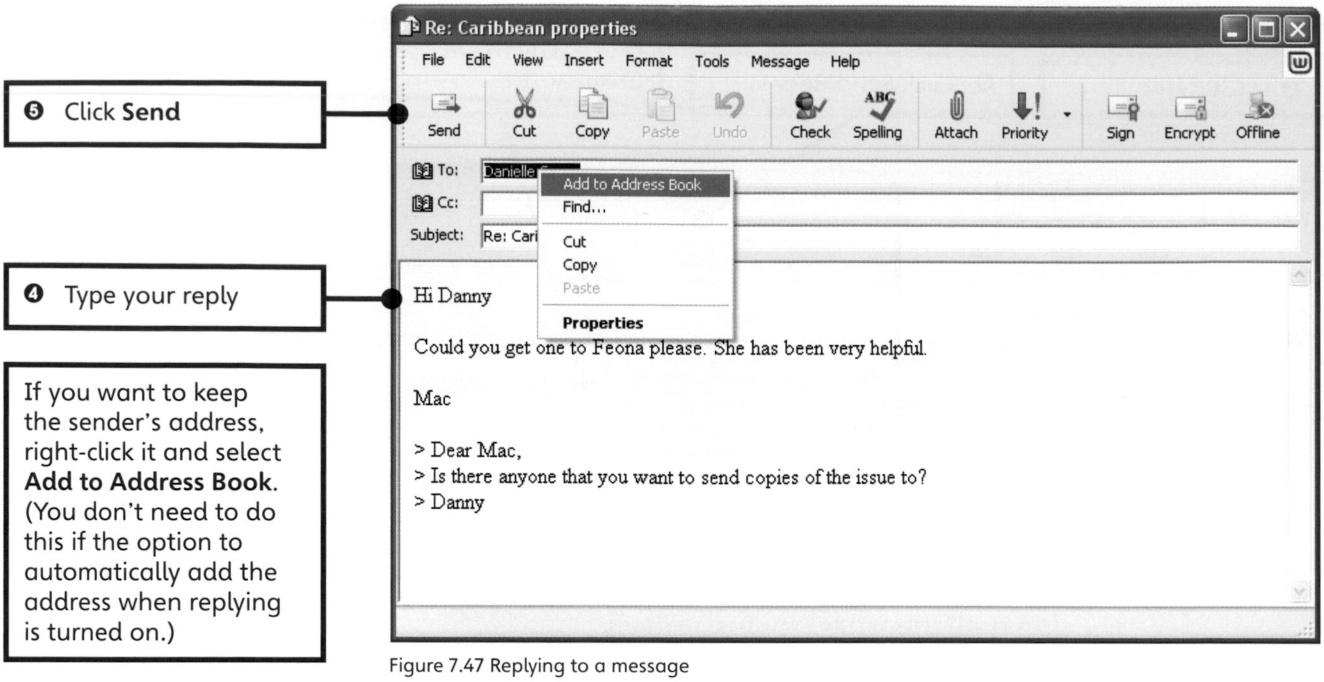

❺ Click **Send**

❹ Type your reply

If you want to keep the sender's address, right-click it and select **Add to Address Book**. (You don't need to do this if the option to automatically add the address when replying is turned on.)

Re: Caribbean properties

File   Edit   View   Insert   Format   Tools   Message   Help

Send   Cut   Copy   Paste   Undo   Check   Spelling   Attach   Priority   Sign   Encrypt   Offline

To: Danielle
Cc:
Subject: Re: Cari

Add to Address Book
Find...

Cut
Copy
Paste

Properties

Hi Danny

Could you get one to Feona please. She has been very helpful.

Mac

> Dear Mac,
> Is there anyone that you want to send copies of the issue to?
> Danny

Figure 7.47 Replying to a message

❶ Select the message in the Header pane.
❷ Click the **Reply** button.
❸ Delete any unwanted headers or other text and add your own comments.
❹ Add your own text.
❺ Click the **Send** button.

Reply to all

If you get a message that has been sent to several people, you can reply to all those listed in the **To:** and **Cc:** boxes. Click the **Reply All** button, instead of **Reply**, and continue as for a normal reply. Your message will be copied to all the recipients of the original message.

Forward (7.6.2.2)

You can send on a message to other people, perhaps after adding your own comments.

❶ Select the message in the Header pane.
❷ Click the **Forward** button.
❸ Type or select the address(es) of the recipient(s).
❹ Delete any unwanted headers or other text and add your own comments.
❺ Click the **Send** button.

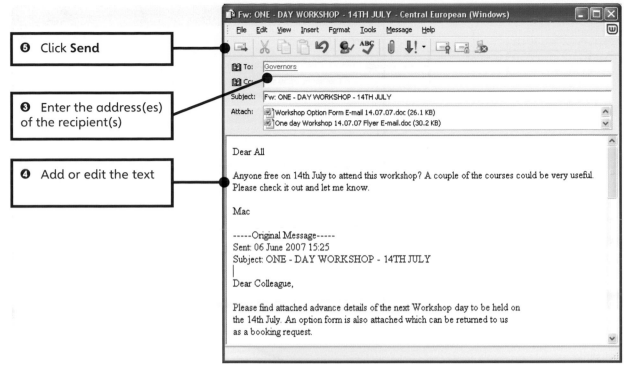

⑤ Click **Send**

③ Enter the address(es) of the recipient(s)

④ Add or edit the text

Figure 7.48 Fowarding a message

Print a message (7.6.2.4)

Most of the time, email can be dealt with entirely on-screen, but sometimes you need a paper copy of a message.

① Select the message.

② If you only want to print part of it, open the message and select the text to print.

③ Click the **Print** button ![Print icon] or open the **File** menu and select **Print...** The **Print** dialogue box will open (Figure 7.49 on page 424).

④ Choose the printer to use, if you have more than one.

⑤ Set the **Page Range** if there are several, or click **Selection** if you have selected part of the text.

⑥ Set the number of copies you want.

⑦ Click **Print**.

Do it!

Print the whole of one message, and selected paragraphs from a second.

Note

Outlook Express does not have a Print Preview facility. That does not matter too much as email is not usually printed out. The main disadvantage is that you cannot tell in advance exactly how many pages a message will take – and all too often the last sheet only has a few lines from the signature or an advert for the mail service! If you want to save paper and ink, select the part that you want printed and use the **Selection** option in the **Print** dialogue box.

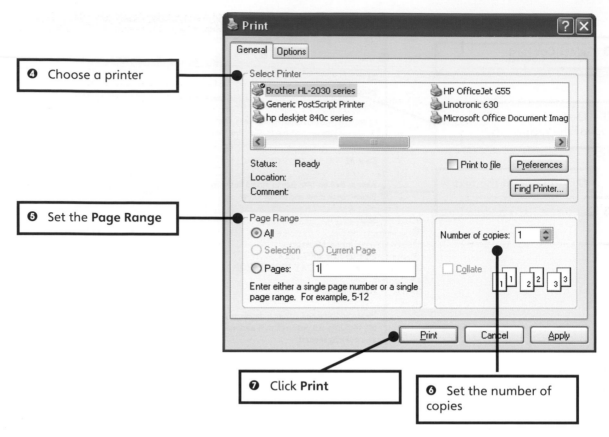

❹ Choose a printer

❺ Set the **Page Range**

❼ Click **Print**

❻ Set the number of copies

Figure 7.49 The **Print** dialogue box

Help (7.6.3.6)

The **Help** system in Outlook Express works in the same way as the one in Internet Explorer – only the content is different! Browsing through the **Contents** is often the best way to get to know the system, but if you need specific help, it is often quicker to try a key word in the **Index** or the **Search** tabs.

❶ Open the **Help** menu and select **Contents and Index**.
❷ Switch to the **Content** tab, if it is not on top.
❸ Click ❖ to open a 'book' of topics.
❹ Click ？ or 🗐 to display a help page.
❺ If a page has a set of links to topics, click one to reach its page.

Do it!

Use the Help system to find out how to reduce the risk of getting email viruses.

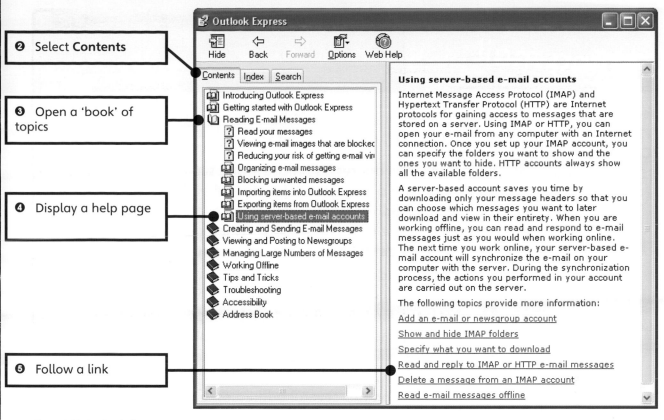

❷ Select **Contents**

❸ Open a 'book' of topics

❹ Display a help page

❺ Follow a link

Figure 7.50 Getting help

Test your understanding

① Set the **Header pane** to show only these columns: **Attachment**, **Flag**, **From**, **Subject**, **Received** and **Size**.

② In the **Send** options, turn off the option to save a copy of sent messages, and turn on the option to put people you reply to into your **Address Book**.

③ If you have a 'welcome' message from your email service provider, print it out. If not, select another message and print that.

④ Use the **Help** system to find out about working offline in Outlook Express.

Sending mail

Learning objectives

By working through this lesson you will learn:
- ◉ about the Address Book
- ◉ about the types of email recipients
- ◉ how to write and send a message
- ◉ how to copy text into a message.

Address Book (7.7.2.1)

Typing an email address is precise – one slip and the message will come back with a 'recipient unknown' label. The simple solution is to use the **Address Book**. Every email system has one. Type in the address once correctly, or add it when replying to a message (page 421), so it's there whenever you want it.

❶ Click the **Addresses** button 📖 .

❷ Click the **New** button 🔲 and select **New Contact...**

❸ Enter the **First**, **Middle** and **Last** names – contacts are normally listed alphabetically by **Display** name (**First + Last**).

❹ Type the email address.

❺ Click **Add**.

❻ If the person has several addresses, add them and set one as the default.

❼ Click **OK**.

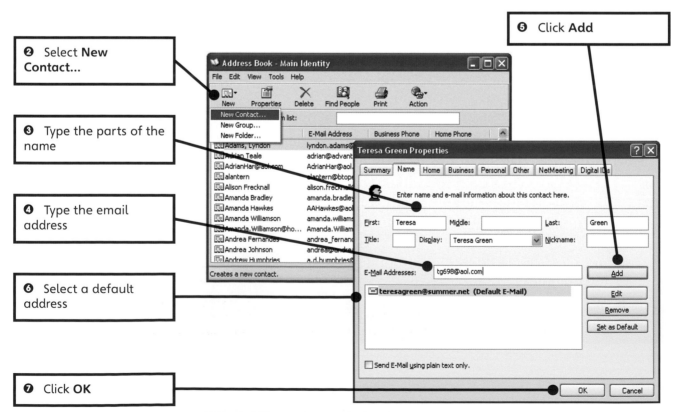

❷ Select **New Contact...**

❸ Type the parts of the name

❹ Type the email address

❻ Select a default address

❼ Click **OK**

❺ Click **Add**

Figure 7.5l Adding an entry into the **Address Book**

Deleting an address

If you no longer need an email address, delete it. A tidy Address Book is easier to use than one filled with old, unwanted addresses.

1 Select the contact in the Address Book.

2 Click the **Delete** button on the toolbar.

Do it!

Find the email addresses of at least three friends or colleagues and enter them into your address book. Copy in the addresses from anyone else who has written to you if you want to write to them at some point.

Types of recipient (7.5.3.4/7.6.1.3)

There are three types of recipients, so there are three ways that you can send messages to people.

- ◉ `To: ->` for the people who you want to read and respond to your message.
- ◉ `Cc: ->` (carbon copy) for those who you want to keep informed, but don't really expect them to reply.
- ◉ `Bcc: ->` (blind carbon copy) sends copies to people without including their addresses in the messages that other people receive. Blind carbon copies are mainly used for mailing lists where people do not usually want their addresses given to strangers. When you are writing to an individual, if you send copies to anyone, use Cc: – people should know who else is reading their mail.

Writing a message (7.6.1.2–4/7.6.1.9)

Messages can be composed and sent immediately if you are online, or composed offline and stored for sending later.

1 Click the **Create Mail** button.

2 Type the address in the **To:** box on the **New Message** dialogue box.

Or

3 Click `To:` by the top line of the **To:** box to open the **Select Recipients** dialogue box – this uses your Address Book.

4 Select a name and click the **To:** button, then **OK** to copy the address.

5 To send copies, either type an address into the **Cc:** text box, or in the Address Book, select the name and click the **Cc:** or **Bcc:** buttons.

Tip!

(7.7.2.2) Add addresses the easy way. When you receive an email you can add the sender's address to your Address Book in two clicks. Select the message in the Header pane, right-click it and select **Add Sender to Address Book**.

| Open |
| Print |
| Reply to Sender |
| Reply to All |
| Forward |
| Forward As Attachment |
| Mark as Read |
| Mark as Unread |
| Move to Folder... |
| Copy to Folder... |
| Delete |
| Add Sender to Address Book |
| Properties |

Figure 7.52 Adding to the Address Book

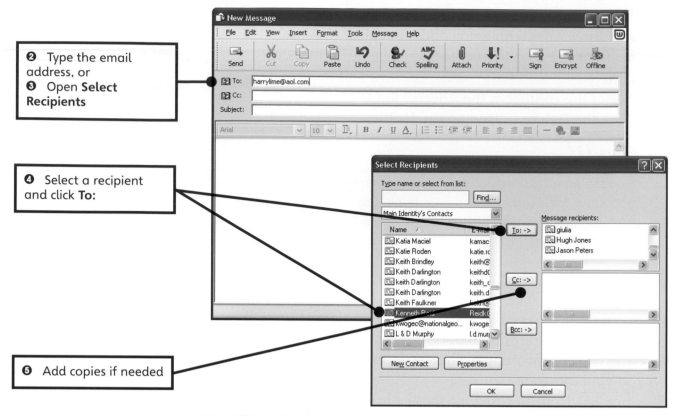

❷ Type the email address, or
❸ Open **Select Recipients**

❹ Select a recipient and click **To:**

❺ Add copies if needed

Figure 7.53 Selecting a recipient

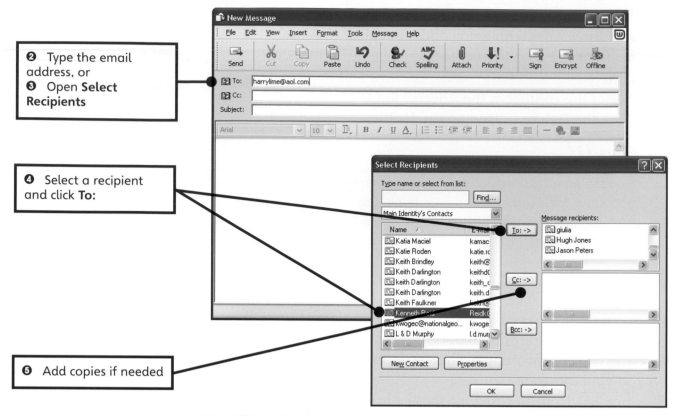

Tip!

If the Formatting toolbar is not visible, it's because you are in **Plain text** mode. Open the **Format** menu and select **Rich Text (HTML)**.

❻ In the **Subject:** field, type a brief note to say what the message is about. This helps your recipients to organise and find their messages. Make your Subject lines brief, but clear.

❼ Type your message.

❽ Use the buttons and options in the **Formatting bar** to set the font, size, style, colour and alignment of the text. (Use them just as you would in Word, Excel or PowerPoint.)

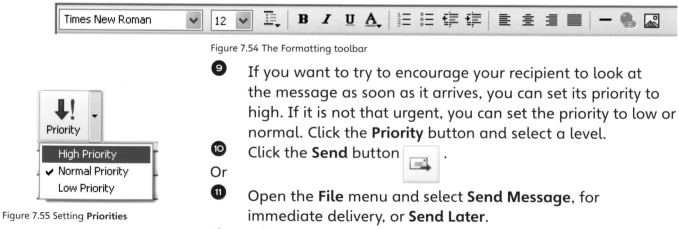

Figure 7.54 The Formatting toolbar

❾ If you want to try to encourage your recipient to look at the message as soon as it arrives, you can set its priority to high. If it is not that urgent, you can set the priority to low or normal. Click the **Priority** button and select a level.

❿ Click the **Send** button.

Or

⓫ Open the **File** menu and select **Send Message**, for immediate delivery, or **Send Later**.

Figure 7.55 Setting **Priorities**

If you choose **Send Later**, the message will be stored in the **Outbox**. Outlook Express will offer to send the messages when you close down or you can send them using the option on the **Tools, Send and Receive** menu.

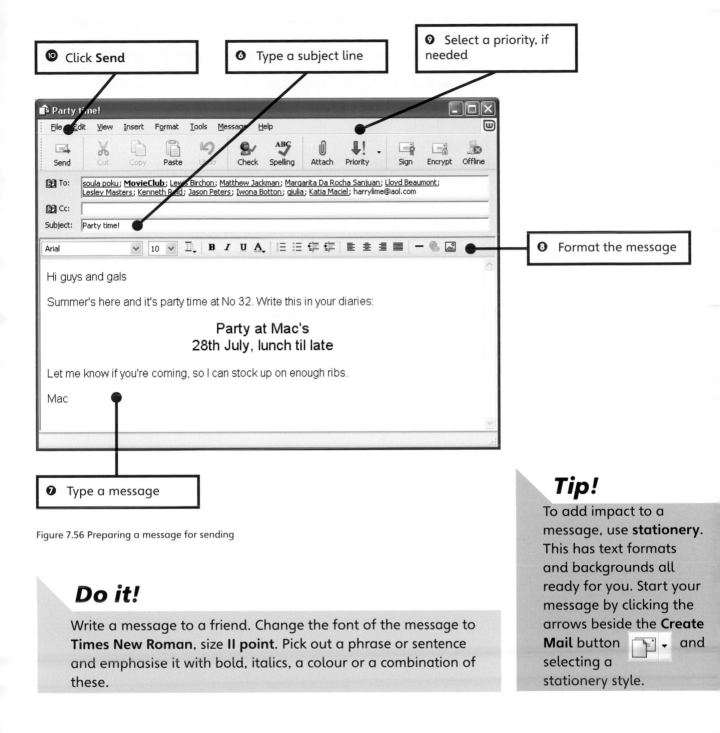

⑩ Click **Send**

⑥ Type a subject line

⑨ Select a priority, if needed

⑧ Format the message

⑦ Type a message

Figure 7.56 Preparing a message for sending

Do it!

Write a message to a friend. Change the font of the message to **Times New Roman**, size **II point**. Pick out a phrase or sentence and emphasise it with bold, italics, a colour or a combination of these.

Tip!

To add impact to a message, use **stationery**. This has text formats and backgrounds all ready for you. Start your message by clicking the arrows beside the **Create Mail** button and selecting a stationery style.

Copying text into a message (7.6.I.5)

You can copy and paste text into a message, just as you can in any other application. Select the text from its source – a Word document, a web page or whatever – copy it, using **Edit**, **Copy** or by clicking the **Copy** button. Then click in the message where you want it to go and use **Edit**, **Paste**, or click the **Paste** button.

Test your understanding

1. Collect as many email addresses as you can from your friends and family and add them to your Address Book.

2. Confuse a friend. Send them an unseasonal greeting – if it's coming up to Christmas, wish them Happy Easter; if it's midsummer, wish them Merry Christmas. Make your message big and colourful using a variety of fonts and other features.

Files by mail

Introduction (7.6.1.6)

Files of any type – graphics, word-processed and spreadsheet documents, audio and video clips – and URL links, can be attached to messages and sent by email. Compared with sending files printed or on disc in the post, email is almost always quicker and often more reliable. It is usually cheaper as well.

If you work in **Rich Text** mode, not **Plain text**, you can insert pictures directly into the message.

❶ Compose the message.

❷ Click the **Attach** button on the toolbar or click **File Attachment...** on the **Insert** menu.

❸ Browse for the file and click **Attach**.

Or

❹ If you are sending a picture in a formatted message, open the **Insert** menu and select **Picture...**

Learning objectives

By working through this lesson you will learn:

◉ how to open and save attached files
◉ how to save a message in draft form
◉ about the spellchecker
◉ about email etiquette.

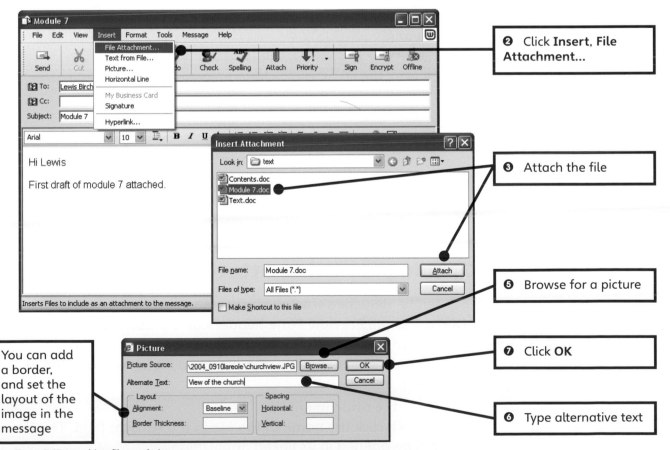

Figure 7.57 Attaching files and pictures

❷ Click **Insert, File Attachment...**

❸ Attach the file

❺ Browse for a picture

You can add a border, and set the layout of the image in the message

❼ Click **OK**

❻ Type alternative text

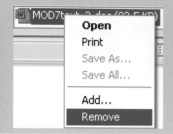
⑤ Browse for the file.

⑥ Type a brief description in the **Alternate Text:** field. If people have chosen not to display images in messages, this is what they will see.

⑦ Click **OK**.

⑧ Carry on with the writing and sending the message as normal.

⑨ The header area will now have a new line, labelled **Attach:**, showing the filename.

Tip!

(7.5.3.3) If you are sending an executable file, or a document with macros, or anything else which might contain a virus, then your message must make it clear that the message really is from you and that the file is safe.

If you are sending any kind of file to someone for the first time, it is always a good idea to send a separate message to let them know it is on the way, then they can alert you if it doesn't arrive. Files may not be delivered for several reasons. Size can be a problem – some email systems set a maximum size, typically 10 MB, and several large photos or a video could be more than that. If the message is rejected because of its size, it is possible that neither you nor your recipient will realise it did not get through. Note that when a file is processed as an attachment, it becomes almost 50 per cent bigger.

Some organisations place limits on attachments. They may limit the size of file that can be sent or received, and they may ban certain types of files, such as programs, screen savers or documents that can have embedded macros. Any kind of executable file can be used to hide a virus.

Opening or saving attached files (7.6.2.3)

Files can be detached from messages as easily as they were attached. If the **Preview Pane** header bar is present, an attached file is shown by a **paperclip**. If it is not, you must open the message in its own window – the attached file(s) will be listed in the **Attach:** line.

❶ Open the attachment list.

❷ Double-click the name of the file in the **Attach:** field. The file will be opened in its linked application.

3 The system may check that you want to open the file. Click **Open** if you are sure that it is safe to do so.

Or

4 Select **File, Save Attachments...**

5 Check the **Save To** location. If it is not where you want to store the file, click **Browse...** and navigate to the folder you want.

6 Click **Save**.

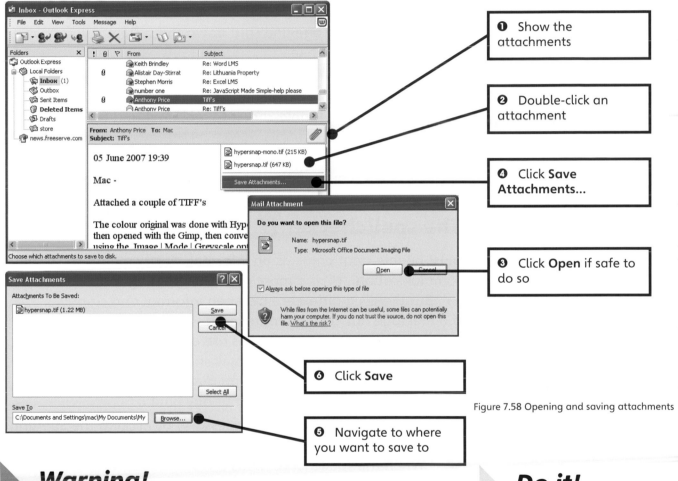

① Show the attachments

② Double-click an attachment

④ Click **Save Attachments...**

③ Click **Open** if safe to do so

⑥ Click **Save**

⑤ Navigate to where you want to save to

Figure 7.58 Opening and saving attachments

Warning!

(7.5.2.3) Attached files may contain viruses. These are programs hidden within programs or documents that will run on your system without you knowing it. At best, they will just send copies of themselves to other people, but more often they will also do damage to your PC, wiping out or corrupting files. Some types of files are more dangerous than others, which is why the system checks with you before opening files. Be very cautious about opening any files. Images (.jpg, .gif and .bmp files) are safe, but do not open any executable files unless you are expecting them and you are sure that they are safe. This also includes documents and spreadsheets that can harbour macros.

Do it!

You will need to ask a friend or colleague to work with you on this exercise.

Create a new message and insert an image. Send the message to your partner. They should send a reply that has an attachment. When it arrives, open it.

Saving a draft (7.6.1.7)

If you run out of time part-way through writing a message or, perhaps you need more information before you can complete it, you can save the message as a draft and come back to it later.

1 Make sure that the message has a **Subject line** – you may need it to identify it later.

2 Open the **File** menu and select **Save**.

3 You may see an alert box, telling you that the message has been saved in your **Drafts** folder. (These can be turned off.)

4 Close the message and shut down the system if you have finished for a while.

Later...

5 In Outlook Express, open the **Drafts** folder. Your message will be listed. Double-click it to reopen it and finish writing it, and/or send it.

6 When you send the letter, the copy in the **Drafts** folder will be deleted automatically.

Figure 7.59 Saving a draft

The spellchecker (7.6.1.8)

Most people treat email as an informal, chatty means of communication. 'Hi' is a more common greeting than 'Dear Sir'. But there's a difference between informal and sloppy. If a message has spelling mistakes, it is more likely to be misunderstood. Spelling mistakes are completely avoidable because Outlook Express has a built-in spellchecker. You can set the spellchecker to run automatically before a message is sent or run it yourself at any time.

1 Start the **spellchecker** (if necessary) by clicking the **Spelling** button.

2 When the spellchecker finds a word it does not recognise, the **Spelling** dialogue box will open.

3 To use a suggestion, pick one and click **Change**.

4 If the word is spelled correctly, click **Ignore**.

5 To add the word to the dictionary so that it is recognised next time, click **Add**.

6 When the check is complete, click **OK**.

Tip!

You can set options to control how the spellchecker works.

1 Click **Options...** on the **Tools** menu to open the **Options** dialogue box.

2 Click the **Spelling** tab and select the options you want.

Do it!

Write a message to a friend or colleague. Copy text from a Word document or other source. Save it as a draft. Close it without sending, then reopen it from the Drafts folder. Spellcheck the message before you send it.

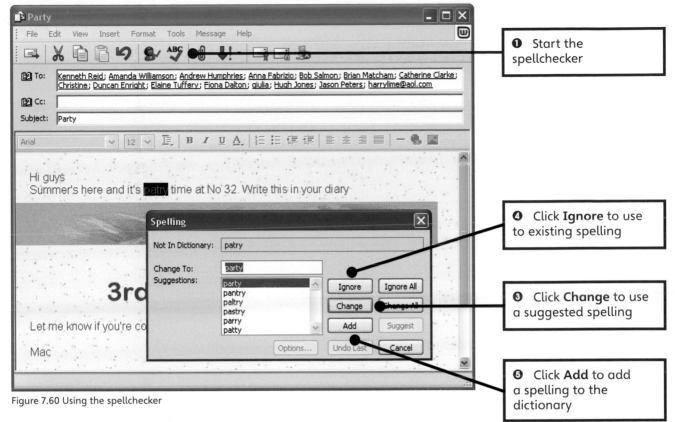

Figure 7.60 Using the spellchecker

The callout boxes in the figure read:

❶ Start the spellchecker

❹ Click **Ignore** to use to existing spelling

❸ Click **Change** to use a suggested spelling

❺ Click **Add** to add a spelling to the dictionary

Email etiquette (7.5.3.2)

Email has its own etiquette (sometimes called 'netiquette'). The rules are not just about being 'nice' – they have a real purpose.

- Give your message a meaningful Subject line. This makes it clear that it is not spam (see page 444) and helps them to see which messages to deal with first. It will also be useful to them when they are organising their old mail.

- The essence of email is speed and efficiency. Keep your messages short and to the point – especially those you send for business purposes. Don't spend much time, if any, formatting them. Save the fancy stationery for special announcements and greetings.

- Don't SHOUT. Using capitals is known as shouting. It's OK to emphasise the odd word this way, but don't shout whole messages.

- Spellcheck your messages! Typing and spelling mistakes look sloppy and they may also lead to misunderstandings. It only takes a moment to run the checker.

- Size can be a problem if the message has an attachment, especially if your recipient has a dial-up connection. Large files take time to download, and this may add to their phone bills. On a standard phone line, email usually comes in at around 3 kbps or 1 MB in 5 minutes.

1. Send a Word document to your tutor or a friend, and ask them to add a note and send it back to you. When you get their reply, save the document file (with a new name or in a different location so that it does not overwrite the original one).

2. Start a new message, with the subject 'Etiquette', but without putting any address in the To: line. Write some notes to remind you of the key points of etiquette. Spellcheck the message and save it in your Drafts folder.

Managing your messages

Sorting the mail (7.7.1.2)

The **Inbox**, and the other mail folders, are normally organised by date, so the newest is at the top or bottom of the list. Messages can be listed in order of any of the details in the headers.

❶ Click the bar at the top of a column to sort messages into order of the items in that column (e.g. click **From** to sort by sender). All those from each sender will then be grouped together, and all in alphabetical order.

❷ Click the bar again to reverse the sort order.

Figure 7.6I Sorting columns

❶ and ❷ Click to sort the column

Do it!

Sort your messages by date, with the newest at the top. Sort them by subject. If there are replies with **Re:** at the start, how do they get sorted? Sort them by size, with the largest at the top (before you can do this, you may have to display the **Size** column (see pages 418–9)).

Finding lost messages (7.7.1.1)

When you are trying to find a lost message, sorting can help. If that doesn't work there is a surer way. You can search through your messages using **Find** to look for names or words in the **From:**, **To:** or **Subject:** lines, or in the text of the messages. You can also search by date.

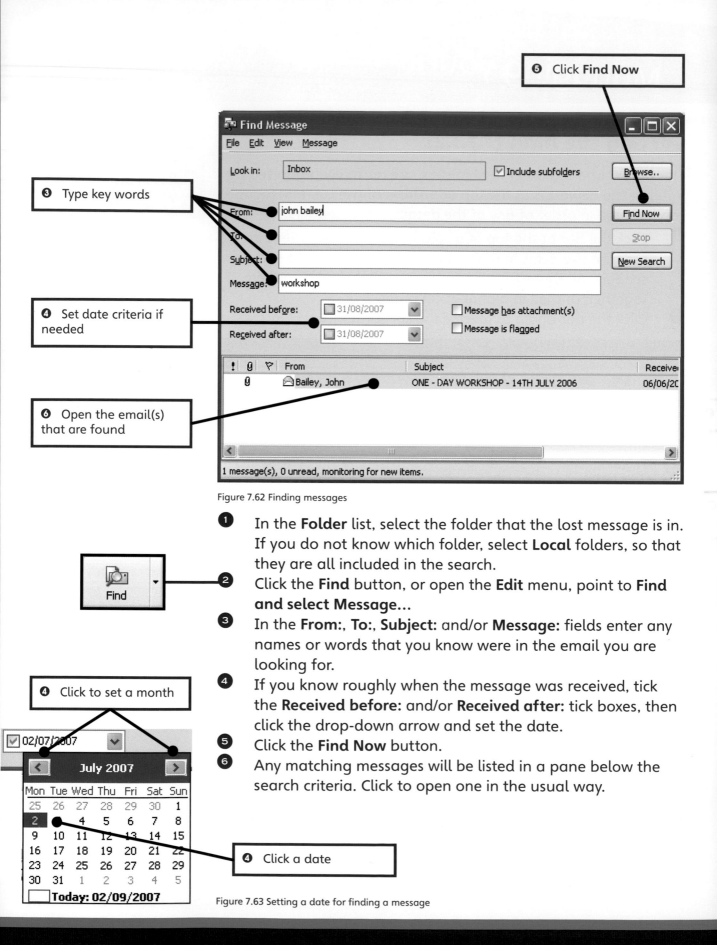

❺ Click Find Now

Find Message

File Edit View Message

Look in: Inbox   ☑ Include subfolders   Browse..

❸ Type key words

From: john bailey   Find Now
To: Stop
Subject: New Search
Message: workshop

❹ Set date criteria if needed

Received before: ☐ 31/08/2007 ▼   ☐ Message has attachment(s)
Received after: ☐ 31/08/2007 ▼   ☐ Message is flagged

!	0	▽	From	Subject	Receiver
	0		Bailey, John	ONE - DAY WORKSHOP - 14TH JULY 2006	06/06/20

❻ Open the email(s) that are found

1 message(s), 0 unread, monitoring for new items.

Figure 7.62 Finding messages

❶ In the **Folder** list, select the folder that the lost message is in. If you do not know which folder, select **Local** folders, so that they are all included in the search.

Find

❷ Click the **Find** button, or open the **Edit** menu, point to **Find** and select **Message…**

❸ In the **From:**, **To:**, **Subject:** and/or **Message:** fields enter any names or words that you know were in the email you are looking for.

❹ Click to set a month

☑ 02/07/2007 ▼

❹ If you know roughly when the message was received, tick the **Received before:** and/or **Received after:** tick boxes, then click the drop-down arrow and set the date.

❺ Click the **Find Now** button.

❻ Any matching messages will be listed in a pane below the search criteria. Click to open one in the usual way.

| ◀ | July 2007 | ▶ |

Mon	Tue	Wed	Thu	Fri	Sat	Sun
25	26	27	28	29	30	1
2		4	5	6	7	8
9	10	11	12	13	14	15
16	17	18	19	20	21	22
23	24	25	26	27	28	29
30	31	1	2	3	4	5

❹ Click a date

Today: 02/09/2007

Figure 7.63 Setting a date for finding a message

Folders for emails (7.7.1.3)

Email needs organising. Even with light use, say two or three incoming messages a day, there could be 1,000 in the Inbox by the end of the year! Treat email as you would postal mail. After you have read and replied to a message, throw it away or store it somewhere else if you want to keep it.

You can create folders at any time. As with folders in Windows Explorer, they can be created inside other folders if you want to subdivide areas.

1. Open the **File** menu, point to **New** and select **Folder...** to open the **Create Folder** dialogue box.
2. Type a suitable, meaningful name.
3. Select the folder in which to create the new one – select **Local Folders** for a top-level one.
4. Click **OK**.

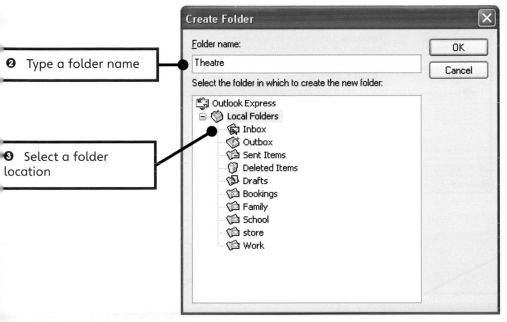

2 Type a folder name

3 Select a folder location

Figure 7.64 Creating an email folder

Moving messages (7.7.1.4)

Once they are in place, it is simple to move messages out of the Inbox and into appropriate folders.

1. Make sure that you can see the target folder. If it is inside another one, you may need to open the top one.
2. Go to the folder containing the message you want to move and select it.

❸ Drag the message across to the target folder and drop it in.

Or

❹ Right-click the message and select **Move to Folder...**

❺ Select the folder and click **OK**.

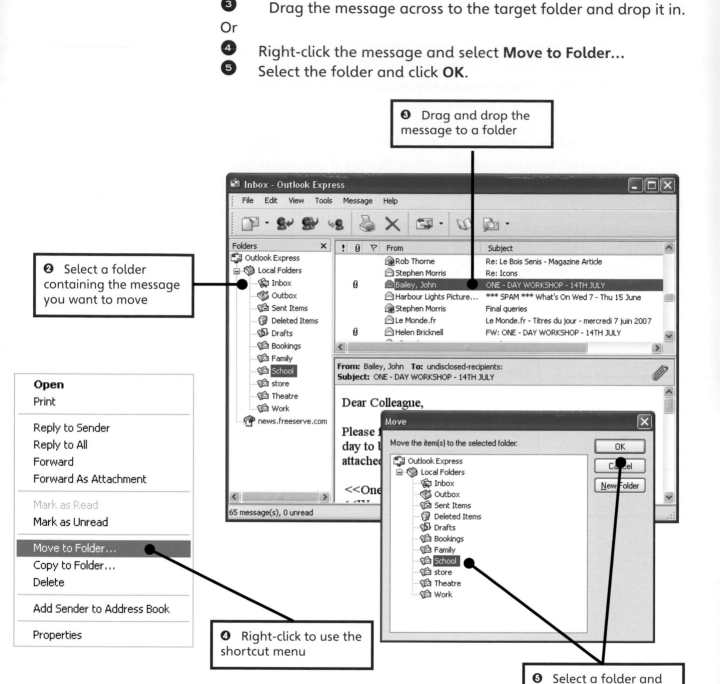

❸ Drag and drop the message to a folder

❷ Select a folder containing the message you want to move

❹ Right-click to use the shortcut menu

❺ Select a folder and click **OK**

Figure 7.65 Moving an email to a folder

Deleting messages and folders (7.7.1.5–6)

Don't let your folders get cluttered with old emails. Once you have finished with a message, delete it.

❶ Select the folder, message or messages – you can delete a whole set at once (use the standard **Shift+click** or **Control+click** techniques to select the set).

② Click [× Delete] . If you are deleting a folder, you will be asked if you really want to delete it. Click **Yes**.

The messages or folder will be transferred to the **Deleted Items** folder. If you delete something by mistake, go and find it in the **Deleted Items** folder and move it back to where it was.

Emptying the Deleted Items folder (7.7.1.7)

The **Deleted Items** folder needs to be emptied from time to time. You can do this by selecting the messages in the folder and deleting them (again), or you can have the folder emptied automatically when you shut down Outlook Express. This is an option on the **Maintenance** tab in the **Options** dialogue box. Use **Tools**, **Options...** to open the **Options** dialogue box and find out what the setting is on your system.

Do it!

Organise your email! Think about the sort of messages you receive and send. Are there any distinct sets? Do they relate to your work, or a hobby or club? Do you get a lot of emails from certain people? Do you want to store any of these for future reference? Set up three or more folders as stores, then move the messages from your Inbox (and Sent Items) into the appropriate folders. You may find it useful to sort your Inbox so that you can select messages more easily.

As you go through your Inbox, delete any messages that you no longer need.

Using flags (7.6.3.3)

If you look at the left side of the **Header pane**, you will see three thin columns. These tell you things about the messages.

- ◉ ⁣ **⁝** **Priority** can be high, normal or low . This is an option you can set when sending a message. In practice, not many people bother with these.
- ◉ ⁣ **◌** **Attachment** shows if there is a file attached to the message.
- ◉ ⁣ **▽** **Flag** is a general-purpose marker. You can use this for selecting messages to process in some other way.

To set flags

① Go through your messages clicking in the flag column to set a flag for those you want to mark, for whatever reason.

② If you set a flag by mistake, click it to remove the flag.

③ Click the flag column header to sort the messages into order, bringing all the flagged ones to one place.

④ Click the first, hold down the **Shift** key and click the last to select them as a group.

The selected messages can then be deleted, moved or printed in one operation.

Mark as read/unread (7.6.3.4)

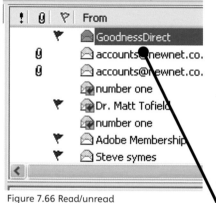

Figure 7.66 Read/unread

When messages first arrive, they are listed in the Inbox in bold. This indicates that they are unread. If you open a message its listing will switch to normal text, to show that it has been read. Sometimes you will want to mark an opened message as unread, perhaps to remind you to read it again properly when you have time. There will be other messages that you may not want to read at all (e.g. email newsletters or copies of messages sent to other people, or things which you might need to refer to later). These can be marked as read, so that they no longer appear in bold.

To mark messages as read or unread

① Select the message(s). (Use **Control+click** to select several at once.)

② Open the **Edit** menu and select **Mark as Read** or **Mark as Unread**.

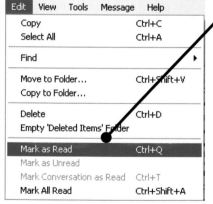

Figure 7.67 Mark as read

Address lists (7.6.2.2/7.7.2.3)

One of the big advantages that email has over the telephone, fax or postal mail is that you can send a message to several people as easily as you can send it to one. This is also one of the big disadvantages... (see page 427).

An address list, or group as Outlook Express calls it, brings together any number of email addresses under a single name, which you can select from your **Address Book** instead of having to pick all the individual addresses.

① Open the **Address Book**.

② Click the **New** button and select **New Group...**

③ Give the new group a name.

④ Click **Select Members**.

⑤ Work through the list of contacts, selecting each person in turn and clicking **Select ->**.

⑥ Click **OK**.

⑦ Back in the **Properties** dialogue box, check the names. If one is there by mistake, select it and click **Remove**.

⑧ Click **OK**.

To write to a group

⑨ Start a new message. Type the group name or click [To: ->] and select it from the **Address Book**. If you do not want the group members to see each others' addresses, use send as Bcc (see page 427).

⑩ Finish and send the message as usual.

Note

No matter how large the group, you only send one message to your mail server. It then sends a copy of the message to every address in the group. Some service providers set limits on how many copies of a message can be sent at one time. This may be as low as 20. Check with your email provider. If necessary, you may have to set up several smaller address lists instead of one large one.

❷ Click **New**, **New Group...**

❸ Type a name for the group

❹ Click **Select Members**

❼ Remove unwanted group members

❽ Click **OK**

❾ Select the group name to send to

❺ Select group members

❻ Click **OK**

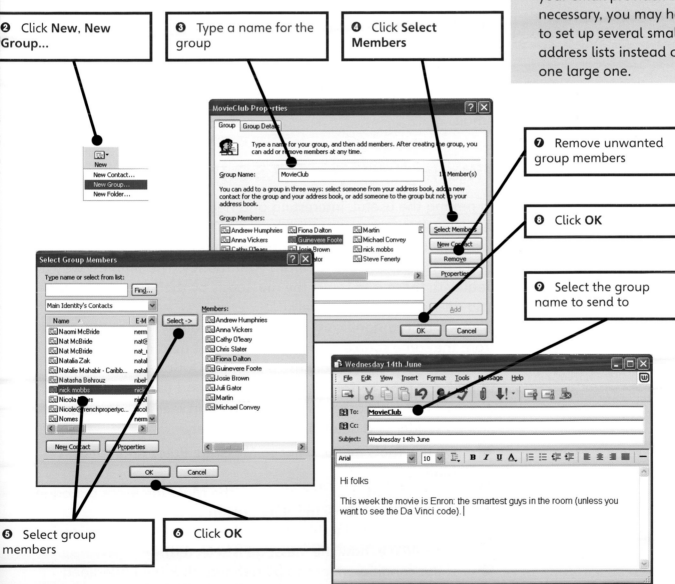

Figure 7.68 Creating and using a group

Email security

Learning objectives

By working through this lesson you will learn:
- ⦿ about digital signatures
- ⦿ how to filter out spam
- ⦿ about other forms of electronic communication.

Digital signatures (7.1.2.3/7.5.2.4)

If email is being used to send confidential information, it is important that the documents should only be read by the intended recipients. **Digital signatures** are part of an encryption system which makes email more secure. The message is encrypted, and your signature and a public key (part of the decoder) attached to the message. Your recipient will have been sent your private key (the other part of the decoder) separately, and so can read your message. Anyone intercepting the mail cannot read it without that private key.

To use digital signatures, you need a digital ID, which you can get from a certification authority. They are not free, which is why they are only used by people who need high levels of security for their email.

Filtering out spam (7.5.2.1)

In among the useful, interesting and necessary email that you receive will be some **spam** (junk mail). These might be adverts for real and imaginary goods, invitations to dubious websites, and other attempts to part you from your money. The simplest way to deal with these is to select the messages by their subject/senders and delete them immediately.

If junk mail is a significant problem, particularly if a lot is coming from the same source, you might like to set up a message rule to deal with it. A rule is an instruction for Outlook Express to look out for a certain type of message and to deal with it automatically. Typically, the rule will pick up messages from a named sender and delete them immediately.

1. On the **Tools** menu, point to **Message Rules** and select **Mail...**
2. If you already have some rules, the **Message Rules** dialogue box will open. Click the **New** button.
3. In the **New Mail Rule** dialogue box, select the **Condition** for the rule (i.e. how the message is selected).
4. If the condition needs to be defined, click the underlined text.

⑤ In the **Definition** dialogue box, enter the values that you want the system to check for. Type them and click **Add**.

⑥ Click **OK**.

⑦ Select the **Action** (i.e. what is to be done with them).

⑧ Back in the **Message Rules** dialogue box, type a name for the rule.

⑨ Click **OK**.

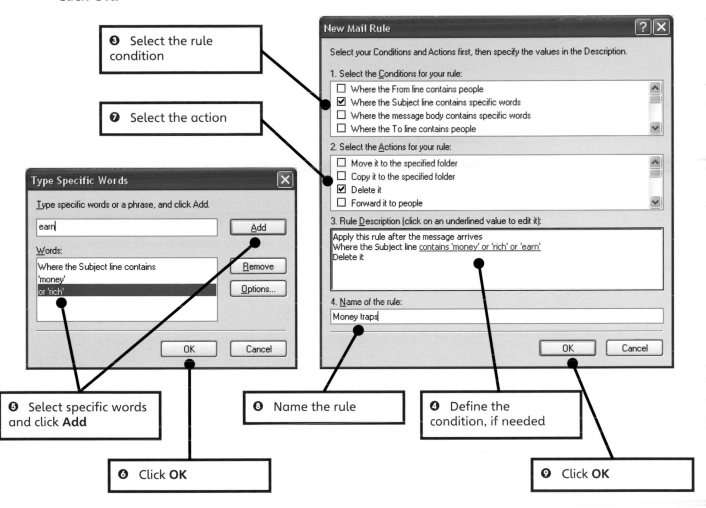

❸ Select the rule condition

❼ Select the action

Type Specific Words

Type specific words or a phrase, and click Add.

earn

Words:

Where the Subject line contains 'money' or 'rich'

Add

Remove

Options...

OK   Cancel

New Mail Rule   ? ✕

Select your Conditions and Actions first, then specify the values in the Description.

1. Select the Conditions for your rule:

☐ Where the From line contains people
☑ Where the Subject line contains specific words
☐ Where the message body contains specific words
☐ Where the To line contains people

2. Select the Actions for your rule:

☐ Move it to the specified folder
☐ Copy it to the specified folder
☑ Delete it
☐ Forward it to people

3. Rule Description (click on an underlined value to edit it):

Apply this rule after the message arrives
Where the Subject line contains 'money' or 'rich' or 'earn'
Delete it

4. Name of the rule:

Money traps

OK   Cancel

❺ Select specific words and click **Add**

❻ Click **OK**

❽ Name the rule

❹ Define the condition, if needed

❾ Click **OK**

Figure 7.69 Message rules

Warning!

(7.5.2.2) **Phishing** and **ID theft** are other dangers for email users. A phishing email is one which appears to come from a bank, credit card company or similar organisation, and which asks people to log on to a site to check their security details. A financial institution never uses email this way, and most warn their customers regularly, but people are still taken in and find their accounts cleared out.

Other forms of electronic communication

Web phones (7.5.1.4)

VoIP (Voice over Internet Protocol) allows people to talk to each other through the Internet, in almost the same way and with almost the same quality as through the normal telephone system. All that's needed is a headset or speakers, a microphone and an account with an Internet phone service, such as Skype. Calls to other users' computers are free. Calls can also be made from a computer to a landline or mobile phone. These are charged at the local rates in the other person's country (plus a small surcharge) rather than at international rates.

Short Message Service (SMS) (7.5.1.3)

Better known as text messaging, this is communication between mobile phones – and beyond. It is called 'short' because there is a limit of 160 characters on any single message.

The basic service is mobile to mobile, but it is also possible to send a text message to a 'landline' phone, where it will be 'read' out by a computer-generated voice. There are also websites which allow you to send texts to mobile numbers.

Instant messaging (7.5.1.5)

Instant messaging services such as Skype and Windows Messenger allow people to exchange text messages, images and files interactively. If the users at both ends have fast broadband connections, the exchanges are almost instant – hence the name.

Virtual communities (7.5.1.6)

People get together online to form virtual communities. 'Virtual' because they never, or rarely, meet face to face. We looked at these in Module 1 (page 35).

Test your understanding

1. Organise your messages. Look through your Inbox and decide on three or four (or more) categories that they could be grouped into. This may be by the kind of person who is writing to you or the sort of thing they are writing about. Set up folders and move into them any old messages that you want to keep.

2. Delete any old messages that you do not want. Check your Deleted Items folder, restoring any deleted by mistake, then empty it.

3. Create an address list of your closest friends. Send an (un)seasonal greeting to them all.

4. Messages without a subject are often spam. Create a folder named Subjectless. Set up a message rule to filter out any message without a subject and move it into this folder. Check the folder from time to time, just in case any of your contacts has written to you without including a Subject line.

Sadly, the growth in the use of IT, both at home and in business, has led to new crimes that exploit it. These illegal activities are commonly known as cyber crimes, and they take many forms: from the annoying program that might cause a message to be displayed on a screen on a certain date to the deliberate attempt to illegally obtain money from private online bank accounts.

Individuals and corporate businesses are both vulnerable to security breaches, and it is vital that everything possible is done to minimise the risk of data falling into the wrong hands.

This module covers the BCS IT User Syllabus specification requirements for IT Security for Users Level I.

MODULE 8.
it security

Learning objectives

By working through this lesson you will learn:
- about spam and malicious programs, and how to protect a computer against them
- about hackers and hoaxes.

Unwanted messages

In among the useful, interesting and necessary email that you receive will be some **spam** (i.e. unwanted messages or junk mail). The spam might be adverts for real and imaginary goods (adware), invitations to dubious websites, and other attempts to part you from your money. The simplest way to deal with these is to delete them from your Inbox immediately.

Most ISPs provide an efficient first line of defence to spam, but obviously they cannot always tell what messages are genuine and what messages are unwanted. If spam is a significant problem, particularly if a lot is coming from the same source, you might like to set up a message rule to filter it. A rule is an instruction for your email software to look out for a certain type of message and to deal with it automatically. Typically, the rule will pick up messages from a named sender and delete them immediately.

Spam can be minimised by installing anti-spam software, but it is difficult to reliably block all spam while still letting genuine email messages through to your computer. One technique used by anti-spam software is to detect keywords (such as those that might be offensive), however spammers (those who send spam) try to find ways around the filters by deliberately misspelling these words. Another technique blocks emails sent from known addresses, but again the spammers often regularly change their addresses to circumvent this filter.

Malicious programs

Viruses are programs designed to cause damage to computer files or, at the very least, cause inconvenience and annoyance to computer users. They are disguised as innocent files, hidden in other programs or documents, but become active once the program is run or the document opened. (A document cannot itself do anything, but it may contain macros – mini programs – which can contain viruses.) A key feature of viruses (and why they are called 'viruses') is that they create copies of themselves and attempt to infect other files and computers.

If a virus infects your computer, it can corrupt files and spread to other computers on your network or belonging to your email contacts. You must take steps to prevent viruses getting into you computer, removing any that do make it through the defences. Viruses can be spread in programs downloaded from the Internet, or passed between computers on disks or flash drives, but are most commonly spread through emails.

Precautions to avoid your PC being infected with a virus include the following:

- You should not share or lend floppy disks or flash drives that could introduce viruses into your system without first checking the files on them for viruses.
- You should take care when downloading files from the Internet. The proliferation of viruses over recent years is partly due to email communication. Never open an email message or an email attachment from someone that you don't recognise – it could introduce a virus to your system.

Tip!

Do not set Outlook Express to automatically display the content of a received message in the Preview Pane. The process of rendering the text contained in an HTML-formatted email to display it can unleash a virus or send an alert to the dubious source letting it know that your email address is valid. If you are unsure of the origin of an email, right click the unopened message header in the **Inbox** and select **Properties**. Click the **Message Source** button on the **Details** tab to display the message content. Scroll down to the message. If the text is in HTML then close the **Properties** windows and delete the email from the **Inbox** without opening it.

There are other types of **malware** (malicious software):

- **Trojan horses** – programs hidden within other legitimate programs and designed to become active under certain conditions, for example a set date or when a specific operation is run. Hackers sometimes use Trojans to record and send passwords or other security information.
- **Spyware** – sends information about the websites you visit and other aspects of your computer use to their hosts. This may just be measuring the effectiveness of web advertising,

Warning!

You must take care when downloading programs or opening email attachments. Software can be infected with viruses or other malware – hidden programs that can damage your computer in a variety of ways. They can destroy files, take over your email and send spam or viruses using your account, steal your credit card details, and more. Software from established, big-name manufacturers will be safe, and those from established download sites will also have been checked. Be very wary of anything from any other sources. Install a virus checker and make sure that it is running, up-to-date and set to check all programs, including emails, that are downloaded onto your computer.

but it can be more intrusive, for example it can also place code on a computer that logs keystrokes as they are typed, thereby recording passwords and other personal data that are then sent to the criminal.

- ◉ **Worm** – a program that copies itself and tries to spread over a computer network. Unlike a Trojan, this is not hidden in another program and they are not usually meant to do any damage to files. They can do damage to networks simply because they can take up processing power and use bandwidth as they copy and spread.
- ◉ **Adware** – software that automatically displays advertisements on a computer's screen.
- ◉ **Rogue dialer** – this malware targets computers that use a dial-up connection to access their ISPs for email and Web access by changing the usual contact phone numbers to premium rate numbers, sometimes leaving the computer connected even though the user has closed the session. The user will be unaware that the rogue dialer has done this until they receive an unusually high phone bill.

The best protection against malware is good anti-virus and anti-spyware software. Both must be updated regularly so that they are able to recognise new malware as it is developed.

Anti-virus software should be installed on all computer systems. This automatically checks for any infected data when the computer is started up, and scans any new files as they are introduced into the computer. Checks can also be run manually on floppy disks, CDs and flash drives before their files are accessed. Hundreds of new viruses are unleashed each month so it is a good idea to install a virus checker that provides an automatic or manual online update service. With the latter, you will automatically receive a message to update. The virus checker software should be capable of not only detecting the virus, but also of removing it from the infected file. This is called disinfecting the file.

Infiltration

The UK Computer Misuse Act (1990) legislates against the unauthorised use of both hardware and software: a process known as 'hacking'. Those who illegally access others' computer systems are called 'hackers', and they might hack either directly at a workstation or over a network (including the Internet). Hacking could be as simple as using somebody else's illegally gained password to access a computer, but circumventing the many security features in today's computer systems is not always so easy. There are many reasons why a hacker might want illegal access to a computer system. They include:

- To obtain data. This might be an individual's passwords, bank account details or other personal information. In a business system, this might be commercial secrets that will give a competitor a market advantage, or to obtain names and email addresses of customers from a database.
- To discredit a company or other body. This might be to 'hijack' or deface a website for political or propaganda reasons.
- To prove a point. A hacker might wish to expose a flaw in a high-profile computer system.
- For fun. Some hackers gain unauthorised access simply to prove to themselves that they can do it.

Although a hacker might have simply found out a password by watching the legal user type it in, it is more usual for the hacker to operate remotely using the Internet. Malware, such as that described in the preceding section, is used to record keystrokes and to exploit loopholes in browser software. Hackers often use sophisticated software and techniques to circumvent security systems.

One way of preventing illegal access via a network connection is to install a firewall. This is hardware or software that controls the flow of data over a network. It allows you to specify which sites, if any, can have access to your machine, and to set the level of access, if any.

Most manufacturers react quickly to shortcomings that are revealed in their software's security. They do this by releasing program updates, called 'patches', that prevent any future exploitation of the loophole.

Warning!

Once a potential security flaw has been revealed in, for example, browser software, it is important to install the manufacturer's 'patch' as soon as it is released. You should set software to download updates automatically as they become available so your computer is protected to the latest security level at all times.

Hoaxes and scams

Among all the malware and security threats that hinder safe use of computer systems are messages that are simply an annoying waste of time. Some constitute spam, others are emails from well-meaning friends and colleagues passing on warnings of viruses, that on investigation turn out to be bogus.

Many hoaxes and scams are very obvious, for instance, an email:

- might ask you to deposit funds in an off-shore bank account to help an individual gain residency in your country, with the promise of repayment at a later date.
- might purport to be from a bank and ask you to visit a website to change your password or give your account details – a practice known as 'phishing' (see page 457).

Tip!

Always check misunderstanding and prevent unnecessary scares by checking the validity of a message. Most hoaxes and scams are well known and can be researched on reputable websites.

● might take the form of 'electronic' chain letter with a threat to the recipient if they do not pass on the message to a given number of new addresses.

● might advise you to delete a file from your disk because it says it is a virus, whereas in reality it is crucial to the correct working of the operating system or other software.

You should never act on any of these or similar messages, other than to delete them.

Others messages are less obvious and are designed to raise false alarm. For example, you might receive notification of a virus – usually a message telling you to look out for and not to open any email with a particular subject. You can check the existence of the virus on your anti-virus software manufacturer's website. If it turns out to be a hoax, it is good practice not to pass on the message to others, so not to propagate unnecessary alarm, and to tell the person who sent you the warning that it is a deception, putting their mind at rest.

Information security

Learning objectives

By working through this lesson you will learn:
- ◉ about controlling access to data
- ◉ about identity theft.

Identity and authentication

The security of data, both on an individual's computer and on a company's networked servers, is vitally important. Access to that data must be controlled to prevent its deletion or it falling into an unauthorised person's hands. The UK Data Protection Act (1998) legislates on the storage of personal data requiring, among other things, that it is safe from unpermitted access.

Most networks require a user to identify themselves by typing a user ID which is then authenticated by typing a password before they can gain access to the computer system. Together, these allow the user to log on to their network account. The user ID assigned to you is open to view. The password is secret and does not appear on the screen when you type it in – the letters may be replaced by asterisks as you type. You can change your password whenever you like.

The network administrator can use network management software to assign which servers and drives an individual can access with their account, and set what rights (e.g. read, write, delete, copy) are allowed.

Warning!

Change your password/PIN at least every month. Change it more often if your company security policy requires you to or if the data you access is particularly sensitive. Your IT help desk staff will be able to tell you how to do this for your company's network, or you can search the **Windows Help and Support Center** on a standalone PC.

Note

Identification and authentication methods such as swipe cards or biometric readers (e.g. fingerprint readers) are used on some computers that could give access to data that needs a high level of security.

Tip!

When leaving a computer unattended, even for a short while, use a password protected screensaver to prevent prying eyes seeing what is on your screen or an unauthorised person using your open network account to access servers or disk drives.

Warning!

Always log off a network when you have finished working on it (and switch off the computer if you are leaving work) unless there is some special reason why you should leave it running and logged on (e.g. monitoring or processing data overnight), in which case you should use an alternative means of preventing access, such as a keyboard lock.

If you are authorised to access particularly sensitive data which only certain people are allowed to view, you may need to enter a personal identification number (PIN) or second password.

You should change your password/PIN regularly in case somebody has found it out. How often you should change it might form part of a company's network management policy, and, indeed, the network operating system might be configured to automatically tell you to do so after defined periods.

If, for any reason, you feel that your password/PIN has been found out, you should change it immediately.

Confidentiality

As explained, access rights are used to protect confidential, commercial and vital data, but they also safeguard the privacy of individuals.

If you are entrusted with authorised access to these types of data, there are some basic rules you should follow when using a password or PIN so that others do not have the opportunity to find it out or use it successfully.

- ◉ Never write down the password/PIN. Commit it to memory.
- ◉ Never tell your password/PIN to another person.
- ◉ Do not use an obvious word or name as a password. A combination of at least six letters and numbers is best.
- ◉ Change your password/PIN regularly.

You should always save confidential data to secure drives on network servers and not to a local drive on a desktop PC, laptop or other portable storage media (see Portable devices, page 459). The data is then less vulnerable to hacking, and automatic backups ensure recovery if the data is accidently deleted.

Warning!

It is better to remember a password/PIN than to use the AutoComplete password feature available in some browsers where the userID is linked to its stored password (and a hacker only needs to find out the ID to gain illegal access).

Identity theft

The use of user IDs and passwords is a strong defence that protects data falling into the wrong hands, so, not surprisingly, the cyber criminal now spends a great deal of time trying to find them out so that they can pose as the bona fide user and enjoy all the access rights of that person. If successful, the criminal has committed **identity theft**.

To minimise being a victim of identity theft, you should be extremely careful of how you give out or dispose of any personal data that could be gathered and used by a thief. The rules about password usage and confidentiality obviously apply, but you should also be careful with all other personal information, both on paper and online, such as credit card numbers and statements, your address, bank account details etc. In fact, it is best to shred or burn personal details that could be illegally gathered over time to build up a portfolio of information that might be used to defraud or discredit you.

Phishing is another danger for email users. A phishing email is one which appears to come from a bank, credit card company or similar organisation, and which asks people to log on to a website to change their security details. The phishing website can look sufficiently genuine to entice a user to enter their online banking details. A financial institution never uses email this way, and most warn their customers regularly, but people are still taken in and find their accounts cleared out.

Tip!

Check with your bank whether or not they are interested in seeing phishing emails you might receive. Some welcome them because they analyse them in an effort to keep ahead of the criminal's next move and perhaps even track them down.

Warning!

Never inappropriately disclose your personal data or that of others to which you are entrusted.

Networks

A network within a company's premises or in a home office is protected by security measures, such as a firewall or proxy server, from the public and less secure Internet. Private, leased network connections are available to those who wish to pay for security, but the rest of us transmit and receive data over the world's public telephone communication channels, be they copper wires, fibre optic cables or microwave links etc. These are inevitably less secure than private networks, thereby making the data they carry more vulnerable to being intercepted and used for illegal purposes.

When banking or shopping online, or when sending confidential or valuable data to a website via a public network, you need to be sure that your data is safe while in transit. Encryption ensures this. If a site uses encryption, data is encoded before sending and can only be decoded by a computer that has the necessary key. Sites that use encryption have digital certificates to guarantee that they are who they say they are.

Secure sites can be recognised by the letters https at the start of the address instead of the usual http.

In a Wi-Fi broadband setup, any Wi-Fi-enabled computer within range of the router may be able to access the Internet – even without the router owner being aware of it. Going online through someone else's Internet connection without their permission is known as 'piggy-backing'.

It is easily stopped. Access to a router can be controlled by setting up a network name and password. This should be done on a home network. It doesn't just stop piggy-backing, it will also prevent outsiders gaining access to your computers and their files. When you configure a router or set up an account on a website, such as an online banking site, you will often be given a default password to let you use it in the first instance. You should change

> **Tip!**
>
> View a website's digital certificate if you want to check that it is safe to send data securely.

this as soon as you have used it for the first time, and thereafter change it regularly as described on page 455.

You should also change any default security settings to those that suit your network usage. This is covered in detail for Microsoft Internet Explorer 7 in Module 7, Safety online, on page 397.

You will need to consult the user guides for firewall and router configuration settings.

Warning!

Keeping default passwords and security settings leaves your computer vulnerable to unauthorised access.

Connectivity

A wireless communication protocol that overcomes some of the limitations of traditional wireless networks, and allows data to be exchanged between IT devices within range of one another, is called Bluetooth. Bluetooth-enabled devices include PCs, laptops, mobile phones, cameras and printers. An advantage of using Bluetooth connectivity is that, unlike a Wi-Fi network, the network devices do not have to be configured individually to communicate with each other. However, security is compromised because of the simpler set-up procedures. Unless some precautions are put in place, a Bluetooth-enabled device is potentially accessible to any other Bluetooth-enabled device within communication range. Here are some security considerations when using Bluetooth connectivity. (You might need to read the relevant user guide to find out exactly how to configure your device.)

- ◉ Turn off Bluetooth or 'hide' your device when you are not using it to transmit or receive files. ('Hide' means set your device to its **non-discoverable** or **non-connectable** mode.)
- ◉ Check the sender is known to you before accepting a file.
- ◉ Set up a password protected connection (sometimes called **pairable** mode).
- ◉ Turn on encryption if your device allows it.

Portable devices

Portable devices (such as laptops/notebooks/tablets, PDAs, mobile phones, disks and flash drives etc.) by their very nature are targets for a thief, but they are also easily lost by the owner. Replacement equipment can be bought and, if the data has been backed up, the owner can continue work after some expense and time. However, confidential business files and personal details can fall into criminal hands, with potentially disastrous consequences, if the portable devices are not properly protected. This protection can include:

- Visible security marks to make hardware less attractive to steal.
- Security cables and locks to make it harder to remove devices.
- Portable storage media must be kept under lock and key when not in use. In transit, they must be protected and monitored at all times.
- Password-protected access to disk drives, folders and files to help to keep data safe.
- A system of signing in and out portable devices to help instil the security and vigilance requirements among staff.

Guidelines and procedures

Learning objectives

By working through this lesson you will learn:
- ◉ about laws and company policies on security and privacy.

Security and privacy policies

Many of the security and privacy considerations discussed in this module are means to comply with UK Acts of Parliament such as:

- ◉ The Copyright, Designs and Patents Act (1988)
- ◉ The Computer Misuse Act (1990)
- ◉ The Data Protection Act (1998)
- ◉ The Electronic Communications Act (2000)
- ◉ The Freedom of Information Act (2000)
- ◉ The Regulation of Investigatory Powers Act (2000).

In the UK, all individuals and companies are subject to the legislations of these Acts, so businesses usually provide staff with guidelines and procedures they can follow to ensure that nobody is breaking the laws. These policies are usually written so they help compliance within the context of the company's type of work. Many companies will provide these guidelines, maybe as part of a staff handbook, and give training to new staff as part of their introduction.

The handbook will usually tell staff where they can get further guidance if they want it. If a company has an IT help desk, its staff should be able to advise on IT security issues in the first instance. The HR/personnel department should be able to help with privacy policy.

Follow the guidelines as published, making sure that you understand each policy item it requires you to follow.

The security guidelines will also tell you who you must notify if you think or know that the company's IT security has been threatened or breached.

Warning!

You must always follow a company's security and privacy guidelines. Failure to do so could lead to disciplinary action or dismissal. Remember that the procedures are often there to comply with legislation, so you could also be breaking a law.

Note

In many companies which have special security or confidentiality needs, the guidelines might be displayed where they can be read as a reminder.

Tip!

Find out from your supervisor who you should approach for advice on security or privacy issues or if you are unclear of the procedure you should follow.

Note

A company's policies could contain many rules on many topics. You might even be required to conduct risk assessments when new procedures are introduced, or even periodically check that the existing procedures are working adequately.

Warning!

A security breach does not necessarily mean that it has been committed by an outsider to the company. It could be a colleague you saw acting negligently or you might have left your laptop in a taxi!

Data security

In a corporate network environment staff are encouraged to use disk space allocated to them on a server. These servers are automatically backed up each night so data can be easily recovered if the user loses the original.

Tip!

An individual in the home environment will not necessarily have access to a secure area to store their data and application software. Nevertheless, it is important that essential data is backed up and the source files of software are kept in case of catastrophe or the need to transfer everything to a new computer.

Keep the regular backup somewhere safe where you can change them periodically (e.g. online storage), but you could consider putting long-term backups and source disks (with other set-up information such as licence numbers etc.) in a locked box and asking a friend or a family member to look after it.

Learning objectives

By working through this lesson you will learn:
- about the importance of backups.

Security

Not all thefts and loss of data occur because the equipment is portable (see page 459). Desktop computers might be stolen in some burglaries or data copied from disk drives to floppy disks or flash drives. To minimise these risks you should do all or some of the following depending on how sensitive the data is:

- Lock the equipment to the desk using a cable lock.
- Keep the equipment in a secure room.
- Use locks on floppy disk drives.
- Do not have floppy disk drives or USB ports.
- Use locks on keyboards.
- Do not permit sensitive data to be stored on the computer's local drives.
- Password protect folders on disk drives.

Backups and safe storage

Computer data can be very valuable and can be all too easily lost, for example because of fire/flood, theft, file corruption, disk crash, virus infection or accidental deletion etc. Backups ensure that you have a recent copy of your data in case disaster strikes. For home users it may be enough to make a backup once a week, or after any significant work has been done or new files loaded. In businesses, backups are typically made on a daily basis, or more frequently, depending on the nature and importance of the data. Large companies will usually have special software and hardware to manage the backups ensuring that copies are made regularly. Backing up data involves copying it to a removable storage device such as magnetic tape, CD-ROM, Zip drive, flash memory etc. The backup media must be clearly labelled.

Backups are a vital lifeline to individuals and companies so they need to be kept safe from theft, fire and flood. Depending on the importance of the data, options for storing backup media include a secure, fireproof, waterproof container/room on or off site. The latter might be an online storage facility.